Tantric Visions of the Divine Feminine

Tantric Visions of the Divine Feminine

The Ten Mahāvidyās

DAVID KINSLEY

MOTILAL BANARSIDASS PUBLISHERS
PRIVATE LIMITED • DELHI

Reprint: Delhi, 2023
First Indian Edition: Delhi, 1998

ISBN: 978-81-208-1522-3 (Cloth)
ISBN: 978-81-208-1523-0 (Paper)

MOTILAL BANARSIDASS
41 U.A. Bungalow Road, Jawahar Nagar, Delhi 110 007
8 Mahalaxmi Chamber, 22 Bhulabhai Desai Road, Mumbai 400 026
236, 9th Main III Block, Jayanagar, Bangalore 560 011
203 Royapettah High Road, Mylapore, Chennai 600 004
Sanas Plaza, 1302 Baji Rao Road, Pune 411 002
8 Camac Street, Kolkata 700 017
Ashok Rajpath, Patna 800 004
Chowk, Varanasi 221 001

Printed in India
BY JAINENDRA PRAKASH JAIN AT SHRI JAINENDRA PRESS,
A-45 NARAINA, PHASE-I, NEW DELHI 110 028
AND PUBLISHED BY NARENDRA PRAKASH JAIN FOR
MOTILAL BANARSIDASS PUBLISHERS PRIVATE LIMITED,
BUNGALOW ROAD, DELHI 110 007

To my friends and teachers
Om Prakash Sharma and Virendra Singh

Contents

Acknowledgments

I first became aware of the group of Hindu goddesses known as the ten Mahāvidyās while conducting research on the goddess Kālī in Calcutta during the academic year 1968–69. Kālī is nearly always listed as the first of this group of ten unusual goddesses and in many ways is the exemplary Mahāvidyā. It was not until 1983–84 in Varanasi, however, that I began to undertake detailed research on this group. With the help of a fellowship from the Canadian Social Sciences and Humanities Research Council, I investigated literary sources and did field research on Mahāvidyā temples, iconography, and worship. I returned to Varanasi in 1992–93 to continue my research, this time with the help of a grant from McMaster University Arts Research Board.

During my research in Varanasi I was fortunate to have the assistance of many people. Om Prakash Sharma was indispensable in helping me locate several Mahāvidyā temples and paintings, putting me in touch with many knowledgeable people, and finding relevant texts. Virendra Singh, who patiently attempted to teach me Hindi, was always encouraging about my work. Mahant Sri Rama Shankar Tripathi of the Kashi Vishvanath temple held frequent useful discussions with me during 1983–84 and translated several relevant Sanskrit texts about the Mahāvidyās for me. Hemendra Nath Chakravarty was especially important in helping me think through the meaning of several of the Mahāvidyās and in locating and translating for me several crucial passages relating to the Mahāvidyās as a group and to individual Mahāvidyās. I also appreciated the many discussions I had with Mark Dyczkowski at his home overlooking Assi Ghat. I remember these chats as a pleasant blend of sober scholarly inquiry and amusing speculation on the mysteries presented by this unusual group of Hindu goddesses.

Doug Abrams Arava, my editor, has made several discerning suggestions that have very much improved this book and has been unwavering in his attentive support throughout its preparation. I owe special thanks also to the three readers who reviewed the manuscript: Kathleen Erndl, Miranda Shaw, and an anonymous reviewer. Their comments and criticisms proved very useful in revising the book. Victoria Wilson-Schwartz, the University of California Press copyeditor, was attentive, constructive, and unhesitant in scrutinizing my prose—to her, thanks very much. I am also grateful to my wife, Carolyn, for the many hours she spent lending this book consistency and clarity, from an early draft through subsequent stages of production.

Introduction

What is one to make of a group of goddesses that includes a goddess who cuts her own head off, another who prefers to be offered polluted items by devotees who themselves are in a state of pollution, one who sits on a corpse while pulling the tongue of a demon, another who has sex astride a male consort who is lying on a cremation pyre, another whose couch has as its legs four great male gods of the Hindu pantheon, another who prefers to be worshiped in a cremation ground with offerings of semen, and yet another who is a haglike widow?

Are these goddesses, who are known as the ten Mahāvidyās, bizarre creations of radical groups within the Hindu tradition, obscure beings whose significance is peripheral to the basic themes of Hindu spirituality? Should we dismiss them as tangential, perhaps even irrelevant, to Hindu religion? After years of studying and musing on them, it seems to me that there is a logic to the group as a whole and that even its most outrageous members, if understood within their proper context, reveal important spiritual truths.

We know the Mahāvidyās from a variety of sources. Many goddess temples across North India contain paintings and images of them. Contemporary lithographs portray them both as a group and individually. *Dhyāna* mantras describe them for liturgical and meditative purposes, and they are the subject of several tantric digests.

The Mahāvidyās have been known as a group since the early medieval period (after the tenth century C.E.).[1] Some of them predated this development and continue to be very well known in their own right, such as the fierce black goddess Kālī. She is also usually the primary, or *ādi*,

Mahāvidyā. Kamalā, who is the same as the very popular goddess Śrī-Lakṣmī, is also a member of the group. Tārā and Tripura-sundarī, lesser known but still far from obscure, are other examples of Hindu goddesses who are popular on their own and as part of the group. On the other hand, Bagalamukhī, Chinnamastā, Dhūmāvatī, and Mātaṅgī are rarely mentioned apart from the Mahāvidyās.

The aim of this study is to reflect on the meaning of the Mahāvidyās, both as a group and as individual deities. As a group, the Mahāvidyās present a curious collection. It is not at all apparent why these particular ten goddesses have become associated with one another. As for the individual goddesses, several are obscure and have received no scholarly attention. In some cases the sources available on individual Mahāvidyās are so limited that it is difficult, if not impossible, to reconstruct their histories or gain a clear impression of their worship. In many respects this study is not definitive or conclusive. I seek here to bring a preliminary ordering to the Mahāvidyā tradition in the hope that it will encourage other scholars to undertake more detailed studies of the group and of its individual members.

Throughout my study of the Mahāvidyās, I was told many times by a number of people—priests, scholars, painters, and practitioners—that the Mahāvidyās are "all one." Sometimes they were responding to a question concerning the significance of the group as a whole and sometimes to one concerning the peculiarities of an individual goddess. I often took this reply to indicate that the person did not have an appropriate answer to the question and that the main point, in any case, was to understand the group as so many manifestations of one (or the) great goddess. Such questions as, "Why does Bagalāmukhī like yellow?" "What does the name Bagalāmukhī mean, and what is its significance?" "Why does Kālī stand on Śiva?" "What is the significance of the name Mātaṅgī?" often elicited a look of incomprehension (why would I want to know this anyway?), followed by the comment that all of the Mahāvidyās are the same: they are all different expressions of the same goddess, who enjoys taking many forms for her own pleasure and the needs of her devotees. I usually took this as a formulaic reply, the kind that Hindus often make to non-Hindus who stand bewildered before the fantastic array of divinity expressed in the immense Hindu pantheon. After a careful study of the individual Mahāvidyās, however, it became apparent to me that in many ways this comment, "They are all one," is important in understanding the significance of the individual manifestations and their worship.

Texts that dwell in detail on the Mahāvidyās—the *Tantrasāra*, *Śākta-*

pramoda, *Śaktisaṁgama-tantra*, and many others—discuss each Mahāvidyā according to a clear structure. That is, the description and worship of each goddess is outlined in very similar terms, no matter how different she may appear from the others. She is made to conform to an accepted structure that has at least two central components: (1) a ritualistic approach to the deity that is individual and tantric in nature and (2) a philosophical/mythological paradigm of the Mahādevī (great goddess) to which the individual Mahāvidyā is compared or equated.

Whether the *sādhaka* (practitioner) worships Kālī or Kamalā, whether one seeks worldly boons or spiritual awareness, set patterns of worship determine how one approaches the deity. The adept must know, "perfect," and repeatedly recite the goddess's mantra (*japa sādhanā*) throughout the worship rituals; carefully select and "protect" a place of worship with the appropriate mantras and *mudrās* (hand gestures); correctly imagine and interiorize the goddess; draw or carefully imagine and worship her yantra; invoke the goddess's hymns, including her hundred- and thousand-name hymns; offer her standard sixteen-part *pūja* (worship), or an abbreviated form of it; and make his or her wish or wishes known to the chosen deity. The overall intent of the worship also has normative aspects. In general, the *sādhaka* seeks to identify with the goddess in question, to have a vision of her, and to gain a boon that is understood to be part of her "store" of grace. In the logic of the worship, if one is able to become the goddess, one can obtain that which she possesses, be it redemptive knowledge or the power to annihilate one's enemies.

This type of worship, generally known as tantric (as opposed to Vedic or *purāṇic*), is strongly individualistic. Tantric texts emphasize its secrecy. The mantras of the goddesses, which are the basic building blocks of tantric worship and represent the essential power of the goddesses, are always disguised and must be decoded by those with special knowledge before their exact components can be understood. A guru, a spiritual master who is expert and accomplished in the worship of a particular goddess, transmits the mantra of that goddess, and other details of worship, to the initiated individual. The guru gives this information only after determining the capability of the adept. Furthermore, the guru chooses the goddess whose peculiarities match the predilections of the initiate. An ideal match is supposedly made according to the guru's superior spiritual intuition and knowledge of both the initiate and the goddess. She becomes the initiate's special goddess, to whom he or she will devote intense energy over a lifetime.

It is uncommon for a person to be initiated into more than one goddess.

Fig. 1. Rājarājeśvarī (Lalitā, Tripura-sundarī), contemporary lithograph.

It is more typical for someone to focus on one particular goddess and to find in her the satisfaction of all his or her worldly and spiritual needs. For the adept, this goddess becomes the Great Goddess. This relationship between the goddess and the practitioner is individual and personal and in this sense is secret. That is, only the devotee and the goddess (and perhaps the adept's guru) know its nature and peculiar features. It is not shared with the public, not even with family members.

The philosophical/mythological model to which most of the individual Mahāvidyās conform is exemplified in the *Lalitā-sahasranāma*, an early thousand-name hymn in praise of Tripura-sundarī in her form as Lalitā. This text attributes several dominant characteristics to Lalitā. It identifies her in a number of ways and in many epithets as the highest reality in the cosmos, identical with certain philosophical absolutes such as *brahman*. As the highest reality, she oversees the three principal cosmic functions: creation, maintenance, and destruction. Related to this role as cosmic queen is her role as slayer of demons. She protects the world and the position of the gods by defeating demons that they have found too formidable. In this respect she is said to transcend or empower the great male gods Brahmā, Viṣṇu, and Śiva, who are often said to be helpless in the face of the demons she defeats. She is identified with the physical creation itself. She is *prakṛti*, the inherent or vital principle of creation. She is also usually identified with *śakti* (the inherent power of creation), *ātman* (the spiritual essence of reality), and *puruṣa* (another term denoting the spiritual aspect of creation). She is often described as the consort of Śiva and in this role is a model wife. She has many benign qualities and grants boons to her devotees, including spiritual attainments and enlightenment. She is also said to have fierce, terrible, frightening aspects, and sometimes she is said to like meat, liquor, and blood (all considered polluting in the Hindu tradition). She is also lovely to behold and erotically powerful.[2]

The ways and extent to which an individual Mahāvidyā conforms to this model vary, to be sure. As one might expect, hymns to goddesses such as Kālī and Chinnamastā paint them in rather fierce tones, while Kamalā and Bhuvaneśvarī are fairly benign in their hymns. But each goddess in her own way approximates the paradigm. From descriptions of Kālī in her *dhyāna* mantras, one might expect her to lack any pacific or nurturing qualities, but her thousand-name hymns describe her as having both. From Dhūmāvatī's *dhyāna* mantras, one would expect that she would lack all positive, beneficent features, but her thousand-name hymn says that she has many such qualities. Conversely, one is surprised to find fierce or terrible aspects to Kamalā, given her strong associations with good fortune, fertility, and royal authority, but such qualities are mentioned. It is also surprising, given the descriptions of most of the Mahāvidyās in their *dhyāna* mantras and the stories about their origins, that every one of them is strongly associated with Durgā in her role as demon slayer.

Each goddess, no matter how remote she may seem from the Great Goddess in other ways, in her thousand-name hymn is associated with protecting cosmic order by slaying demons. This is striking, given how different some of the Mahāvidyās appear to be from each other.

These texts seem to make the point that, indeed, in the case of the Mahāvidyās, "all are one." The origin myths of the group as a whole also make this point, saying that all ten forms arose from one goddess (Satī, Kālī, or Durgā) and all are different facets, aspects, or *avatāras* of that goddess. The hymns to the individual goddesses also seem to make the point by suggesting that an adept who delves deeply enough into any one of the Mahāvidyās will find them all in her. They inhere in each other and represent different facets of a single, multifaceted being. The adept or devotee need not worship all ten Mahāvidyās to gain their assortment of blessings or *siddhis*. He or she need only cultivate an intense and sustained rapport with one goddess to discover the blessings of all.

But why would one want to receive the blessings of such goddesses in the first place? Why would a Hindu practitioner go out of the way to establish rapport with a goddess who is outrageous or bizarre? What are the blessings to be had from these unusual goddesses? An important key to understanding, or appreciating, the Mahāvidyās, I think, lies precisely in their radical or outrageous aspects. It is true that some of the Mahāvidyās are benign deities, associated with such worldly boons as wealth, fecundity, and security. However, most of the Mahāvidyās are associated with marginality, inauspicious qualities, pollution, and death; they might be termed *antimodels*, especially for women. By antimodels I mean that their roles violate approved social values, customs, norms, or paradigms. For example, the most powerful approved model for Hindu women for centuries has been the goddess Sītā, who is the ideal *pati vratā* (a wife devoted to her husband). Hindu women for generations have been socialized to view Sītā as an ideal to imitate in their own lives. Sītā's husband is the be-all and end-all of her existence. Her thoughts and actions, wishes and dreams, all focus on him; her life only has meaning in relation to him. Most of the Mahāvidyās, however, either are independent from males or dominate (sometimes humiliate) them in one way or another. Many of the Mahāvidyās seem to mock the *pati vratā* ideal and to present an alternative social role that is almost its exact opposite. These goddesses, if they allow males in their presence at all, demand to be served by them.

Several of the Mahāvidyās also subvert the strong emphasis in the Hindu tradition on avoiding pollution. Death, which is highly polluting in Hindu culture, is a dominant theme in Mahāvidyā iconography and worship. Several Mahāvidyā goddesses dwell in cremation grounds and sit on corpses. Several wear garlands of severed heads (always male) or hold severed heads. Several receive blood sacrifice, always of male victims. Several like blood (which is itself polluting), perhaps need it, and sometimes are said to be smeared with it. Several of the Mahāvidyā goddesses are also sexually aggressive. Sexual fluids are polluting in Hindu culture, and the sexually powerful nature of the Mahāvidyās suggests that they are in a polluted state. They are often shown having sex, always in the so-called dominant or reverse position, that is, on top of their consorts. In the case of Mātaṅgī, we have a goddess who prefers pollution and who requires her devotees to be in a state of pollution when they offer her polluted substances, such as menstrual blood.

In many ways the goddess Kālī, who is almost always named as the first of the Mahāvidyās, is the prototype of the group in terms of being what I have termed an antimodel. She haunts cremation grounds. She wears a garland of severed human heads, which are often gushing blood that smears her body. She holds a freshly severed head in one of her hands. She receives blood sacrifice at her temples. She rides a ghost or a corpse as her vehicle. She is almost always naked. She is aggressive and is often standing on her male consort. She is sexually powerful and is shown having sex astride her consort (who sometimes lies on a funeral pyre). Her companions are ghosts, jackals, and female furies. Her hair is wild and unbound. Her tongue lolls out grotesquely, rudely, suggesting an insatiable, indiscriminate hunger and thirst. Kālī insults, subverts, and mocks the social status quo, particularly as it defines proper behavior for women.

Appreciating the liberating potential of antimodels, it seems to me, is one way of appreciating the Mahāvidyās. It is a theme I take up at several points in the book. I argue that it is a feature of certain aspects of tantric spirituality in particular, but I also think that it is a muted theme in much of the nontantric Hindu tradition as well. There is an insistence in Hinduism that the world as it appears to us is a show, that there remains hidden from our normal view an aspect of reality that is different, perhaps shockingly different, from our ego-centered way of apprehending it. The world is not the way we like to think it is, and the sooner we realize that, the quicker we will make progress in acquiring spiritual maturity. The Mahāvidyās, as antimodels, are awakeners, visions of the divine that challenge comfortable and comforting fantasies about the way things are in the world.

PART I

The Mahāvidyās as a Group

The Ten Mahāvidyās

The order in which the Mahāvidyās are given varies somewhat, as do the goddesses included in the group. In contemporary sources, however, the following goddesses in the following order are most common: (1) Kālī, (2) Tārā, (3) Tripura-sundarī (Ṣoḍaśī), (4) Bhuvaneśvarī, (5) Chinnamastā, (6) Bhairavī, (7) Dhūmāvatī, (8) Bagalāmukhī, (9) Mātaṅgī, and (10) Kamalā. The ten are described in most sources as follows:

1. Kālī is black, which in fact is what her name means. She has a fierce countenance, stands on the supine body of the god Śiva, and has four arms. Her upper left hand holds a bloodied cleaver and her lower left hand a severed head. Her right upper hand makes the sign "fear not," and her lower right hand makes the gesture of bestowing boons. She is naked, apart from a garland of severed heads and a girdle of severed arms; her hair is unbound and disheveled; and she is often standing in a cremation ground or on a battlefield. She is almost always mentioned as the first of the Mahāvidyās and occupies a preeminent place in the group. In some texts and in some settings, the other Mahāvidyās are understood to arise from her and to be her different forms.

2. Tārā is usually given as the second Mahāvidyā, and in appearance she is similar to Kālī. She is dark; her left foot is placed on a corpse or on Śiva; she wears a tiger skin; her hair is tied in a long braid; she is pot-bellied and has four arms. In her left hands she holds a knife and a sev-

Fig. 2. The ten Mahāvidyās, contemporary lithograph.

ered head, and her right hands make the signs of giving favors and granting fearlessness. She often stands in the midst of a cremation fire.

3. Ṣoḍaśī (also known as Tripura-sundarī, Lalitā, and Rājarājeśvarī) is a beautiful young girl of sixteen with a red complexion. She is sometimes shown astride Śiva in sexual intercourse. They are on a pedestal or couch supported by the gods Brahmā, Viṣṇu, Rudra, and Indra. Some descriptions say that the four gods who support her pedestal are Brahmā, Viṣṇu, Rudra, and Yama. Sometimes she is said to sit on a lotus that emerges from the navel of Śiva, who is reclining below her. Her four arms hold a noose, goad, bow, and arrows.

4. Bhuvaneśvarī, who is said to nourish the three worlds, holds a piece of fruit in one of her four hands, makes the sign of assurance with another, and holds a goad and a noose in the other two. Her breasts are large and ooze milk. She has a bright, light complexion and smiles pleasantly.

5. Chinnamastā has cut off her own head with a sword. Her left hand supports her head on a platter, and her right hand holds the sword with which she cut it off. Three jets of blood gush from her neck: one stream enters the mouth of her severed head; the other two jets enter the mouths of two female companions. Chinnamastā stands on the copulating bodies of the goddess Rati and her husband Kāma, the god of sexual lust. They in turn are lying on a lotus or sometimes a cremation pyre. Sometimes Chinnamastā (with her head chopped off) is shown astride Śiva, copulating with him as he lies beneath her. Her hair is loose, and she is naked.

6. Bhairavī has a fierce appearance; her primary role in the cosmic process is destruction. Her complexion is said to be as bright as thousands of rising suns. She wears a garland of skulls and clothes made from the skins of demons she has killed; her feet and breasts are covered with blood. Her four hands hold a rosary and a book and make the signs of fearlessness and granting wishes. The *Kālikā-purāṇa* says that her eyes roll from intoxication and that she stands on a corpse.[1]

7. Dhūmāvatī is tall, with a pale complexion and a stern, unsmiling face. She is dressed as a widow, in white clothes with no adornments. Her clothes are dirty and her hair disheveled. She is toothless, her breasts long and pendulous, and her nose large and crooked. She is hungry and thirsty, has a quarrelsome nature, and rides a crow or is seated on a chariot. She holds a winnowing basket and sometimes a trident.

8. Bagalāmukhī, "she who has the head of a crane," usually sits on a throne of jewels, which is sometimes in the midst of a body of water. She is dressed in a yellow *sārī*. In one hand she holds a club, with which she

Fig. 3. *Left to right, top to bottom*, the Mahāvidyās Kālī, Tārā, Ṣoḍaśī, Bhuvaneśvarī, and Chinnamastā.

Fig. 4. *Left to right, top to bottom*, the Mahāvidyās Tripura-bhairavī, Dhūmāvatī, Bagalā, Mātaṅgī, and Kamalā.

is about to beat a dark-complexioned enemy. With another hand she is pulling his tongue. Sometimes she sits on a corpse, and in some cases she has a crane's head, or a crane is her vehicle, or *vāhana*.

9. Mātaṅgī has several different forms. Usually she is a beautiful young woman with a dark or black complexion. The moon adorns her long hair, and she sits on a jeweled throne. She wears a beautiful robe and a garland of flowers. Her four hands hold a goad, noose, sword, and club. Her eyes are described as intoxicated from passion.

10. Kamalā is a beautiful young woman with a golden complexion. Two elephants flank her and pour pitchers of water on her while she sits on a lotus and holds lotuses in her hands. She is clearly a form of the goddess Lakṣmī, one of whose common epithets is Kamalā, "lotus."

This list of the Mahāvidyās is not unvarying. Lists or depictions of the Mahāvidyās almost always include Kālī, Tārā, Chinnamastā, Bagalāmukhī, Tripura-sundarī (Ṣoḍaśī), and Dhūmāvatī, but the others are sometimes excluded. At times, well-known goddesses such as Durgā, Annapūrṇā (she who is full of food), and Kāmākhyā (she whose eyes express desire) may be included in the list, which is the case in the *Cāmuṇḍā-tantra*.[2] At other times obscure goddesses such as Vāśalī, Bālā, and Pratyaṅgirās will be included.[3] In addition, the order in which the Mahāvidyās are given varies, although Kālī is almost always named as the first of the group and Tārā as the second.[4] The number of Mahāvidyās also varies. The *Niruttara-tantra* lists eighteen Mahāvidyās,[5] while the *Nārada-pañcarātra* says that there are seven million Mahāvidyās.[6]

Typical Literary and Iconographic Contexts

The Mahāvidyās are prominent primarily in tantric literature and in a few late *śākta purāṇas* and *upa purāṇas* (minor, later, or subsidiary *purāṇas*). The *tantras* contain little narrative material about the Mahāvidyās. They are primarily interested in providing the details of how to worship the Mahāvidyās and do not dwell on the meaning of their symbolism or stories that feature them. A typical tantric treatment of a Mahāvidyā includes, first, her mantra, which is believed to represent her essence; a devotee seeking the goddess's blessing or power must repeat it continually. Next, the goddess's *dhyāna* (meditation) mantra describes her physical appearance in some detail; again, the devotee is to fill his or her mind with this description of the goddess while ritually approaching her. The text also gives the goddess's *rahasya* (essence or secret), which is usually similar to her *dhyāna* mantra. It also lists her *kvaca* (armor), usually in the form of a prayer to protect her devotee on all sides. A *tantra* usually includes the goddess's *nāma stotra*, a list of her names or epithets. Sometimes it describes her yantra (a schematic drawing generally composed of circles, triangles, and stylized lotuses), along with directions for constructing and meditating upon it. In addition to this, the text sometimes gives directions for routine *pūjā* (worship), in which various items are offered to the goddess.

In *purāṇic* literature, only a few late texts mention the Mahāvidyās. They do, however, contain fairly detailed stories about the origin of the Mahāvidyās as a group. These myths are important in providing interpretive contexts for the group as a whole.

Certain goddess hymns also mention the Mahāvidyās. For example, they are named in the *Durgā-cālisā*, a famous hymn of forty verses to the goddess Durgā. They are also mentioned in the *Kāmākhyā-cālisā*. A hymn to the goddess Gaṅgā says that the Mahāvidyās Tārā, Dhūmāvatī, Mātaṅgī, and Bhairavī are her manifestations.[7] The purpose of their inclusion in such hymns is to demonstrate that the main deity being praised—for example, Durgā, Kāmākhyā, or Gaṅgā—appears in many forms throughout the world and that all goddesses are simply her manifestations.

Iconographically, the Mahāvidyās are often shown as a group in goddess temples. Their images are usually painted on the temple walls; more uncommonly, they may be represented by stone or metal images. Sometimes the presiding goddess of the temple in which the Mahāvidyās are depicted is herself one of them. In the Kālī-bārī temple dedicated to the goddess Kālī in Simla, for example, the Mahāvidyās are painted on the walls surrounding the *garbha gṛha*, the inner shrine room, which houses an image of Dakṣiṇā-kālī. Kālī herself is depicted among the Mahāvidyās.[8] In a temple to Dhūmāvatī in Varanasi, similarly, the Mahāvidyās are painted on the interior of the outer walls and include the usual group. Again in Varanasi, at the Lakṣmī Kund temple, the images of the Mahāvidyās are painted around the inside door frame of the main entrance to the temple and include Kamalā (a form of Lakṣmī).

In other cases, the Mahāvidyās are depicted in temples dedicated to goddesses who are not among the Mahāvidyās. Images of the Mahāvidyās are carved on pillars of a gate at Naina-devī temple in the district of Bilaspur in Himachal Pradesh. They are shown on the interior walls of a temple dedicated to Caraī-devī-mātā in Siddhapur on the outskirts of

Dharmsala in Himachal Pradesh. Caraī-devī is a local deity; her temple was established by truckers who sought the goddess's protection for their union building. At a Cāmuṇḍā-devī temple located about fifteen kilometers from Dharmsala, the Mahāvidyās are painted on the interior walls of the central shrine. An inscription states that the goddesses have been depicted according to the *Śākta-pramoda*, a well-known text that describes the Mahāvidyās. When I asked why the Mahāvidyās were depicted in the temple, the priest replied that Cāmuṇḍā-devī was a form of Kālī, the chief of the Mahāvidyās. In his mind, then, this temple is an example of the type in which the Mahāvidyās appear as a group in a temple dedicated to one of them. Hindu texts, however, almost always distinguish Cāmuṇḍā-devī from Kālī, and they are different in appearance.

Two other temples whose primary deity is not a Mahāvidyā are interesting because they are related to Satī and the origin of the Mahāvidyās. The temple of Jvālāmukhī-devī in Himachal Pradesh prominently depicts the Mahāvidyās on the walls of a large pavilion, separate from the main shrine, which houses an image of Durgā.[9] Jvālāmukhī-devī's temple is said to be the place where the goddess Satī's tongue fell when her body was chopped up by Viṣṇu and so is one of the *śākta pīṭhas*, sacred goddess sites scattered all over India.[10] As this is the case, Jvālāmukhī is associated with Satī, who, as we shall see below, is said to be the origin of the Mahāvidyās in certain mythological accounts of their origin. Similarly, the famous Kāmākhyā-devī shrine near Gauhati in Assam is said to be the place where Satī's yoni (vulva) fell to earth. The hillside on which the main shrine is located has small shrines to each of the Mahāvidyās.

At the Bajreśvarī-devī temple in Kangra, large paintings in an alcove called the *śakti bhavan* show the Mahāvidyās. The Amber Fort, about eleven kilometers east of Jaipur in Rajasthan, has a temple to Śilā-devī; a large double door at the main entrance to the temple depicts the ten Mahāvidyās.[11] In the Durgā Saptaśatī temple in Nagawa, just south of Varanasi, they are painted in a row on one of the inner walls of the main shrine.[12] The Mahāvidyās are also shown in bas-relief on the exterior walls of the temple at the Ramakrishna Math in Varanasi.

Temples dedicated to the group of Mahāvidyās themselves are rare, in my experience. Indeed, I have been able to find only one. In the section of north Calcutta known as Cossipore, near the cremation ground on the Hoogly River, is a small temple dedicated to the Dasamahāvidyās. It contains ten (*dasa*) images of the Mahāvidyās. Ṣoḍaśī is in the center and is larger than the rest. On her right, from the most distant to the closest, are Bagalā, Mātaṅgī, Kamalā, and Dhūmāvatī. On her left, from

Fig. 5. Dhūmāvatī, Durgā Saptaśati temple, Nagawa, Varanasi.

closest to farthest, are Kālī, Tārā, Bhuvaneśvarī, Bhairavī, and Chinnamastā. The temple enshrines several *liṅgams* (phalluses), connoting the presence of Śiva and suggesting his connection with the Mahāvidyās.

The presence of the Mahāvidyās at the Kāmākhyā temple at Kāmarūpa in Assam is unusual in the abundance and variety of images throughout the site.[13] This temple is an important *śākta* center according to many texts, because it is the place where Satī's yoni fell to earth, and hence her *adi pīṭha* (primordial or original seat). It is also strongly associated with the Mahāvidyās. Stone yonis in the main temple represent the Mahāvidyās Ṣoḍaśī, Mātaṅgī, and Kamalā. Indeed, some informants identify Kāmākhyā herself with Ṣoḍaśī. The other Mahāvidyās (and other goddesses as well) have small shrines or temples located nearby.[14] Several of these smaller shrines are associated with Śiva *liṅgams*. The Tārā temple is quite large and resembles the central shrine. The Bhairavī shrine has images of the other nine Mahāvidyās on the walls near the ceiling. The central representations of the Mahāvidyās in these shrines usually are not anthropomorphic and are sometimes difficult to see at all, as they are obscured by flowers, clothing, or offerings or are located in underground caves that are open for *darśan* (viewing by devotees) only on special occasions. Sometimes this representation is a yoni and is associated with a spring (as in the main shrine as well).

The Mahāvidyās are prominent iconographically in two large goddess festivals in Bengal, Durgā Pūjā (Navarātra) and Kālī Pūjā (Dīvalī). During Durgā Pūjā, artisans construct thousands of large clay images featuring Durgā as Mahiṣamardinī (the slayer of the buffalo demon Mahiṣa). These images are usually part of an elaborate tableau that includes the goddesses Sarasvatī and Lakṣmī and the gods Gaṇeṣa and Kārtikeya. Traditional renditions of this divine tableau have a halolike panel called the *cāl citra* (literally, "roof picture") behind and encircling the central image of Durgā. This frame depicts deities or scenes from Hindu mythology. It often shows the Mahāvidyās, giving the unmistakable impression that they are different forms of the goddess Durgā.

During Kālī Pūjā, devotees establish clay images of Kālī all over Bengal. The images are often set in a tableau featuring Śiva, Ramakrishna, and Bāmākhepa (two famous Bengali Kālī devotees) or some aspect of Kālī mythology or iconography. In recent years, Kālī's tableau has included the other Mahāvidyās. I saw two examples of this during Kālī Pūjā in October 1992. Both sets of Mahāvidyā images were set up in central Calcutta, and both featured Kālī in the center of the row of ten goddesses. Her image was far larger than the others; it was clear that she held the preeminent position. Indeed, a man at one of the *pandals* referred to the Mahāvidyās as "the ten Kālīs." For the most part, the images were faithful duplications of the tantric *dhyāna* mantras that describe the appearance of the Mahāvidyās.[15]

The Mahāvidyās as Forms of the Mahādevī

Both literary and iconographic materials give the general impression that the ten Mahāvidyās are different forms of an overarching, transcendent female reality, who is usually referred to simply as the

Fig. 6. Durgā surrounded by the Mahāvidyās, contemporary lithograph.

Mahādevī (great goddess). An underlying assumption of many *śākta* texts is that the highest reality is the Great Goddess, and this infinitely great being manifests herself in a wide variety of forms. Indeed, this is perhaps the central feature of Hindu *śākta* theology in those texts.[16] Many myths in *śākta* literature describe a goddess, or the goddess, as producing other goddesses from her own body. In such cases she often announces that she assumes different forms at different times to maintain cosmic stability,[17] to bless a particular devotee, or out of a sense of sport or playfulness. The theological idea is that ultimate reality, which is female in essence and form, displays herself in a great variety of ways for different purposes. Some texts even say that wherever a female being exists, there the goddess reveals herself, being present in every female form.[18] This theme is strong and obvious in the case of the Mahāvidyās. Their presence in *devī* temples seems to state: "The goddess enshrined in this place assumes many forms." The Mahāvidyās are the concrete expression of the idea of "many forms." In the case of goddesses who are identified with a particular place, and who are not well known outside their local areas, association with the Mahāvidyās lends them a cosmic, universal, transcendent dimension. The presence of the Mahāvidyās in a goddess temple identifies a local or regional goddess with an all-India mythology or symbolic structure, lending her a certain prestige.

There is evidence that the ten *avatāras* ("descents" or incarnations) of Viṣṇu are the model for the ten Mahāvidyās as expressions of the Mahādevī; that is, the Mahāvidyās represent, at least to some extent, a *śākta* version of the Vaiṣṇava idea. Comparison of the Mahāvidyās to the *avatāras* of Viṣṇu places a premium on their role as maintaining and sustaining the cosmic and moral orders. Individually and as a group, their positive, world-supporting natures are emphasized. The *Guhyātiguhya-tantra*, for example, lists the Mahāvidyās and identifies each with one of Viṣṇu's *avatāras:* Kālī is said to have become Kṛṣṇa, Chinnamastā to have become Narasiṁha, and so on.[19] The *Toḍala-tantra*, in chapter 11, also equates the ten Mahāvidyās with the ten *avatāras.*[20] An article on Tārā in Hindi says that the ten *avatāras* come from the fingernails of the Mahādevī and that the Mahāvidyās, which are also her forms, are like the *avatāras* in that they are created to help overcome *adharma* (evil or immorality).[21] The *Muṇḍamāla-tantra* compares the ten Mahāvidyās to the ten *avatāras.*[22] A contemporary Hindi work also compares the Mahāvidyās to the *avatāras.*[23] Another contemporary Hindi work on Tantra says that the Mahādevī takes on different forms from time to time to defeat demons, and the Mahāvidyās are such forms.[24] Iconographically the two groups are also associated. At the temple at the Ramakrishna Math in Varanasi, the ten *avatāras* are sculpted on two exterior walls, five to a side. The Mahāvidyās are on the other two walls. The juxtaposition of the two groups suggests that the Mahāvidyās are the female counterparts of the ten *avatāras*.

A *śākta* devotee and teacher in Varanasi, Swami Sadhananda Shastri, told me that the Mahāvidyās correspond to the "*avatāras*" (I put the term in quotations because several of the examples of male deities that he mentioned are not actually Viṣṇu *avatāras*): Bagalāmukhī is Vāmana, Kamalā is Viṣṇu, Kālī is Kṛṣṇa, Tārā is Rāma, Bhairavī is Rudra, Chinnamastā is Matsya, Mātaṅgī is Brahmā, Dhūmāvatī is Varāha, Ṣoḍaśī is Śiva, and Bhuvaneśvarī is the formless *brahman* (the absolute). He stated that, like the *avatāras* of Viṣṇu, the Mahāvidyās were created to play positive functions in the world. Tārā, for example, was created to defeat the thousand-headed Rāvaṇa, who appeared after Rāma's defeat of the ten-headed Rāvaṇa. The thousand-headed Rāvaṇa could be slain only by a woman, and so the Great Goddess took the form of Tārā to kill him. Kālī was created to eat and drink the blood of demons who threaten the world, and Chinnamastā, he said, was created to delude the demons at the churning of the ocean so that they would not get their share of the nectar of immortality. Chinnamastā took their share of the nectar, drank it, and then killed herself so that they were deprived of it. Ṣoḍaśī was created to arouse Śiva to sexual activity so his creative powers could stimulate the world. Bhuvaneśvarī was created to save the world when it was taken under the waters of the cosmic ocean and thus plays the same role as the boar *avatāra* of Viṣṇu. Kamalā was created to spread wealth in the world. Mātaṅgī, who is the same as Sarasvatī, according to Swami Shastri, was created to spread music and education and to help human beings acquire liberating wisdom (*jñāna*). Bagalāmukhī was created to paralyze enemies. Dhūmāvatī was created to spread disease. Although this may not seem a very positive cosmic role, we might suppose that Dhūmāvatī spreads disease to punish the wicked and support the moral order.[25]

Although an important aspect of *śākta* theology stresses the place of the Mahādevī in upholding the cosmic order and the Mahāvidyās are sometimes likened to Viṣṇu's *avatāras* as playing positive cosmic roles, the Mahāvidyās seem only tenuously connected to this type of activity in most tantric and *purāṇic* texts that mention them. In most cases, as we shall see, the emphasis seems to be not so much on maintaining cosmic order and defeating demons as on the diversity of forms the Mahādevī assumes and, by implication, the insistence that, through her many forms, she pervades all aspects of reality. That there are ten Mahāvidyās as a group, however, does seem best explained on the analogy of the ten *avatāras* of Viṣṇu, which is an ancient, well-known, and popular feature of Hindu mythology. In fact, this explanation is supported by certain texts and by present-day informants.

Mahāvidyā Origin Myths

I have come across five versions of the origin of the Mahāvidyās as a group. In one of these versions, the Mahāvidyās are different forms of the goddess Satī; in a second version they are forms of the goddess Pārvatī; in a third they arise from the goddess Kālī, herself one of the Mahāvidyās; in a fourth they are forms of the goddess Durgā; and in a fifth they are said to arise from the goddess Śatākṣī, who is also identified with Śākambharī and Durgā.

1. THE MAHĀVIDYĀS AS FORMS OF SATĪ

Of the five versions of the Mahāvidyās' origin, I have found only two that are firmly attested in literary sources. We shall look first at the most detailed version. In the *Mahābhāgavata-purāṇa* and the *Bṛhaddharma-purāṇa*, which are both late *śākta upa purāṇas*, probably written in eastern India after the fourteenth century C.E., the origin of the ten Mahāvidyās is recounted as part of the story of Dakṣa's sacrifice. This tale is ancient in the Hindu tradition and well known all over India. It is also an important *śākta* myth, being the prelude to the story of the origin of the *śākta pīṭhas*, which are sacred centers of goddess worship throughout India.[26] In early versions of the story, the Mahāvidyās do not appear; they enter it for the first time in these two relatively late *purāṇas*. By including their origin in this myth, of course, the authors of these texts have lent the Mahāvidyās considerable prestige, as the myth is well known and central to *śākta* mythology.

The account of the origin of the Mahāvidyās in the *Bṛhaddharma-* and *Mahābhāgavata-purāṇas* is as follows.[27] Once upon a time, Dakṣa decided to undertake a great sacrifice. He invited all the inhabitants of heaven, ali the gods and goddesses, except his daughter, Satī, and his son-in-law, Śiva. Dakṣa was not fond of Śiva, as he disapproved of Śiva's odd habits and antisocial nature. Śiva, the archetypal yogi, was fond of inhabiting lonely places and cremation grounds and surrounding himself with ghosts and goblins. When he was not going about completely naked, he wore animal hides. He often smeared his body with ashes and spent time in isolated meditation. To Dakṣa, he did not seem a fitting husband for his daughter, and so Dakṣa deliberately did not invite him or Satī to his sacrifice. Śiva himself was indifferent to this snub, but Satī was outraged and determined to attend her father's sacrifice in order to disrupt it and berate her father. Śiva, however, forbade her to go.

Now the story departs from earlier versions by introducing in an account of the origin of the Mahāvidyās. Forbidden by Śiva to attend the sacrifice, Satī becomes enraged and accuses him of neglecting her. In her anger her eyes become red and bright and her limbs tremble. Seeing her fury, Śiva closes his eyes. When he opens them, a fearsome female stands before him. As he looks at her, she becomes very old, her graceful appearance disappearing. She develops four arms, her complexion becomes fiery and her hair disheveled, her lips are smeared with sweat, and her tongue lolls out and begins to wave from side to side. She is naked except for a garland of severed heads; she wears the half moon as a crown. Standing before Śiva, she blazes like a million rising suns and fills the world with earth-shattering laughter.

Śiva is afraid and tries to flee. He runs around in all directions, but then the terrible goddess gives a dreadful laugh, and Śiva is too petrified to move. To make sure that he does not flee from her terrible form, Satī fills the directions around him with ten different forms (the Mahāvidyās). In the *Mahābhāgavata-purāṇa*, when Śiva asks who these goddesses are, Satī answers that they are her "friends."[28] Wherever Śiva goes or looks, he sees a dreadful figure, and his fear increases. Unable to flee, he stands still and closes his eyes. When he opens them, he sees before him a smiling woman whose face is as pleasing as a lotus blossom. She is black, her breasts are large, and she is naked. Her hair is disheveled, and she glows with the brilliance of a million suns. Śiva asks: "Where is my beloved Satī?" She replies: "Do you not see Satī standing before you?"

Śiva then asks who the other goddesses are who surround him and is told their names: Kālī, Tārā, Kamalā, Bhuvaneśvarī, Chinnamastā, Ṣoḍaśī, Sundarī, Bagalāmukhī, Dhūmāvatī, and Mātaṅgī. In relation to Śiva, who is facing south, Kālī is in front of him (to the south), Tārā above him, Chinnamastā to his right (west), Bhuvaneśvarī to his left (east), Bagalā behind him (north), Dhūmāvatī to the southeast, Tripura-sundarī to the southwest, Mātaṅgī to the northwest, and Ṣoḍaśī to the northeast.[29] At one point, the *Mahābhāgavata-purāṇa* (77.4–11) locates the Mahāvidyās

Fig. 7. Satī and Śiva surrounded by the Mahāvidyās, contemporary lithograph.

relative to the goddess Kāmākhyā, who is identified with Kālī. Kāmākhyā (or Kālī) is in the center, seated on a corpse that is lying on a lotus that is resting on a lion. The text identifies the corpse as Śiva, the lotus as Brahmā, and the lion as Viṣṇu, so the goddess is supported by the three great male deities of the Hindu pantheon. The Mahāvidyās are arrayed around the central figure, who faces south.[30] None of these enumerations of the Mahāvidyās elaborates their individual appearances or characteristics. The *Bṛhaddharma-purāṇa* does say that Tārā represents time and that Chinnamastā is emaciated and dreadful,[31] but for the most part the two texts content themselves with making general comments about the group as a whole.

In both accounts, Satī, in her terrible, black form, which is sometimes said to be Kālī, tells Śiva that these ten goddesses are her different forms. "All these figures are my excellent forms, and I abide in manifold forms."[32] In the *Bṛhaddharma-purāṇa* the Mahāvidyās as a group are said to cause trouble and conflict among people, but also to give spiritual liberation (*mokṣa*).[33] They are also said to bestow the powers of *māraṇa* (the ability to cause a person's death simply by willing it), *uccāṭana* (the ability to make one's enemy sick by willing it), *stambhana* (the ability to immobilize a person), the power to control another's speech, the power of remaining young oneself while causing another to grow old, and the power to attract another to oneself.[34] The *Bṛhaddharma-purāṇa* also says that when Brahmā creates the world and Viṣṇu maintains it, they use the powers of the Mahāvidyās "like two arms."[35] These references suggest that the Mahāvidyās are associated with magical powers, which may be acquired by worshiping them.

After the Mahāvidyās have surrounded Śiva and he has been told who they are, he acquiesces to Satī's wish and says that she may attend her father's sacrifice. In the *Mahābhāgavata-purāṇa*, Tārā merges with Kālī at this point, and the other forms disappear.[36] Satī, in the form of Kālī, then goes off to Dakṣa's sacrifice and kills herself by throwing herself on the sacrificial fire. In the *Bṛhaddharma-purāṇa* account, Satī leaves the Mahāvidyās behind with Śiva, instructing them to look after him in her absence. She explains that she has created these forms to attend Śiva when she is away.[37] Then Satī, taking on a form that wears a tiger skin and has disheveled hair, a fearsome face, and fiery red eyes, heads off to Dakṣa's sacrifice, flying through the sky. The rest of the story conforms to the account in the *Mahābhāgavata-purāṇa.*

In the version of the origin of the Mahāvidyās that is given in the *Bṛhaddharma-* and *Mahābhāgavata-purāṇas*, there are several important points to be noted.

First, the myths make clear that Satī, or the goddess in the form of Satī, is a superior power to Śiva. He forbids her to attend her father's sacrifice, but she forces him to let her go by overwhelming him with her numerous and terrible forms. Both accounts of the story stress the fact that Śiva is afraid of the goddess in her terrible forms and tries to flee. The fact that the goddess is able to physically restrain Śiva dramatically makes the point that she is superior in power. The theme of the superiority of the goddess over male deities is common in *śākta* texts, so the story is stressing a central *śākta* theological principle.

Second, the *Bṛhaddharma-* and *Mahābhāgavata-purāṇa* account of the origin of the Mahāvidyās stresses their terrifying aspects. Although other texts describe some of the Mahāvidyās as pleasant, beautiful, and mild of manner, here they are, as a group, awful and frightening. The one goddess the story does describe in detail, the initial form taken by Satī, is particularly fearsome, and Śiva reacts to it by closing his eyes or trying to run away. This account stresses the dramatic effects the Mahāvidyās have on Śiva. He is frightened and repelled by them. They are terrible, not pleasing, in form.

Third, this version of the Mahāvidyās' origin emphasizes that the ten goddesses are manifestations of Satī, or of the Great Goddess, who has taken the form of Satī. When Śiva asks who the Mahāvidyās are, Satī tells him they are her forms or her friends. The myth makes clear that the Mahāvidyās are extensions of Satī's power. They embody her will and wrath and succeed in bending Śiva to her wishes.

Fourth, the appearance of the Mahāvidyās takes place in the context of husband-wife and father-daughter tensions. Dakṣa insults his daughter by not inviting her to his home for the sacrifice, and Śiva offends her by not allowing her to go to her paternal home. The Mahāvidyās are, at least to some extent, the embodiments of an offended wife and daughter. They are the embodiments of female fury precipitated by male neglect and abuse.

The cult of the goddess Nandā-devī of Garwahl in Himachal Pradhesh illustrates the potential danger posed by unfairly restricting a woman's freedom to return to her native village (the domain of her father), whether the impediments are caused by the father or the husband. Although local Garwahli literature stresses that a woman is totally transformed when she marries, becoming part of her husband's lineage, Garwahli women insist that females remain strongly identified with, influenced by, and related to their home families and villages, their *maits.* Both men and women share the belief that a woman has the ability to effectively curse her husband or her father if she is impeded from maintaining contact with her home village. The bride who has gone away, the "out-married village daughter" (*dhiyāṇī*), should continue to be respected by her home village and must be invited back for all its important festivals and events. A village that neglects to do this risks her destructive curse, which could be ruinous. In the cult of the goddess Nandā-devī, a yearly pilgrimage wends its way through many local villages where she is worshiped, and this represents her return to her native village. If this pilgrimage is not undertaken, the goddess will be offended and assume that she is no longer loved and respected. Such implied neglect or indifference would court her wrath.[38]

A similar situation exists in the story of Satī. Her *mait* is not fulfilling its duty to her, because her father has not invited her home for his elaborate sacrifice. Furthermore, her husband, in forbidding her to return to her home village, is showing her serious disrespect. Both Śiva and Dakṣa become the targets of her anger. In the logic of the Nandā-devī cult, Satī returns to her home village enraged at her father's lack of respect for her and immolates herself in her father's sacrificial fire. He and his home are cursed and eventually destroyed by Śiva and his hosts when Śiva hears of Satī's death.

A fifth important point about this version of the origin of the Mahāvidyās is that these goddesses are associated with magical powers and have little or no connection with upholding the order of dharma.[39] They do not resemble the *avatāras* of Viṣṇu in either nature or function. They do not appear in order to defeat demons who threaten the stability of the world but in order to frighten Śiva into allowing Satī to attend her father's sacrifice. Their primary role in the story is to overpower an opponent, in this case, Śiva. The *Bṛhaddharma-purāṇa* says that the Mahāvidyās have been created to produce conflict and trouble among people[40] and that they confer the power to kill at will, to immobilize one's enemies, and so on. Indeed, the effect they have on Śiva underlines this aspect of their nature. Śiva is alternately frightened into fleeing and frozen with fear. Although other myths concerning individual Mahāvidyās suggest their world-supporting function, and in several instances the Mahāvidyās are compared to the Vaiṣṇava *avatāras*, this version of their origin only hints at world-supporting characteristics. Although some of the individual Mahāvidyās are more strongly associated with magical powers than others, as we will see below, this version of the group's origin says that the group as a whole grants these powers.

2. THE MAHĀVIDYĀS AS FORMS OF PĀRVATĪ

The second version of the origin of the Mahāvidyās was told to me by the *mahant* (chief priest) of the Kashi Vishvanath temple in Varanasi, Sri Rama Shankar Tripathi, who in turn was told the story by a *tāntrika* friend of his. The *tāntrika* said the story was to be found in "all the Tantra *śāstras*," but as yet I have not been able to find it in any written source. According to this version, Śiva is living with his second wife, Pārvatī (whom he married after Satī killed herself), in her father's house in the mountains. One day, Śiva decides to leave. Pārvatī asks him to stay, but he refuses. When he attempts to leave, she prevents him from doing so by blocking the ten doors of the house with her ten forms, the Mahāvidyās. The esoteric meaning of the myth, according to the *tāntrika*, is based on an allegory. The house represents the human body, and the blocking of the ten doors means the blocking, or controlling, of the ten bodily apertures: two eyes, ears, and nostrils, plus the mouth, anus, penis or vagina, and *brahmarandhra* (an aperture at the top of the head). In this allegorical interpretation, Śiva's desire to leave Pārvatī's house presumably signifies the individual's desire to indulge the senses willfully, to act without yogic discipline and control.

This version bears similarities to the first version of the Mahāvidyās' origin. As in the first one, the Mahāvidyās appear in order to restrain Śiva, to bend him to the goddess's will. He wants to leave his father-in-law's house, but she wants him to remain. The Mahāvidyās force the issue in Pārvatī's favor. It is also clear in this version that the Mahāvidyās are all forms of one goddess, in this case, Pārvatī. They represent various aspects of the goddess. As in the first version also, the appearance of the Mahāvidyās is the result of marital tension. In this case, however, the goddess's father seems to play little or no role. This version of the story also emphasizes the superiority of the goddess over Śiva. The fact that Śiva and Pārvatī are living at her father's house in itself makes this point, as it is traditional in many parts of India for the wife to leave her father's home upon marriage and become a member of her husband's lineage and live in his home among his relatives. That Śiva dwells in Pārvatī's house implies her priority in their relationship. Her priority is also demonstrated in her ability, through the Mahāvidyās, to thwart Śiva's will and assert her own.

This story lends itself to an allegorical interpretation of the Mahāvidyās as aspects or powers of the human organism, states of consciousness perhaps, rather than as world-supporting or cosmic powers. The teller's emphasis on their role in yogic concentration, or perhaps *sādhanā* (religious endeavor) generally, suggests that the Mahāvidyās are associated with facets, aspects, dimensions, or characteristics of the human organism, which in Tantra is understood to be the universe in microcosm. In fact, this interpretation of the Mahāvidyās is supported by some tantric texts. The *Śaktisaṁgama-tantra*, for example, says that the Māhavidyās are connected with the five senses (sound, touch, color or sight, flavor, and smell) and the five elements (ether, air, fire, water, and earth).[41] Although the *Śaktisaṁgama-tantra* does not specify which Mahāvidyā is connected with each sense or element, it is clear that they are associated with the fundamental makeup of humans.

The association of the Mahāvidyās with *siddhis* (magical powers) is also implied in this second version of their creation. Such powers are acquired by means of *sādhanā*, which almost always includes yogic practices aimed at controlling or enhancing the senses. We shall treat the idea of the Mahāvidyās as *siddhis* in more detail below.

3. THE MAHĀVIDYĀS AS FORMS OF KĀLĪ

The third version of the origin of the Mahāvidyās is found in a contemporary Hindi book about the worship of Tārā.[42] According to this version, Śiva is living with the goddess Kālī in the Satya Yuga, the first and most perfect of the four periods of a world cycle. Eventually he grows restless and decides he is tired of living with Kālī. He gets up, and when she asks him where he is going, he answers: "Wherever I wish!" She does not reply, and he begins to wander off. However, in whichever direction Śiva goes, a form of Kālī appears, one of the Mahāvidyās: first Kālī herself, then Tārā, Ṣoḍaśī, Bhuvaneśvarī, Bagalāmukhī, Bhairavī, Kamalā, Dhūmāvatī, Mātaṅgī, and Chinnamastā. Seeing these goddesses, Śiva loses his yearning to leave Kālī and wander about, having gained the knowledge (*vidyā*) that she pervades the entire cosmos and that wherever one goes she is there in one of her forms.

This version of the myth is obviously related to the first two in several respects. The Mahāvidyās arise as manifestations of a particular goddess, who is said to be Śiva's spouse. As in the other two versions, the goddess (Kālī, in this case) creates the Mahāvidyās to prevent Śiva from leaving or fleeing. This version also gives no indication that the Mahāvidyās play a role similar to the Vaiṣṇava *avatāras*. Unlike the first two versions, however, there is less emphasis on marital tension, although the implication is that Śiva is going against Kālī's wish by trying to leave her and wander about. This version also does not indicate that the Mahāvidyās are terrible or frightening (they are not even described) or that Śiva is afraid of them. The story does not even say that the Mahāvidyās prevent Śiva from leaving. It simply says that Kālī fills the whole cosmos with her forms.

The central point of this version of the origin of the Mahāvidyās, a point implicit in the other versions, is that it is impossible to go where the goddess is not. To depart (or flee) from her is impossible, as she pervades the entire cosmos in one form or another. She is everywhere; indeed, she is identical with the cosmos itself. The story as told here also places a premium on the Mahāvidyās as revealing knowledge (*vidyā*), in this case, knowledge that Kālī pervades all of reality. In this sense, the story interprets the Mahāvidyās, not as *avatāra*-type figures who maintain the cosmos, nor as manifestations of magical powers or states of consciousness, but as sources of wisdom. The point of this version of the story is Śiva's enlightenment, which the Mahāvidyās bring about.

4. THE MAHĀVIDYĀS AS FORMS OF DURGĀ

Contemporary oral tradition, supported by certain iconographic evidence, supplies yet a fourth version of the origin of the Mahāvidyās. According to this version, the Mahāvidyās appear when the great battle queen Durgā confronts the demons Śumbha and Niśumbha. The myth of Durgā's defeat of these demons constitutes the third episode of the *Devī-māhātmya* and is also told in several other *purāṇas.*[43] Although none of the texts that describe this battle mentions the Mahāvidyās, several people have told me that they fight in it as a group. Moreover, individual Mahāvidyās are sometimes associated with the myth, and there is, as we shall see, considerable iconographic evidence to support this version of the Mahāvidyās' origin. A contemporary Hindi book on Tantra also alludes to this version of the origin of the Mahāvidyās: the author states that, in the beginning, the male gods were threatened by demons and appealed to the Mahādevī, who defeated the demons by taking on different forms, including the nine Durgās[44] and the ten Mahāvidyās.[45]

The *Devī-māhātmya* is the most famous and revered of all Hindu *śākta* texts. It was probably written around the sixth century C.E. and today occupies a central position in *śākta* circles. Several commentaries have been written on it, and several subsidiary texts have arisen as addenda to it.[46] It is not surprising, therefore, that people associate the Mahāvidyās with this famous text. The nature of the text also invites such association, particularly the third episode featuring the defeat of Śumbha and Niśumbha. The theology of the *Devī-māhātmya* is summed up in that episode. Durgā is said to underlie or pervade the cosmos; to create, maintain, and periodically destroy it according to the rhythmic sequences of Hindu cosmology (12.33–35); and to assume different forms from time to time when

Fig. 8. Durgā with the Mahāvidyās, contemporary lithograph.

cosmic balance is threatened by enemies of the gods (11.38–51). The theology of the text is succinct: "Though she is eternal, the goddess becomes manifest over and over again to protect the world" (12.32). This is very similar to the Vaiṣṇava *avatāra* theology.[47] When associated with this type of theology, the Mahāvidyās' function becomes primarily that of upholding and protecting cosmic order. We have already seen that other texts compare the Mahāvidyās to the *avatāras*, so it is not surprising that some Hindus think they appear in the *Devī-māhātmya*, even though they do not.

Another feature of the third episode of the *Devī-māhātmya* makes it understandable that the Mahāvidyās would be thought to arise there. In the course of the battle, Durgā produces several goddesses to help her. She brings forth Kālī while confronting the demons Caṇḍa and Muṇḍa (7.3–22) and calls upon her again for help in defeating Raktabīja (8.49–61). During the battle a group of seven goddesses, collectively known as the Mātṛkās, is created from certain male gods to help defeat the demons. They are Brahmāṇī, created from Brahmā; Māheśvarī, created from Śiva; Kaumarī, created from Kārtikeya; Vaiṣṇavī, created from Viṣṇu; Vārāhī, created from the boar *avatāra* of Viṣṇu; Narasiṁhī, created from the man-lion *avatāra* of Viṣṇu; and Aindrī, created from the god Indra (8.12–20). Later in the battle, when Durgā confronts the demon Śumbha himself, he challenges her to single combat, and she agrees, saying that her battle companions are only her different forms (10.2–5). She then absorbs the Mātṛkās and Kālī into herself. The *Devī-māhātmya* describes the nature of the Mātṛkās as wild and fierce. They are furious warriors and near the end of the battle dance wildly, intoxicated on the blood of their slain victims (8.62).[48] The third episode, then, includes the creation of a group of goddesses who bear certain resemblances to the Mahāvidyās, giving rise to the tradition that the Mahāvidyās themselves appear in the *Devī-māhātmya*. It is also the case that other texts compare individual Mahāvidyās to the Mātṛkās or give them Mātṛkās' names as epithets. The Mahāvidyā Tripura-bhairavī, for example, in her *sahasranāma stotra* (thousand-name hymn) in the *Śākta-pramoda*, has the following epithets: Brahmāṇī, Maheśvarī, Kaumarī, Vaiṣṇavī, Vārāhī, Cāmuṇḍā, and Indrāṇī.[49] They are the same as the names of the Mātṛkās in the *Devī-māhātmya*, except that the *Śākta-pramoda* substitutes Cāmuṇḍā for Nārasiṁhī. The Mahāvidyā Bhuvaneśvarī has among her many epithets Vaiṣṇavī, Brahmāṇī, Nārasiṁhī, Maheśvarī, and Vārāhī.[50]

There is also iconographic support for this fourth version of the origin of the Mahāvidyās. Contemporary religious art typically shows the

Fig. 9. Durgā surrounded by the Mahāvidyās, contemporary lithograph.

Mahāvidyās surrounding a central goddess, none other than Durgā (in her form of Mahiṣamardinī, slayer of the demon Mahiṣa) and the central figure of the *Devī-māhātmya*. While contemporary art also depicts the Mahāvidyās surrounding Śiva and Satī as the central figures, the configuration with Durgā in the center is just as common, if not more common, at least in the areas with which I am most familiar, Varanasi and Calcutta. The depiction of the Mahāvidyās on the *cāl citras* of the Durgā images set up for Durgā Pūjā also reinforces the tradition that the Mahāvidyās arise to help Durgā defeat demons and restore the stability of the cosmos. At the Durgā Saptaśati temple in Nagawa, just outside Varanasi (a temple dedicated to the *Devī-māhātmya*, popularly known as the *Saptaśati*), paintings of the Mahāvidyās on a wall of the inner shrine also dramatically associate the Mahāvidyās with Durgā, and specifically with Durgā as she appears in the *Devī-māhātmya*. From these examples it is easy to conclude that the Mahāvidyās are forms of Durgā, and as Durgā is primarily a battle queen, it is also logical to assume that the Mahāvidyās play the role of supporting Durgā in her attempts to protect the cosmic order.[51]

This version, then, differs markedly from the first three in its view of the role and nature of the Mahāvidyās. This version does not mention marital tension, the goddesses do not appear in order to frighten or control Śiva, they are not associated with magical powers, and they are in a battlefield rather than a domestic setting. Their association with the *avatāras* of Viṣṇu is heightened and stressed.

Stories associated with individual Mahāvidyās also tend to suggest this fourth version of their origin. An image maker in Varanasi, for example, told me that Dhūmāvatī was created by Durgā in her battle with Śumbha and Niśumbha and that she helped defeat these demons by employing acrid smoke, "like tear gas," against them. Dhūmāvatī, "she who abides in smoke," is here interpreted as having a special weapon with which she defeats demons for the welfare of the world. Similarly, I have been told that Bagalāmukhī has often appeared in battles, where she has deluded the enemy (often the Pakistanis) into making critical blunders. Swami Sadhananda Shastri, a tantric practitioner from Varanasi, whom I mentioned earlier as comparing the Mahāvidyās to the *avatāras*, noted a world-maintaining function for each of the Mahāvidyās.[52]

Several people have also told me that famous gods and heroes of Hindu mythology employed the Mahāvidyās, or the powers gained through worshiping them, in their conquest of demons. Śiva killed Tāraka, Kṛṣṇa defeated Kaṁsa, Rāma killed Rāvaṇa, and Indra killed Vṛtra with the help of the Mahāvidyās. Likewise, Hanuman, with the aid of the Mahāvidyās, defeated the female demon who tried to stop him from jumping to Lanka. That is, by propitiating the goddesses he was able to acquire the magical power of becoming very small and thus was able to enter the mouth of the female demon and destroy her from inside.[53] Indeed, at the Sankat Mochan temple in Varanasi, a famous Hanuman temple, the Mahāvidyās are depicted around the ceiling of the porch in front of the shrine containing the main Hanuman image.

When we look at the individual Mahāvidyās in detail, as we shall do below, it also becomes apparent that they are often associated with Durgā the demon slayer and the *Devī-māhātmya* myths. To take just one example at this point, Bhuvaneśvarī in her *sahasranāma stotra* in the *Rudrayāmala* has among her names several that directly identify her with Durgā, the forms Durgā takes in the *Devī-māhātmya*, and the actions she performs there. She is called She Who Destroys Madhu and Kaiṭabha, She Who Slays Mahiṣāsura, and She Who Slays Śumbha and Niśumbha. These three names, that is, identify her with all three episodes of the *Devī-māhātmya* as the slayer of the principal demons.[54] She is also called Śivadūtī, Cāmuṇḍā, and She Who Destroys Raktabīja, all of which are epithets of Durgā or one of Durgā's forms in the *Devī-māhātmya*. She is also called by the name Durgā itself.[55]

5. THE MAHĀVIDYĀS AS FORMS OF ŚATĀKṢĪ

The fifth version of the origin of the Mahāvidyās is told in the *Devī-bhāgavata-purāṇa*. As in the fourth version, they arise to defend the world against demons. Once upon a time the demon Durgama gained control over the universe and forced the gods into subservience. The gods appealed to the Mahādevī for help. She appeared in a form having innumerable eyes, all of which shed tears on seeing the pitiable plight of the gods, human beings, and the earth as a result of demonic oppression. She was duly named Śatākṣī (she who has one hundred eyes). She then distributed fruits and vegetables from her own body to feed the starving beings of the earth, which was suffering from drought. For this reason she was named Śākambharī (she who bears vegetables). A fierce battle then began between the goddess and the demon and his armies. The goddess created several groups of goddess allies to help her in this fight, and among them were the Mahāvidyās. The text says that these goddesses are her principal *śaktis* and have emerged directly from her body. It names them in the following order: Kālikā, Tāriṇī, Tripurā, Bhairavī, Kamalā, Bagalā, Mātaṅgī, Tripura-sundarī, Kamākṣā, Tulajā-devī, Jambhinī, Mohinī, and Chinnamastā.[56] The *Devī-bhāgavata-purāṇa* does not mention the Mahāvidyās again. At the end of the battle the goddess is named Durgā because she killed the demon Durgama.

There are two important points to note about this version of the origin of the Mahāvidyās. First, they are created to defeat demons and defend the cosmic order, as in version 4. In this sense they function like the *avatāras* of Viṣṇu. They are forms of the Mahādevī created for a specific purpose. Second, they are mentioned along with other groups of goddesses: the Guhya-kālīs, who are said to number ten thousand, and two other groups, numbering thirty-two and sixty-four. The group of sixty-four may allude to the sixty-four *yoginīs.* According to the text, the goddess (called Mahādevī, Māheśvarī, Śatākṣī, Śākambharī, and Durgā, among other names) has many forms and multiplies herself as needs arise. In the *Devī-bhāgavata-purāṇa* this is a very common theme. Throughout this treatise on goddess mythology and philosophy, a central theme is the overarching reality of the Mahādevī, the highest principle in the universe, indeed, the universe itself. According to this text, she manifests herself in many female forms, and all goddesses are manifestations of her.[57]

CONCLUSIONS

Having reviewed these five versions of the origin of the Mahāvidyās, we can now draw some general conclusions about what they tell us about these goddesses.

The Mahāvidyās are related to Śiva. The goddesses from whom the Mahāvidyās are created are usually associated with Śiva as his spouse. The first three versions feature Satī, Pārvatī, and Kālī as his wife or consort. Several of the individual Mahāvidyās, as we shall see below, also have strong associations with Śiva, reinforcing this point.

Śiva is subordinate to the goddesses. In versions 1–3, the Mahāvidyās limit, frighten, or control Śiva. Indeed, this is the reason they were created in these three versions. The Mahāvidyās demonstrate the superior might of the goddess in question, her ability to overpower Śiva. Versions 1–3, that is, emphasize the superiority of the goddess to Śiva. A common theme in *śākta* theology, and in many tantric texts as well, is that Śiva is ultimately dependent upon *śakti.* This theme is succinctly and vividly expressed in the well-known saying, "Śiva is a mere *śava* (corpse) without *śakti.*" This theme of Śiva's dependence upon *śakti* is perhaps expressed most clearly in version 2, which features Kālī as the source of the Mahāvidyās. In this version, Śiva wishes for independence. He wants to leave Kālī but cannot, because she pervades the cosmos in her various forms. There is nowhere that she is not. It is impossible to exist apart from her. This theme is also implicit in versions 1 and 3.

The Mahāvidyās are fierce goddesses. In version 1, the Mahāvidyās as a group are dreadful and frightening. Versions 2, 3, and 4 imply their fierce nature but do not make it explicit. The frightening nature of the Mahāvidyās is also attested in most descriptions of individual Mahāvidyās. Kālī, Tārā, Bagalā, Dhūmāvatī, and Chinnamastā are nearly always frightening, terrible, and fierce. Tripura-sundarī (Ṣoḍaśī), Bhairavī, Mātaṅgī, and Bhuvaneśvarī are often said to have fearsome characteristics. Only Kamalā is consistently presented as benign. In characterizing tantric religion generally as "more rugged than tender,"[58] the authors of a recent book on Tantrism might well be describing the Mahāvidyās, who in fact feature prominently in tantric religion.

The Mahāvidyās are associated with magical powers. Version 1 explicitly, and versions 2 and 3 implicitly, link the Mahāvidyās to magical, meditative, or yogic powers. Many other texts about the Mahāvidyās emphasize this association, particularly in the case of certain individual Mahāvidyās, such as Bagalāmukhī. These powers are often used to control other people, usually adversaries, and include the power to bring about whatever one wills, to attract other people to oneself, to immobilize someone or make that person mute, to cause someone to flee, to make others grow old prematurely while remaining young oneself, and to kill someone simply by willing it. The fact that in versions 1–3 a goddess is able to control Śiva with the Mahāvidyās reinforces the idea that they are associated with magical or meditative powers. We might say that in these three versions, the goddess in question controls Śiva with her magical or meditative powers.

Male-female tensions and female independence. In versions 1 and 2, the Mahāvidyās emerge against a background of male-female tensions, and there may be the implication of such tension in version 3 as well. This tension arises when the goddess feels abused, ignored, or insulted by her father or husband. In version 1, Satī becomes furious and transforms herself into such a horrible, frightening being that Śiva can barely stand to look at her. The Mahāvidyās are forms of this being, further personifications of Satī's wrath. Version 1 makes clear, and versions 2 and 3 imply, that the goddess, Śiva's spouse in each case, has a will of her own and is perfectly capable of exercising that will even if it means going against her husband or father. The point cannot be missed in version 1: Satī is not content to remain a passive, obedient, submissive wife if she is sufficiently provoked. She contains aspects and powers that easily overwhelm and frighten her husband.

The fact that the individual Mahāvidyās are not submissive consorts of male deities reinforces the emphasis in versions 1–3 that the goddess is an independent being. Most of the individual Mahāvidyās are not depicted with a male consort, and when they are, as in the case of Kālī, Tārā, and Tripura-sundarī, for example, they dominate him (both Kālī and Tārā are shown standing on the supine body of Śiva, while Tripura-sundarī is usually shown sitting on him).

World maintenance. Versions 4 and 5 differ markedly from versions 1–3 in stressing the world-maintaining function of the Mahāvidyās. Versions 4 and 5 cast the Mahāvidyās in the familiar role of forms of the goddess Durgā or the Mahādevī, created by her to defeat demons who have usurped the position of the gods. The extent to which individual Mahāvidyās are described or featured as world maintainers or demon slayers varies a good deal. Kālī is well known as a demon slayer and is often featured in the role. Others, however, such as Dhūmāvatī and Bagalā, are only rarely described in this capacity. For the most part, with the exception of Kālī, world maintenance is a minor theme in stories of the individual Mahāvidyās.

Group versus individual character of the Mahāvidyās. Finally, it is important to note that the Mahāvidyās as a group in these five versions of their origin often function or are described quite differently from the individual Mahāvidyās. As was just noted, the world-maintaining aspect of the Mahāvidyās is stressed in versions 4 and 5 but figures only weakly in the worship, mythology, and symbolism of the individual Mahāvidyās. Version 1 implies that all the Mahāvidyās are associated with magical powers and that they all create conflict among people. However, the extent to which the individual Mahāvidyās are characterized this way varies a good deal. Bagalāmukhī, for example, is strongly associated with these characteristics, but Kamalā hardly at all.

Interrelationships among the Mahāvidyās

As a group, the Mahāvidyās present a curious collection of goddesses. If there is an internal coherence to the group that explains how its members are related to each other, it is not readily apparent. Neither in textual sources nor in the contemporary oral tradition have I been able to discover an obvious pattern or logic to the inclusion of these ten goddesses in the same group. There are hints in some texts, and some of my informants have speculated about the question. These hints and speculations cover a wide range of possibilities.

1. FORMS OF THE GREAT GODDESS

Many texts and the contemporary oral tradition say that the Mahāvidyās are "all forms of the goddess," that "they are all one." Indeed, this is clearly the case. One Mahāvidyā is often explicitly equated with another or with several others. To take just one example, among the names of Bhuvaneśvarī in her *sahasranāma stotra* from the *Rudrayāmala* are Mātaṅgī (v. 10), Bhairavī (v. 12), Kālikā (v. 15), Ugra-tārā (v. 19), Tārā (v. 20), Sundarī (v. 10), Chinnamastā (v. 60), and Kamalā (v. 6).[59] The impression is difficult to avoid that each Mahāvidyā is one facet of a multifaceted Great Goddess and that each facet contains all the others—that if one observes intensely and carefully enough, one will find all forms inhering in each particular form.

What continues to be perplexing, however, is why this particular combination of ten goddesses has come to express the rather basic *śākta* theological theme that the Great Goddess has many forms. With the exception of Kālī, Kamalā, and to some extent Tripura-sundarī and Tārā, the goddesses who make up this group are not very well known. Indeed, some of the Mahāvidyās are obscure. If the intention of Mahāvidyā mythology and iconography is to illustrate the idea that the goddess takes many forms, one would have thought that some of the more popular goddesses, such as Durgā and Sarasvatī, would have been included in the group. The choice of the ten goddesses who make up the Mahāvidyās as illustrative of this idea, then, is not obvious and still begs the question concerning the essential interrelatedness of the group.

2. ŚAIVITE ASSOCIATIONS

Versions 1–3 of the origin of the Mahāvidyās stress that they issue from Śiva's wife or consort and are all forms of this goddess. It therefore seems that one characteristic of the group that lends it coherence is that all of the Mahāvidyās are wives or consorts of Śiva, or strongly associated with Śiva. The problem here is that when we look at the Mahāvidyās individually, as we shall do below, we find that some of the Mahāvidyās have a stronger affiliation with Śiva than others, that Dhūmāvatī is a widow and has no consort (although, as we shall see, one of her individual origin myths relates her to Satī), and that Kamalā is the wife of Viṣṇu, not Śiva. Moreover, an explanation of the interrelationship of the Mahāvidyās as centered in their relationship to Śiva breaks down outside these three versions. The emphasis on the independence of the goddess from whom the Mahāvidyās arise, and on the independence of several individual Mahāvidyās, also tends to attenuate this feature as the key to explaining the logic of their interrelationship.

3. SISTERS

In answer to my question concerning how the Mahāvidyās relate to each other, a priest at the Dhūmāvatī temple in Varanasi suggested that they are all sisters. Other groups of goddess sisters exist in Hinduism. The seven goddesses who form a protective circle in the desert around the city of Jaiselmer in western Rajasthan, for example, are said to be sisters. The priest at the Dhūmāvatī temple said that Lakṣmī (Kamalā) is the older sister of Dhūmāvatī and that Ṣoḍaśī (Sundarī) is younger than the others. He was uncertain about the relative ages of the other Mahāvidyās. This idea is not found in textual sources and seems unknown to most of my contemporary informants. It therefore seems less than satisfying as the key to understanding the interrelationship of the Mahāvidyās.

4. STAGES IN WOMEN'S LIVES

A related idea is that the Mahāvidyās represent different stages or aspects of a woman's life cycle. In ancient Greek religion, the divine feminine was said to reveal herself in three main forms, corresponding to the "three ages of woman": maiden, mother, and crone. I have also learned that the Nine Durgās, a group of goddesses in Varanasi who are said to be different forms of Durgā,[60] are considered by a female devotee of Durgā to represent the differing stages of the goddess's (and by extension a woman's) life cycle.[61] This scheme has some plausibility vis-à-vis certain goddesses in the Mahāvidyā group. Dhūmāvatī, for example, might represent the goddess in old age. She is usually shown as aged and is nearly always described as a widow. Other members of the group, particularly Ṣoḍaśī (Sundarī), are said to be sixteen years old. Other Mahāvidyās, such as Bhairavī in her form as Annapūrṇā-bhairavī, have matronly qualities.

One problem is that other members of the group do not seem to fit this scheme. Moreover, there is little or no emphasis on the motherhood of the Mahāvidyās. Although they are sometimes called Mā, they are not shown with infants or children, and their independence from male consorts is stressed. The married and motherly aspects of the female life cycle are minimized in the mythology of the Mahāvidyās. This scheme also, then, seems unsatisfactory as the key to understanding the interrelationships of the group.

5. STAGES OF CREATION AND DESTRUCTION

One of the most common *śākta* theological formulas for presenting or describing the multiform nature of the Mahādevī is to think of her as functioning in three ways, corresponding to the functions of the male *trimūrti* (the great male deities, "having three forms": Brahmā, the creator; Viṣṇu, the maintainer; Śiva, the destroyer). That is, in her creative aspect the Great Goddess manifests herself as Mahāsarasvatī (corresponding to Brahmā), in her role as maintainer of the cosmos, as Mahālakṣmī (corresponding to Viṣṇu), and as destroyer of the cosmos, as Mahākālī (corresponding to Śiva). It has been suggested to me that the Mahāvidyās might be divided along these lines, that they represent symbols of the cosmic process of creation, preservation, and destruction, which the goddess oversees or embodies. Indeed, a contemporary practical guide to Tantra for aspirants says: "Mahāmāyā becomes Ṣoḍaśī and creates the world, then she becomes Bhuvaneśvarī and maintains the world, and then she becomes Chinnamastā to destroy the world."[62]

Another author supports this idea. He sees seven stages of creation and three stages of dissolution of the universe symbolically expressed in the Mahāvidyās as given in their usual order: Kālī represents the primordial void prior to creation, Tārā represents the first manifestations of creation, Tripura-sundarī represents the creation of time, and so on.[63] The problem with this particular attempt is that the last mentioned of the Mahāvidyās, Kamalā, is thereby associated with destruction, exactly the opposite of her character: she is traditionally associated with abundance and fertility. The other Mahāvidyās also do not fit at all neatly into this scheme, so it seems highly unlikely that the usual sequence in which they are named is meant to suggest seven stages of creation and three of dissolution.

It is possible to categorize some individual Mahāvidyās under the three functions of creation, maintenance, and destruction. That is, some of them are associated with preservation, such as Lakṣmī; others with destruction, such as Kālī and Tārā; others with creation, such as Bhuvaneśvarī and Ṣoḍaśī. Few of the individual Mahāvidyās, however, are primarily images of cosmogonic functions. Kālī and Kamalā are members of the well-known *śākta trimūrti*, the tripartite cosmogonic formula that says that Mahāsarasvatī creates the world, Mahālakṣmī maintains it, and Mahākālī destroys it, but the other members of the group do not neatly fit the formula. Some of the individual Mahāvidyās have little or no apparent connection with any cosmogonic function. Therefore, this approach to the interrelationship of the Mahāvidyās also seems unsatisfying.

On the other hand, some individual Mahāvidyās are associated with all three goddesses (Mahāsarasvatī, Mahālakṣmī, and Mahākālī) and all three of their cosmic functions. So, for example, in the *sahasranāma stotra* of Bhuvaneśvarī from the *Rudrayāmala*, Bhuvaneśvarī is called Sarasvatī (v. 16), She Who Creates and Sustains the World (v. 52), Kamalā (v. 6), Mahālakṣmī (v. 65), and Kālikā (v. 18).[64] In fact, the tendency is usually to associate a particular Mahāvidyā with a wide range of characteristics and functions and to equate her with all three cosmic functions, not just one.

6. THE THREE *GUṆAS*

A related approach to explaining the interconnections among, or the underlying logic of, the Mahāvidyās is to think of them as symbols of the three *guṇas* (qualities). In this approach, each Mahāvidyā corresponds to one of the three constituents of the created universe: *sattva* (purity), *rajas* (energy), or *tamas* (ignorance). Indeed, the three goddesses of the *śākta trimūrti* discussed above are also sometimes associated with the three *guṇas:* Mahāsarasvatī with *sattva*, Mahālakṣmī with *rajas*, and Mahākālī with *tamas*. The three *guṇas* are often related to colors: *sattva* is white, *rajas* is red, and *tamas* is black. In the case of the Mahāvidyās, John Woodroffe says that according to the *Kāmadhenu-tantra* Tārā is identified with *sattva guṇa* and the achieving of *kaivalya*, yogic bliss; Ṣoḍaśī, Bhuvaneśvarī, and Chinnamastā are associated with *rajas guṇa;* and Dhūmāvatī, Kamalā, Bagalā, and Mātaṅgī are related to *tamas guṇa*.[65] The *Mahānirvāṇa-tantra* associates the individual Mahāvidyās with the three *guṇas* in the same way.[66] It has also been suggested to me that the complexions of the Mahāvidyās, which vary in color, might be the key to identifying them with the three *guṇas*. So, for example, Kālī, Tārā, and Mātaṅgī, who have black or dark complexions, would be associated with the *tamas guṇa*, while Bhairavī, who has a red complexion, would be associated with the *rajas guṇa*. Mahāvidyās with golden or light complexions, such as Bagalā, Dhūmāvatī, and Chinnamastā, would be related to *sattva guṇa*.

This of course divides the Mahāvidyās quite differently from Woodroffe's scheme based on the *Kāmadhenu-tantra*. Another problem that arises here concerns the compatibility of the color of an individual Mahāvidyā's complexion with what we know of her nature and functions. Kālī, who would be linked with *tamas*, is known in many texts as the symbol of the highest knowledge, while the *tamas guṇa* is equated with delusion, lust, and sloth. Bagalāmukhī, who is usually said to have a golden or light complexion, is often associated with the acquisition of magical powers with which one can satisfy worldly desires, but the *sattva guṇa*, with which she would be identified in terms of her color, is related to purely spiritual qualities. So this formula also cannot easily be applied to the Mahāvidyās to explain their coherence as a group.

7. THREE MOODS

Yet another tripartite scheme used to describe the nature of the goddess and her many manifestations is found in the *Kālikā-purāṇa*, where it is said that the Mahādevī has three forms or moods: amorous, angry, and benevolent. She assumes these forms, the text says, according to her whims. In her amorous form she holds a yellow garland and stands on a red lotus on a white corpse. In her angry form she holds a sword and stands directly on a corpse. In her benevolent mood she rides a lion.[67] The *Kālikā-purāṇa* also says that the goddess Tripurā is adored in three aspects: Tripura-bālā (the virgin), Tripura-sundarī (the beautiful), and Tripura-bhairavī (the terrible).[68]

This schema applies fairly well to certain Mahāvidyās, such as Dhūmāvatī and Kālī, who are primarily terrible manifestations. But when we look at each of the Mahāvidyās in detail, it becomes obvious that they usually have all three of these characteristics. In many cases, it is difficult to determine which of the three "moods" a Mahāvidyā best expresses. While the schema is certainly suggestive, I do not find in it the key to explaining the inner coherence of the ten goddesses who form the Mahāvidyās.

8. FIERCE AND PEACEFUL FORMS

Another common way of schematizing the various forms of the Mahādevī in *śākta* theology is to say that she reveals or expresses herself in fierce (*raudra*) and peaceful (*saumya*) forms.[69] Similarly, informants have suggested to me that the Mahāvidyās may be divided into fierce and peaceful manifestations of the Mahādevī. According to this scheme, Kālī, Tārā, Bagalā, Chinnamastā, and Dhūmāvatī might be included under the *raudra* forms of the Mahādevī, while Ṣoḍaśī, Bhuvaneśvarī, Kamalā, Mātaṅgī, and Bhairavī might be included under the *saumya* forms.

Apart from the fact that I have not found any texts that apply this schema to the Mahāvidyās, certain Mahāvidyās are difficult to classify as either fierce or peaceful. Sometimes an individual Mahāvidyā has several different forms, some more fierce than others. Others seem ambiguous vis-à-vis such a dichotomy; for example, Dhūmāvatī is described as quarrelsome and has inauspicious characteristics, but she is not actually said to be fearsome or terrible. Bhairavī also presents somewhat of a problem, for although her name means "the frightful one," her descriptions often depict her as peaceful. Also, if the primary purpose of selecting ten goddesses to illustrate this dichotomy were the rationale for the Mahāvidyās, it is strange that certain goddesses who are unambiguous examples of either the *raudra* type, such as Cāmuṇḍā, or of the *saumya* type, such as Sarasvatī, are omitted from the group. It is true that the Mahāvidyās include examples of both the *raudra* and *saumya* types, but as a structure to explain all ten of the goddesses the polarity remains unsatisfying.

9. DYNAMIC AND STATIC ASPECTS OF THE DIVINE

Another way of classifying goddesses is to think of them as expressing either the dynamic or static nature of reality. A tantric scholar in Varanasi suggested to me that the goddesses among the Mahāvidyās who sit or stand on or otherwise dominate a male figure (these would include Kālī, Tārā, Bagalā, Bhairavī, Tripura-sundarī, and sometimes Chinnamastā) might illustrate the dynamic aspect of the goddess, while the others (Dhūmāvatī, Mātaṅgī, Kamalā, and Bhuvaneśvarī) illustrate the static aspect. Again, while this schema might be helpful in suggesting how certain *śākta* theological themes are reflected in the Mahāvidyās, it applies more clearly to certain Mahāvidyās than others and seems forced in cases where the particular goddess illustrates neither pole in any clear way.

10. KNOWLEDGE AND IGNORANCE (CONCEALMENT)

Another way of classifying manifestations of the goddess according to two polarities is to say that her forms are *vidyā* or *avidyā*, that is, some of her manifestations are meant to get rid of ignorance and delusion and grant liberating knowledge (the *vidyā* forms), while other forms are meant to veil reality and delude beings as to its true nature (the *avidya* forms).[70] According to this scheme, Kālī might belong to the former type of manifestation, symbolizing the nature of ultimate truth, while Kamalā, who is approached primarily for worldly rewards, might belong to the latter. The other Mahāvidyās might be arranged in similar fashion.

The problem here is that a goddess such as Kālī, about whom so much is written, and who has such an ancient and widespread cult, clearly plays both roles. To assign a particular Mahāvidyā to one pole or the other is difficult in many cases. Which type of goddess, *vidyā* or *avidyā*, for example, is Dhūmāvatī or Mātaṅgī? A case might be made for either pole. Likewise with most of the Mahāvidyās. Also, I have yet to find any text that divides the Mahāvidyās in this fashion.

11. THE LUNAR PHASES

A tantric scholar suggested to me yet another approach to explaining the interrelationships of the Mahāvidyās, one that identifies them with the different lunar *tithis* (the thirty days of the waxing and waning moon). According to this scholar, Kālī is identified with the new moon (*amavasya*) and Ṣoḍaśī with the full moon (*pūrṇimā*). These two goddesses represent completeness of knowledge, according to this scheme, in two different ways, both equally valid. Kālī represents complete knowledge in terms of transcendence. Like the new moon, she is beyond what can be perceived and circumscribed. Or perhaps one could say that Kālī represents knowledge gained by getting rid of all false knowledge, by shedding ignorance, while Ṣoḍaśī represents knowledge gained by acquiring increasing amounts of knowledge until one is filled with wisdom. The former would be suggested in the *tithis* of the waning phase of the moon, while the latter (Ṣoḍaśī) would be suggested in the *tithis* of the waxing moon. Ṣoḍaśī, whose name means "the sixteenth," represents complete knowledge or wisdom in terms of being all-inclusive. As the sixteenth, she includes all the other fifteen *tithis*. The other Mahāvidyās are associated with the waxing and waning lunar *tithis* according to which of the poles they most resemble. The tantric scholar suggested that Chinnamastā, who is close in nature or meaning to Kālī, would represent the first and second waning lunar *tithis*, while Bhuvaneśvarī and Kamalā, both of whom are associated with abundance, would represent the last four *tithis* prior to the full moon.

Again, although this approach may be helpful in the case of a few of the Mahāvidyās, it seems forced in most. The extent to which a particular Mahāvidyā approximates knowledge as transcendent or knowledge as all-inclusive is usually difficult to determine.

12. LEFT- AND RIGHT-HANDED GODDESSES

Some informants have suggested to me that the Mahāvidyās are interconnected through their association with the right- or left-handed paths in Tantrism. Tantrism describes two paths, left and right, as means to achieving spiritual fulfillment. The left-handed path is restricted to those of heroic nature, is described as dangerous, and employs the infamous *pañca tattva* ritual in which the aspirant partakes of five forbidden things: meat, fish, wine, a particular type of grain (possibly a drug of some kind), and illicit sexual intercourse. Tantric texts sometimes specify which path should be used in worshiping particular Mahāvidyās. The *Śaktisaṁgama-tantra*, for example, says that Kālī, Tārā, Sundarī, Bhairavī, Chinnamastā, Mātaṅgī, and Bagalā are fond of the left-handed path, while Bhuvaneśvarī, Dhūmāvatī, and Kamalā should be worshiped by the right-handed path.[71] However, in many cases texts specify that both paths are appropriate, and in practice most of the goddesses who belong to the Mahāvidyās are worshiped by practitioners of both paths. It is difficult, therefore, to designate particular Mahāvidyās as belonging either to the left- or the right-handed paths.

If one is attempting to divide the Mahāvidyās between right and left, it is relevant to consider images in which they are arrayed in the ten directions, with a goddess or Śiva in the center. One might expect that the goddesses on the central deity's left side are those worshiped primarily by means of the left-handed path and those on the right, by the right-handed path, but that is not the case. According to the *Mahābhāgavata-purāṇa*, Tārā, Ṣoḍaśī, and Tripura-sundarī are located to the left (the east), while Bhairavī, Chinnamastā, and Bhuvaneśvarī are to the right. These six goddesses do not correspond in any consistent way to the left- and right-handed paths.

13. STAGES OF CONSCIOUSNESS

Finally, the Mahāvidyās might be understood as symbols of the stages (or types) of consciousness experienced by tantric aspirants in their progressive spiritual development. Each goddess confers a certain type of perfection, blessing, or awareness. These perfections (*siddhis*) or types of consciousness, meditative states, or moods (*bhavas*)[72] might be understood as progressive, some presupposing or being more inclusive than others. Several informants independently of each other suggested this approach to the Mahāvidyās, and it has some textual support.[73] In this approach, Kālī is understood to represent unfettered, complete knowledge of self and of ultimate reality, fully enlightened consciousness that has transcended all limitations of egocentricity.[74] She is symbolic of the ultimate goal of tantric *sādhanā* (spiritual exercise). Tārā, who is very similar to Kālī in appearance, symbolizes a high or expanded state of awareness, but a state that has not entirely transcended physical and personal limitations. Bagalāmukhī represents a state of sharply focused consciousness, an intensified will that is capable of directly influencing people with whom the adept comes in contact. Kamalā and Bhairavī symbolize lower states of consciousness, in which the adept is preoccupied with satisfying bodily and mental needs. The other Mahāvidyās symbolize states of consciousness that arise between the adept's preoccupation with worldly, bodily, or personal needs and desires and the eventual dawning of the fully enlightened consciousness represented by Kālī.

In tantric religion, the progressive nature of *sādhanā* is often described as the awakening, arising, and ascent of *kuṇḍalinī śakti*. This female power or energy is depicted as a coiled and slumbering serpent at the base of the spine in a *cakra* (center), pictured as a lotus. Through meditative techniques, the aspirant awakens this power and causes it to ascend by way of the central channel, the *suṣumnā nāḍī*, which traverses the body along the line of the backbone. As the *kuṇḍalinī* rises, it passes through six other *cakras*, also represented as lotuses, and awakens or invigorates them as it reaches them. Different *bhavas*, "spiritual moods" or states of consciousness, are sometimes associated with the awakening of each *cakra*. According to one adept, when *kuṇḍalinī śakti* awakens in the *mūladhāra cakra*, one experiences a feeling of dissatisfaction with ordinary life. That is, *kuṇḍalinī sādhanā* represents a desire to go beyond or to expand normal consciousness.[75] Ultimately, the *sādhaka* (aspirant) seeks to have the *kuṇḍalinī* rise to the topmost *cakra* at the crown of the head, where she unites with Śiva and creates the bliss of awakening (*mahāsukha*).

In interpreting the Mahāvidyās as states of consciousness, meditative states, or mental perfections (*siddhis*), one might think of them as symbols of the nature of the mental states associated with the seven *cakras* of *kuṇḍalinī* yoga.[76] There is, in fact, evidence that the Mahāvidyās are associated with the *cakras*, and with the *kuṇḍalinī* generally. It is said of Bhuvaneśvarī, for example, that she sleeps in the *mūlādhāra cakra*, the lowest *cakra*, where the *kuṇḍalinī* sleeps.[77] It is also said that Bhuvaneśvarī cuts the knots of (or awakens) the *cakras* and rises to meet Śiva, which means that she is equated with the *kuṇḍalinī*.[78] Another example is Tripura-bhairavī, who is called Sat-cakra-krama-vāsinī (she who abides in the six *cakras*).[79]

Lending credibility to this approach to the Mahāvidyās is the *tantras*' ranking of different paths. Many *tantras* name seven (sometimes nine) different paths and describe and rank them, usually from inferior (in which the aims are worldly) to superior (in which the aims are transcendent). A standard list of the seven paths, in ascending order, is: Vedācāra, Vaiṣṇavācāra, Śaivācāra, Dakṣiṇācāra, Vāmācāra, Siddhāntācāra, and Kaulācāra. The *Śaktisaṁgama-tantra* says that the highest path, the Kaulācāra, comprises the *kula*, the family of worshipers, who know the truth that reality is comprised of *śakti* and Śiva.[80] The *Mahānirvāṇa-tantra* says that the Kaulācāra path includes the performance of the *pañca makāra* (five essentials) ritual and is only entered upon after the aspirant has been initiated by a guru.[81]

A good example of goddesses representing progressive states of perfection is found in the Śrīvidyā cult. In ritually and meditatively moving from the outward parts of the Śrīvidyā *cakra*, which represents the entire cosmos, to the center, the adept acquires different *siddhis*, or perfections. The outer *siddhis* are less powerful and more worldly in nature, while the inner *siddhis* are both more spiritual and more powerful. These *siddhis*, furthermore, are personified as goddesses.[82]

There is even a tradition that associates particular goddesses with each of the seven *cakras*. Dākinī is associated with the *mūlādhāra cakra*, Rākinī with the *svādhiṣṭhāna cakra*, Lakṣmī with the *maṇipura cakra*, Kākinī with the *anāhata cakra*, Śākinī with the *viśuddha cakra*, Hākinī with the *ājñā cakra*, and Nirvāṇa-śakti with the *sahasrāra cakra*.[83] For the most part, these goddesses are hardly known outside this context, and of the seven, only Lakṣmī, whom we may identify with Kamalā, is a Mahāvidyā.

What is missing in order to make the association of the Mahāvidyās with the *cakras* and ascending states of consciousness a convincing interpretation of the interrelationship of the Mahāvidyās is a clear tradition that asserts a hierarchy or progressive ranking of the ten goddesses[84] and consistently identifies each one with specific paths, *siddhis*, or *cakras*. Although a certain Mahāvidyā may sometimes be identified with a particular path, *siddhi*, or *cakra*, there is seldom a consistent pattern, except, perhaps, in the case of Kālī, who is often identified with the Kaulācāra path, which is considered the highest. Although we find Mahāvidyās associated with *kuṇḍalinī śakti*, the *mūlādhāra cakra*, or the *cakras* generally, it is rare to find Mahāvidyās assigned to each of the other *cakras* in a predictable way. It is also curious that there are ten, not seven, Mahāvidyās if they are meant to be symbols of the progressive stages of consciousness experienced by aspirants in *kuṇḍalinī* yoga. Although I am inclined to see in this approach a helpful framework for thinking about the meaning of the Mahāvidyās as a group and as individual goddesses, the evidence is too thin to say with assurance that this is the key to understanding how they relate to each other within the group.

We seem left, then, with no entirely satisfactory key to understanding the connections among the Mahāvidyās. Perhaps the best we can hope for is to combine all the possibilities we have mentioned, or some subset of them, in our efforts to discern the coherence of the group, to understand how such a curious mix of goddesses has come together to form the ten Mahāvidyās.

Worship of the Mahāvidyās

The Mahāvidyās are approached in a variety of ritual contexts, and the worship of one Mahāvidyā may differ from that of others. Some of the Mahāvidyās, for example, have ancient and widespread cults that existed, and still exist, quite apart from the Mahāvidyās as a group. This is the case with Kālī, Tārā, Tripura-sundarī, and Kamalā, for example. In general, though, we can think of their worship as taking place primarily in two contexts: in temples, where they are served by priests and where people come to take part in public worship, and in temporary places marked off by individual aspirants, where worship is undertaken in tantric fashion, either right-handed or left-handed. Although temple and tantric styles of worship have some similarities, they are quite different in mood and style.

TEMPLE WORSHIP

The extent to which individual Mahāvidyās are worshiped in temples varies considerably. There are Kālī and Lakṣmī temples throughout India, and these two goddesses have been widely worshiped in such settings since ancient times. Other members of the Mahāvidyās, such as Dhūmāvatī, Bagalā, and Chinnamastā, however, are not well known at all outside the group, and there are very few temples dedicated specially to them anywhere in India. As for temples dedicated to the Mahāvidyās as a group, I know of only the one mentioned above in Calcutta, although the Mahāvidyās are depicted as a group in many goddess temples across North India.

A worshiper in a temple approaches a Mahāvidyā primarily as a devoted servant attending a royal mistress. The whole structure of Hindu temple *pūjā* is patterned on the model of a subject serving a royal person. The proper mood of the devotee is that of humble supplication before a superior being from whom one makes requests and to whom one offers respectful service and homage. The standard sixteen-part *pūjā*, which is performed daily, often several times daily in large temples, consists of actions that are thought appropriate for a servant or subject toward a superior, royal figure. The devotee who comes to the temple—the royal court—also brings offerings appropriate to the particular deity. Several of the Mahāvidyās like blood offerings (which are made in the form of animal sacrifices), in addition to the typical flowers, incense, and fruit. Kālī, Chinnamastā, Tārā, and Bagalāmukhī all have a reputation for being pleased by blood offerings, although practices vary from temple to temple.

Worship of the Mahāvidyās in temples invites an open, public approach to them as powers who are able to grant devotees blessings and favors and who are pleased with devotional service and the public festivals and celebrations that are a part of every temple's annual cycle. In the context of temple worship, the individual Mahāvidyās are perceived as very similar to other Hindu deities. They are thought of as great beings who have an objective existence outside the devotee and who live in heavenly places or special, sacred dwellings constructed for them on earth. In this context, the ritual actions of the devotee are directed outward toward the powerful being, who is affirmed to exist outside, above, or beyond the worshiper.

TANTRIC WORSHIP

The majority of texts that mention the Mahāvidyās are tantric. Indeed, it is probably fair to refer to the Mahāvidyās as primarily tantric goddesses, by which I mean that the proper framework in which to understand them is tantric. It is clear that they are typically approached by means of tantric rituals and that their worship is to be interpreted according to tantric principles. Although many tantric texts give the specific details for sixteen-part *pūjā* (discussed above), such *pūjā* takes on a somewhat different meaning in a tantric context, as we shall see.

In tantric worship, which is generally referred to as *sādhanā*, or spiritual exercise, the aspirant seeks to achieve an awakened or enlightened state of consciousness through techniques that are physical, mental, ritualistic, and spiritual at the same time. A central theme in tantric *sādhanā* is the identification of the macrocosm with the microcosm, which is represented by the human organism, specifically by the *sādhaka*, the practitioner or adept. Through meditation techniques, rituals, images, mantras, yantras, and *maṇḍalas* (schematic diagrams), the adept systematically identifies parts, aspects, or dimensions of himself or herself with parts, aspects, or dimensions of the cosmos. The deities are thought of as aspects of the cosmos that correspond to aspects of the human organism—mental, physical, or both. The aim of tantric *sādhanā* is to establish identity with the deity worshiped, to appropriate that deity, or to awaken that deity within oneself, and then to offer it *pūjā*, which in effect means worshiping the divinity within oneself. Or, conversely, one worships the deity residing within in the hope of awakening in oneself the reality that it represents.

The self-divinization of tantric *sādhanā* may have several results. The adept may acquire an expanded self-awareness, that is, the wisdom of self-knowledge, which is often said to be tantamount to achieving *mokṣa* (*mukti* or "liberation"). That is, tantric *sādhanā* may result in redemptive transformation. Or such *sādhanā* may lead to heightened sense perception, the acquisition of *siddhis* through which the adept excels at one of the senses or even transcends the limitations of sensory perception. These *siddhis*, in turn, may lead to enjoyments impossible before achieving such perfections. Or tantric *sādhanā* may result in an intensified or expanded mental capacity or power that enables the practitioner to achieve feats of self-control or control over others. We have already seen, and will see in more detail below when we discuss the Mahāvidyās individually, that all of these results, or "fruits"—redemptive wisdom, increased sensory perception, worldly boons, and magical powers—are associated with worship of the Mahāvidyās.

We can get a good idea of how the Mahāvidyās are worshiped according to tantric principles and rites from a brief description of *sāmanya pūjā*, ordinary or regular worship of the goddess, as described in the *Kālikā-purāṇa*, a fourteenth-century text devoted to the goddess in the form of Kālī.[85] Though the text does not describe tantric worship of the Mahāvidyās per se, it provides a rather detailed outline of the stages of tantric worship, which can be adapted to any given deity. The ritual may be done almost anywhere, although the text does recommend certain sites, such as a mountaintop or a cave, and says that the ritual is more potent if done at a place sacred to whichever form of the goddess is being worshiped. The ritual may be performed at any time and does not require a priest. It is done by an individual by and for himself (let us imagine that the adept is a male in the following description, although the adept could be female). A physical image of the goddess is not necessary. The ritual probably takes no longer than an hour and could be done in abbreviated form in considerably less time. The *Kālikā-purāṇa* describes a continuous set of actions, but we can think of the ceremony as having four parts: (1) preparation, (2) meditation, (3) worship of the goddess herself, and (4) concluding rites.

The opening rites of *sāmanya pūjā* aim primarily at purification of the adept and the delimitation of an appropriate place within which to perform the ceremony.[86] The adept bathes, sips water (signifying internal purification), and asks the goddess to rid his mind of any impurities. He also recites certain mantras at this point to expel potentially harmful spirits.

The adept next purifies the place of worship by sprinkling water on the ground. He carefully inspects the items to be used in the ritual to insure that they are unblemished. Flowers to be offered, for example, should be free from insects. Items are also purified by means of mantras and water. The adept then draws a yantra (a schematic diagram) representing the particular goddess to be worshiped. In the case of the Mahāvidyās, each has her distinctive yantra or *maṇḍala*.

In the second phase of the ceremony, the adept performs a series of acts that are primarily mental to further purify himself. In general, this part of the rite aims at the adept's symbolic death and dissolution. The text says that the body is composed of impure elements—mucus, feces, urine, and so on—and as such is unfit to be an instrument of worship. The adept's symbolic death is followed by his mental re-creation of the world and, most important, by the appearance of the goddess herself.

Assuming the correct posture and practicing breath control, the adept begins a ritual that releases his life force, his *jīva*, from his body. He imagines his *jīva* passing through different stages, each connected with an element: earth, water, fire, air, and sound. Finally, identifying himself with space, he imagines his life force leaving his body through the top of his head. This signals his symbolic death.

The adept then symbolically dissolves his body, which as a microcosm of the universe also represents the physical world as a whole. He imagines his body dissolving, then imagines it burning on a funeral pyre, then imagines the ashes blowing away, and finally imagines a shower of pure nectar cleaning the place where his body had lain and been burned. In effect, the adept has destroyed the cosmos and himself by reducing them to their elemental constituents. His ultimate purification is now complete, and he is ready to be reborn.

Re-creation of the cosmos, and the rebirth of the adept, begins with the adept pronouncing the seed syllable (*bīja*) of the goddess. He then visualizes the different parts of the cosmos, often in the form of letters, syllables, or mantras. He completes the re-creation of the cosmos by visualizing the goddess herself seated on a throne in the center of the world, which is imagined as her particular *maṇḍala*. Next he identifies himself with the goddess by placing a flower that he has been holding in his hands on top of his head and saying: "I am this." The adept reinforces his deification with *mudrās* (hand gestures) and mantras that identify parts of the cosmos with parts of his body. Having provided himself with a new, divine body (actually identified with the goddess herself), he is now prepared to undertake worship of the goddess herself.

This begins with inward worship. That is, the adept imagines the goddess and her attendants dwelling in his heart. He pictures the goddess by reciting her *dhyāna* mantra, which often describes her in great detail. He then transfers the goddess from his heart into the yantra he has drawn on the ground by exhaling through his right nostril onto a flower that he holds in his hand. Her transference to the yantra can also be done with *mudrās*, hand gestures with which the adept "catches" the goddess and places her in the yantra. The adept now praises the goddess with hymns and treats her as an honored guest by offering her various articles, physically or mentally. The actions are similar to temple *pūjā*, but in contrast to elaborate and costly temple *pūjā*, in this ceremony the adept offers the goddess little more than purified water and flowers. The text instructs the adept, throughout this part of the ceremony, to constantly repeat the goddess's special mantra, which is said to be identical with the goddess herself.

Outward worship of the goddess in the *maṇḍala*, who can be any of the ten Mahāvidyās, closes with a final offering, usually consisting of rice or some other grain. The adept may also make a blood offering. An entire chapter in the *Kālikā-purāṇa* suggests offerings appropriate to the goddess and the rewards that may be expected from them. Among the

Mahāvidyās, Kālī, Tārā, and Chinnamastā are fond of blood offerings, so these are recommended in their worship, while Mahāvidyās like Kamalā do not receive such offerings.

The adept now dismisses the goddess by circumambulating the flower that represents her and mentally visualizing her return to her normal abode: heaven, the adept's heart, or some particular holy place. If the goddess is visualized as returning to the worshiper's heart, the adept smells the flower that represents her, inhaling her, as it were, and then places the flower on his head. With the worship of the goddess complete, he finishes the ceremony by erasing the yantra or *maṇḍala* and disposing of the remains of the offerings. The remains are considered especially potent and dangerous and must be handled with great care. Fierce goddesses are associated with these leftovers and must be propitiated before the ceremony is complete.[87]

Sāmanya pūjā is a ritual through which the worshiper is deified. After ritually undertaking one's own death and dissolution, one re-creates the world and oneself. In this act of re-creation, the goddess is identified with the worshiper. The two are declared essentially one. In this sense, *sāmanya pūjā* is worship of one's own inner sacred essence as well as of a superior divine being. Or perhaps one could say that in *sāmanya pūjā*, which is essentially tantric in nature, one reveres one's highest or most essential nature, which is identified with the goddess.

During *sāmanya pūjā*, then, which is the likely setting for worship of the Mahāvidyās, the emphasis is upon individual meditation and identification with the goddess in question. Unlike temple worship, the goal is to inwardly realize the presence of the goddess in the aspirant. Although *sāmanya pūjā* perceives the goddess in question to be both a superior being who exists outside the *sādhaka* and an inward dimension or aspect of the worshiper, the emphasis, particularly in comparison to temple worship, is on the latter.

The Mahāvidyās are also worshiped in a format known as the left-handed (Vāmācāra) path in Tantrism. This type of worship is characterized primarily by the *pañca tattva* or *pañca makāra* ritual, the ritual of the "five forbidden things." According to the *tantras*, it is reserved for the few of heroic nature who are capable of undertaking it without harming themselves in the process. The *sādhaka* must partake of five things that are ordinarily forbidden or are highly polluting: meat, fish, wine, *mudrā* (a type of grain that may have hallucinogenic properties), and sexual intercourse with a woman who is not one's wife (the ritual is described from a male point of view). The ritual is done under the guidance of a guru.

Individual texts differ over whether this rite is to be done alone or in a group. Texts devoted to the Mahāvidyās often refer to the *pañca tattva* ritual, indicating that at least some of the goddesses are worshiped in this context.

The logic or intention of this ritual appears to be related to perceiving or intensely realizing the basic truth that all of reality, all things, are pervaded by *śakti*, the goddess herself, or *brahman*. By partaking of forbidden things, one affirms that ultimately there is nothing that is not the goddess, that nothing is polluting, for she pervades all.[88] Such distinctions as "pure" and "polluting" impose artificial qualifications on the manifestation of the goddess as the physical world. The *pañca tattva* ritual seeks to abolish a mentality that perceives the world according to artificial human constructs, that perceives the essentially unified world that is the goddess (or *brahman*, with which the goddess is often identified) as fractured and divided.

The precise connection between the Mahāvidyās and the left-handed path, and the *pañca tattva* ritual specifically, is not entirely clear. Their worship may include this ritual, but some may be worshiped by either the right- or left-handed paths. Perhaps the fierce or inauspicious qualities of some of the Mahāvidyās that are worshiped according to the left-handed path relate to the logic of the *pañca tattva* ritual, in which the adept is forced to confront and partake of forbidden things. Some of the Mahāvidyās, particularly Kālī, Tārā, Dhūmāvatī, and Chinnamastā, are identified with such harsh realities as death, destruction, old age, and decrepitude. By confronting these deities, and one's fears, one gains release from the inhibitions and constraints they can generate.

The Mahāvidyās and Magical Powers

We have already touched on the association of the Mahāvidyās with magical powers, but it is so persistent that we should discuss it in more detail before turning to a treatment of the individual goddesses. Hindu literature is full of stories in which individuals, often demons, undertake ascetic and meditative practices in order to acquire special abilities with which they hope to achieve power, wealth, sex, or some other worldly pleasure or reward. In these stories, it is clear that they employ meditative and ascetic practices to attain selfish, worldly goals rather than what we might think of as spiritual ones. Texts on yoga say that one can acquire special powers (*siddhis*) by practicing yoga, but warn against indulging in them and thereby perverting the spiritual quest.[89]

Other Hindu texts deal specifically with magical powers. The *Dāmara-tantra*, for example, is devoted entirely to describing the use of mantras to acquire *siddhis*, particularly healing ones, but also the kinds often associated with the Mahāvidyās, such as causing strife, paralyzing or obtaining victory over an enemy, and attracting a person of the opposite sex.[90] The *Phetkārinī-tantra* describes six magical powers (*ṣaṭ karmāṇi*): *śānti* (pacification), *vaśīkaraṇa* (subjugation), *stambhana* (immobilization or paralyzing), *uccāṭana* (eradication), *vidveṣaṇa* (sowing dissension), and *māraṇa* (causing death).[91] This text, which is named after Kālī as "the howling one" (Pheṭkārinī), has chapters on several of the Mahāvidyās, thereby associating the quest for magical powers with the Mahāvidyās specifically. The six magical acts are also described in the *Śalya-tantra*, the *Dattātreya-tantra*,[92] and the *Uḍḍāmara-tantra*.[93] The *Kālarudra-tantra* "describes destructive rites to be executed with the help of *mantras* of fearsome goddesses such as Dhūmāvatī."[94] The *Ṣaṭkarmadīpikā* and the *Kāmaratna* are also preoccupied with magical acts.[95] The *Śāradā-tilaka-tantra* (23.122ff.) mentions a list of six magical practices: *śānti* (cure of disease and the expulsion of evil spirits), *vaśya* (bringing others under one's control), *stambhana* (paralyzing the activity of others), *vidveṣa* (causing dissension), *uccāṭana* (compelling someone to leave home), and *māraṇa* (killing by will).[96] The *Bṛhaddharma-purāṇa* says that the Mahāvidyās as a group give the powers of eradication, attracting, paralyzing, killing by wishing it, making a person sick, controlling speech, causing a person to get old, and preserving one's youth. These are said to be the duties of the Mahāvidyās.[97]

Other groups of goddesses are identified with specific *siddhis* in some tantric texts. In the Śrīvidyā school of Tantrism, which is dominant in South India, we find a group of ten *yoginīs* (female beings endowed with magical powers) who personify ten *siddhis:* the powers to make small, to become light, to become large, to become superior, to control others, to have an irresistible will, to enjoy, to gain all of one's desires, to obtain anything, and to control desires.[98] In this case, the goddesses not only grant these powers but actually represent, or are identical with, them.

Individual Mahāvidyās are often associated with magical powers. Mātaṅgī is said to give all kinds of *siddhis*, especially the power by which whatever one says comes true (*vāk siddhi*).[99] Kālī has a long history of association with magical powers. In the Bengali *maṅgal kāvyas*, Kālī is often the main deity and bestows magical powers on her devotees. In the *Kālikā-maṅgal-kāvya*, for example, the hero Sundara succeeds in finding and winning the heroine, Vidyā, by means of magical powers acquired in worshiping Kālī.[100] In the *Śākta-pramoda*, Śiva says that Dhūmāvatī is worshiped primarily for the *siddhi* of killing one's enemies.[101] Also in the *Śākta-pramoda* we read this prayer to Chinnamastā: "Give me *siddhis* and destroy my enemies."[102] The Mahāvidyā who is most consistently associated with magical powers is Bagalāmukhī. The *Bagalāmukhī-rahasya* says that she is worshiped for paralyzing, eradication, and control over the planets. Different recipes are given to achieve these different powers. To achieve the ability to kill at will, one should burn mustard oil and blood of a she-buffalo in a sacrificial fire, while for eradication one should burn the feathers of a crow and a vulture.[103] The *Śākta-pramoda* says that worship of Ṣoḍaśī (Tripura-sundarī) gives knowledge of all and makes one wealthy, immune to poison, authoritative in speech, and free from sickness.[104]

The importance of magical powers in the worship of the Mahāvidyās might be understood from at least two points of view. First, and perhaps obviously, worship generally can be prompted by specific desires, frustrations, and needs. A deity is approached for help. In this sense, it is not surprising to find the Mahāvidyās associated with granting a range of blessings and powers. Other deities also bestow a variety of blessings, including magical powers.

Second, the adept worships the Mahāvidyās by developing and employing mental capacities through meditation. Tantric yoga is supposed to awaken one's consciousness, to expand and intensify it. That magical powers as well as transformative wisdom might be associated with this process is understandable, and many of the magical powers that are specified relate directly to mental powers. In exploring and expanding one's consciousness, one discovers new dimensions to one's psychic capacities. Like the *kuṇḍalinī* serpent rising and awakening the *cakras*, causing the lotuses to bloom, the adept awakens aspects or dimensions of his consciousness and realizes that his mental or psychic capacities are much greater than he might have imagined. Insofar as the Mahāvidyās might be thought of as aspects or stages of consciousness in the spiritual quest, the association of *siddhis* with them is not surprising.

The Significance of the Term *Mahāvidyā*

A literal translation of the term *mahāvidyā* is "great knowledge," while a somewhat less literal translation might be "supreme (or superior or complete) knowledge (or wisdom)." There are several possibilities for what the name tells us about the nature and function of the Mahāvidyās. It is not obvious why these ten goddesses should have been so designated, but several explanations are possible.

I have been told by two scholars of Tantrism in Varanasi[105] that the term *dasamahāvidyā* as it applies to the ten goddesses is technical and means the "ten great mantras," *vidyā* generally being used in this technical sense in tantric contexts. In his commentary on the *Lalitā-sahasranāma*, Bhāskararāya says: "The difference between *Mantra* and *Vidyā* is that the former has reference to male deities and the latter to female ones."[106] Indeed, the first order of business in many tantric texts that discuss or describe the Mahāvidyās is to give their mantras, which consist of a few syllables. The mantra, it is often said, is highly secret and extremely powerful. It is a given in the tantric context, in fact, that the mantra is identical with the goddess. It is not that the mantra *belongs to* the goddess, which is the way one is often tempted to understand the relationship between the deity and the mantra; the situation, rather, is that the mantra *is* the goddess. Jan Gonda says: "The essence of a *mantra* . . . is the presence of the deity: only that *mantra* in which the *devatā* has revealed his or her aspects can reveal that aspect. The deity is believed to appear from the *mantra* when it is correctly pronounced."[107]

There is a long-standing tradition in Hinduism that sound is the essence of reality. The idea of *śabda brahman* is ancient: ultimate reality in its most essential form is expressed in sound. Philosophical schools of great sophistication, such as the Sphoṭa school,[108] are based on theories of sound and vibration as the essential and basic constituents of reality. Related to this emphasis on the priority of sound as basic to the nature of ultimate reality is the equally ancient emphasis in Hinduism on the potency of mantras, or sacred utterances. Reciting mantras, particularly Vedic mantras, is an essential part of most Hindu rituals. Indeed, many rituals are believed to be impotent unless qualified priests pronounce the mantras correctly. Traditionally, furthermore, only a select group of people, certain Brahmans, knew Vedic mantras and were prohibited from uttering them where they might be heard by unqualified people, such as women or any members of lower castes. Mantras were usually taken from sacred texts, and their power was believed to be almost unlimited; a high-caste male elite guarded them closely.

Similarly in tantric *sādhanā*, the mantras that a *sādhaka* receives from his or her guru are secret and regarded as extremely powerful. The mantra of a goddess, for example, is transmitted to a *sādhaka* by a guru secretly in a ritual; the guru has chosen the particular mantra as suitable to the adept. Despite the impression that mantras are public because they are in printed editions of the *tantras* and that one might freely invoke them for their effect, mantras are in fact transmitted by a spiritual master during a carefully supervised spiritual undertaking.

The idea, then, that the ten goddesses who constitute the Mahāvidyās are essentially ten mantras, and that the term *dasamāhavidyā* may literally mean the "ten great mantras," is understandable. What is also significant is that the goddess—who is the mantra—appears or exists only when the mantra is invoked. She remains in latent form until a particular adept invokes her through the mantra that is her animating essence. It is in this sense, perhaps, that the emphasis upon the adept and the goddess being one might be understood in the tantric context. One cannot and does not exist without the other.

It is difficult, however, to leave the matter of the term *mahāvidyā* here. Indeed, several people have commented on the significance of the term without emphasizing, or even mentioning, its reference to the mantras of the ten goddesses. The term *vidyā* means "knowledge" and can refer to practical knowledge, knowledge of arts and sciences, or transformative knowledge. The name, then, according to some, is related to the idea that the ten goddesses bestow or reveal certain types of knowledge. One contemporary scholar says: "These [the Mahāvidyās] are the representatives of transcendent knowledge and power, the sources of all that is to be known."[109] Another scholar refers to the Mahāvidyās as "ten objects of transcendental knowledge . . . signifying the various degrees and stages of existence."[110] Another scholar says that the Mahāvidyās are so called because they are the "sources of all that is to be known."[111] Yet another scholar maintains that the Mahādevī causes bondage and in this capacity is referred to as *avidyā*, but that she also causes liberation and in this capacity is referred to as *vidyā*. The ten Mahāvidyās, then, are ten forms in which the goddess brings about enlightenment by means of liberating knowledge.[112] Yet another scholar equates *vidyā* with *śakti*, which, he says, underlies and pervades all things. Indeed, he equates *vidyā* with *brahman* itself, ultimate reality. *Vidyā*, like *brahman*, is *saccidānanda* (being, consciousness, and bliss). The Mahāvidyās, then, embody or transmit ultimate power and complete knowledge.[113]

Each of these interpretations of the term *mahāvidyā* goes beyond the technical meaning of "mantra" to apply the more encompassing meaning, "knowledge," to the ten goddesses. Viewing the goddesses as those who grant great knowledge or wisdom is in keeping with a general association between goddesses and knowledge throughout *śākta* literature. We find many textual references to goddesses, or the Great Goddess, as identical with, or associated with, knowledge and intellect or other mental attributes related to knowledge and wisdom. In the *Devī-māhātmya*, Durgā is referred to as Mahāvidyā twice (1.58 and 11.21) and as Vidyā (1.44 and 4.8). It is clear, furthermore, that her identification with *vidyā* in these verses is related to liberating knowledge. Durgā is also associated with *buddhi*, "intellect," four times in the *Devī-māhātmya*.[114] In the concluding scene of the *Devī-māhātmya*, the goddess grants the merchant Samādhi liberating knowledge (*vidyā*) (13.16). In the *Brahma-vaivarta-purāṇa*, Durgā is also associated with *buddhi* and is called Buddhirūpā, "she whose form is intellect."[115] Durgā is also identified with *cetanā*, "consciousness," in the *Devī-māhātmya* (5.13). In the *Mahābhāgavata-purāṇa*, the goddess is said to be supreme knowledge, *parāvidyā*, and in this form to manifest herself in different goddesses: Gaṅgā, Durgā, Sāvitri, Lakṣmī, and Sarasvatī.[116] Several of the epithets included in the *Lalitā-sahasranāma*, a famous goddess hymn, identify the goddess with knowledge and wisdom: Mahābuddhi, "great intelligence" (no. 223), Vijñānabhanarūpiṇi, "she whose form is a mass of knowledge" (no. 253), Prajñātmikā, "she who is wisdom itself" (no. 261), Mati, "intelligence" (no. 445), Vidyā, "knowledge" (no. 549), Ātmavidyā, "knowledge of *ātman* ('self' or soul)" (no. 583), Mahāvidyā, "great knowledge" (no. 584), and Jñānadā, "she who bestows knowledge" (no. 643).[117] The *Devī-bhāgavata-purāṇa* frequently refers to the principal goddess of the text as Vidyā or Brahmavidyā, "the knowledge of *brahman* (the highest reality)."[118] Perhaps the earliest examples of female beings bearing the name Vidyā are found in the *Mahābhārata*. A female being named Vidyā is mentioned as a member of Pārvatī's entourage (3.221.20), and a group of female beings called the Vidyās are described attending the god Brahmā (2.11.15).

The connection between the technical meaning of *mahavidyā* as "great mantra" and interpretations that emphasize the term as meaning "knowledge" or "wisdom" resides in the tantric belief that mantras awaken consciousness and expand the senses and intellect. The difference is only one of means and ends. Mantras are the means to realizing the goal of knowledge. In this sense, the ten Mahāvidyās are the ten great mantras by means of which knowledge is gained, awakened, or discovered within.

Concluding Observations

The ten Mahāvidyās form a distinctive group of deities. Although it includes some well-known goddesses, such as Kālī and Lakṣmī, most of them are little known apart from this group, and several of the goddesses are strikingly unusual (Chinnamastā, Dhūmāvatī, and Bagalāmukhī in particular). The group does not particularly manifest characteristics and functions that typify *śākta* Hinduism, yet they are often said to represent the Mahādevī in her diverse forms. Several texts and secondary sources imply that they sum up, or circumscribe in some fashion, the main features of the Mahādevī. Nonetheless, the group lacks many features considered central to *śākta* theology and religion.

For example, the group lacks the close association with sacred places that is an important feature of Hindu goddess traditions. Kālī, outside the Mahāvidyās, has many famous temples, and at these sacred places she is often connected to the myth of the *śākta pīṭhas*, which has a geographical theme. The most famous of such Kālī temples is Kālighāṭ (after which the city of Calcutta is named). Similarly, apart from the Mahāvidyās, Tārā has several important sacred places. Tārāpīṭh in Birbhum district of Bengal is perhaps the most famous. Lakṣmī (Kamalā) also has many well-known temples of regional or local importance that tie her to the local culture and land. However, this geographical aspect of Kālī, Tārā, and Kamalā is barely even mentioned in the context of their roles among the Mahāvidyās. The texts that discuss and describe the Mahāvidyās do not seem to be interested in reflecting upon or promoting the ways in which these goddesses are associated with sacred geography in their independent cults. In the same vein, the *śākta pīṭha* myth is rarely mentioned, even though in the myth the *pīṭhas* all arise from the body of Satī, who is the origin of the Mahāvidyās in the *purāṇic* accounts (see above). It is also interesting that the Mahāvidyās as a group and individually are rarely associated with such geographical goddesses as Gaṅgā, even though the *Mahābhāgavata-purāṇa* tells the stories of both Gaṅgā and the origin of the Mahāvidyās. It is difficult to resist the conclusion that the meaning and function of the Mahāvidyās are only very weakly related to sacred geography, even though it is often extremely important in the case of other goddesses and goddess cults. To use Diana Eck's expression, the Mahāvidyās, as a group and as individuals, lack a clear "locative aspect," which is a particularly distinctive feature of Hinduism and much Hindu goddess worship.[119] The Mahāvidyās have little or no connection with "organic symbols" of the sacred,[120] such as mountains, rivers, river banks, or river confluences.

The Mahāvidyās lack another characteristic that typifies many Hindu goddesses. They have little or no connection with motherhood, fecundity, and growth. Although they may have names that connect them with creation in a general way, particularly in their *nāma stotras* (hymns consisting of names or epithets), they are not depicted as mothers, and they are rarely referred to by maternal epithets. Similarly, they are only very weakly connected with fecundity and growth, which are important themes in the cults of other goddesses, even in the cults of Kamalā and Kālī apart from their associations with the Mahāvidyās.[121] The Mahāvidyās are seldom worshiped for progeny or fertility.

Another notable feature of Hindu goddesses is their role as consorts. Many of them are associated with particular gods as wives or consorts. Among the Mahāvidyās this role is extremely weak. They are almost always depicted or described without reference to a consort. Although they may bear epithets in their *nāma stotras* that associate them with a male deity, usually Śiva, he is rarely depicted with them, and when he is, he is subordinate to them. For example, Kālī and Tārā are shown standing on his supine body, and Tripura-sundarī is shown sitting on a throne whose legs are the four male gods (Brahmā, Viṣṇu, Śiva, and Rudra). Both as a group and as individual goddesses within the group, the Mahāvidyās are independent. It is particularly striking in the case of Kamalā, who is otherwise known to be Viṣṇu's consort, that he is not depicted with her when she is shown as one of the Mahāvidyās. Her *dhyāna* mantra describes her without him, preferring the very ancient image of Gaja-lakṣmī, in which she is flanked by elephants showering her with water from their trunks or from pots. It is not her wifely associations and functions that are significant in her role as a Mahāvidyā.

The function of the Mahāvidyās in maintaining cosmic order, dharma, is also weak. For many goddesses, particularly the demon-slaying Durgā, their role as guardian and maintainer of dharma is central. As we have discussed above, the Mahādevī's assumption of appropriate forms to defeat demons and maintain cosmic balance and harmony is an important facet of *śākta* theology in many texts. Indeed, the Mahāvidyās are sometimes compared to the *avatāras* of Viṣṇu, or the *avatāras* are said to be identical with or to have arisen from the Mahāvidyās. Their *nāma stotras* also give individual Mahāvidyās epithets that suggest a world-maintaining role. Their iconography and mythology, however, do not emphasize it, for the Mahāvidyās as a group or as individuals.

Although the Mahāvidyās are not strongly associated with geographical features or maternal, consort, or dharma-upholding functions, they do have other characteristics that might help us begin to understand their distinctive nature as a group and as individual goddesses. The Mahāvidyās are independent deities, having only a weak connection with a male deity. In the case of individual Mahāvidyā who are known to be consorts of male deities outside the context of the Mahāvidyā cult, such as Kālī, Tārā, and Kamalā, this association is played down or ignored when they are approached as Mahāvidyās. Even the origin myth of the Mahāvidyās, though featuring Satī, Śiva's wife, stresses her decision to act independently of her husband and her success in bending him to her will. When the Mahāvidyās as individuals are shown with a male consort, they dominate him, standing on his supine body, assuming the "superior" position in sexual intercourse, or sitting on a throne or couch supported by male deities. In short, where male deities do appear, they are subordinate and subservient to the Mahāvidyās.

The Mahāvidyās, with a few exceptions, are fearsome. They dwell or are worshiped in cremation grounds, sit on corpses, wear garlands of severed heads or skulls, are naked and smeared with blood, and have disheveled hair. They tend to be rough, not soft, in nature. This fierce aspect overshadows their boon-conferring, indulgent nature.

In the context of Tantrism, and in terms of many of their names, they are associated with *sādhanā* (spiritual exercises). They are associated also with mental and psychic powers (*siddhis*) and heightened states of consciousness.

Finally, they are associated with mantras. They are mantras, they exist where their mantras are uttered, and their most essential form is as mantras. They are, unquestionably, powerful sounds. In this respect, they are tied inextricably to human beings, without whom they would remain only latent. It is when a *sādhaka* invokes the mantra of a goddess that she "comes alive." The Mahāvidyās, that is, as mantras, represent or symbolize aspects of awareness, consciousness, or mental capacity associated with mantra *sādhanā* (spiritual discipline that employs sacred sounds). In a sense we could say that each Mahāvidyā represents a style of spirituality appropriate to the *sādhaka* as determined by the guru who has bequeathed to him or her a special mantra, that is, a special goddess.

Next we will turn our attention to the individual Mahāvidyās. We will often find ideas and themes that apply to the Mahāvidyās as a group being reiterated and emphasized in the iconography and mythology of a particular goddess. On the other hand, each goddess also has her peculiarities: unique features that are only weakly stressed in the group as a whole.

PART II

The Individual Mahāvidyās

Kālī

The Black Goddess

She is the terrible one who has a dreadful face. She should be meditated upon as having disheveled hair and a garland of freshly cut human heads. She has four arms. In her upper left hand she holds a sword that has just been bloodied by the severed head that she holds in her lower left hand. Her upper right hand makes the gesture of assurance and her lower right hand, the sign of granting favors. She has a bluish complexion and is lustrous like a dark cloud. She is completely naked, and her body gleams with blood that is smeared all over it from the garland of bleeding severed heads around her neck. Her ear ornaments are the corpses of children. Her fangs are dreadful, and her face is fierce. Her breasts are large and round, and she wears a girdle made of severed human hands. Blood trickles from the corners of her mouth and makes her face gleam. She makes a terrible sound and lives in the cremation ground, where she is surrounded by howling jackals. She stands on the chest of Śiva in the form of a corpse. She is eager to have sexual intercourse in reverse fashion with Mahākāla. She wears a satisfied expression. She smiles.[1]

She is lustrous like a dark cloud and wears black clothes. Her tongue lolls, her face is dreadful to behold, her eyes are sunken, and she smiles. She wears the crescent moon on her forehead and is decorated with serpents. She drinks wine, has a serpent as a sacred thread, is seated on a bed of snakes, and wears a garland of fifty human heads that hangs all the way down to her knees. She has a large belly, and the thousand-hooded serpent Ananta looms above her head. Śiva is present as a boy beside her. She makes a loud, laughing sound, is very dreadful, but bestows the desires of the aspirant.[2]

> She is like a mountain of collyrium, and her abode is in the cremation ground. She has three red eyes, her hair is disheveled, and she is awful to look at because of her emaciated body. In her left hand she holds a jar full of liquor mixed with meat, and in her right hand she holds a freshly severed head. She is eating raw flesh, she is naked, her limbs are adorned with ornaments, she is drunk on wine, and she smiles.[3]

Although the order, number, and names of the Mahāvidyās may vary, Kālī is always included and is usually named or shown first. She is also affirmed in many places to be the most important of the Mahāvidyās, the primordial or primary Mahāvidyā, the *ādi* Mahāvidyā.[4] In some cases it seems apparent that the other Mahāvidyās originate from Kālī or are her differing forms. In one of the accounts of the origin of the Mahāvidyās as a group, it is explicitly stated that they arise from Kālī when Śiva wishes to leave her.[5] In the origin account given in the *Mahābhāgavata-purāṇa*, Satī takes on the form of a goddess who resembles Kālī before actually multiplying herself into the ten Mahāvidyās. Although Kālī is not specifically named, Satī first turns into a dark, frightening, naked, four-armed goddess with disheveled hair and a garland of skulls (which is just how Kālī is usually described), and then creates from herself the other forms.[6] Furthermore, in early accounts of Satī's confrontation with Śiva over her right to attend her father's sacrifice—accounts in which the Mahāvidyās do not appear—Satī does turn herself into Kālī and in her Kālī form convinces Śiva to let her go.[7] The *Śaktisaṁgama-tantra* proclaims Kālī's priority explicitly: "All the deities, including the Mahāvidyās, Siddhi-vidyās, Vidyās, and Upa-vidyās, are different forms that Kālī assumes."[8]

Kālī's place as the primary Mahāvidyā, the first among the goddesses, is reinforced by the fact that she lends the group as a whole her own characteristics. Her character, attributes, and nature are shared by the others. She is typical, perhaps even paradigmatic, as the *ādi* Mahāvidyā. And her symbolic meaning, I think, often helps to uncover the meaning of some of the other goddesses in the group. As we shall see below, according to some interpretations Kālī reveals or symbolizes the ultimate goal suggested or implied in the other Mahāvidyās. She completes the others, as it were.

Given Kālī's central role among the Mahāvidyās, it is important to consider in some detail her history prior to her association with them. Kālī appeared quite early in the Hindu tradition, and by the late medieval period, when the cult of the Mahāvidyās arose, she was by no means an obscure goddess: she had achieved a clearly defined mythology and character and a cult that was popular throughout India. It is quite clear,

Fig. 10. Kālī, contemporary painting.

furthermore, that Kālī's character has remained fairly intact in the context of the Mahāvidyās. That is, her role in the group is not based on a selective use of her characteristics, although there are some aspects of her nature and mythology that are preferred over others, as we shall see. It is also important to look at Kālī's central role in Tantrism generally before seeking to understand her meaning in the context of the Mahāvidyās.

The Early History of Kālī

The earliest references to Kālī date to the medieval period (around 600 C.E.). They usually place her on the periphery of Hindu society or on the battlefield. The *Agni-* and *Garuḍa-purāṇas* involve Kālī for success in war and victory over one's enemies. She has an awful appearance: she is gaunt, has fangs, laughs loudly, dances madly, wears a garland of corpses, sits on the back of a ghost, and lives in the cremation ground. She is asked to crush, trample, break, and burn the enemy.[9] In the *Bhāgavata-purāṇa*, Kālī is the patron deity of a band of thieves whose leader tries to secure her blessing in order to have a son. The thief kidnaps a saintly Brahman youth with the intention of offering him as a blood sacrifice to Kālī. The effulgence of the virtuous youth, however, burns Kālī herself when he is brought near her image. Emerging from her image, infuriated, she kills the leader and his entire band. She and her host of demons then decapitate the corpses of the thieves, drink their blood until drunk, and throw their heads about in sport. She is described as having a dreadful face and large teeth and as laughing loudly.[10] Kālī's association with thieves is also seen in her role as patron deity of the infamous Thugs, who specialized in befriending and then murdering travelers.[11] Kālī is also pictured in the Bengali *maṅgal kāvyas* as bestowing magical powers on thieves to help them in their criminal deeds.[12]

Kālī's association with the periphery of Hindu society (she is worshiped by criminals, tribals, and members of low castes in uncivilized and wild places) is also evident in an architectural work of the sixth to eighth centuries, the *Mānasāra-śilpa-śāstra.* It says that Kālī's temples should be built far from villages and towns, near cremation grounds and the dwellings of Caṇḍālas (very low-caste people).[13] Kālī's association with areas outside or beyond the borders of civilized society is also clear in a eleventh-century C.E. Tamil text, the *Kalingattuparaṇi*, which says that her temple is located in a desert where the trees are withered and the landscape is barren.

The description of the temple itself underlines Kālī's awful, uncivilized nature. The temple is constructed of bones, flesh, blood, heads, and body parts of enemies killed in battle. The severed heads are used as bricks, the blood is used to make mortar, elephant tusks serve as roof trusses, and on top of the enclosure walls (a common feature of South Indian temples) "the severed heads of peacocks, the heads of men offered as sacrifice, the heads of young babies also severed in sacrifice and blood-oozing flesh as standards were placed as beautifying elements."[14] The temple is "cleansed" daily with blood instead of water, and flesh is offered to the goddess instead of flowers. The fires consuming the corpses of sacrificial victims also serve as lamps.

The description of the worshipers and the *pūjā* at the temple is equally horrific. A graphic account is given of a devotee chopping off his own head as an offering to the goddess.[15] Warriors also offer their heads to the goddess to demonstrate their fearlessness. *Yoginīs* frequent the temple and arrive there with swords and severed heads, in appearance like Kālī herself. The temple is "full of blood, flesh, burning corpses, vultures, jackals and goblins."[16] Kālī herself is seated on a couch of five ghosts (*pañca preta*) with a corpse as a pillow. She sleeps on a bed made of flesh.[17]

Kālī's most famous appearances on the battlefield are found in the *Devī-māhātmya*. In the third episode, which features Durgā's defeat of the demons Śumbha and Niśumbha and their allies, Kālī appears twice. Early in the battle, the demons Caṇḍa and Muṇḍa approach Durgā with readied weapons. Seeing them prepared to attack her, Durgā's face becomes dark with anger. Suddenly the goddess Kālī springs from her forehead. She is black, wears a garland of human heads and a tiger skin, and wields a skull-topped staff. She is gaunt, with sunken eyes, gaping mouth, and lolling tongue. She roars loudly and leaps into the battle, where she tears demons apart with her hands and crushes them in her jaws. She grasps the two demon generals and in one furious blow decapitates them both with her sword (7.3–22). Later in the battle, Kālī is summoned by Durgā to help defeat the demon Raktabīja. This demon has the ability to reproduce himself instantly whenever a drop of his blood falls to the ground. Having wounded Raktabīja with a variety of weapons, Durgā and her assistants, a fierce band of goddesses called the Mātṛkās, find they have worsened their situation. As Raktabīja bleeds more and more profusely from his wounds, the battlefield fills with his duplicates. Kālī finally defeats the demon by sucking the blood from his body and throwing the countless duplicate Raktabījas into her gaping mouth (8.49–61).

In these two episodes, Kālī emerges to represent Durgā's personified

Fig. 11. Kālī and Durgā, contemporary lithograph.

wrath, her embodied fury. Kālī plays a similar role in her association with Pārvatī. In general, Pārvatī is a benign goddess, but from time to time she exhibits fierce aspects. When this occurs, Kālī is sometimes described as being brought into being. In the *Liṅga-purāṇa*, Śiva asks Pārvatī to destroy the demon Dāruka, who has been given the boon that he can only be killed by a female. Pārvatī enters Śiva's body and transforms herself from the poison that is stored in Śiva's throat. She emerges from Śiva as Kālī, ferocious in appearance, and with the help of flesh-eating *piśācas* (demons) attacks and defeats Dāruka and his hosts. Kālī, however, becomes so intoxicated by the blood lust of battle that she threatens to destroy the entire world in her fury. The world is saved when Śiva intervenes and calms her.[18] Kālī appears in a similar context elsewhere in the same text. When Śiva sets out to defeat the demons of the three cities, Kālī is part of his entourage. Adorned with skulls and wearing an elephant hide, her eyes half-closed in intoxication from drinking the blood of demons, she whirls a trident. She is also praised, however, as the daughter of Himālaya (the mountain range personified as a god), a clear identification with Pārvatī (who is Himālaya's daughter). It seems that, in the course of Pārvatī's preparation for war, Kālī appears as her personified wrath, her alter ego, as it were.[19]

In the *Vāmana-purāṇa*, Śiva calls Pārvatī "Kālī" (the black one) because of her dark complexion. Hearing him use this name, Pārvatī takes offense and undertakes austerities to rid herself of her dark complexion. After succeeding, she is renamed Gaurī (the golden one). Her discarded dark sheath, however, is transformed into the furious battle queen Kauśikī, who subsequently creates Kālī in her fury. So, again, although there is an intermediary goddess (Kauśikī), Kālī plays the role of Pārvatī's dark, negative, violent nature in embodied form.[20]

Kālī makes similar appearances in myths concerning both Satī and Sītā. In the case of Satī, Kālī emerges when Satī's father, Dakṣa, infuriates his daughter by not inviting her and Śiva to a great sacrificial rite. Satī rubs her nose in anger, and Kālī appears.[21] This story, of course, reminds us of one of the accounts of how the Mahāvidyās as a group originated, the one in which they come forth as Satī's embodied anger. In the case of Sītā, Kālī arises as her fierce, terrible, bloodthirsty aspect when Sītā's husband, Rāma, is confronted with such a terrible monster that he is frozen with fear. Sītā, transformed into Kālī, handily defeats the demon.[22]

In her association with Śiva, Kālī's tendency to wildness and disorder persists. Although sometimes he is said to tame or soften her, at times she incites Śiva himself to dangerous, destructive behavior. A South Indian tradition tells of a dance contest between the two. After defeating Śumbha and Niśumbha, Kālī takes up residence in a forest with her retinue of fierce companions and terrorizes the surrounding area. This distracts a local devotee of Śiva from his austerities, and he asks Śiva to rid the forest of the violent goddess. When Śiva appears, Kālī threatens him, claiming the region as her own. Śiva challenges her to a dance contest and defeats her when she is unable (or unwilling) to match his energetic *tāṇḍava* dance. That Śiva should have to resort to his *tāṇḍava* dance to defeat Kālī suggests the motif of Kālī inciting Śiva to destructive activity, as this particular dance is typically performed at the end of the cosmic age and destroys the universe. Descriptions of the dance dwell on its destructive aspects.[23]

Although Śiva defeats Kālī in the dance contest and forces her to control her disruptive habits, we find few images and myths depicting her as docile. Instead, we repeatedly find Śiva and Kālī behaving in disruptive ways, inciting each other, or Kālī in her wild activity dominating an inactive or corpselike Śiva. In the first type of relationship, the two appear dancing together in such a way that they threaten the world. Bhavabhūti's *Mālātīmādhava* describes the pair as they dance wildly near the goddess's temple. Their dance is so frenzied that it threatens to disrupt the cosmos. Pārvatī stands by frightened as she watches them.[24]

Iconographic representations of Kālī and Śiva nearly always show Kālī as dominant. She is usually standing or dancing on Śiva's supine body, and when the two are shown in sexual intercourse, she is on top of him. Although Śiva is said to tame Kālī in the myth of the dance contest, it seems clear that she is never finally subdued by him; she is most popularly represented as uncontrollable, more apt to provoke Śiva himself to dangerous activity than to renounce her own wildness.

In terms of her early history, then, we can say that Kālī is primarily a goddess who threatens stability and order. Although she may be said to serve order in her role as slayer of demons, more often than not she becomes so frenzied on the battlefield, intoxicated on the blood of her victims, that she herself begins to destroy the world that she is supposed to protect. Thus, even in the service of the gods, she is dangerous and likely to get out of control. In association with other goddesses, she emerges to represent their embodied wrath and fury, a frightening, dangerous dimension of the divine feminine that is released when these goddesses become enraged or are summoned to take part in war and killing. In relation to Śiva, she appears to play the opposite role from that of Pārvatī. Pārvatī calms Śiva, counterbalancing his antisocial or destructive tendencies; she brings him within the sphere of domesticity and with her soft glances urges him to moderate the destructive aspects of his *tāṇḍava* dance. Kālī is Śiva's "other wife," as it were, provoking him and encouraging him in his mad, antisocial, disruptive habits. It is never Kālī who tames Śiva but Śiva who must calm Kālī. Her association with criminals reinforces her dangerous role vis-à-vis society. She is at home outside the moral order and seems to be unrestrained by it.

Kālī's Preeminence in Tantrism

Despite Kālī's terrible appearance, gruesome habits, and association with the periphery of civilization in many early references, she eventually achieved great popularity and prominence in the Hindu tradition. Of particular interest is the centrality that Kālī achieved in the tantric tradition, which for our purposes is especially significant. She figures prominently in tantric texts in Kashmir, particularly in the works of Abhinavagupta. In a philosophy that portrays reality as essentially the interaction of two principles, Śiva and Śakti, Kālī is often designated as one of the forms assumed by Śakti. Many different forms of Kālī are mentioned: in *Tantraloka*, Abhinavagupta mentions thirteen.[25] It is clear that tantric *sādhana* (spiritual endeavor) featuring Kalī was common in Kashmir at an early period.[26] An important image in Kashmir Tantrism is the *śakti cakra*, described as a wheel of energy symbolizing the evolution and dynamics of consciousness. Sometimes the main wheel has additional wheels within it, representing different types of consciousness, or phases in the cognitive process, and these wheels are identified with "the twelve Kālīs."[27]

Kālī is even more popular and dominant in the Tantrism of eastern India, particularly Bengal. Many tantric texts written in Bengal include manuals for her worship; they describe her appearance, mantra, and yantra and give hymns in her praise (*nāma stotras*), typically listing either 108 or 1,000 names. In tantric digests such as the *Tantrasāra*, *Śāktapramoda*, and *Prāṇatoṣiṇī*, she plays a central role and is said to have several forms, of which the following are described in detail: Dakṣiṇa-kālī, Mahākālī, Śmaśāna-kālī, Guhya-kālī, Bhadra-kālī, Cāmuṇḍā-kālī, Siddha-kālī, Haṁsa-kālī, and Kāmakalā-kālī.[28] Kālī is widely worshiped according to tantric rites throughout eastern India, and this tradition is probably quite ancient. It is important at this point to reflect in a general way on how Kālī came to achieve such a central position in Tantra.

An underlying assumption in tantric ideology is that reality is the result and expression of the symbiotic interaction of male and female, Śiva and Śakti, the quiescent and the dynamic, and other polar opposites that produce a creative tension. Consequently, goddesses in Tantrism play an important role and are affirmed to be crucial in discerning the nature of ultimate reality. Although Śiva is usually said to be the source of the *tantras*, the source of wisdom and truth, and Pārvatī, his spouse, to be the student to whom the scriptures are given, many of the *tantras* emphasize the fact that it is Śakti (personified as Pārvatī, Kālī, and other goddesses) who is immediately present to the adept and whose presence and being underlie the adept's own being. For the tantric adept it is her vitality that is sought through various techniques aimed at spiritual transformation; thus it is she who is affirmed as the dominant and primary reality.

Although Pārvatī is usually said to be the recipient of Śiva's wisdom in the form of the *tantras*, it is Kālī who seems to dominate tantric iconography, texts, and rituals. In many places, Kālī is praised as the greatest of all deities or as the highest reality. The *Nirvāṇa-tantra* says that the gods Brahmā, Viṣṇu, and Śiva arise from her like bubbles from the sea, endlessly appearing and passing away, leaving their source unchanged. Comparing them to Kālī, says this text, is like comparing the puddle of water in a cow's hoofprint to the waters of the sea.[29] The *Nigama-kalpataru* and the *Picchilā-tantra* declare that, of all mantras, Kālī's is the greatest.[30] The *Yoginī-*, *Kāmākhyā-*, and *Niruttara-tantras* all proclaim Kālī the greatest of the Vidyās, divinity itself; indeed, they declare her to be the essential form (*svarūpa*) of the Mahādevī.[31] The *Kāmadā-tantra* states unequivocally that she is attributeless, neither male nor female, sinless, the imperishable *saccidānanda* (being, consciousness, and bliss), *brahman* itself.[32] In the *Mahānirvāṇa-tantra*, too, Kālī is one of the most common epithets for the primordial Śakti.[33] In one passage, Śiva praises Kālī as she who devours time, who alone remains after the dissolution of the universe, and who is the origin and destroyer of all things.[34]

Why Kālī, instead of some other goddess, attained this preeminent position in Tantrism is not entirely clear, but the explanation may lie in certain tantric ideological and ritual presuppositions. Tantrism generally is oriented toward ritual. By means of certain rituals (exterior and interior, bodily and mental), the *sādhaka* (religious adept), seeks to gain *mokṣa* (awakening, or the bliss of self-knowledge). A consistent theme in this endeavor is the uniting of opposites or the seeing beyond opposites (male-female, microcosm-macrocosm, sacred-profane, auspicious-inauspicious, pure-polluted, Śiva-Śakti). Tantrism teaches there is an elaborate, subtle

Fig. 12. Kālī within her yantra, contemporary lithograph.

geography of the body that must be learned and controlled. By means of the body, including both physical and subtle bodies, the *sādhaka* can manipulate levels of reality and harness the dynamics of those levels to the attainment of the desired goal. With the help of a guru, the *sādhaka* undertakes to gain his or her goal by conquest, to use his or her own body and knowledge of that body to bring the fractured world of name and form, the polarized world of male and female, sacred and profane, pure and polluted, good and bad, back to wholeness and unity.

Sādhanā takes a particularly dramatic form in left-handed Tantrism. In the attempt to realize the nature of the world as thoroughly pervaded by the one *śakti*, the *sādhaka* (here called the *vīra*, "hero") undertakes the ritual of the *pañca tattva*, the "five (forbidden) things" or "truths". In a ritual context and under the supervision of a guru, the *sādhaka* partakes of wine, meat, fish, parched grain (perhaps a hallucinogenic drug of some kind), and sexual intercourse. In this way one overcomes the distinction (or duality) of clean and unclean, sacred and profane, and breaks one's bondage to a world that is artificially fragmented. The adept affirms in a radical way the underlying unity of the phenomenal world, the identity of *śakti* with the whole creation. Heroically, one triumphs over it, controls and masters it. By affirming the essential worth of the forbidden, one disarms it of its power to pollute, degrade, and bind, and changes that negative power into spiritually transformative energy.[35]

The figure of Kālī conveys death, destruction, terror, the all-consuming aspect of reality. She is also a "forbidden thing," or the forbidden par excellence, for she is death itself. The tantric hero does not propitiate, fear, ignore, or avoid the forbidden. During the *pañca tattva* ritual, the adept boldly confronts Kālī and thereby assimilates and overcomes her, transforming her into a vehicle of salvation. This is particularly clear in the *Karpurādi-stotra*, a short work in praise of Kālī, which describes the *pañca tattva* ritual as performed in the cremation ground (*śmaśāna sādhanā*). Throughout this text Kālī is described in familiar terms. She is black (v. 1), has disheveled hair and blood trickling from her mouth (v. 3), holds a sword and a severed head (v. 4), wears a girdle of severed arms, sits on a corpse in the cremation ground (v. 7), and is surrounded by skulls, bones, and female jackals (v. 8). It is she, when confronted boldly in meditation, who gives the *sādhaka* great power and ultimately salvation. In Kālī's favorite dwelling place, the cremation ground, the *sādhaka* meditates on every terrible aspect of the black goddess and thus achieves the desired goal.

> He, O Mahākālī, who in the cremation-ground, naked, and with dishevelled hair, intently meditates upon Thee and recites Thy *mantra*, and with each recitation makes offering to Thee of a thousand *Akaṇda* flowers with seed, becomes without any effort a lord of the earth.
>
> O Kālī, whoever on Tuesday at midnight, having uttered Thy *mantra*, makes offering even but once with devotion to Thee of a hair of his *Śakti*

[his female companion] in the cremation-ground, becomes a great poet, a lord of the earth, and ever goes mounted upon an elephant. (vv. 15–16)[36]

The *Karpurādi-stotra* clearly makes Kālī more than a ferocious slayer of demons who serves Durgā and Śiva on the battlefield. In fact, she is by and large removed from the battle context. She is the supreme mistress of the universe (v. 12), she is identical with the five elements (v. 14), and in union with Śiva (who is identified as her spouse) she creates and destroys the worlds. Her appearance also has been modified, befitting her exalted position as ruler of the world and the object of meditation by which the *sādhaka* attains liberation. In addition to her terrible aspects (which are insisted upon), there are now hints of another, benign dimension to the goddess. So, for example, she is no longer described as emaciated or ugly. In the *Karpurādi-stotra* she is young and beautiful (v. 1), has a gently smiling face (v. 18), and makes gestures with her two right hands that dispel fear and offer boons (v. 4). These positive features are apt, because Kālī no longer is a mere shrew, the distillation of Durgā's or Pārvatī's wrath, but is she through whom the hero achieves success, she who grants the boon of liberation, and she who, when boldly approached, frees the *sādhaka* from fear itself. She is here not only the symbol of death but the symbol of triumph over death.

Kālī as the Exemplary Mahāvidyā

Several of Kali's prominent characteristics set the tone for the Mahāvidyās as a group, and several individual Mahāvidyās clearly reflect her character. Moreover, according to several informants, Kālī alone among the Mahāvidyās, or to the fullest extent, reveals the nature of ultimate reality and symbolizes fully awakened consciousness.

In several of their origin myths, the Mahāvidyās arise when a goddess (Satī, Pārvatī, or Kālī) exerts her independence from her husband, invariably Śiva. In this sense, the Mahāvidyās are symbols of female independence. Kālī dramatically illustrates this. She is rarely, if ever, depicted or described as playing the role of the compliant, subservient wife. She is not characterized by the attributes of a *pati vratā*, a woman totally devoted to her husband, obedient to his wishes and compliant to his will in every way. As Śiva's consort, she violates that stereotype. She dominates him, inciting him to destructive frenzy, standing on his body, or assuming the upper position, the "man's position," in sex.

Kālī also deviates shockingly from the appearance of the ideal wife, who wears her hair tightly bound and is modestly but carefully attired and adorned with attractive ornaments. Kālī is naked, immodestly displaying herself. Her "ornaments" are awful, disgusting: she wears a string of severed heads or skulls as a garland and a string of severed arms as a girdle; infant corpses dangle from her ears. Her hair is completely unbound and ratty, in keeping with her wild nature. She is often smeared with blood, which is highly polluting and inauspicious.

Kālī is also sexually powerful. While early descriptions of her emphasize her gaunt, sometimes skeletal, appearance, with sunken eyes, withered, dangling breasts, and wrinkled skin, in later texts her haglike appearance is greatly attenuated, and she is often said to be eternally young, with full and firm breasts and a beautiful, smiling face. In later texts, especially the *tantras*, she is sexually aggressive and is often shown or described as having sex with Śiva. In her *sahasranāma stotra* (thousand-name hymn) many names emphasize her vigorous sexual appetite or her sexual attractiveness. She is called She Whose Essential Form Is Sexual Desire, Whose Form Is the Yoni, Who Is Situated in the Yoni, Who Is Adorned with a Garland of Yonis, Who Loves the Liṅgam, Who Dwells in the Liṅgam, Who Is Worshiped with Semen, Who Dwells in an Ocean of Semen, Who Is Always Filled with Semen, and many other such names.[37] In this respect, Kālī also violates the idea of the controlled woman who is sexually satisfied by marriage. Kālī is sexually voracious, and dangerous because of this.

Kālī denotes freedom, particularly freedom from societal norms. She dwells outside the confines of normal society. She prefers the cremation ground, which is a place avoided by those who live within society. She lives in the forests or the jungle, among uncivilized people. Her loose hair and nudity suggest that she is totally unrestrained, totally free from social and ethical roles and expectations. In the same vein, she is an outsider, beyond convention. She is worshiped by criminals and outcastes. She is unrefined, raw in appearance and habit. And she is powerful, full of energy, perhaps because of being an outsider, a breaker of boundaries and social models.

Some of these characteristics seem important among the other Mahāvidyās. Tārā is very close to Kālī in appearance and character and shares with her the role of independent outsider. Chinnamastā is even more shocking in appearance than Kālī and rudely breaks the model of the subdued, controlled, obedient wife, mother, or daughter. She suggests energy out of control to the point of self-destruction. Mātaṅgī, particularly

Uccișța-mātaṅginī, as we shall see, has strong associations with the jungle and with pollution. Bagalāmukhī is a fierce goddess associated with black magic. Dhūmāvatī is the essence of the inauspicious: an ugly, withered old widow with a quarrelsome temperament. It is difficult to resist the conclusion that many of the Mahāvidyās, in a vein similar to Kālī, are deliberately depicted as breaking stereotypes of the properly socialized female. They are symbols of the "other," of ways of being female that male-dominated mainstream society sees as dangerous.

Kālī's Tongue: Tasting the Forbidden

Two features that typify Kalī's appearance—her unbound, wild hair and her lolling tongue—seem particularly apt expressions of her (and by extension, the Mahāvidyās') "otherness," her nontraditional, boundary-stretching, role-shattering, liminal character. Both of these features have been the subject of recent scholarly work.

One of the most distinctive features of Kālī's appearance is her grotesquely lolling tongue. In her *dhyāna* mantras (meditation mantras) and iconography, she is almost always shown with her mouth open and her tongue hanging out. In her early history, where she is depicted as a wild, bloodthirsty goddess who lives on the edges of civilization or as a ferocious slayer of demons who gets drunk on the blood of her victims, her lolling tongue seems to suggest her great appetite for blood, as does her gaunt and emaciated figure. She is famished and extends her tongue grossly to satisfy her huge appetite, which is all-consuming.

Most contemporary Hindu informants interpret the lolling tongue of her best-known image, Dakṣiṇā-kālī, quite differently. They see it as an expression of her being disconcerted: Kālī is embarrassed when she inadvertently finds herself standing on Śiva, her husband. The Dakṣiṇā-kālī image shows her in the moment of recognizing her husband as she stands on him. She is abashed and "bites her tongue."

In recent work, Jeffrey Kripal suggests another interpretation of Kālī's tongue, one that seems much more in keeping with the image of Kālī in tantric literature and practice as a goddess who subverts social norms and challenges the socialized ego.[38] According to Kripal, Kālī's lolling tongue has two primary meanings in the context of Tantra: (1) sexual gratification and (2) consumption of the forbidden or polluted.

Kālī's lolling tongue as denoting sexual gratification or the desire for sexual indulgence seems plausible. In Dakṣiṇā-kali images, Śiva sometimes has an erection, and in some *dhyāna* mantras and iconographic representations of Kālī she is having sex with him. In both cases her tongue lolls out. This interpretation is substantiated by a story recorded in Orissa. Durgā became angry when she found out that she could defeat the buffalo demon only if she showed her genitals to him. She did so, but then went on a terrible rampage.

> Her anger grew so terrible that she transformed herself, grew smaller and black and left her lion mount and started walking on foot. Her name then became Kali. With tongue lolling out and dripping with blood, she then went on a blind, destructive rampage, killing everything and everyone in sight, regardless of who they were. The gods and the people became extremely worried and appealed to Siva for help. Mahadev agreed and lay himself down, sleeping on the path on which the furious, black and naked Kali was coming. In her blinded anger she did not see him and stepped on his chest. At that moment Siva's penis became erect and entered Kali. At that instant Kali recognized her husband and pulled out her tongue in ecstasy and her anger disappeared.[39]

Kālī's tongue also hangs out in contexts that are not even remotely sexual, however, where neither gratification nor embarrassment seems a likely interpretation. She is often pictured in cremation grounds without a male consort, for example, and invariably her tongue is lolling. How might her tongue in these instances be interpreted within a tantric framework? On the basis of his careful examination of a group of passages describing the tantric *sādhanā* of Ramakrishna, Kripal argues that Kālī's tongue denotes the act of tasting or enjoying what society regards as forbidden, foul, or polluted, her indiscriminate enjoyment of all the world's "flavors."

The passages in question concern Ramakrishna's habit while undertaking tantric *sādhanā* of eating feces, sometimes his own, and drinking wine and urine. During his tantric *sādhanā*, Ramakrishna sought to realize the state of consciousness in which all things are perceived to be essentially one, or essentially unified and related. He is said to have held his own feces in one hand and sandal paste (a particularly fragrant and pure substance) in the other and contemplated their essential sameness.[40] Ramakrishna's use of his own feces in his *sādhanā* worried and even revolted some of his friends, who began to think him mad. An acquaintance, probably trying to dissuade Ramakrishna from his ways, rebuked him by saying that anyone can handle their own feces, but to handle the feces of another is what really marks one as a knower of *brahman*. As was his habit, Ramakrishna took this rebuke as a challenge. He summoned Kālī, and she entered his body. "At that moment, possessed by the goddess and her lolling tongue, the saint went down to the river where people defecate and urinate. There he took clay laced with feces and touched it to his tongue, 'and he felt no disgust.' "[41]

Kālī's gaping mouth and lolling tongue, her appearance and habits generally, are unquestionably repulsive to our ordinary sensibilities. In Tantra, this is probably precisely the point. What we experience as disgusting, polluted, forbidden, and gruesome is grounded in limited human (or cultural) consciousness, which has ordered, regimented, and divided reality into categories that serve limited, ego-centered, selfish conceptions of how the world should be. Kālī, in her rude way, deconstructs these categories, inviting those who would learn from her to be open to the whole world in all of its aspects. She invites her devotees, like Ramakrishna, to dare to taste the world in its most disgusting and forbidding manifestations in order to detect its underlying unity and sacrality, which is the Great Goddess herself.

Kālī's Hair: Pollution and Dissolution

Another striking feature of Kālī is her loose, disheveled hair. I have never seen a depiction of Kālī with bound or braided hair. Some of the other Mahāvidyās, such as Chinnamastā, Bagalāmukhī, and Dhūmavatī, are also typically shown with wild hair. In some cases, as in the Durgā Saptaśatī temple in Nagawa, near Varanasi, all the Mahāvidyās are depicted with disheveled hair. Unkempt hair contrasts strikingly with the way adult Hindu women wear their hair and the way the hair of most goddesses is depicted. What might be the significance of Kālī's unbound hair? Two general interpretations seem likely.

Women's braided or bound hair suggests conformity to social convention and probably also acceptance of social control. Married women part their hair in the middle and pull it back tightly in a braid. The part is often marked with red, which symbolizes the woman's married state. Girls who have reached puberty also usually wear their hair bound in some fashion. Loose hair is very uncommon. Along with Kālī's other unconventional features—her nudity, her standing atop her husband or consort, her dwelling in cremation grounds, and her rude, lolling tongue—her messy, loose, tangled hair emphasizes her socially marginal character, her disdain for convention.[42] Kālī is free from convention, wild and uncontrolled in nature, and not bound to or limited by a male consort.

Kālī's unbound hair may also have a broader, indeed cosmic, significance, suggesting dissolution itself. Considering Kālī's identification with the cremation ground and death, her loose hair may suggest the end of the world. Her hair has come apart and flies about every which way; order has come to an end; all has returned to chaos. The "braidedness" of social and cosmic order comes to an end in Kalī's wild, unbound, flowing hair.

A second interpretation of Kalī's disheveled hair seems plausible. In certain circumstances, almost all associated with impurity and pollution of some kind, Hindu women do unbind their hair. In particular, they unbind it during menstruation.[43] Perhaps the best-known example of this in Sanskrit literature is the case of Draupadī in the *Mahābhārata*. Her husband, Yudhiṣṭhira, wagers her and loses her. Draupadī, at the command of Duryodhana, an opponent of Yudhiṣṭhira, is dragged into the assembly hall and made to undress. The text notes that she is menstruating and that her hair is disheveled. Commenting on this scene, Alf Hiltebeitel says, "These two facts are not unrelated. Draupadī's hair is dishevelled *because* she is menstruating. The *Mahābhārata* draws here on a well known prohibition on wearing the hair braided during menstruation, and not binding it up until the ritual bath that ends the period of impurity."[44] In addition to wearing their hair unbound during menstruation, women in the Punjab also unbind their hair following childbirth, intercourse, and the death of their husbands. That is, women wear their hair unbound when they are in a state of pollution.[45]

I have been unable to find textual verification for the suggestion that Kālī's disheveled hair indicates that she is menstruating. But since she symbolizes the subversion of social order and decorum and represents a confrontation with, or at least the acknowledgment of, the forbidden (represented by the polluted), it seems likely that we are meant to understand her as menstruating.

Kālī as an Expression of Ultimate Reality

Kālī is also considered the exemplary Mahāvidyā because she most completely reveals the ultimate truth. She is the *ādi* Mahāvidyā, the primordial Mahāvidyā. In one of her *sahasranāma stotras* (there are

Fig. 13. Kālī's hair, contemporary lithograph.

several of these addressed to Kālī), she is called She Who Is Knowledge of the Self, She Who Is Knowledge of *Brahman*, She Whose Form Is the Highest *Brahman*,[46] and Mistress of the Mahāvidyās.[47] Kālī's preeminent position in such epithets as these implies that in some way she reveals the ultimate truth. In Tantrism, which is ritually oriented and spiritually pragmatic, ultimate truth is perhaps confirmed and realized only by means of *sādhanā*, is revealed only to adepts who have worshiped Kālī. It is tempting, nevertheless, to speculate on just how Kālī reveals ultimate truth.

One approach is to interpret Kālī's most important form, Dakṣiṇā-kālī, symbolically, allegorically, or mystically, as some contemporary Hindu writers and practitioners have done. They find that esoteric truths can be gleaned from Kālī's image, truths that are not obvious, that are not immediately suggested by her appearance. Based on the information I have been able to gather, this esoteric or mystical interpretation of Kālī as exemplifying ultimate truth runs as follows.[48]

The overall image of Dakṣiṇā-kalī, first of all, teaches philosophical or cosmological truths. Kālī's standing on Śiva, for example, is often interpreted as symbolizing the interaction of Śiva and Śakti and the ultimate superiority of the latter. The image, that is, is taken as an icon suggesting the essential nature of reality as Śiva and Śakti and the priority of Śakti. Another interpretation also finds cosmological significance in the image.

> Śiva was born from the goddess Kālī. She is the only uncreated being. Śiva was needed for creation, so she created him by her own action. She created sperm in her womb and made love to herself. She made a mistake in creating the world and started to destroy it. Brahma told Śiva to stop the destruction—so he stretched himself down before her. To avoid killing him, she stopped destroying the world. Śiva insisted that she re-create the destroyed part, so she vomited it out. She had swallowed the whole world. That is why her tongue is sticking out when she stands on Śiva.[49]

The name Dakṣiṇā-kālī, according to a contemporary author, implies Kālī's preeminent position. The name comes from the story that when Yama, king of the dead, who lives in the south (*dakṣiṇa*), heard Kālī's name, he ran away in fear and ever since has been unable to take her devotees to his kingdom. That is, worship of Kālī overcomes death, and so she is the one who overwhelms the ruler of the south (Yama) and is called Dakṣiṇā-kālī. The name is also derived, according to some informants, from *dakṣiṇa*, the name for the gift given to a priest after a ritual without which the ritual is not effective. Kālī is that reality without which nothing would be effective. She is the underlying *śakti*.

Several informants have also suggested to me that the name Dakṣiṇā-kālī refers to the fact that Kālī places her right (*dakṣiṇa*) foot on Śiva's chest in this particular iconographic depiction. Lending credibility to this is the fact that several informants have mentioned a form of Kālī known as Vāma-kālī (leftward-tending Kālī), in which Kālī is shown with her left foot on Śiva's chest. Vāma-kālī is said to be extremely dangerous and rarely worshiped except by people of heroic nature. Depictions or descriptions of Vāma-kālī are rare. Finally, she is called Dakṣiṇā-kālī because she is worshiped by Dakṣiṇā-bhairava, that is, Śiva, who is often said to be the highest reality.[50]

Kālī's four arms represent the complete circle of creation and destruction, which is contained within or encompassed by her. She represents the inherent creative and destructive rhythms of the cosmos. Her right hands, making the *mudrās* of "fear not" and conferring boons, represent the creative aspect of Kālī, while the left hands, holding a bloodied sword and a severed head, represent her destructive aspect.[51] Her three eyes represent the sun, moon, and fire, with which she is able to observe the three modes of time: past, present, and future.[52]

The bloodied sword and severed head also symbolize the destruction of ignorance and the dawning of knowledge. The sword is the sword of knowledge, or desireless *sādhanā*, that cuts the knots of ignorance and destroys false consciousness (the severed head).[53] Kālī opens the gates of freedom with this sword, having cut the eight bonds (*paśu*) that bind human beings.[54] In addition to signifying false consciousness, the bleeding severed head is said to signify the outflow of *rajas guṇa* (passionate proclivities), which completely purifies the adept, who becomes totally composed of *sattvic* (spiritual) qualities in his or her awakening to truth.[55] The severed head is also interpreted as that of a child and thus as symbolizing the nature of the accomplished devotee or practitioner, who, like Ramakrishna, has achieved the innocence of a child.[56]

Kālī's lolling tongue and sharp fangs are interpreted as symbolizing the conquest of *rajasic* power (the red tongue) by *sattvic* power (the white teeth). That is, Kālī is totally *sattvic*, totally spiritual in nature, having transcended any impurities inherent in the other two *guṇas*.[57]

Kālī's blackness also symbolizes her all-embracing, comprehensive nature, because black is the color in which all other colors merge; black absorbs and dissolves them. Or black is said to represent the total absence of color, again signifying the *nirguṇa* (beyond qualities) nature of Kālī as ultimate reality.[58] Either way, Kālī's black color symbolizes her transcendence of all form.[59]

Kālī's nudity has a similar meaning. It symbolizes that she is completely beyond name and form, completely beyond the illusory effects of *māyā* (false consciousness), completely transcendent. Her nudity is said to represent totally illuminated consciousness, unaffected by *māyā*.[60] Kālī is the bright fire of truth, which cannot be hidden by the clothes of ignorance, represented by *māyā*. Such truth simply burns them away.[61]

Kālī's dwelling place, the cremation ground, has a similar meaning. The cremation ground denotes a place where the five elements (*pañca mahābhūta*) are dissolved. Kālī dwells where dissolution takes place. In terms of devotion, worship, and *sādhanā*, this denotes the dissolving of attachments, anger, lust, and other binding emotions, feelings, and ideas. The heart of the devotee is where this burning away takes place, and it is in the heart that Kālī dwells. The devotee makes her image in his heart and under her influence burns away all limitations and ignorance in the cremation fires. This inner cremation fire in the heart is the fire of knowledge, *jñānāgni*, which Kālī bestows.[62]

Kālī's *āsana* (seat), which is none other than the supine body of Śiva (sometimes said to be a corpse or corpselike), symbolizes that her devotees have given up their entire lives for her, having offered her their very breath. Having sacrificed themselves (their egos) to her, devotees die and become corpselike. It is only then that Kālī enters their hearts, freeing them from all worldly cares. Kālī's standing on Śiva signifies her blessing of her devotees.[63]

Another interpretation says that Śiva represents the passive potential of creation. In the philosophy of yoga he represents *puruṣa* (literally, "male"), the unchanging, unqualified aspect of reality, while Kālī represents the active *prakṛti* (nature or the physical world). In this interpretation, Kālī and Śiva together symbolize ultimate reality.[64]

Another interpretation of Kālī's standing on Śiva, or engaging in reverse sexual intercourse with him (*viparīta rati*),[65] is that it symbolizes meditative involution, by means of which one "de-creates" the universe in order to experience the blissful union of Śiva and Śākti. The theme of yogic meditation "going against the stream," reversing the creative processes, is ancient. The inversion of traditional male and female roles in the Dakṣiṇā-kālī image might suggest this inverse process.[66]

The garland of severed heads represents the sounds of the alphabet and symbolizes Kālī as *śabda brahman*, the underlying essence of reality as manifest in sound, particularly the primordial sound, *om*. Some texts specify the garland of heads or skulls to be fifty and to represent the fifty Sanskrit letters.[67] From the various sound seeds (*bījas*), all creation proceeds, and Kālī is identified with this underlying power.[68] Her girdle of severed arms represents the destruction of devotees' karma. The arms symbolize deeds, actions—karma—and the binding effects of this karma have been overcome, severed, as it were, by Kālī *sādhanā* or devotion. She has blessed the devotee by cutting him free from karma.[69]

Other images or forms of Kālī reinforce these associations with ultimate reality or ultimate spiritual realization. Guhya-kālī, who is described as having sunken eyes, fearful teeth, a constantly moving tongue, matted hair, and a large belly, is replete with serpent ornaments and companions. Her sacred thread is a serpent; she is seated on a bed of serpents; the thousand-headed cosmic serpent Ananta is above her head; and she is surrounded by serpents.[70] The symbolism of serpents is complex, but in this case it indicates Kālī's cosmic supremacy. Like Viṣṇu, for example, she is protected by Ananta, which indicates that she is a primordial, creative force. Serpents are also held to possess mystic wisdom and great wealth, both of which they obtain from their association with the interior of the earth. They are symbols of transformation, being able to shed their skins and become new beings. Serpents are liminal figures in that they pierce different cosmic zones, the earth and the underworld. As beings who live both on the earth and in the earth, they move between cosmic planes and also between states of being, between the realms of the living and the dead. Kālī is "at home" with these mysterious, powerful, liminal beings, which suggests her transformative nature and power.

Many of the *dhyāna* mantras of the different forms of Kālī also mention her drinking wine or blood, holding cups or empty skulls filled with wine or blood,[71] or being intoxicated. Siddha-kālī drinks blood from a skull held in her left hand. Guhya-kālī and Rakṣā-kālī (sometimes called Mahākālī) sip wine. Śmaśāna-kālī carries a skull full of wine in her right hand and is said to be intoxicated all the time. Although there are several possible interpretations of this characteristic feature of Kālī, her intoxication suggests altered consciousness, perhaps the dawning of liberated consciousness, in which the restrictions and limitations of convention are overcome.

The overwhelming presence of death imagery in all depictions of Kālī also might be interpreted as symbolizing the transformative nature of the goddess, and hence her association with ultimate knowledge, wisdom, and enlightenment. What is a more dramatic image of radical change than death, the greatest transformation a human being experiences? In association with the chopped heads and skulls that adorn almost all of her forms, the death imagery (corpses, cremation grounds, severed body parts) suggests that Kālī stands at the threshold of change, that she is the guide who takes the aspirant from one state of being, one state of consciousness, to another—that she is the mistress of change and transformation.

The way in which Kālī is worshiped in the tantric tradition may also suggest her association with ultimate reality. According to Swami Annapurnananda, tantric *sādhanā to* Kālī is applied or practical Advaita Vedānta (monism), in which one seeks to discern the underlying identity between oneself and ultimate reality, *brahman*, represented by Dakṣiṇā-kālī. In the process of undertaking *sādhanā* to Kālī, one produces her image out of oneself, worships it by identifying with it, and then dismisses it back into oneself. In this process (described in Part I), one ritually and mentally undertakes one's own death and destruction, after which one re-creates the cosmos with Kālī at the center. Such rituals as *nyāsa*, in which one suffuses one's body with the seed syllables of the deities, thus identifying with the different aspects of the cosmos, and *bhūta śuddhi*, in which the adept imagines the dissolution and re-creation of the cosmos, are ritual devices whereby one's limited, ego-centered identity is subverted. The process aims at expanding the adept's identity so widely and universally that there is no sense of "I" or "me" remaining. The goal is to identify completely with Kālī, who is the symbol of the absolute, beyond name and form, beyond individuality and specificity.

In certain aspects of Kashmir Śaivism, which might be described as dynamic idealism, the stages and rhythms of consciousness are affirmed to be the ground of reality and are identified with twelve Kālīs. That is, Kālī, in her differing forms, is symbolic of consciousness itself and of the processes whereby cognition and knowledge take place. As identical with these processes, then, Kālī is taken to be the innermost essence of reality and the most appropriate symbol of that essence.[72]

Conclusion

Kālī might be thought of as the goddess who sets the tone for the rest of the Mahāvidyās in two ways. First, she suggests a being who is liminal in nature, who dwells on the boundary of society and threatens, subverts, or challenges the status quo. For Tantrism, she is an appropriate symbol of rituals and meditative techniques that seek to confront, appropriate, and overcome forbidden, feared, "polluting" realities. As the embodiment of the polluted, feared, and loathed, she can, if confronted boldly by the aspirant, grant liberation, freedom from subservience to conventionality.

Second, Kālī might be thought of as a symbol of ultimate reality, an embodiment of the highest truths. By interpreting her features and habits allegorically and imaginatively, which is a widely accepted and practiced approach to understanding her, the adept can glimpse secrets that point to certain central truths of the Hindu tradition. In this latter approach, Kālī's dramatic, often offensive, always shocking appearance is not necessarily to be taken literally. Her real meaning is not obvious to the uninitiated; it reveals itself only to imaginative and spiritually sensitive interpretation.

It is interesting to note that most insiders, that is, the native Hindus, prefer to interpret Kālī allegorically, while most outsiders, that is, Westerners, prefer to focus on her surface attributes, appearance, and habits. I do not think the two approaches contradict each other. In many cases they are complementary. It is clear, however, that many Hindus, even tantric Hindus, who are supposedly intent on subverting the mentality of the status quo, are uncomfortable with interpretations of Kālī that too strongly emphasize her outrageous, shocking features and habits as central to her significance.

Tārā

The Goddess Who Guides through Troubles

In lists of the Mahāvidyās, Tārā almost always follows Kālī. This suggests a certain importance in the group. Indeed, she is more like Kālī in appearance than any of the other Mahāvidyās. As we shall see below, interpretations of her significance often come close to those of Kālī.

Tārā occupies a central place in Tibetan Buddhism and to a great extent plays the role of a Tibetan national deity. In her Buddhist context, she is almost always a benevolent, compassionate, gentle, playful young woman who indulges her devotees and never lets them come to harm. In her Hindu context, on the other hand, particularly as one of the Mahāvidyās, Tārā is almost always fierce, often horrible to behold, and potentially dangerous. Although Tārā also has fierce aspects in Buddhism and benign ones in Hinduism, she generally manifests gentle features in the former and fierce ones in the latter. Historically, it is likely that the Hindu Mahāvidyā Tārā developed from the Buddhist bodhisattva Tārā and that the Hindu preference was for her fierce manifestations.

Tārā's Place in Buddhism

Tārā seems to have been important in the Buddhist tradition first and to have become known in the Hindu tradition later. The earliest reference to Tārā, in Subandhu's *Vāsavadattā*, which was probably written in the seventh century, puts her in a Buddhist context. The reference occurs as part of a pun and reads: "The Lady Twilight was seen, devoted to the stars and clad in red sky, as a Buddhist nun [is devoted to Tārā and clad in red garments]."[1]

In Buddhist tantric mythology and iconography, Tārā belongs to the family of the Dhyāni Buddha Amoghasiddhi, but she is also related to the bodhisattva Avalokiteśvara, who is in the family of the Dhyāni Buddha Amitābha. In one account of Tārā's origin, all the creatures of the world begin to lament when Avalokiteśvara is about to achieve *nirvāṇa* (final liberation and freedom from rebirth), which means he will leave the world behind. Hearing them, Avalokiteśvara sheds a tear of compassion for the suffering of all beings. That tear becomes Tārā, who is thus understood to be the essence of the essence of compassion.[2] As we shall see, Tārā's essential nature in Tibetan Buddhism is that of a compassionate savior who rescues her devotees from peril. Her inclusion in the Amitābha family therefore seems fitting, since both Amitābha and Avalokiteśvara are renowned for their great compassion.

Tibetan Buddhists know other legendary or mythological accounts of Tārā's origin. One legend identifies Tārā with the wives of the first great Tibetan king, Songsten gampo (617–50 C.E.). The king himself is said to have been an incarnation of Avalokiteśvara, while his Chinese wife is said to have been an incarnation of Green Tārā and his Nepalese wife an incarnation of White Tārā (there are several different forms of Tārā in Buddhism, as we shall see).[3] Another Tibetan legend, ancient and pre-Buddhist in origin, says that the Tibetan people arose from the union of a monkey and a rock ogress. By the fourteenth century, however, when Buddhism dominated Tibet, the monkey had come to be identified with Avalokiteśvara, and the rock ogress, despite her lustful nature, with an incarnation of Tārā.[4] An interesting aspect of these Tibetan legends is that they associate Tārā with the origins of the Tibetan people and the Tibetan royal line. They affirm that she is dear to the Tibetan people in a special way. She is in a legendary sense their queen and mother.[5]

Historically, Tārā was known in Tibetan Buddhism as early as the eighth century, that is, around the time when Buddhism was introduced to Tibet from India. Until the time of Atīśa (eleventh century), however, the worship of Tārā does not seem to have been very widespread there. Atīśa is usually associated with popularizing the cult of Tārā in Tibet; biographical accounts emphasize the many visions he had of her and his special devotion to her. Atīśa is credited with translating a series of Sanskrit texts about Tārā into Tibetan. The texts were soon circulated as a coherent cycle and came to be known by the name *Cheating Death*.[6] Another text that was to become popular in Tibet was also brought there and translated in the eleventh century, by the spiritual master Darmadra. *Homages to the Twenty-One Tārās* to this day is well known to most Tibetans.[7]

Despite Tārā's many forms and functions it seems clear wherein lies her extraordinary power and appeal in the Tibetan context. She is approached primarily as a savior, as a being who specializes in dramatic appearances when her devotees call on her in dire circumstances. She is often said to rescue her devotees from such desperate predicaments as being lost in an impenetrable forest, foundering in a storm at sea, being under threat of imminent execution, or being trapped and bound in prison.[8] In many folk stories Tārā appears at the request of her devotees to snatch them from the jaws of death.[9] Tārā's compassion for suffering beings, then, is revealed primarily in her role as the cheater of death. In this sense her chief blessing to her devotees is a long life. Other stories featuring Tārā also emphasize that regular worship of Tārā brings about longevity.[10] In Tibetan monastic traditions, when novices are initiated into the ceremonies in honor of Tārā, the rituals are referred to as an "initiation into life."[11] Unlike goddesses who are associated with life as embodiments of fertility, Tārā is approached primarily as the one who protects, preserves, and saves life. She is not a fertility goddess (although she does give her blessing in this way from time to time)[12] but a greatly compassionate being who cannot tolerate the suffering of her devotees.

Although Tārā's primary appeal in Buddhism seems to be as the cheater of death, the prolonger of life, and a charming, playful young girl, she does have a variety of forms, some of which are fierce, even terrifying. *Homages to the Twenty-One Tārās*, probably her most popular hymn of praise, contains several verses that invoke Tārā in fierce forms.

Homage, Lady who annihilates the heroes of Māra,
TURE, the terrible lady,
slaying all enemies
by frowning the brows of her lotus face.

. . . .

Homage, Lady who strikes the earth with her hand,
who pounds upon it with her feet,
shattering the seven underworlds
with the sound HŪM made by her frowning brows.

. . . .

Homage, Lady who strikes with the feet of TURE,
whose seed is the form of the syllable HŪM,
shaking Mount Meru, Mandāra, Kailāśa,
and all the triple world.[13]

A particularly fierce form of Tārā is Tārā Kurukullā.[14] She is described as follows:

> Homage and praise to her
> who stands in the dancing pose
> haughty with furious rage,
> who has a diadem of five skulls,
> who bears a tiger's skin.
> I pay homage to the red one,
> baring her fangs, whose body is frightful,
> who is adorned with the five signs of ferocity,
> whose necklace is half a hundred human heads,
> who is the conqueress of Māra.[15]

Tārā Kurukullā's special power lies in her ability to subjugate and destroy evil spirits or one's personal enemies.[16] Through the rituals in which Kurukullā is invoked, she comes to reside in the practitioner himself (the texts almost always assume a male adept). The rituals thus require a strong and accomplished adept, for Kurukullā is a potent force. The adept dresses in red garments and visualizes himself taking on the form of the goddess. Then he recites her mantra ten thousand times. Then he makes certain offerings to her and asks her to subjugate the person or demon who is the object of the rituals.

> When these preliminaries are complete, when he has firmly grasped the vivid appearance and ego of the goddess, the visualization is ready to be performed. Light radiates forth from a HRIH in the practitioner's heart and places the person to be subjugated, naked and with unbound hair, upon a wind maṇḍala arisen from YAM: that is, the seed of wind transforms into the round shape symbolic of the air element, and this wind propels forward the person to be subjugated; he is bound around the neck by a noose radiated from the practitioner's—Kurukullā's—lotus flower, drawn forward by an iron hook stuck into his heart, summoned by the strength of the mantra, and laid down helpless upon his back before the practitioner's feet. If the person to be subjugated is male, the text adds, Kurukullā's iron hook is stuck into his heart; if female it is stuck into her vagina.[17]

Other fierce forms of Tārā in Buddhism include Mahāmāyā-vijayavāhinī-tārā,[18] who is called The Blue She-Wolf,[19] and Mahācina-tārā. Mahācina-tārā (also known as Ugra-tārā) is described in both Buddhist and Hindu sources. Here is an account from a Buddhist work, the *Sādhanamālā:*

The worshiper should conceive himself as (Mahācina-Tārā) who stands in the Pratyālīḍha attitude [an aggressive pose in which the left foot is put forward], and is awe-inspiring with a garland of heads hanging from the neck. She is short and has a protruding belly, and her looks are terrible. Her complexion is like that of the blue lotus, and she is three-eyed, one-faced, celestial and laughs horribly. She is in an intensely pleasant mood, stands on a corpse, is decked in ornaments of snakes, has red and round eyes, wears the garments of tigerskin round her loins, is in youthful bloom, is endowed with the five auspicious symbols, and has a protruding tongue. She is most terrible, appears fierce, with bare canine fangs, carries the sword and the Kartri in the two right hands and the Utpala and Kapāla [skull] in the two left. Her Jaṭāmukuṭa [bound-up hair] of one coil is brown and fiery and bears the image of Akṣobhya within it.[20]

Vasiṣṭha and Mahācina-tārā

It is likely that Tārā first became important in Indian Buddhism and then, after being introduced into Tibet, assumed a central position there. Her place in Hinduism is not as prominent as it is in Tibetan Buddhism: she probably entered the Hindu tradition through Buddhist tantric influence. Clear indications of Tārā's Buddhist affiliation remain in Hindu sources. She is said, for example, to have Akṣobhya set in her hair. Akṣobhya, "the unperturbed one," is said to be an epithet of Śiva, but it is also the name of a Buddha. In the *Rudrayāmala* and *Brahmayāmala*, furthermore, Tārā is sometimes called Prajñāpāramitā (the perfection of wisdom), which is definitely a Buddhist name.[21]

The most convincing testimony to Tārā's earlier Buddhist association is a myth that features the sage Vasiṣṭha's attempts to worship Tārā. Once upon a time, he did austerities for ten thousand years, but got no results. He went to the god Brahmā and asked for a powerful mantra that might help him. Brahmā told him about the glory of Tārā. It is through Tārā's power, he said, that he creates the world, Viṣṇu protects it, and Śiva destroys it. She is infinitely more glorious than millions of suns, she is the source of all light, and she reveals the Vedas. Brahmā then told Vasiṣṭha to recite the Tārā mantra for success. Vasiṣṭha went to Kāmākhyā, the famous goddess shrine in Assam, and undertook Tārā's worship. After one thousand years he still was unsuccessful. At this point the sage became angry and was about to curse Tārā for her indifference. The whole earth trembled in fear, and even the gods were disturbed. At that moment Tārā appeared in front of Vasiṣṭha. She told him that he had been wasting his time because he did not understand her or know how to worship her. She said that Vasiṣṭha did not know her appearance in the form of Cīna-tārā and that she could not be propitiated through yoga and austerities. "Only Viṣṇu in the form of Buddha knows my form of worship," she said, "and to learn this kind of worship you have to go to China." Tārā then disappeared.

Vasiṣṭha went to Tibet to find out what to do. Near the Himalayas, he had a vision of the Buddha surrounded by many beautiful girls and intoxicated with wine. They were all naked, drinking and carousing. Vasiṣṭha was shocked and refused an invitation to take part in the frolic. Then a voice from the sky said to him: "This is the best way of worshiping Tārā. If you want immediate success, you have to adopt this type of worship." Vasiṣṭha then took refuge in Viṣṇu in his form as the Buddha and asked to be instructed in this method. The Buddha revealed to him the *kula mārga*, a tantric type of *sādhanā* (spiritual practice), warning him that it was very secret. A central feature of this path is the ritual of the five forbidden things. With this ritual, and on this path, one can live in the midst of good and bad things while remaining aloof from them, the Buddha told him. On this path there is no need for traditional types of rituals. Worship is mental and not physical. All times are auspicious; nothing is inauspicious; there is no difference between pure or impure; there are no restrictions on what one can eat or drink; worship can be done any place and any time; a friendly attitude toward women should be cultivated, and worship of women should be practiced.

Receiving this knowledge from the Buddha, Vasiṣṭha did the ritual of the five forbidden things and became a very powerful *sādhaka* (religious adept). He went to Tārāpur to practice his new spiritual path. This place, now known as Tārāpīṭh, is located in Birbhum district in Bengal and is the place where the famous adept Bāmākhepa (1843–1911) did his *sādhanā*. It is located near a cremation ground.[22]

This myth makes several important points. First, the proper worship of Tārā is associated with the Buddha, who is understood to be a form of Viṣṇu.[23] That is, the myth implicitly acknowledges that Tārā worship is derived from Buddhism. Second, the type of worship is tantric, specifically of the left-handed type featuring the ritual of the five forbidden things. Third, Vasiṣṭha's going north to discover the true form and worship of Tārā suggests Tibetan influence. Fourth, the myth mentions Kāmākhyā in Assam and Tārāpīṭh in Bengal as important centers, which implies that worship of Tārā in Hinduism was strong and perhaps centered in eastern India.

The Fierce Tārā of Hinduism

There are several forms of Tārā described in Hindu sources, but nowhere do we find the playful, charming girl that dominates her iconography in Tibetan Buddhism. Nearly every description of Tārā in Hindu sources stresses her fierce, often horrifying, appearance and reminds us of the terrifying Tārā Kurukullā and Mahācina-tārā of the Buddhist tradition. While Tārā is said to have benign and compassionate aspects in the Hindu setting (see below), these tend to be overshadowed by her terrible ones. The *dhyāna* mantra for Ugra-tārā from the *Mantra-mahodadhiḥ* describes her thus:

> I meditate upon the Divine Mother of the three worlds, who is sitting on a white lotus situated in the centre of the waters enveloping the entire universe. In her left hands she holds a knife and a skull and, in her right hands, a sword and a blue lotus. Her complexion is blue, and she is bedecked with ornaments. . . . She is decorated with three beautiful serpents and has three red eyes. Her hair is bunched into a single plait of tawny colour. Her tongue is always moving, and her teeth and mouth appear terrible. She is wearing a tiger skin around her waist, and her forehead is decorated with ornaments of white bone. Sage Akṣobhya, in the form of a serpent, is situated on her head. She is seated on the heart of a corpse, and her breasts are hard. Thus should one meditate on Bhagavatī Tārā, who is the mistress of all three worlds.[24]

Other forms of Tārā are equally forbidding. The *dhyāna* mantra of Tārā in her form as Nīla-sarasvatī from the *Tantrasāra* is as follows:

> I bow to you mother Nīlasarasvatī. You give well-being and auspiciousness. You are situated on the heart of a corpse and are advancing aggressively. You have three fearful, bright eyes. You carry a skull bowl, scissors, and a sword. Your form shines like a blazing fire. Give me refuge. Give me golden speech. Please let your gracious nectar drench my heart, remover of pride. You are decorated with snakes as ornaments, you wear a tiger skin as a skirt, you ring a bell loudly, and wear a garland of chopped off heads. You are frightening and remove fear.[25]

Another of her *dhyāna* mantras from the *Tantrasāra* describes her as follows:

> Tārā should be conceived as emerging from a white lotus. She advances with her left foot forward, and she is dreadful in appearance. She is short in stature and has a protruding and long belly. She wears a garland of skulls

Fig. 14. Tārā, 1926, Jaipur, Rajasthan. Ajit Mookerjee Collection of Tantric Art, National Museum, Delhi.

> and a tiger skin for a skirt. She is eternally young. Her forehead is decorated with a row of five skulls. She has a lolling tongue; she is very dreadful and has four arms in which she carries a sword, a pair of scissors, a cut head, and a lotus. She has a smiling face. Her hair is in the form of a matted *jaṭā* (a braided knot) on which sits Akṣobhya in the form of a serpent. Her complexion is like that of the bright moon. She has three eyes; she stands on a blazing funeral pyre; her teeth are dreadful; she is adorned with ornaments.[26]

Tārā's description and character in Hindu texts emphasize two important and related features that are absent from the Buddhist Tārā: (1) she is strongly associated with the goddess Kālī, whom she closely resembles, and (2) she is often located in the cremation ground. Both of these associations emphasize her fierce, terrifying nature and distinguish her from the gentle forms of Tārā that dominate Tibetan Buddhism.

The similarities in appearance between Kālī and Tārā are striking and unmistakable, especially in the two most common images of each goddess, Dakṣiṇā-kālī and Ugra-tārā. They both stand upon a supine male figure, often discernible as Śiva but sometimes said to be an anonymous corpse. Sometimes the figure they stand upon is being consumed in a cremation fire. Both goddesses are black, dark blue, or blue-black. Both are naked or wear minimal clothing, sometimes a tiger skin. Both wear a necklace of severed heads or skulls and a girdle of severed arms. Both are usually shown in the cremation ground. Both have a lolling tongue, and blood oozes from their mouths. Their appearances are so strikingly similar that it is easy to mistake one for the other. Indeed, they are often said to be manifestations of each other; for example, in their thousand-name hymns they share many epithets as well as having each other's names as epithets. Tārā, for example, is called Kālikā, Ugra-kālī, Mahākālī, and Bhadra-kālī.[27] The devotional poetry of Ramprasad Sen, an eighteenth-century Bengali saint, uses the names Kālī and Tārā interchangeably. At time it seems that Ramprasad favors the name Tārā when explicitly referring to the goddess's more benign or gentle aspects, but this is not consistent.[28]

Like Kālī, furthermore, Tārā in her Hindu context enjoys blood. In her hymn of a hundred names from the *Muṇḍamālā-tantra*, she is called She Who Likes Blood, She Who Is Smeared with Blood, and She Who Enjoys Blood Sacrifice.[29] The *Tārā-tantra* describes Tārā's delight in both animal and human blood but says that the latter is more pleasing to her. The blood of devotees is to be taken from specified parts of the body, such as the forehead, hands, breast, head, or area between the eyebrows; some of these areas may correspond to the different *cakras,* spiritual cen-

Fig. 15. Tārā, by Molaram, late eighteenth century, Garwahl, Himachal Pradesh. Bharat Kala Bhavan, Benares Hindu University, Varanasi.

ters within the body (5.15). Throughout this text, the worship of Tārā is described as part of left-handed tantric rites, in which wine, meat, and sexual union figure prominently; in this respect also, Tārā resembles Kālī. That is, her worship seems to play upon the power of the forbidden and the attempt to transmute forbidden objects or acts into spiritually transformative instruments.

Like Kālī, Tārā is also associated with Śiva, although not as consistently as Kālī is. The male figure beneath her feet is often identifiable as Śiva, and many of her names associate her with Śiva. She is called, for example: Śivā (the feminine form of Śiva), Śankara-vallabhā and Hara-vallabhā (both mean "beloved of Śiva"), Hara-patnī (wife of Śiva), Dear to Bhairava (Bhairava is a form of Śiva), and Wife of Mahābhairava.[30] Tārā also wears her hair knotted on top of her head in a *jaṭā*, the style of an ascetic, which is the way Śiva wears his. This associates her with the world of asceticism and yogis, Śiva's world par excellence.

Although we find Tārā linked with Śiva by her epithets and iconography, there are few myths about her in Hindu texts, and scarcely any that connect her with Śiva. In the oral tradition, however, I have come across a particularly intriguing story about the two. The myth begins with the churning of the ocean. Śiva has drunk the poison that was created from the churning of the ocean, thus saving the world from destruction, but has fallen unconscious under its powerful effect. Tārā appears and takes Śiva on her lap. She suckles him, the milk from her breasts counteracting the poison, and he recovers.[31] This myth is reminiscent of the one in which Śiva stops the rampaging Kālī by becoming an infant. Seeing the child, Kālī's maternal instincts come to the fore, and she becomes quiet and nurses the infant Śiva.[32] In both cases, Śiva assumes the position of an infant vis-à-vis the goddess. I have also been told that the particular form of Bhairava Śiva associated with Tārā is Baṭuk-bhairava, the bachelor Bhairava (Śiva), who is an adolescent. That is, the oral tradition seems to see the relationship between Tārā and Śiva as that of mother and son as well as that of wife and husband.

Tārā in Hinduism is also strongly associated with the cremation ground. The figure she stands upon is often said to be either a corpse or a *preta* (ghost) and is often shown being cremated. In some depictions of Tārā, cremation fires are visible in the background. Jackals are also often shown. It is common for worship manuals to specify that Tārā should be worshiped in the cremation ground, usually in the dead of night. Tārā's epithets also sometimes associate her with the cremation ground. For example, in both her *kvaca* (a type of invocation that literally means "armor") and her thousand-name hymn, she is called Śmaśāna-bhairavī (terrible one of the cremation ground).[33] In this respect also, Tārā resembles Kālī. They both haunt cremation grounds, and their temples are often established in or near them. Kālī's most famous temple, Kālighāṭ, is adjacent to one of the largest cremation grounds in Calcutta, and Tārāpīṭh temple, probably the most famous of Tārā's temples, is similarly located next to a cremation ground. Although cremation grounds are generally believed to be sacred places in Hinduism, and temples to other deities may be established in or near them, Kālī and Tārā are consistently associated with such sites. Indeed, Tārā is sometimes said to be the fire of the cremation pyre itself, the personified expression of this awesome, religiously powerful symbol.

Despite the variations in sequence found among lists of the Mahāvidyās, Kālī and Tārā are almost invariably named as first and second, respectively. There is little doubt that this signifies their preeminent position in the group, particularly insofar as they are described in very similar terms. That is, it seems that Tārā's position as second only to Kālī in importance is directly related to her being so similar to Kālī in appearance. If Kālī in her form as Dakṣiṇā-kālī is taken to be the highest expression of wisdom (*vidyā*), liberating knowledge, which many texts imply and contemporary informants insist upon, then Tārā, listed just after Kālī and appearing so much like her, must be a close approximation of that highest truth. We might think of Tārā as Kālī's first, least-diffused, least-refracted emanation, an expression of ultimate truth that is very close to the original totality. Or we might think of Tārā as the penultimate stage in the progressive sojourn toward complete dissolution of the ego in its merging with the absolute, the penultimate stage in the *pralaya* (cosmic dissolution) of the ego, as it were. A modern commentator says that "at the time of *pralaya*, Tārā becomes furious and changes into Kālī."[34]

The Symbolic Significance of Tārā

Most of the symbolic meanings associated with Kālī apply to Tārā. Indeed, she appears to be a variant expression of Kālī, a kindred spirit, as it were, who expresses the same truths as Kālī, only in a slightly different form. She dominates the male figure associated with her. She stands upon Śiva or a male corpse, or she mothers the infant Śiva. Like Kālī, Tārā suggests the preeminence or dominance of Śakti in a vision of the cosmos that is constituted or pervaded by Śiva and Śakti.

Like Kālī also, Tārā is primarily a liminal symbol. She embodies and expresses realities that belong to the edges of the civilized order or that tend to be excluded as dangerous or polluting. Like Kālī, she is naked or dressed in animal hides. Her hair is disheveled, and she stands on, as opposed to standing by or kneeling before, her male associate. Like Kālī, she reverses the expectations of the female role in male-dominated Hindu culture. She is unrestrained, wild, and dominant. As primordial power, she is uncircumscribed and uncontrolled.

Like Kālī also, she is identified with destruction. Kālī is strongly associated with the dissolution of all things through the wearing down by time. Tārā, on the other hand, is more strongly linked to destruction by fire. She is often identified with the actual fires of cremation and thus represents the final destructive but purifying force that marks the transition from life to death or from one type of existence to another. As the cremation fire, that is, she is more than just a destructive force: she is purifying and transformative. As we shall see below, there are creative and transformative aspects to Tārā's character. She is also identified with the excess heat of the sun. A contemporary author says that Tārā appears as the first manifestation of creation after *pralaya* in the form of the sun. The primordial sun burns extravagantly, wildly, and dangerously and must be tempered with offerings of grain. Tārā represents its untamed, excessive heat, which can completely dry up the creation by consuming the sap of life in all creatures.[35] The same author points out that even the snakes that adorn Tārā are part of her destructive nature. By emitting poisonous gas at the end of the world, they destroy it.[36] He also interprets the skull that Tārā holds, and sometimes drinks from, as an emblem of her role as mistress of destruction. According to him, the head is the primary repository of *rasa*, the sap of life. Tārā consumes this in her destructive bent.[37]

Tārā's necklace of skulls and girdle of severed arms suggest the same meanings as in the case of Kālī. The skulls (which are sometimes said to correspond in number to the number of letters in the Sanskrit alphabet) probably are meant to suggest the sounds of the alphabet and to associate Tārā with *śabda brahman*, the primoridal creative force in the form of sound. They almost surely also suggest her destructive aspect and are meant to signify death. The girdle of severed arms signifies her destruction of accumulated karma, which frees the individual from bondage to *saṁsāra* (the realm of rebirth). Her sword and scissors, like Kālī's sword, symbolize her ability to cut through the fetters that bind a person to ignorance and limited consciousness. With her sword she certainly destroys, but this destruction can be positive and transformative. A contemporary devotee of Tārā understands the severed heads she wears as symbolizing her elimination of the mind that is overwhelmed by ignorance or crippled with limited consciousness. "She does want to kill you—the false you, the limited personality which has accrued over so many births. . . . When she cuts off your head, your mind becomes firm, unwavering in its concentration, which enables you to succeed."[38] Of the girdle of severed arms, the same devotee says: "Most people clothe themselves in their karmas, and She wants to cut them off, remove them from you completely."[39]

The Gentler Side of the Hindu Tārā

Several aspects of Tārā's iconography differ from Kālī's, some of them suggesting a dimension to Tārā that is less destructive and more maternal than the fierce Tārā we have looked at so far. Tārā is said to have large, full breasts and to be "potbellied." It is not clear if she is pregnant, but these features do suggest her maternal character. One informant interprets Tārā's large breasts and swollen belly as suggesting that she represents the first impulse toward creation and individuation. Kālī is the void, *nirguṇa brahman* (ultimate reality without qualities), as it were, reality in its complete, essential form, or *pralaya* (cosmic dissolution). Tārā, so closely resembling Kālī in most ways, but differing from her in the large breasts and swollen belly, has attributes of creation. She is filled with the universe, which is about to emerge from the void.[40] Conversely, Tārā may be seen as the last stage just prior to dissolution, represented by Kālī. She wears some clothes (Kālī does not), suggesting less-than-complete freedom, for example. In either case, Tārā is close to Kālī, either as the first step toward creation or the last stage prior to dissolution.[41]

Despite Tārā's strong connection with destruction, there are indications that she is understood as a creative, nourishing, maternal presence as well. This is most clear in her hymn of one thousand names. She is called, for example, Jaleśvarī (mistress of rain), Jagaddhātrī (mother of the world, world nurse), Pṛthivī and Vasudhā (both mean "earth"), Vṛkṣamadhyani-vāsinī (she who dwells in trees), Sarvavamayī (she who creates everything), and She Who Likes Fresh Flowers.[42]

Tārā is also said to be a savior of her devotees and in this respect reminds us of the Tibetan Buddhist Tārā. In many places it is said: "She who takes one across *saṁsāra*, she is Tārā."[43] Access to her is easy: her mantra, which has power to enlighten, is said to be accessible to all without special initiation or qualification. She gives her blessing readily and does not require her devotees to do *pūjā* (worship), *japa* (repetition of her name), or *dhyāna* (meditation) or make any effort to win her favor.[44] She is called Saṁsāratāriṇī (she who carries across the ocean of *saṁsāra*),[45] and her name is said to be derived from the meaning "to cross over," implying that she helps beings cross the ocean of ignorance to enlightenment. Some iconographic representations show her with an oar in her hand, emphasizing her role in ferrying her devotees across the river of *saṁsāra*.[46] A contemporary author says: "She helps to cross over three types of problems: bodily, those associated with fate, and those associated with material happiness. The meaning of Tārā is she who liberates, 'The Liberator.' "[47]

Some texts describe Tārā as living on an island to which devotees are taken by boat. She herself is sometimes said to be the chief deity in transporting them across the lake.

> There is a great hall called "mānas" whose middle enclosure comprises the nectar-lake. There is no way to get into it save the conveyance of a boat. There is the great śakti, Tārā by name, who controls the gate. There are many attendants of Tārā who are dark like the blue lotus and are sporting in the waters of the lake with thousands of boats of jewels. They come to this shore [presumably *saṁsāra*, or "this world"] and go back to the other shore [presumably *mokṣa* or *mukti* (the state or condition of liberation from rebirth), or Tārā's heaven]. There are millions of boat-women under Tārā who are in the prime of youth. They dance and sing the most sacred fame of the goddess. Some hold oars and others conches in their hands. They are drinking the nectar-water of the lake and going hither and thither on hundreds of those boats. Of these śaktis who guide the boats and have dark colour the chief one is Tārā, the mother who can calm the floods. . . . Thus Tārā, the mother, surrounded by various boats and herself occupying a large boat, shines exceedingly.[48]

One of the most dramatic Hindu images of Tārā's gentler aspect is found at Tārāpīṭh temple in Bengal, where she is shown suckling Śiva, whom she holds on her lap. The myth in the oral tradition of this temple that explains this maternal appearance of Tārā is a variation and elaboration of the story of the sage Vasiṣṭha, who went to China to find the true method of worshiping Tārā. There he found devotees worshiping her with rites using women, meat, and intoxicants. According to the Tārāpīṭh tradition, the Buddha, after initiating Vasiṣṭha into this left-handed tantric worship, instructed him to return to India to practice his new *sādhanā*. He was instructed to go to Bengal, to the very place, in fact, where Tārāpīṭh was subsequently established near the Dwaraka River. The Buddha, with his superior mystical insight, knew this spot to be sacred to Tārā. Vasiṣṭha positioned himself on a seat of five human skulls and proceeded to recite the Tārā mantra three hundred thousand times. Tārā was pleased with his *sādhanā* and appeared to him. She offered him a boon, and he requested that she reveal herself to him in her maternal aspect, as a mother suckling Śiva at her breast, the image the Buddha had described to him. She manifested this form to Vasiṣṭha, and it then turned to stone; this became the central image of Tārāpīṭh temple.[49]

> The stone image of Ugratārā which was seen by Vasiṣṭha had actually existed before that time. The eye of Satī (some say the third or spiritual eye) which fell to earth at Tārāpīṭh turned to stone and sprang up in the form of the image which Vasiṣṭha saw. This statue relates to the story of Śiva (as Nīlakaṇṭha) having saved Creation by drinking poison which had emerged from the ocean after it had been churned. He was stricken with burning in the throat from the poison, which caused his throat to turn

Fig. 16. Tārā of Tārāpīṭh, contemporary lithograph.

blue [hence he is called Nīlakaṇṭha, "blue throat"]. To relieve burning, Śakti offered Śiva her breast, which he took and was relieved.[50]

As we have already indicated in a few instances, Tārā's terrifying or fierce aspects also may be interpreted in positive ways that conform to her role as "the liberator." The cremation fire that she represents or often stands in is said to symbolize the burning of the dross of one's past karma, the purifying of one's mind of ignorance, the burning away of attachments.[51] Her scissors and sword are said to represent her role in cutting through the bonds that keep people in ignorance and self-delusion. The severed heads represent the destruction of false ideas and self-enchantment. Her standing on a corpse represents, according to one modern commentator, her "triumph over calamities."[52]

In short, although Tārā's appearance and habits initially seem to be almost totally terrifying and fearsome, she has a gentler side. She is a savior who takes special care of her devotees, and in this respect she reflects the personality of the gentle Tārā of Tibetan Buddhism. The Hindu Tārā's means of helping her devotees are more abrasive and frightening than those of the Tibetan Buddhist Tārā, but the end result—liberation—is similar. The Hindu Tārā tends to shock her devotees into liberating knowledge, while the Tibetan Tārā overwhelms them with compassion.

Worship of Tārā at Tārāpīṭh

Although the Hindu Tārā is not as widely worshiped as Kālī or Lakṣmī, there are several temples dedicated to her in North India and Nepal. Compared to Chinnamastā, Bagalāmukhī, Mātaṅgī, and Dhūmāvatī—Mahāvidyās who receive barely any public worship—Tārā has a fairly flourishing temple cult. Perhaps her most famous temple is at Tārāpīṭh in Birbhum district of rural Bengal. The temple is not particularly large, and the flow of worshipers is modest, but the temple and deity are widely known, and Tārāpīṭh is reputed to be a very powerful center of goddess worship. The temple's founding myths, its type of worship (which includes blood offerings), the hymns sung there, the powers of the nearby tank, and the inhabitants and rituals of the adjacent cremation ground combine to give a good picture of Tārā worship.

There are two mythical traditions that tell of the origin of the Tārāpīṭh temple. The first is the story about the sage Vasiṣṭha. The second concerns the well-known story of the dismemberment of Satī's corpse and the establishment of the *śākta pīṭhas* ("seats of *śakti*," places sacred to goddesses) throughout India. Wherever a piece of her body fell, a center of goddess worship was established. According to the Tārāpīṭh myth, Satī's third, or spiritual, eye fell to earth at the place where the temple is now located. It was this sacred *pīṭha* that the Buddha saw with his mystical vision and to which he directed Vasiṣṭha. These two mythical traditions, then, combine to associate the temple with the Satī myth, and hence an all-India goddess network, and with left-handed tantric worship brought from the north, the source of Buddhist Tārā worship.

The central image of Tārā depicts her nursing Śiva and thus emphasizes her maternal, protective, and nourishing aspects.[53] Tārā's presence in a busy temple, where she is worshiped with traditional rituals on a regular basis, also mitigates the fierce aspect that is dominant in her Hindu manifestation. As the center of an active temple, she is carefully tended by priests and approached routinely with petitions from her devotees. She holds court in her temple and dispenses favors to the faithful like an understanding mother. In her aspect as the nursing mother and as the center of attentive priests and devotees who are regularly serving and supplicating her, Tārā at Tārāpīṭh has a domesticated quality. The tank adjacent to the temple also emphasizes her benign aspect. This "tank of life" is reputed to have the power to restore the dead to life and to heal most maladies. Pilgrims routinely bathe in it before and after worship of the goddess in the temple.

Tārā's benign, maternal aspects are also emphasized in devotional poems associated with Tārāpīṭh and often sung there by worshipers. As in the case of Bengali Kālī devotion, these poems exploit the metaphor of the goddess as mother and cast the devotee in the role of her loving, dependent child, whom she cannot deny. The following poem by Gyan Babu, the organizer of an *āśrama* (ashram) in Tārāpīṭh, is a good example of this genre.

Come, come to Tārāpīṭh,
If you want to see "Mā,"
Here you will get the touch of your own Mother,
There is no doubt about it.
Here there is no distinction of caste,
Because my Mā is the Mother of the universe,
Only call out "Mā, Mā,"
Mother will place you on her lap.
Come here and see,

Mother sitting with spread lap,
To relieve the burning sensation of poison,
She is breast-feeding Nīlakaṇṭha ["blue throat," i.e., Śiva],
If you come here you will see Vāmākhepā,
The Mother's darling son.
He ate with jackals and the gods,
Calling them his brothers,
To give rice to the hungry,
The mother is calling her children,
Wherever you may be,
Come, come, come here.[54]

Tārā's fierce aspect and her association with left-handed tantric *sādhanā* with its often fearsome rites, however, reveal themselves in the practice of blood sacrifice at the temple and the importance of the nearby cremation ground. Her frightening aspect is also seen in the metal image of her that is usually available to worshipers for *darśan* (viewing). This three-foot-tall image recalls the *dhyāna* mantras of Ugra-tārā cited above. She has four arms, wears a garland of skulls, and has a lolling tongue. She is fierce in appearance, and while this is not the primordial image around which the temple was built (that image being equated with the rough stone image), it is the one that most worshipers see.

Blood sacrifices are offered to Tārā daily. Normally two or three goats are offered each day, but on festival days, such as Durgā Pūjā and Kālī Pūjā, one hundred fifty to two hundred goats may be sacrificed. The animals are almost always offered to the goddess by individual worshipers as part of a vow that the goddess will be given a sacrificial victim in return for some favor she has done for the devotee. Before being slain, the animals are bathed in the tank to purify them. The worshipers also undergo purification rituals in the temple prior to the sacrifice. The animals, almost always goats, are killed at a sacrificial pit near the temple. Within the sandy enclosure is a two-pronged stake that holds the animal firm while a priest decapitates it in one blow with a special sword. After it has been killed, a bit of blood is taken in a pot and offered to the image in the temple. The sacrificial pit itself is revered by worshipers; some dip their fingers in the blood of a freshly killed animal and mark their foreheads with it.[55]

In iconographic representations and descriptions of Tārā, she typically stands on a corpse, which often lies on a cremation fire. In her most popular Hindu forms she haunts cremation grounds and is associated with death and destruction. An important element of the religious atmosphere at Tārāpīṭh is the large cremation ground or cremation grove, located near the temple. Here is where the Bengali saint Bāmākhepā (or Vāmākhepā in Sanskrit) (1843–1911) lived and undertook his spiritual exercises for several decades prior to his death. His name may be translated as the mad or crazy (*khepā*) follower of the left-handed path (*vāmā* means "left"). Indeed, he behaved like a lunatic, which is often said to be one of the marks of a saint.[56] Legend says that, after Bāmākhepā had been meditating on Tārā for a long time in the cremation ground, surrounded by corpses, funeral pyres, and jackals, Tārā appeared to him in a burst of flames in her dreadful form and then took him to her breast.[57] A tradition at Tārāpīṭh says that Bāmākhepā was an incarnation of Tārā's fierce husband, Śiva, in his form as Bhairava. Like Bhairava, the legend says, Bāmākhepā was fierce and mad on the outside but full of mercy on the inside.[58]

The cremation ground has been a site of tantric *sādhanā* for generations and continues to be so used today. Several *sādhakas* dwell more or less permanently in the cremation ground, which is probably an ancient tradition, and wandering *sādhakas* often visit it for extended periods. It is a place where *śmaśāna sādhanā* (spiritual practices appropriate to cremation grounds) and *śava sādhanā* (spiritual practices using a corpse) may be performed. It is included on the itinerary of many pilgrims to Tārāpīṭh and is an integral part of the sacred complex. It reinforces the theme apparent in much Tārā iconography that she favors cremation grounds and that it is appropriate to propitiate her there.

Tripura-sundarī

She Who Is Lovely in the Three Worlds

Tripura-sundarī, who also appears in lists of the Mahāvidyās under the names Ṣoḍaśī, Lalitā, Kāmeśvarī, Śrīvidyā, and Rājarājeśvarī, is often cited third, after Kālī and Tārā. She is also sometimes said to be, along with Kālī and Tārā, an *ādi* (primordial) Mahāvidyā, which suggests that she occupies a high place in the group, that she, like them, represents a complete vision of reality.[1] According to other sources, she represents the penultimate vision of enlightened consciousness, a stage of consciousness suffused with *sattvic* qualities but lacking the completeness of fully enlightened consciousness, represented by Kālī, which is beyond all quality and form, *nirguṇa*.[2]

Her *dhyāna* mantra describes her as follows: "She shines with the light of the rising sun. In her four hands she holds a noose, a goad, arrows, and a bow."[3] Further details of her appearance are found in the famous hymn in her praise, the *Lalitā-sahasranāma*, where she is said to be seated on a throne like a queen (names 2 and 3), to wear jewels (names 13 and 14), to have the auspicious marks of a married woman (names 16–25), and to have heavy breasts and a thin waist (name 36); the crescent moon adorns her forehead, and her smile overwhelms Śiva, himself the lord of desire (Kāma) (name 28). She has as her seat the corpses of Brahmā, Viṣṇu, Śiva, and Rudra (name 249) and is attended by Brahmā, Viṣṇu, Śiva, Lakṣmī, and Sarasvatī (name 614).

She is often depicted iconographically as seated on a lotus that rests on the supine body of Śiva, which in turn lies on a throne whose legs are the gods Brahmā, Viṣṇu, Śiva, and Rudra. In some cases the lotus is growing out of Śiva's navel. In other cases it is growing from the Śrī *cakra*, the yantra

Fig. 17. Tripura-sundarī, by Molaram, late eighteenth century, Garwahl, Himachal Pradesh. Bharat Kala Bhavan, Benares Hindu University, Varanasi.

of Tripura-sundarī. In this rendering of the goddess, she is self-emergent, as the Śrī *cakra* is identical with the goddess herself (see below). In one instance she is said to sit on Śiva's lap in his form as Kāmeśvara, "lord of desire."[4] The *Vāmakeśvara-tantra* says that Tripura-sundarī dwells on the peaks of the Himalayas; is worshiped by sages and heavenly nymphs; has a body like pure crystal; wears a tiger skin, a snake as a garland around her neck, and her hair tied in a *jaṭa;* holds a trident and drum; is decorated with jewels, flowers, and ashes; and has a large bull as a vehicle.[5]

The *Saundaryalaharī* and the *Tantrasāra*[6] describe her in detail from her hair to her feet. The *Tantrasāra dhyāna* mantra says that she is illuminated by the jewels of the crowns of Brahmā and Viṣṇu, which fell at her feet when they bowed down to worship her.[7] It is interesting to note that in the *Tantrasāra* she is not associated with Śiva in any obvious way, as she is in other descriptions.

Mythology and Characteristics

Tripura-sundarī (Ṣoḍaśī) was a very well-known and important tantric goddess before she was grouped with the Mahāvidyās. She occupies a prominent position in both Kashmiri and South Indian Tantrism. She has been worshiped from a very early period in South India, where she is central in a movement of considerable sophistication and popularity, the Śrīvidyā cult. Although she is often described in anthropomorphic fashion, her cult, which still flourishes throughout India, but particularly in the South, centers on worship of and meditation on her mantra, the Śrīvidyā mantra, and her yantra, the Śrī *cakra*. This worship is done almost exclusively in private and in tantric fashion.[8]

The earliest reference to Śrīvidyā (the form of the goddess as mantra) is in the Tamil work *Tirumantiram*, by Tirumular, who lived in the seventh century C.E. By the ninth century, the cult of Śrīvidyā was mentioned in Sanskrit works, and several texts celebrating her are attributed to the great philosopher from South India, Śankara (788–820). Several texts in which Tripura-sundarī is featured appeared about the same period in Kashmir, where she became a significant goddess. Of particular note is the *Vāmakeśvara-tantra*, which attracted several important commentaries. During the thirteenth and fourteenth centuries, the cult of Śrīvidyā expanded greatly in both Kashmir and South India, with several notable commentaries being written on earlier works. Her cult eventually became popular in Bengal, with certain northern variations, and now her worship and fame have spread throughout India.

Despite the tendency of Śrīvidyā worship and ritual practice to remain private and esoteric, there are popular hymns to the goddess with a strong devotional flavor. The *Navavaraṇakirthis* by Muttusvami, a composer of classical Karnatik music, contain some famous examples, and in actual practice such hymns are sung in public, outside an esoteric tantric setting.[9]

Although there are not many temples where Tripura-sundarī is worshiped in anthropomorphic form, she has become identified with certain important goddesses in South India. Her presence in many temples is marked by the Śrī *cakra*, rather than an anthropomorphic image. Sometimes another goddess will be shown associated with the Śrī *cakra*, thus identifying her with Tripura-sundarī, whose essential form is identical with the Śrī *cakra*. At the temple of the famous South Indian goddess Mīnākṣi of Madurai, for example, coins are sold depicting Mīnākṣi in anthropomorphic form on one side and the Śrī *cakra* on the other. Pictures of Mīnākṣi standing above a Śrī *cakra* are also sold there. Another example is the goddess Akhilandeśvarī of Tiruchirappalli, who is shown wearing Śrī *cakras* as earrings.[10] In other cases the appearance of a particular goddess may be so similar to Tripura-sundarī's that it is difficult not to associate or identify the two. This is the case with the goddess Kamākṣi of Kanchipuram, whose depictions differ from those of Tripura-sundarī in only very minor ways. The Śrī *cakra* is also shown in Kamākṣi's iconography.[11]

In Varanasi there is a temple to Rājarājeśvarī, a common epithet of Tripura-sundarī. It is said that she has the power to attract people and that one can feel the pull of her strength when taking her *darśan* (viewing her image). No one is strong enough to spend the night in her temple, and after awhile she drives people crazy who stay in her presence. Her priests do not last long. I was told that she is an unmarried goddess, but there is a *liṅgam* outside her temple, suggesting the presence of Śiva. There is also a Rājarājeśvarī temple in the village of Bangaramu in Uttar Pradesh. The *garbha gṛha* housing the image is flanked by two Śiva *liṅgams*. The image of the goddess holds weapons and is of a dark complexion. The supine figure of Śiva lies in front of it. Painted panels on the front of her throne show five male deities, each seated on a lotus with different numbers of petals. Brahmā, Viṣṇu, and Śiva are distinguishable and may represent the legs of the throne on which the goddess sits, a common theme in her descriptions, where the gods are said to support her.[12]

I also have been told of a temple to Haṁseśvarī-devī, an epithet of Tripura-sundarī, in the village of Bansberia near Hooghly in Bengal. The temple is six stories tall, and the central image is of Tripura-sundarī, who sits on a lotus that emerges from the navel of Śiva, who is reclining on another lotus that in turn rests on an image of the Śrī *cakra*. There are fifteen black *liṅgams* in the temple and a sixteenth that is white. The sixteenth may symbolize Tripura-sundarī as Ṣoḍaśī, "she who is the sixteenth" or "the one who goes beyond or includes the fifteen lunar *tithis*" (lunar days; see below). The temple also has three staircases, one on the right of the image, another on the left, and a third descending into the temple. These probably represent the three *nāḍīs* (veins or arteries) of *kuṇḍalinī* yoga and, taken together, the whole of reality. A temple of similar design to Tripura-sundarī is currently under construction in Varanasi.[13]

Tripura-sundarī is also an important goddess in the Nepali town of Bhaktapur. There she is associated with a group of goddesses called the Astamātṛkās, the "eight mothers." These eight goddesses, each of whom has a shrine, or *pīṭha*, form a protective circle around the city of Bhaktapur. In the center is Tripura-sundarī's shrine. As the ninth and central goddess of the group, she is understood to be preeminent among the others, to be the supreme goddess.[14] It is also interesting to note that among the Astamātṛkās are two of the other Mahāvidyās, Kālī and Lakṣmī.[15]

The central tale in the mythology of Tripura-sundarī concerns her defeat of the demon Bhaṇḍa. According to this myth, Śiva destroyed Kāma, the god of love, when he sought to distract Śiva from his meditation. Subsequently, one of Śiva's *gaṇas* (companions or followers) makes an image of a man from Kāma-deva's ashes. This man then appeals to Śiva to teach him a powerful mantra, which Śiva obligingly does. By reciting the mantra, one gains half the might of one's adversary. Śiva also grants the man rulership of the world for sixty thousand years. Śiva praises the man with the words "Bhaṇḍ! Bhaṇḍ!" ("Good! Good!"), but because he was born from Śiva's anger when he burned up Kāma, he turns into a dangerous, wrathful demon. He builds a city rivaling in glory the city of the gods ruled over by Indra. When Bhaṇḍa attacks Indra, Indra, at the bidding of the sage Nārada, calls on Tripura-sundarī for help. Indra also instructs his allies to propitiate the goddess by offering her their own flesh and blood with Vedic rites. At the end of these rites the goddess appears and agrees to help the gods. In the meantime, the sixty thousand years granted to Bhaṇḍa to rule the world have expired.

With Indra's city still under siege, the gods arrange the marriage of Śiva and Tripura-sundarī. After some time the goddess, with her female associates (*śaktis*), goes off to battle Bhaṇḍa and his army. Tripura-sundarī produces many weapons from the noose and goad that she carries in her hands. Bhaṇḍa is amused by the army of females and predicts that they will be as ineffective in battle as the name of their leader, Lalitā (soft and delicate), suggests. Tripura-sundarī and her army, however, turn out to be superior to Bhaṇḍa and his army. In the course of the battle the two chief protagonists, Tripura-sundarī and Bhaṇḍa, produce various beings from their bodies. Bhaṇḍa creates a number of demons that are well known in Hindu mythology, and Tripura-sundarī counters by bringing forth a corresponding deity or *avatāra* to defeat the demon. Bhaṇḍa, for example, creates Hiraṇyākaśipu. Lalitā in turn produces Prahlāda, who in the well-known Vaiṣṇava myth defeats Hiraṇyākaśipu. Bhaṇḍa brings forth Rāvaṇa, and Tripura-sundarī creates Rāma from one of her fingernails. In the course of the battle Bhaṇḍa also creates Mahiṣāsura. The goddess responds by producing Durgā, who is ornamented with jewelry given to her by many male gods. Durgā then slays Mahiṣāsura, as she does in the famous *Devī-māhātmya*. Finally, the goddess defeats Bhaṇḍa himself. After the battle, the gods, led by Kāma-deva's wife, Rati, implore Tripura-sundarī to restore the god of love, whom Śiva had destroyed. She does so, and desire is restored to the world. The gods praise her in unison.[16]

The myth establishes certain central characteristics for Tripura-sundarī. Her primary role is to protect the well-being of the gods and cosmic stability. She herself is the source of several of Viṣṇu's *avatāras*, whom she creates to defeat particular demons in the battle with Bhaṇḍa. Tripura-sundarī is said to have other forms, actually referred to as *avatāras*. These include the goddesses Kālī, Kumārī, Caṇḍikā, Bhārati, and Gaurī.[17] This myth, and other passages enumerating her different manifestations created to sustain the world, establish Tripura-sundarī as a transcendent cosmic guardian, the source of well-known deities and *avatāras*, the great director behind the scenes, the ultimate overseer of the cosmic processes. In the *Lalitā-sahasranāma* she is called She from Whose Ten Fingernails Spring the Ten Forms of Viṣṇu (name 88). The same text gives her names that emphasize her role as a warrior, for example, She Who Slays Demons (name 318), She Who Grants Boons to Warriors (name 493), Ruler of Armies (name 691), She Who Is Worshiped by Warriors (name 777), and Mother of Warriors (name 836). In short, the myth and hymns to her depict Tripura-sundarī as a great battle queen similar to Durgā and underline her role as guardian of cosmic order.

Complementing her role as a warrior are Tripura-sundarī's royal characteristics. In the *Lalitā-sahasranāma* she is worshiped by kings (name 305). She takes pleasure in ruling (name 686) and subdues all the worlds (name 698). One of her most popular epithets is Rājarājeśvarī, "queen of kings." Another of her names, Śrī, associates her with sovereignty. However, she is distinguished in many ways from the goddess, also called Śrī, who is Viṣṇu's consort, and is more commonly associated with Śiva, as we shall see below.

On a more cosmic scale, Tripura-sundarī undertakes the three principal cosmic functions of creation, maintenance, and destruction. She either performs these functions by herself or creates and directs Brahmā, Viṣṇu, and Śiva in these roles. In the *Saundaryalaharī*, the entire universe is formed from a tiny speck of dust from her foot. From that speck Brahmā fashions the universe, which Viṣṇu, in his form as Vāsuki, the many-headed serpent, can barely support (v. 2). In the *Lalitā-sahasranāma*, she sits on the five corpses of Brahmā, Viṣṇu, Rudra, Iśvara, and Sadāśiva (name 249). In the hymn of a thousand names to her in the *Vāmakeśvara-tantra*, she is called Mistress of All, Mother of the World, and Mother of the Vedas.[18]

She is the quintessence of auspiciousness (*saubhāgya*) and in this respect resembles the goddess Śrī, Viṣṇu's consort. She is described, often in great detail, as lavishly adorned with ornaments and fine clothing. She is said to give all blessings, grant all desires, embody purity (*suddhā*), and be calm, peaceful, and completely suffused with *sattvic* qualities.[19]

Tripura-sundarī is also often described as extremely attractive, beautiful, and erotically inclined. The *Lalitā-sahasranāma* details her charms from head to foot (vv. 13–51), and the majority of the *Saundaryalaharī* is similarly preoccupied with her attractive appearance. She is often said to give desire, to suffuse the creation with desire, and to be the actual form of desire—that is, the god of desire, Kāma-deva—or his wife, Rati. In the *Lalitā-sahasranāma* she is called The Desirable One (name 321), She Who Is Filled with Erotic Sentiments (name 376), She Whose Form Is the Desire of Women (name 454), She Who Causes Emotion (name 466), She Who Enchants (name 562), She Whose Form Is Sexual Desire (name 796), and She Who Overflows with Desire and Pleasure (name 863). The *Saundaryalaharī* says that Kāma, the god of love, who bewitches the whole world, received his powers by a glance from the goddess (v. 6). It is also said there that a worn-out old man, ugly and sluggish in the arts of love, can be restored to sexual attractiveness and vigor by her glance (v. 13). The *Prapañcasāra-tantra* says that her worship has such an amorous effect that celestial females such as *gandharvas, yakṣas,* and *siddhas* come to the *sādhaka* "with gazelle-like eyes, breathing heavily, their bodies quivering . . . and moist with the pearly sweat of passion; and throwing away their ornaments and letting their clothes fall from about them, bow themselves before him and offer to do his will."[20] The several names that associate or identify her with the female sexual organ in her thousand-name hymn in the *Vāmakeśvara-tantra*[21] also suggest the erotic character of the goddess.

In the *Kālikā-purāṇa*, Bālā-tripura-sundarī (young girl who is beautiful in the three worlds) is said to be the symbol of beauty and sexuality and is worshiped by adoring a living girl in either the right- or left-handed tantric manner.[22] The *Yoginī-tantra* enjoins the devotee to contemplate the image of a naked sixteen-year-old girl and to think of each part of her body being assimilated to his own.[23] In the *Tripurā-rahasya*, Tripurā creates nine *śaktis,* several of whom have erotic associations: Kāmeśvarī, Bhagāmālinī (having a garland of yonis), Nityalinnā (always moist), and Bheruṇḍā (pregnant), for example.[24]

Such names also suggest Tripura-sundarī's association with fertility and growth. The *Lalitā-sahasranāna* calls her She Who Is Vitality (name 767),

She Who Gives Life (name 783), and She Whose Form Is Life (name 784). The hymn of her thousand names in the *Vāmakeśvara-tantra* calls her The Mother Who Oversees Birth.[25] She is often associated with the earth itself and is said both to create and uphold it. Related to her nature as the power underlying vigor and growth is her association with nourishment and food. In the *Lalitā-sahasranāma* she is called Mahī and Dharā, both meaning "the earth" (names 718 and 955), and is identified with nourishment (name 444) and food itself (name 699). She is also called Jagaddhātrī, "world nurse" (name 935).

For the most part, Tripura-sundarī is characterized by names and features that emphasize her beautiful, auspicious, pure, fertile, and gracious nature and that associate her with wealth, royal power, the protection of the order of dharma, and the defeat of demons. She is often described as the patient, obedient wife of either Śiva or Viṣṇu. Other features of Tripura-sundarī, however, suggest aspects of her nature that deviate from this portrait. In places she is said to be frightening, wild, and perhaps dangerous. Although none of her principal names (Tripura-sundarī, Śrīvidyā, Ṣoḍaśī, Lalitā, or Rājarājeśvarī) suggests this aspect of the goddess, there is no denying its presence in many of the texts that describe her. In contrast to the usual descriptions of Tripura-sundarī as clothed in radiant garments and glowing jewels are passages in the *Vāmakeśvara-tantra* where she is naked or clothed in animal hides and wears her hair in a *jaṭa*, an ascetic's knot.[26] She carries a skull, wears ashes, and has a snake as a necklace; she has a large and long tongue, fearful fangs, disheveled hair, and the form of a skeleton.[27]

In many ways she resembles Kālī, with whom she is sometimes identified.[28] There is even a myth explaining the identity of Tripura-sundarī and Kālī. In the *Prāṇatoṣinī* (probably written in Bengal in the seventeenth century), we are told that once upon a time Śiva referred to Kālī by her name in front of some heavenly damsels who had come to visit, calling her "Kālī, Kālī" ("Blackie, Blackie"), which she took to be a slur against her dark complexion. She left Śiva and resolved to rid herself of her dark complexion through asceticism. Later, the sage Nārada visited Kailāsa and, seeing Śiva alone, asked where his wife was. Śiva complained that she had abandoned him and vanished. With his yogic powers Nārada discovered Kālī living north of Mount Sumeru and went there to see if he could convince her to return to Śiva. He told her that Śiva was thinking of marrying another goddess and that she should return at once to prevent this. By now Kālī had rid herself of her dark complexion but did not yet realize it. Arriving in the presence of Śiva, she saw a reflection of herself with a light complexion in Śiva's heart. Thinking that this was another goddess, she became jealous and angry. Śiva advised her to look more carefully, with the eye of knowledge, telling her that what she saw in his heart was herself. The story ends with Śiva saying to the transformed Kālī: "As you have assumed a very beautiful form, beautiful in the three worlds, your name will be Tripura-sundarī. You shall always remain sixteen years old and be called by the name Ṣoḍaśī."[29]

The Names Tripura-sundarī, Ṣoḍaśī, and Lalitā

The texts dealing with Tripura-sundarī often reflect on the significance of her names, which are usually thought to hold hidden or mystical meanings. These reflections elicit further aspects of her character and additional associations with ideas and themes in Hindu philosophy, mythology, and spiritual practice. The names that receive the most attention are Tripura-sundarī, Ṣoḍaśī, and Lalitā.

The name Tripura-sundarī, whose most obvious and apparent meaning is "she who is beautiful in the three worlds," typically prompts speculation concerning various triads known to Hindu philosophy, mythology, and *sādhanā* (spiritual practice). In the process of associating Tripura-sundarī with these triads, the texts often imply that she is identical with ultimate, essential, or complete reality in one way or another. The *Kālikā-purāṇa* gives several interpretations in this vein. She is called Tripurā, the text says, because she is identical with the triangle (*trikoṇa*) that symbolizes the yoni and that forms her *cakra* (see below). The triangle in the Śrīvidyā cult, as we shall see, is a primordial form from which the creation proceeds and is clearly related to the generative power of the yoni. She is called Tripurā also because her mantra (discussed below) has three clusters of syllables. Here Tripurā is identified with the alphabet, from which all sounds and words proceed and which is often understood to occupy a primordial place in tantric cosmology. She is threefold, furthermore, because she expresses herself in Brahmā, Viṣṇu, and Śiva in her roles as creator, maintainer, and destroyer of the universe. She is threefold also because she represents the subject (*mātā*), instrument (*māna*), and object (*meya*) of all things. Here again she is identified with reality expressed in terms of speech, which involves a speaker, what is said, and objects to which the words refer.[30]

The *Kamakalā-vilāsa* (vv. 13–40) speculates that Tripura-sundarī is triple faceted because she represents three kinds or colors of *bindu* (seed or essence): red, white, and mixed. This probably refers to sexual fluids: red being female sexual fluid; white, semen; and mixed, the union of the two.[31] The meaning here is that the goddess represents both of the sexual polarities in the universe and their ultimate union. The same text says that she is triadic because she has her abode in Soma, Sūrya, and Agni, that is, in the moon, sun, and fire. She is thus all-pervasive and all-inclusive, as are light and fire. Further, the text speculates, she is triadic because she is identified with the three principal goddess *pīṭhas*, or sacred centers: Kāmarūpa, Jālandhara, and Pūrṇagiri. She is triple natured also because she embodies the three principle powers of *icchā śakti* (will), *jñāna śakti* (consciousness, knowledge), and *kriyā śakti* (doing, action).[32]

In his commentary on the *Lalitā-sahasranāma*, Bhāskararāya says that the goddess is called Tripura-sundarī because "she is older than the three persons (Brahmā, Viṣṇu, and Rudra)."[33] He also says that the goddess is triple natured because she is identified with the three main channels of the subtle body in *kuṇḍalinī* yoga that represent cosmic totality.[34] Bhāskararāya comments further on the triple nature of the goddess: "There are three Devas, three Vedas, three fires, three energies, three notes (*svaras*), three worlds, three abodes, three sacred lakes, three castes. . . . Whatever in the world is threefold, such as the three objects of human desire, all these, O divine one, really belong to your name."[35] Śivānanda says that the goddess is triple natured because she "has the nature of Śiva, Śakti, and Ātman."[36]

The name Ṣoḍaśī seems to be of less interest to commentators, but there is some speculation on its hidden significance. Literally, the name means "she who is sixteen." It is common for deities to be described as eternally sixteen years old, which is considered the most beautiful and vigorous human age. This is exactly how the name is interpreted in the myth, recounted above, in which Śiva renames the transformed Kālī both Tripura-sundarī and Ṣoḍaśī.[37] The name is also understood to mean "she who has sixteen (good) qualities."[38] More esoterically, the name can mean "the sixteenth" or "she who is the sixteenth." In this case it probably refers to the phases of the moon, the lunar *tithis*, of which there are fifteen in the bright half of the lunar month (*śukla pakṣa*) and fifteen in the dark half (*kṛṣṇa pakṣa*). These *tithis* are often personified as goddesses. As the sixteenth, Ṣoḍaśī is that which is beyond the phases, or the rhythms of time. Or she may be understood as the additional element that lends to the individual *tithis* the impetus to wax and wane, the reality that underlies cosmic rhythms and impels the cosmos along an orderly course. As the cusp of the lunar phases, she is the mysterious element that transcends and yet encompasses all things.[39] "The addition of a sixteenth element to an established set of fifteen is analogous to the addition of a fourth element to established triads. The 'sixteenth' element deliberately plays on the symbolism of 'plus one,' that is, a set of three or fifteen plus one more element. . . . The sixteenth element, like the fourth in a set of threes, subsumes and encompasses the others as well as completes the symbolic pattern of meanings."[40]

The name Lalitā, "she who is lovely," "the lovely one," is also said to have universal, cosmological, or mystical significance. Bhāskararāya says:

> The wise say, "The word *lalitā* has eight meanings, namely brilliancy, manifestation, sweetness, depth, fixity, energy, grace and generosity; these are the eight human qualities." The *Kāma-śāstra* says: Lalitā means erotic actions and also tenderness; as she has all the above-mentioned qualities, she is called Lalitā. It is said also, "Thou art rightly called Lalitā for thou hast nine divine attendants [in the Śrī *cakra*, see below] and your bow is made of sugar-cane, your arrows are flowers, and everything connected with you is lovely (*lalitā*)."[41]

It seems clear that commentators on the meaning of Tripura-sundarī's names begin with the assumption that she is the highest reality, or reality itself, and find in her epithets mystical meanings that affirm this. Whether she is called Lalitā, Ṣoḍaśī, Tripura-sundarī, or one of several other common names, she is the cosmic queen from whom everything originates, in whom everything inheres, and by whom everything will be dissolved.

The Śrīvidyā Mantra and the Śrī *Cakra*

The goddess Tripura-sundarī's identity with the Śrīvidyā mantra and the Śrī *cakra* yantra have been elaborated by theorists of the Śrīvidyā cult. While we might be tempted to refer to the Śrīvidyā mantra as her mantra, and the Śrī *cakra* as her yantra, as symbols in sound and diagram of the goddess whom we imagine in anthropomorphic form, practitioners of the cult insist, on the contrary, that the mantra is she, that the *cakra* is she, herself.[42] Indeed, they say that the anthropomorphic image of the goddess, the deity described in myths and praised in hymns, who has characteristics and a physical appearance and who undertakes actions and plays roles, is a gross form that, to some extent, hides her essential nature. In the view of the Śrīvidyā cult, this physical, anthropomorphic aspect of the goddess is her *sthūla* form, which is considered crude compared to her illuminative (*śūkṣma*) and supreme (*parā*) manifestations, which in turn are identified with her forms as mantra and *cakra*, respectively.[43]

Both mantras and yantras are central to Tantric *sādhanā*. However, Tripura-sundarī, in the Śrīvidyā cult, expresses more clearly than any of the other Mahāvidyās the importance of mantras and yantras in the worship and conceptualization of these goddesses. It is appropriate, then, to dwell here in more detail on the significance of mantra and yantra by analyzing how they express and relate to Tripura-sundarī. The first point that must be emphasized is that the mantra and yantra are affirmed in the cult to be unmediated revelations, not human or cultural constructs. Nor are they partial revelations: they are not simply clues to, or aspects of, the transcendent goddess. They *are* the goddess in her purest, highest, most intense form. We might think of the mantra and the yantra as forms of grace. That is, the goddess has given these complete expressions of herself to certain spiritually advanced people in the Śrīvidyā cult.

As explained in Part I, the mantra and yantra are not public. That is, although they may be available to the uninitiated (the mantra is now available in print in many places, and the yantra is displayed in many books and temples), their potency depends upon their being transmitted to individual adepts by spiritual masters (gurus). For uninitiated or spiritually unqualified people to recite or devote themselves to the mantra or yantra is ineffective; the goddess's reality and inherent power will not be realized. Bhāskararāya says: "The devotion of the inept to the external ostentation [of the *śrīvidyā*], being without aptitude for what is necessary, is like a body in which life has perished, or a puppet from which the strings are detached."[44]

Becoming spiritually qualified to benefit from the inherent power of the goddess in her mantric (or yantric) form demands extended spiritual preparation under the guidance of a guru, during which the adept learns the significance of the mantra (and yantra). The power of the mantra remains latent unless the practitioner understands its special, sacred significance. It is during preparation for initiation that the guru communicates this to the student. This instruction, which introduces the adept to "an elite form of spirituality, linked to the concept of favorable karma acquired over the course of countless previous births,"[45] culminates in an elaborate ritual in which the master transmits the Śrīvidyā mantra to the

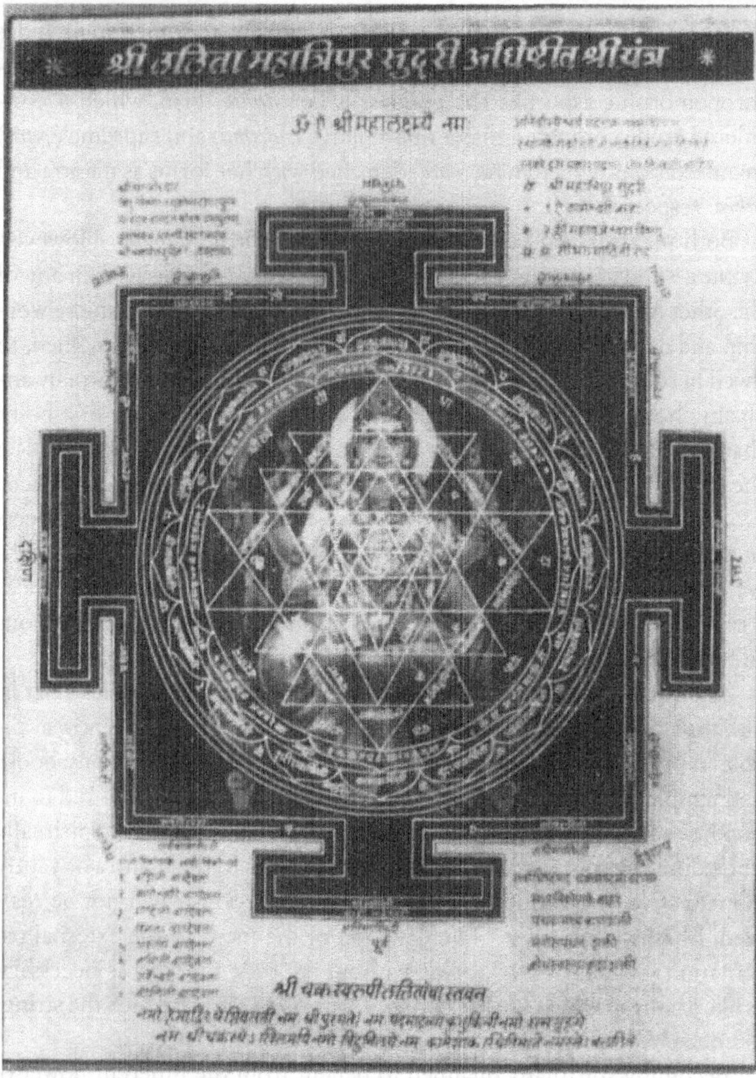

Fig. 18. Tripura-sundarī with the Srī yantra, contemporary lithograph.

student. This ultimate revelation of the goddess makes her fully accessible to the initiate. At this point the guru may also give the initiate a physical form of the Śrī *cakra* for his or her personal use in *sādhanā*.

In learning the significance of the mantra, the student first comes to appreciate that the mantra (or yantra) is a full expression of the goddess.

Beginning with this assumption, the adept is then prepared to appreciate the esoteric or mystical meanings of the individual parts of the mantra (or yantra) and its overall correspondence to other symbols or expressions of ultimate reality in the Hindu tradition. That is, the student, under the instruction of the guru, learns to discern in the mantra every aspect and dimension of cosmological, spiritual, and existential truth. As in the case of the goddess's names, so here the hidden meanings of the sacred expression are elaborately drawn out. Each syllable of the mantra, each line and angle of the yantra, is infused with meaning (or suffused with meaning, depending upon one's point of view) and is gradually absorbed by the spiritual adept in his or her ongoing devotion and use of the mantra. One way of thinking about the mantra as containing all reality, according to Bhāskararāya, is to think of the mantra as a seed containing in potential form the entire or full-grown plant. "As a banyan tree is found in its seed, so [the mantras] contain everything and are complete."[46] Creation proceeds from seed mantras to language (especially Sanskrit), to other languages (which, according to Brahmanical tradition, all derive from Sanskrit), to other sounds, and finally to all sounds in creation. Throughout the whole cosmos, then, the seed mantras exist as the essential form or power of reality.

To give an example of how the Śrīvidyā mantra is interpreted as containing the fullness and essence of ultimate reality, let us see how those in the tradition of the Śrīvidyā cult discern in the Śrīvidyā mantra the presence of the Gāyatrī mantra, the mantra from the Ṛg-veda in praise of the sun, "the most holy passage of that most holy scripture."[47] The Śrīvidyā mantra consists of fifteen syllables that have no literal meaning: *ka, e, ī, la, hrīṁ, ha, sa, ka, ha, la, hrīṁ, sa, ka, la, hrīṁ*. The Gāyatrī, on the other hand, consists of many more than fifteen syllables and has a literal meaning: it praises the sun. Bhāskararāya finds that each syllable of the Śrīvidyā mantra contains one or several syllables from the Gāyatrī and, therefore, that the Gāyatrī inheres in the Śrīvidyā mantra. He lists the correspondences by associating specific sounds in the two mantras; for example, *ka = tat, e = savitur vareṇyam, ī = bhargo devasya dhi-*, and so on through both mantras.[48] The Śrīvidyā mantra is also divided into three parts, or three peaks (*kūṭas*). Just as cosmological, mystical, or meditative triads are found hidden in the name Tripura-sundarī, so each peak of the mantra is compared to a cosmological, spiritual dynamic. There is the peak concerned with the power of speech, the peak concerned with the power of desire, and the peak concerned with the underlying *śakti* of the cosmos. Brahmā, Viṣṇu, and Śiva; the moon, the sun, and fire; the three *guṇas* (*sattva*, *rajas*, and *tamas*)—these and other triads are identified with the three peaks. In this way the triple-peaked mantra is seen to correspond to the cosmos, or the cosmos is seen to inhere in the three parts of the mantra.[49]

The mantra is also held to have six esoteric or mystical meanings (*artha*). Bhāskararāya describes them as follows: the first is that the mantra is identical with the supreme goddess, Tripura-sundarī; the second is that the mantra is identical with the five basic elements and the thirty-six *tattvas* (categories of creation); the third is the identity of the self (*ātman*), the guru, and Śiva, which are represented by the three "peaks"; the fourth is the identity between the mantra and the planets, the senses and their objects, and the material and spiritual worlds; the fifth is that the mantra is related to the *cakras* in the body; and the sixth is that ultimately all is one, that the mantra and everything to which it is compared coinhere in an indivisible unity.[50]

Inextricably related to the Śrīvidyā mantra and equally central to the Śrīvidyā cult is the Śrī *cakra*, the yantra form of the goddess Tripura-sundarī.[51] The yantra is to be held in the mind or worshiped in a physical manifestation. Like the mantra, the yantra is not an abbreviated or schematic representation of the anthropomorphic goddess. The Śrī *cakra* is the goddess herself in complete, unmediated form; it fully contains and expresses her. Like the mantra, the Śrī *cakra* is the self-revelation, the self-expression of the goddess in her most essential form. As the *svarūpa* (own form) of the goddess, who encompasses all of reality, everything inheres in the Śrī *cakra;* all of reality and the very nature of reality can be read in terms of it. If we think of the mantra as the expression of ultimate reality (*brahman*) in the form of sound, then we can think of the Śrī *cakra* as the very form of *brahman* in schematic or visual form. The *cakra* is essentially made up of nine triangles, five pointing downward and four pointing upward (in some cases five are pointing upward and four are pointing downward), which overlap each other and create many subsidiary triangles; these in turn are located within an eight-petaled lotus, which in turn is within a sixteen-petaled lotus; the lotuses are surrounded by four circles; and the whole is enclosed within four gates of triple lines. In the very center of the Śrī *cakra* is a dot, the *bindu.*

The Śrī *cakra* expresses the essential nature of ultimate reality as the interaction and mutual coinherence of Śiva and Śakti, male and female, potentiality and actuality. The *bindu* in the center represents their absolute union and identity, while the rest of the *cakra* represents their evolution into the cosmos. The five downward-pointing triangles represent

Śakti, while the upward-pointing triangles represent Śiva. They overlap to represent the mingling, interaction, and mutual influence of these two powers. The predominance of Śakti in this rendering of the *cakra* implies her dominant position in the creation. Each petal of each lotus has a presiding female deity. These *śaktis* are attendants or guardians of the central deities, Śiva and Śakti in union in the *bindu*. There are also attendant deities at the outer gates who are often associated with *siddhis*, spiritual or magical powers or perfections acquired by the *sādhaka* in his or her spiritual sojourn. In general, the *siddhis* associated with the outermost deities are the least powerful and least difficult to acquire, while those associated with the innermost deities are the most difficult to acquire and the most spiritually potent.[52]

The Śrī *cakra* can be read from the center to the outer gates, or conversely from the outer gates to the center. In the former case, one imagines the creation of the world as one moves from the center outward. This sequence is called *sṛṣṭikrama*. One identifies oneself with the expanding creation and understands one's spiritual prowess and awareness to be expanding along with the cosmos. In the reverse process, the *sādhaka* imagines the gradual dissolution of the cosmos and its reintegration into the *bindu*, which is without name and form. This sequence is called *saṁhārakrama*, and in the course of it one imagines one's own dissolution and gradual reintegration into the One represented by the *bindu*. In both cases the Śrī *cakra* is read as a schematic rendering of one's own spiritual journey. In either case, the exercise, which is undertaken ritually, is held to be spiritually transformative.

In the Śrīvidyā cult, the Śrīvidyā mantra and the Śrī *cakra* are interpreted as two different expressions of the same goddess. In both cases it is affirmed that the goddess herself is fully expressed and that each expression, mantra and yantra, reveals the essential dynamics of cosmic evolution and dissolution. In a ritual context, the mantra and yantra are interconnected and reinforce each other. It is fair to say that the goddess Tripura-sundarī is most intensely and completely revealed in the Śrīvidyā cult when a spiritually mature adept, invoking her mantra while implicitly understanding its subtle meanings, imaginatively or in actuality constructs the Śrī *cakra*.

It is clear that the way in which the other Mahāvidyās are presented in many *tantras* and tantric compendiums also puts a premium on their mantras and yantras. Each of the goddesses is intimately connected with these expressions and is appropriated ritually in all her power by means of these "devices." The centrality of mantra and yantra in the worship of

Tripura-sundarī and specifically in the Śrīvidyā cult should not be taken as idiosyncratic. Their use is typical of tantric *sādhanā.* The emphasis on mantra and yantra also underlines the fact that Tripura-sundarī, and the other Mahāvidyās as well, are only fully realized, understood, and expressed existentially by individual *sādhakas* in ritual contexts. The goddesses are born, as it were, by means of *sādhanā.* Their reality is inextricably connected with the ritually induced experiences of their devotees.

Bhuvaneśvarī

She Whose Body Is the World

> Her complexion is vermillion in color. She has three eyes and wears a crown resplendent with jewels. She has the disk of the moon on her brow and has a smiling face. Her breasts are high and firm. In her two hands she holds a red lotus and a bowl filled with jewels. She is very peaceful and amiable. Her right foot rests on a jeweled jar. In this way one should meditate upon the supreme mother goddess.[1]

> She is the color of lightning and is seated on a red lotus. She has three eyes and is naked. She is adorned with pearls of many colors. She has twenty arms in which she holds a sword, spear, club, disc, conch, bow, arrows, scissors, trident, mace, garland, and makes the boon-conferring gesture and the assurance gesture. She has a smiling face.[2]

Origin Myth

The only myth I have found that mentions the origin or emergence of Bhuvaneśvarī appears in a contemporary Hindi source. It says that in the beginning the sun, Sūrya, appeared in the heavens. *Ṛṣis* (sages) offered *soma* (a sacred plant) so that the world might be created. The sun then created the three worlds (*lokas* or *bhuvanas*). At that time Ṣoḍaśī (Tripura-sundarī) was the main power, or *śakti*, through whom Sūrya created them. Having created the worlds, or having empowered the sun to do so, the goddess assumed an appropriate form and pervaded and directed the triple world. In this form she became known as Bhuvaneśvarī, "mistress of the world." The author also says that Bhuvaneśvarī

Fig. 19. Bhuvaneśvarī, nineteenth century, Jaipur, Rajasthan. Ajit Mookerjee Collection of Tantric Art, National Museum, Delhi.

remains unmanifest until the world is created. That is, Bhuvaneśvarī is particularly associated with the visible, created world.[3] The myth also emphasizes that Bhuvaneśvarī is a form of Ṣoḍaśī (Tripura-sundarī).

Bhuvaneśvarī as the Embodiment of the Physical World

More than any of the other Mahāvidyās, with the possible exception of Kamalā, Bhuvaneśvarī is associated and identified with the earth, the creation in general, and the underlying energy that brings it to be and pervades it. She embodies the characteristic dynamics and constituents that make up the world and that lend creation its distinctive character. In this sense, as we shall see, she is identified with the *mahābhūtas* (the basic physical elements) and *prakṛti* (nature or the physical world). Her name itself stresses this, Bhuvana (mistress of the world), as do several of her epithets, such as Mahāmāyā, Sarveśi (mistress of all), Bhuvaneśi (a synonym for Bhuvaneśvarī), Sarvarūpā (she whose form is all), Viśvarūpā (she whose form is the world), She Who Makes All the Worlds, She Who Dwells in the Five Basic Elements, She Who Makes the Basic Elements.[4] The *Bhuvaneśvarī-stotra* praises her as the form of the five *bhūtas* (elements) and as the moon and the sun.[5] Her hundred-name hymn from the *Rudrayāmala* says that she is each of the five basic elements.[6] The *Devībhāgavata-purāṇa* says that the universe rests on Bhuvaneśvarī, arises from her, melts away into her, and, while it exists, is identified with her. Bhuvaneśvarī is also identified with *prakṛti*.[7] The world is said to emerge from her as a web emerges from a spider or as sparks emerge from fire.[8] Other Mahāvidyās are associated with the physical world and creation, particularly in their thousand-name hymns, as well as with the cosmic rhythms of creation, maintenance, and destruction, but this emphasis is the most sustained and consistent in regard to Bhuvaneśvarī.

Bhuvaneśvarī does not seem to have had a widespread cult of her own prior to being incorporated into the Mahāvidyās. Some early sources refer to her, however, or to goddesses very like her. The *Prapañcasāra-tantra*, for example, which is attributed to Śankara, and if not actually written by him is probably a quite early South Indian tantric text, extols the goddess Prapañceśvarī, "mistress of the fivefold world." The description of her closely resembles that of Bhuvaneśvarī in later literature. At one point, for example, the text says that she has the luster of a thousand rising suns,

Fig. 20. Bhuvaneśvarī, by Bhatuk Ramprasad. Printed with the permission of Dr. Bhanu Shanker Mehta, Varanasi.

wears the crescent moon on her head, holds a noose and a goad, and makes the gestures of giving boons and bestowing fearlessness (11.16). The *bīja* mantra (seed mantra) of this goddess is also the same as Bhuvaneśvarī's, namely, *hrīṁ.* In tantric philosophy and practice the *bīja* mantra *is* the goddess herself in her most essential and complete form, so the identity of the goddess of the *Prapañcasāra-tantra* and the later goddess Bhuvaneśvarī is implied (although the *bīja* mantra *hrīṁ* is used for other goddesses besides these two). Prapañceśvarī is undoubtedly an early expression of Bhuvaneśvarī, or at least her prototype.

Prapañca, the term used in this text for "world," refers to the fivefold (*prapañca*) nature of the creation, that is, the five basic elements—ether, fire, water, wind, and earth—which constitute the physical creation. The name Prapañceśvarī, "she who is mistress of the fivefold world," associates the goddess with the material creation and thus with *prakṛti.* As *prakṛti* this goddess is tangibly present in the physical world; indeed, she is the world. Her reality is immediate and her presence immanent and accessible. A hymn in praise of Prapañceśvarī in the *Prapañcasāra-tantra* stresses this identification with the physical world.[9] She is called Pradhāna (the receptacle of all matter), Prakṛti, and She Who Is the Form of the Elemental World (v. 1).[10] In one place she is praised as each of the five elements (*bhūtas*) and its corresponding physical sense (*indriya*): "Obeisance to Thee in the form of sound and ether, / Salutation to Thee in the form of touch and air, / Obeisance to Thee in the form of sight and fire, / Salutation to Thee in the form of taste and water, / Obeisance to Thee in the form of earth with its quality of smell" (v. 5).[11] She is further praised in vividly concrete terms as manifest in "ear, skin, eyes, tongue and nose, and in the form of mouth, speech, arms, legs, organs of excretion and generation" (v. 6).[12] She is also praised as manifest in mountains, oceans, stars, islands, and even the netherworlds (v. 18). She is, in short, the goddess who is "the form of the whole Universe: Who pervadest all" (v. 6).[13]

In her manifestation as a Mahāvidyā, Bhuvaneśvarī is often described in three forms that are very similar in appearance. They have different complexions, however: gold, red, and bluish. As these three forms probably correspond to the three *guṇas* that make up the fabric of material creation, they suggest in another way Bhuvaneśvarī's identification with the material world.[14]

The Cosmic Queen

Prapañceśvarī and her later manifestation as Bhuvaneśvarī are goddesses whose power and reality go beyond the physical creation itself. They are also identified with that from which the physical creation proceeds and that which governs the physical creation. They are the source of all and that into which all dissolves at the end of the cosmic cycle. This aspect of Prapañceśvarī-Bhuvaneśvarī's character is often expressed in terms of her overseeing the three cosmic functions of creation, maintenance, and destruction. She is the cosmic queen, she who pervades the creation and from whom it emerges and into whom it eventually dissolves. Her hymn of praise in the *Rudrayāmala* says that she is the mother of Brahmā, Viṣṇu, and Śiva and the cause of their forms and functions, that is, the cause of creation, maintenance, and destruction.[15] In her thousand-name hymn from the *Rudrayāmala*, she is called She Who Is the Cause of Mahāpralaya (the great cosmic dissolution).[16] In the *Prapañcasāratantra*, Śiva says in her praise: "Whatever is knowable, is she herself. This movable and immovable world during the *mahāpralaya* goes to rest in her."[17] She is also called Jagaddhātrī, "she who nurses the world," or "world nurse."[18] The *Devī-bhāgavata-purāṇa* says that she directs and upholds everything.[19] That is, she is the source of the vitality that pervades the physical creation as well as being identical with the creation itself. A particularly dramatic image of Bhuvaneśvarī's cosmic role occurs in the *Mahātantra*, a Vaiṣṇavite *tantra:* she is the fig leaf that supports Viṣṇu when he lies on the cosmic ocean during *pralaya.*[20]

Bhuvaneśvarī not only nourishes the creation, she protects it. She does this by assuming various forms to combat demonic forces and preserve or restore cosmic order. Her thousand-name hymn from the *Rudrayāmala* calls her the slayer of Mahiṣāsura, the slayer of Śumbha and Niśumbha, the destroyer of Raktabīja, and the destroyer of Madhu and Kaiṭabha,[21] roles that associate her with the *Devī-māhātmya* and the demon-slaying protector of the cosmos, Durgā, who incarnates herself in appropriate forms to maintain the welfare of the world. In the same hymn, Bhuvaneśvarī is also linked to the three goddesses who are associated with the cosmic functions, the *śākta* version of the male *trimūrti:* Sarasvatī (creation), Lakṣmī (maintenance), and Kālī (destruction).[22]

The *Bīja* Mantra *Hrīṁ*

In her role as creator and pervader of the cosmos, Bhuvaneśvarī is often identified with Sarasvatī, particularly as the goddess of speech. She is called Vāgeśvarī, "mistress of speech,"[23] and is identified with *śabda brahman,*[24] ultimate reality in the form of sound. That is, Bhuvaneśvarī is identified with the created order and with its essence as sound.

An analysis of Bhuvaneśvarī's *bīja* mantra, *hrīṁ*, illustrates her embodiment of creation and the stages in the creative process and also shows the centrality of *bīja* mantras for all of the Mahāvidyās. We are in the habit of referring to the *bīja* mantra as belonging to a particular goddess, but in fact, as was made clear in the case of Śrīvidyā (see the chapter on Tripura-sundarī), the *bīja* mantra is the goddess herself, and her physical, anthropomorphic image is considered her *sthūla*, or gross form, a refracted or imperfect representation of her. We are so used to thinking of a deity in physical, anthropomorphic form, and so unused to thinking of one as a sound, that it is unnatural for us to look to the *bīja* mantra as the essential manifestation of the goddess. In tantric philosophy and *sādhanā*, however, the mantra has priority over the physical image of the goddess. It is not surprising, therefore, to find commentaries or analyses that elaborate the entire cosmos in terms of a given mantra. It is simply assumed that the mantra, which is the goddess herself, contains all of reality, that the mantra is the cosmos in its essential form. The literal translation, "seed," may mislead us; "essence" would be better, for in tantric thought, the cosmos represents a refraction of the essential being of the goddess, which is the mantra itself. A seed is only realized or completed in the growth of a tree, but in the tantric view, the mantra is already complete, the emerging cosmos a natural and necessary effect, or emanation, of the mantra. We can thus appreciate the great secrecy with which mantras are guarded in tantric tradition. The mantra is ultimate power and creativity, the essential revelation of the goddess herself, indeed, the goddess herself made accessible to the *sādhaka*.

The explication of Bhuvaneśvarī's *bīja* mantra (*hrīṁ*) is the subject of chapter 4 of the *Prapañcasāra-tantra*. There we find each of the four components of the mantra—*ha*, *ra*, *i*, and *ṁ* (*bindu*)—interpreted as basic phases or constituents of the cosmic creative process. Different letters of the alphabet are said to proceed from each of the four components of the mantra, along with certain deities and certain aspects of the physical creation. The creation proceeds from the mantra on three levels: sound, deities, and the physical creation. Within the physical creation, furthermore, the creative pattern repeats itself in the maturation of the embryo. The letters of the alphabet are said to have a threefold character—solar, lunar, and fiery—and to correspond to the goddess in her threefold aspect of sun, moon, and fire.[25] That from which all emanates, the mantra itself, is referred to as the *paramātman*, the supreme or transcendent self or soul. In the physical creation, the goddess is the sun from whom the planets and constellations derive. In terms of sound she is the Gāyatrī mantra, the most sacred verses of the Vedas. She is also said to be *kuṇḍalinī śakti* and as such is the energizing element of the human organism that is awakened in *sādhanā* or in the recitation of mantras. She is said to sleep in the *mūlādhāra cakra* and as *kuṇḍalinī* to rise up through the *cakras*, breaking the knots within them and liberating the worshiper.[26] Letters (sounds), deities, and the physical constituents of the creation, then, are inextricably associated in the creative process that emerges when the *bīja* mantra *hrīṁ* is uttered. From the tantric perspective, of course, all of these emanations—sound, deity, constituents of the material world, aspects of the human organism—are subsidiary to the mantra itself, to the goddess herself, who is complete and self-contained.

The Bhuvaneśvarī Yantra

Yantras have an important place in the worship of all of the Mahāvidyās. As mentioned above, the Śrī *cakra*, the yantra particular to Tripura-sundarī, is considered identical with the deity in question. Although the yantras of differing deities vary in design, and though the deities and powers represented may also vary, the overall structure and logic of the yantra, particularly among the Mahāvidyās, are consistent. Similarly, the overall purpose of worshiping the yantra, the way in which it is worshiped, and its role in tantric *sādhanā* are also consistent among the Mahāvidyās.

To understand the context in which the Mahāvidyās are worshiped, it is important to look in detail at yantra *sādhanā* (the construction and worship of a yantra), and Bhuvaneśvarī's may be taken as representative. It is simpler than some (such as the Śrī *cakra*) and more complex than others. It combines the basic shapes and patterns of the other yantras and depicts a series of deities and powers that are common to most of the other Mahāvidyās. The method of worshiping the Bhuvaneśvarī yantra also is typical and can be extended, in most of its features, to all of the other Mahāvidyā yantras. I will therefore give a detailed description of the Bhuvaneśvarī yantra from the *Tantrasāra* as an example of this aspect of Mahāvidyā worship.[27]

In the center of the yantra one is to imagine a *bindu*, a spot, dot, or "seed," or the seed syllable of Bhuvaneśvarī, *hrīṁ*, but in actual pictures of the yantra the center is usually blank. Around the center are two interlocking or superimposed triangles, one pointing down and the other up. Together they form a six-pointed star. Around these triangles is a circle with eight petals (an eight-petaled lotus), and around this another lotus of sixteen petals. The outermost boundary of the yantra is a three-lined rectangular frame containing four gates or entrances.

In overall design, the yantra is intended to represent the emergence of the cosmos from the center to the edges, so its details are usually given from the middle outward. The *bindu* symbolizes the conjunction of Śiva and Śakti in harmonious tension. It may also represent *ambikā śakti* and *śāntā śakti* conjoined (discussed below). The *bīja* mantra is the goddess herself in her essential being. When the *bindu* or the mantra begins to expand, pulsate, or vibrate (all three terms are sometimes used), the first thing that appears is a point where two emerging polarities combine in harmonious tension; this is followed by two additional pairs coming into being, each of which creates another point. These three points form the first, innermost triangle and are are called *pīṭhas* (seats). The three pairs are *icchā śakti* (the power of will) and *vāmā śakti* (the leftward power); *jñāna śakti* (the power of knowledge) and *jyeṣṭhā śakti* (the elder power); and *kriyā śakti* (the power of action) and *raudrā śakti* (the fierce power). Together these three *pīṭhas* represent the triple nature of creation as will or desire (*icchā*), knowledge (*jñāna*), and action (*kriyā*), which is a common schema in Tantrism. A fourth pair, forming a fourth *pīṭha*, is to be imagined in the middle of the triangle (this is *ambika śakti* and *śāntā śakti*), and together the four *pīṭhas* are said to represent the four Mahāpīṭhas, or places sacred to the goddess, on the Indian subcontinent—Kāmarūpa, Jālandhara, Pūrṇagiri, and Uddiyāna—which mark the four "corners" of India. The downward-pointing triangle, representing the yoni, also may be thought of as the goddess Śakti, the upward-pointing one as Śiva; overlapping each other, the two triangles are said to be Śakti and Śiva in union or sexual embrace. The downward-pointing triangle also may be thought of as creation or emanation (or exhalation), the upward-pointing one as dissolution (inhalation), and the two together as symbolizing the basic rhythm of the cosmos.

On the eight petals of the inner lotus are the following goddesses, beginning in the east (at the top of the diagram) and going clockwise toward the south: Jayā, Vijayā, Ajitā, Aparājitā, Nityā, Vilāsinī, Dogdhrī, and Ghorā; in the middle is Maṅgalā. Four goddesses stand at the four cardinal directions around the inner pericarp of the inner lotus: Gaganā (east), Raktā (south), Karālikā (north), and Mahoccuṣmā (west). At the six apexes of the triangles in the center are the following divine pairs, beginning in the east and going clockwise toward the south: Gāyatrī and

Brahmā, Sāitrī and Viṣṇu, Sarasvatī and Rudra, Śrī and Dhanapati (Kubera), Rati and Kāma, and Puṣṭi and Gaṇeśa. At the interstices of the inner circle at the north and south are Śankhanidhi (wealth of the conch, that is, the sea) and Padmanidhi (wealth of the earth).

On the tips of the eight petals of the inner lotus are the following goddesses, beginning in the east and going clockwise toward the south, most of whom are forms of Rati: Anaṅga-kusumā (east), "who longs for union with Kāma"; Anaṅga-kusumaturā (southeast), "who really longs for union with Kāma"; Anaṅga-madanā (south), Kāmi-devī; Anaṅga-madanaturā (southwest), Bhuvana-pālā (west), "who protects the world"; Anaṅga-vedyā (northwest), "who is known by Kāma"; Śasti-rekhā (north), "crescent moon," signifying an adolescent girl; and Gagana-rekhā (northeast), "moon crescent," signifying a prepubescent girl. If these forms of Rati are read in reverse order, they may imply the transformation of a young girl into a sexually mature woman. It is not clear why maturation should follow the counterclockwise direction, when the emergence of the cosmos takes place in clockwise fashion in the construction or emergence of the yantra.

In the eight spaces between the eight inner petals of the lotus are the following *śaktis*, beginning in the east and going clockwise: Anaṅga-rūpā-devī, Anaṅga-madanā-devī, Bhuvana-vegā-devī, Bhuvana-pālikā-devī, Sarva-śiśira-devī, Anaṅga-vedanā-devī, and Anaṅga-mekalā-devī. Several of these goddesses are also forms of Rati. In the sixteen petals of the outer lotus there are the following *śaktis*, beginning in the east and proceeding clockwise to the south: Karālinī (dreadful), Vikarālinī (very dreadful), Umā, Sarasvatī, Śrī, Durgā, Uṣas, Lakṣmī, Śruti, Smṛti, Dhṛti (the power of support), Śraddhā, Medhā (merit), Mati (right discernment), Kānti (beauty), and Āryā (nobility).

In the outer rectangle, at the four gates and the four corners, are the following deities: Indra (east), Agni (southeast), Yama (south), Nirṛti (southwest), Varuṇa (west), Vāyu (northwest), Soma (north), and Iśāna (northeast). Brahmā is between the east and northeast and Ananta between the west and southwest, representing, perhaps, the zenith and the underworld. The ten Lokapālas (guardians of the directions) and their *vāhanas* ("vehicles," usually animals) and weapons are also spread around this outer perimeter. Their weapons are the *vajra*, *śakti*, *daṇḍa*, *khaḍga*, *pāśa*, *aṅkuśa*, *gada*, *śūla*, *padma*, and *cakra*.

Yantras are used in different religious contexts for different reasons. A yantra may be inscribed on a silver, gold, or copper plate and be set up for worship in a temple or in a private home. Generally *pūjā* done to such a permanent form of the yantra is of the sixteen-part type. In that case the yantra is worshiped as a whole, as the goddess herself, and not in all its particulars. The yantra also may be constructed on paper and, with some personal modifications made by a competent guru, be worn on the body as an amulet or as a portable *mūrti* (image) of the goddess for purposes of worship.

The yantra is also used for individual tantric *sādhanā*. In this case the general aim of the *sādhaka* is "to identify with the deity, in this case Bhuvaneśvarī, and in doing so to obtain the powers that are in her store."[28] In this type of *pūjā*, the yantra is worshiped in each of its individual parts. That is, each of the *śaktis*, goddesses, or deities is individually worshiped by the invocation of a mantra, in this case, often the Bhuvaneśvarī mantra. The worship of the yantra itself is preceded by rituals of purification that include banishing inimical spirits and invoking guardian deities. The sequence in which the elements in the yantra are invoked may vary, and the actual worship may be either mental (in which case the yantra is imagined to reside in the *sādhaka's* heart) or outward and physical. In the *Tantrasāra* and *Śākta-pramoda*, the Bhuvaneśvarī yantra is described from the center outward, and the deities are invoked in clockwise order. That is, the yantra represents the emergence of the cosmos in a spiraling, clockwise fashion. The invocation and worship of the different elements, then, reiterate the creation of the world.

There is some indication, however, that the yantra (or at least the yantras of some of the other Mahāvidyās) may be worshiped from the outside inward, and in a counterclockwise, inwardly spiraling order. In the *Mantra-mahodadhiḥ*, for example, the Tārā yantra is worshiped from outside to inside, although each layer or covering is worshiped in a clockwise direction.[29] For the Chinnamastā yantra, worship is prescribed from outside to inside. "Worship of Chinnamastā Devī should begin from the outer-most covering and proceed in an inverse order."[30] In such cases the theme of "going against the stream" comes to mind. In classical yoga, the practitioner de-creates the various elements of *prakṛti*, going against the natural rhythms of creation, in an attempt to still or transcend the limitations of the physical world. Classical yoga is the process of dissolving the creation in order to transcend it.

Tantric yoga aims to unite the practitioner with the deity. When worship proceeds from the outside of the yantra to the inside, we might think of the *sādhaka* as distilling or reducing the creation to a single point, the central *bindu* or seed mantra of the goddess. Having thereby concentrated the goddess's essence, the adept then identifies with that.

The basic shapes and design of the yantra are significant. The triangle and lotus dominate the yantras of all ten Mahāvidyās, and in this respect the Bhuvaneśvarī yantra is typical. The triangle, particularly when pointing downward, is a symbol of the yoni and symbolizes creation, generation, and reproduction. The lotus, too, is a creative symbol in Indian religion and in Tantrism also represents the yoni. It is often a symbol of the living cosmos, which is understood to be organic in nature. The blossoming lotus is likened to the maturing, emerging cosmos. As the seat of a deity or spiritual being, the lotus also denotes spiritual authority and command, spiritual perfection, purity, and completeness. Both the triangle and the lotus can be understood as female symbols of growth, emergence, and life energy.

The outer layers or coverings are the same in all the Mahāvidyā yantras, square or rectangular. These outer coverings, which constitute the four gates or means of access to the interior, are inhabited by armed male deities. In general structure, then, the yantra has a male-dominated, square outer perimeter, within which is a female-dominated, circular, and triangular center. The inner petals and points are dominated by female beings, and many of them, particularly in the Bhuvaneśvarī yantra, are forms of Rati, consort of Kāma, the god of desire. That is, the inner dynamics of the yantra are female oriented and erotic, while the outer layers or coverings (*āvaraṇas*) are male oriented and associated with weapons. We might think of the overall structure of the yantra as presenting a vision of the world in which an armed, male-dominated exterior protects a female-dominated interior that is sexually dynamic. At the very center, of course, is the *bindu*, which represents female and male (Śakti and Śiva) in harmonious tension or balance.

Bhuvaneśvarī's Beauty, Attractiveness, and Symbols

Bhuvaneśvarī's beauty is mentioned often. The *Tantrasāra* describes her as having a golden complexion and a beautiful face, framed with flowing hair the color of black bees. Her eyes are broad, her lips full and red, her nose delicate. Her firm breasts are smeared with sandal paste and saffron. Her waist is thin, and her thighs, buttocks, and navel are lovely. Her beautiful throat is decorated with ornaments, and her arms are made for embracing. Śiva is said to have produced a third eye to view her more thoroughly.[31] In her hundred-name *stotra* (hymn) in the *Śākta-pramoda*, she is said to be a beautiful young girl, to have a smiling face, and to have an attractive sexual organ. She is said to be the triangle itself (the schematic representation of the yoni).[32]

The beauty and attractiveness of Bhuvaneśvarī might be understood as an affirmation of the physical world. *Śākta* and tantric thought and practice do not denigrate the world or consider it illusory or delusory, as do some other aspects of Indian thought. Tantra has a strong strain of world affirmation, which insists that underlying all of reality is the power, the *śakti*, of ultimate reality. The physical world, the rhythms of creation, maintenance, and destruction, even self-infatuation and the hankerings and sufferings of the human condition, are all affirmed to be Bhuvaneśvarī's play, her exhilarating, joyous sport.

Bhuvaneśvarī never ceases to attend to the world, and this is the reason, one author states, that she has three eyes.[33] She nourishes the world that she oversees and protects. Indeed, she is said to be food itself, on which all creatures depend. Her smiling face reveals her gracious attitude toward the world and all those creatures who depend upon her for sustenance.[34] The gestures of conferring boons and removing fear also express her gracious attitude toward the world, particularly toward her devotees.

The goad and noose held by Bhuvaneśvarī suggest control. According to an informant in Varanasi, the goad means that she controls evil forces or inner hindrances, such as anger, lust, and any obsession that interferes with spiritual development. The noose, according to the same informant, symbolizes the different bodily sheaths that hide, and therefore bind, the spiritual essence of a person, the *ātman*. The goddess therefore helps discipline the devotee with her goad, while at the same time she is the power that masks one's true identity. She is both liberating knowledge and *māyā*; she both gives liberation and withholds it. Another source interprets the goad, the noose, and the two hand gestures (conferring boons and fearlessness) in terms of the stages in spiritual endeavor, *sādhanā:* the noose and goad help *sādhakas* control their *indriyas* (sensory perceptions), and when this is accomplished through her grace, they achieve fearlessness and receive blessings from her. Dharma, or proper moral behavior, is also a form of control, and Bhuvaneśvarī uses it to guide people. In this sense her noose and goad may symbolize dharma.[35]

The red lotus and jeweled drinking bowl full of jewels that she holds are symbols of growth and wealth. The jewels represent abundance and riches, while the lotus represents the vigor inherent in the living world.

Fig. 21. Bhuvaneśvarī, by Molaram, late eighteenth century, Garẘahl, Himachal Pradesh. Bharat Kala Bhavan, Benares Hindu University, Varanasi.

Bhuvaneśvarī also wears the crescent moon on her forehead, which, according to an informant in Varanasi, represents the power of replenishment. This symbolizes that Bhuvaneśvarī is the inner essence of the created world, which empowers it to continue to reproduce itself endlessly with renewed vitality.

Like many deities, and spiritual masters, Bhuvaneśvarī sits on a lotus. This suggests a commanding position and also the seat from which creation sometimes takes place. Brahmā, for example, sits on a lotus growing from Viṣṇu's navel, and from this powerful and dynamic seat he creates the world. Tripura-sundarī, similarly, sits on a lotus and represents the creation as well as the cause of creation. The lotus seat symbolizes spiritual mastery and triumph as well: perfection that is grounded in the world like the roots of a lotus, and yet transcends that world. It is a symbol of authority, purity, and transcendence. Bhuvaneśvarī is called She Who Wanders in the Physical World, but she is also called, in the same hymn, She Who Wanders in the Void.[36] She is the world but also transcends it, as its source and as its container at dissolution.

Devotion to Bhuvaneśvarī, finally, is said to bring the devotee auspiciousness, the power of attracting and controlling others, the power of *vak siddhi* (according to which anything one says happens), and victory over enemies. In this respect, her worship emphasizes gaining material success and well-being, which is appropriate for a goddess who is so strongly identified with the physical world.

Chinnamastā

The Self-Decapitated Goddess

Victory to the light of the world, giver of a good ending to the universe, to her whose forehead is lovely with charming locks.[1]

I meditate upon the Goddess Chinnamastā who is seated in the centre of the Sun's disk and holds in her left hand her own severed head with gaping mouth, her hair is dishevelled and she is drinking the stream of blood gushing out from her own neck. She is seated on Rati and Kāmadeva who are engaged in sexual dalliance, and she is rejoicing with her friends Dākinī and Varṇinī.[2]

She stands in an aggressive manner with her leg put forward. She is holding her own severed head in one hand and a sword in the other. She is naked and happily drinks the blood that gushes from her headless body. She has three eyes and is adorned with a blue lotus at her heart. One should meditate on Chinnamastā, who has the complexion of a red hibiscus flower. She stands on Kāma and Rati, who are joined in sexual intercourse. To her right is Varṇinī, who is possessed by *rajas guṇa*, who is white in color, with loose hair, and who holds a sword and a skull cup. She happily drinks the blood gushing from the *devī*'s severed neck. On her left is Dākinī, who also drinks blood flowing from Chinnamastā's headless body. She is possessed by *tamas guṇa* and enjoys the world in its state of dissolution. One should meditate on this goddess who bestows blessings on her devotees.[3]

Possible Prototypes

Chinnamastā does not have a widespread independent cult in Hinduism and does not seem to have had a very developed history prior

Fig. 22. Chinnamastā, contemporary lithograph.

to her appearance as one of the Mahāvidyās. Like Tārā, however, she also appears in tantric Buddhism, where she is known as Vajra-yoginī (discussed below). Although we are unable to find early references to Chinnamastā or evidence of an early cult associated with her, certain goddesses, or images of female beings, have been suggested as her prototypes because of some peculiarity they share with her, such as being headless, naked, bloodthirsty, or violent.[4]

Several examples have been discovered in India of nude goddesses squatting or with their thighs spread to display their sexual organs. These figures, some very ancient, usually depicted in stone bas-relief, often have their arms raised above their bodies and are headless or faceless. Their headless condition is not the result of subsequent damage but an intentional part of the image. The combination of nudity and headlessness, it has been suggested, may indicate that Chinnamastā had an ancient prototype in India.[5] The arresting iconographic feature of these images is their sexual organs, which are openly displayed. If the headlessness of the figures suggests death or self-destruction, it lacks the force of the Chinnamastā icon. More likely, the headlessness of the nude figures simply focuses attention on their generative physiology and creativity. Although the Chinnamastā image includes an emphasis on sexual activity, life, and nourishment (discussed below), the central iconographic characteristic of the goddess is her shocking self-decapitation.

Other nude goddess figures have been suggested as possible prototypes of Chinnamastā. One of these is the fierce, wild goddess Koṭavī. Koṭavī is usually associated with battlefields and is sometimes included among the lists of Mātṛkās.[6] Sometimes she is an opponent of Viṣṇu, and the *Viṣṇu-purāṇa* (5.32–33) and *Bhāgavata-purāṇa* (10.63.20) describe her as naked, disheveled, and of such disgusting appearance that Viṣṇu has to turn his head away from her lest he become incensed by her. In this myth she tries to protect the demon Baṇāsura, who is her son in the *Bhāgavata-purāṇa* account. Although descriptions of Koṭavī emphasize her nudity and wild appearance, she seems quite different in character from Chinnamastā. Her typical haunt is the battlefield, not the cremation ground (although both are places of death), and she seems to be a fierce demoness whose primary role is to terrify or distract enemies during battle. Her character is usually malevolent. Chinnamastā's character is fierce, but not necessarily malevolent, and although in her thousand-name hymn she is associated with the battlefield,[7] she is rarely shown there in her iconography.

A South Indian hunting goddess called Korravai is similar in name and character to Koṭavī. She is fierce, bloodthirsty, and wild. She receives blood sacrifices and haunts the battlefield, where she grants victory. Again, it has been suggested that she may be another expression of the type of goddess that inspired Chinnamastā.[8] Chinnamastā, however, is not usually described as a warrior goddess, and what rivets the viewer's attention is her self-decapitation. Although in her thousand-name hymns Chinnamastā is said to like blood, and at her few shrines and temples she receives blood sacrifices, the emphasis with Chinnamastā, unlike Korravai, is not so much on her demanding and receiving blood as on her giving her own blood to her devotees.

There are, in fact, many goddesses and spirits in the Hindu tradition who haunt battlefields, are nude, fierce, and bloodthirsty, or have a strong association with fertility, all of which relate to aspects of the goddess Chinnamastā. Chinnamastā, however, seems to be the only goddess who decapitates herself in order to nourish her devotees.

Origin Myths

I have discovered four accounts of Chinnamastā's origin or emergence. The first two are in written texts and are very similar, while the third and fourth, both very brief, I have found only in oral versions.

Version 1 is found in the *Prāṇatoṣinī-tantra*, which in turn attributes the story to the *Nārada-pāñcarātra*.

> One day Pārvatī went to bathe in the Mandākinī River . . . with her attendants, Jayā and Vijayā. After bathing, the great goddess's color became black because she was sexually aroused. After some time, her two attendants asked her, "Give us some food. We are hungry." She replied, "I shall give you food but please wait." After awhile, again they asked her. She replied, "Please wait, I am thinking about some matters." Waiting awhile, they implored her, "You are the mother of the universe. A child asks everything from her mother. The mother gives her children not only food but also coverings for the body. So that is why we are praying to you for food. You are known for your mercy; please give us food." Hearing this, the consort of Śiva told them that she would give anything when they reached home. But again her two attendants, Ḍākinī and Varṇinī, begged her, "We are overpowered with hunger, O Mother of the Universe. Give us food so we may be satisfied, O Merciful One, Bestower of Boons and Fulfiller of Desires."
>
> Hearing this true statement, the merciful goddess smiled and severed her head with her fingernails. As soon as she severed her head, her head fell on the palm of her left hand. Three bloodstreams emerged from her

> throat; the left and right fell respectively into the mouths of her flanking attendants and the center fell into her mouth. After performing this, all were satisfied and later returned home. (From this act) Pārvatī became known as Chinnamastā.[9]

The second version of the origin of Chinnamastā is also from the *Prāṇatoṣinī-tantra*, which in this case attributes the story to the *Svatantra-tantra*. The story is told by Śiva:

> I shall tell you of the emergence of Chinnamastā. In the Kṛta Yuga on Mt. Kailāsa, the best of mountains, Mahāmāyā was engaged in Mahāvrata with me (sexual intercourse). At the time of my seminal emission, she appeared fierce and from her body two *śaktis* emerged who became her two attendants known as Dākinī and Varṇinī. One day Caṇḍanāyikā with her two attendants went to the bank of the Puṣpabhadrā River. When it was noon, her hungry attendants asked Caṇḍikā, "Please give us food." Hearing this, the smiling and auspicious Caṇḍikā looked in all directions and severed her head. With the left bloodstream, she satisfied Dākinī, with the right one, she satisfied Varṇinī and from the center one, she drank her own blood. After playing in this way, she replaced her head on her body and assumed her original form. At dusk, they returned home. When I saw her pale appearance, I suspected that she was abused by another. This infuriated me. From this anger a portion of me arose and became known as Krodha Bhairava. This happened on the day of Vīrarātri. Thus Chinnamastā was born on Vīrarātri.[10]

This version is also told in the *Śaktisaṁgama-tantra* (which attributes it to the *Prāṇatoṣinī-tantra*), but with a few additional details. According to this text, the goddess was in reverse sexual intercourse with Śiva (she was on top), and she dismounted Śiva before he ejaculated. Her attendants appeared when she went outside. This text says that at the river the goddess and her attendants played in the water for some time. The rest of the story is the same as the *Prāṇatoṣinī* account.[11]

A third version was told to me by Rama Shankar Tripathi of the Kāśī Viśvanāth temple in Varanasi, who said that it had been told to him by a friend of his who is a tantric *sādhaka*. In a war between the gods and demons, the gods realized they could not win, and so they prayed to Mahāśakti, the Great Goddess, for help. She was pleased with their prayer and asked Pracaṇḍacaṇḍikā to help them. After killing all the demons, Pracaṇḍacaṇḍikā remained enraged and cut off her own head and drank her own blood. Pracaṇḍacaṇḍikā is the first name given to Chinnamastā in her thousand-name hymn in the *Śākta-pramoda*.

Swami Sadhananda Sastri, a *śākta* practioner in Varanasi, told me the fourth version. Chinnamastā appeared, he said, after the gods and demons churned the ocean. Chinnamastā took the demons' share of the resulting *amṛta* (the nectar of immortality) and drank it herself. Then she killed herself by cutting off her own head, to deprive the demons of their share of immortality. This is how she enabled the gods to achieve their superior position.

Implications of the Origin Myths

These origin myths highlight certain themes that are important in interpreting Chinnamastā. Like several other Mahāvidyās, she is associated with Śiva. In the first two stories, she is said to be Pārvatī. She also acts independently of Śiva or dominates him. In the second version of the story, she engages in reverse sexual intercourse with him and dismounts him before he ejaculates. There is no explicit mention of tension between the two (although this might be implied in her dismounting Śiva before he ejaculates), but she is depicted as dominant sexually.

In the third version of her emergence, Chinnamastā slays demons for the benefit of the world. A common theme in goddess mythology, as in the *Devī-māhātmya*, stresses the impotence of the male deities, who must call on the goddess for help. Chinnamastā assumes the protective role of an *avatāra*. In this particular case, though, she is described as becoming so enraged that she loses control and cuts off her own head. This theme of a goddess getting out of control after battle, usually because she is intoxicated from drinking the blood of her victims, is also familiar. Kālī sometimes dances in a drunken frenzy after battle and has to be brought to her senses by her husband, Śiva. The Saptamātṛkās (seven mothers) who help Durgā defeat Śumbha and Niśumbha in the third episode of the *Devī-māhātmya* also are said to dance wildly after killing demons and becoming drunk on their blood (8.62).[12] In version 3, Chinnamastā is understood as an ambivalent figure. She is powerful and effective in battle, able to defeat the demons and rescue the gods, but she is dangerous. When her fury is unleashed, it can be indiscriminately destructive, indeed, self-destructive. In this account Chinnamastā is not directly connected with Śiva. She is more closely connected with Durgā, Kālī, and the Mātṛkās and with the theme of preserving cosmic order.

In the fourth account of Chinnamastā's origin, the theme of maintaining cosmic stability by combating demons remains central. But this version introduces the theme of self-sacrifice. In version 3 the goddess decapitates herself inadvertently, in a fit of frenzy, while in version 4 she does so as a gesture of self-sacrifice for the gods. Her action here is reminiscent of Śiva's saving the world by drinking the poison stirred up at the churning of the ocean. In both cases a deity acts selflessly to protect the world, at the cost of personal harm.

The first two accounts emphasize maternal self-sacrifice. In both accounts, the reason for Chinnamastā's act of self-decapitation is the hunger of her two companions. Although initially she tries to put them off, eventually she feeds them on her blood, which she releases by cutting off her own head. In demanding to be fed, the companions address her, in the first account, as Mother of the Universe, challenging her to satisfy them. What is striking about the myth is that she chooses to feed them, not from her breasts, but with her blood, released in an act of violence. Instead of drinking her maternal milk, they drink her life blood.

Closely related to the theme of self-sacrifice in the first two versions is the theme of nourishment. These accounts stress the hunger of her companions. They look to her for satisfaction, which they receive in dramatic fashion. The myths tend to downplay the violence or drama of her cutting off her own head. In both accounts, after having a nice meal, which Chinnamastā herself partakes of by drinking from the middle stream of blood, she puts her head back on, and they all go home. The only aftereffect seems to be that she has acquired a somewhat pale complexion, which upsets Śiva. The story is mainly about hunger and its satisfaction. The self-sacrificing, nourishing intent of Chinnamastā is emphasized by P. Pal: "The obvious implication here is of primal sacrifice and renewal of creation. The goddess sacrifices herself, and her blood, drunk by her attendants, renews or resuscitates the universe. . . . Therefore beheading her own head is a temporary expedient to provide food and appears to be a more sanguinary manifestation of the goddess as Śākambharī [she who bears vegetables] and Annapūrṇā [she who is full of food]."[13]

The origin (or emergence) myths of Chinnamastā touch on several themes that are significant in her symbolism and worship. Other important themes in her iconography, however, are not mentioned in her myths. Her iconography and worship, although elaborating on some of the themes above, also suggest new ones that further enrich her religious significance.

Head Offerings

The Chinnamastā icon is dominated by severed heads. Particularly arresting is the goddess's own severed head, which she herself has cut off. Her two companions, Ḍākinī and Varṇinī (sometimes referred to as Jayā and Vijayā), standing on either side of her, are also often holding severed heads. All three heads are typically on platters of the type used in making offerings. In fact, the imagery of offering a head is unmistakable in many iconographic representations of Chinnamastā.

Animal sacrifice is fairly common in the Hindu tradition, and the typical way of killing the victim is to decapitate it. Indeed, since the Vedic period (when animal sacrifice to both male and female deities was common), most blood sacrifices have been to goddesses. In contemporary Hinduism, which inherits a tradition that is many hundreds of years old, blood sacrifice almost invariably is associated with certain goddesses. Daily sacrifices are made at many goddess temples, usually of goats and chickens. In almost all cases, the animal's head is cut off and offered to the image of the goddess, often on a platter. Hindu texts sometimes mention human sacrifice, and there are examples of its having been done in the past for certain goddesses.[14]

There is also a tradition of voluntarily offering one's head to a goddess. The eleventh-century C.E. Tamil text *Kalingattuparaṇi* contains a gruesome description of a Kālī temple in South India: "Like the roaring sound of ocean waves, the shouts of heroes offering their heads in return for the bestowal of boons were echoing all over the area."[15] In another passage from this text, "the process of offering a head is portrayed. The sacrificer cut his head at the bottom of the neck and placed it on the hands of Kālī. The head thus presented sang the greatness of Kālī while the remaining trunk stood saluting the Goddess."[16] In Pallava sculpture particularly, but elsewhere as well,[17] the theme is quite common, although whether the sculptures depict actual devotional suicide by self-decapitation is not certain. In Kṣemendra's *Bṛhatkāthamañjarī*, a washerman and his brother-in-law cut off their heads in a fit of devotional fervor to the goddess Gaurī. An inscription dated 991 C.E. from the Kannada area tells of a loyal subject named Katega, who offered his head to the goddess Guṇḍadabbe to fulfill a vow when the king succeeded in fathering a son.[18] In the Tamil epic *Śilappadihāram*, the goddess Aiyai, who is worshiped by hunters, receives blood sacrifices and accepts the blood that flows from the severed heads of her devotees.[19]

There is also a story associated with the Jvālāmukhī temple in Himachal Pradesh that features a head offering. A devotee of the goddess Jvālāmukhī named Dhyanu wished to visit her temple but was prohibited by the emperor Akbar, who claimed the goddess had no power. The emperor permitted Dhyanu to proceed if he agreed to leave his horse behind and permit Akbar to kill it. If the goddess was able to revive the horse, Akbar said, he would spare Dhyanu's life. Dhyanu accepted the challenge. Akbar duly killed his horse and locked the body in a room. At Jvālāmukhī's temple, Dhyanu did devotion to the goddess, but she did not appear or answer his pleas to prove her power to the emperor. In desperation, Dhyanu decided to offer his own head to the goddess. Taking a sword, he was about to cut off his head, when she appeared and granted him the boon of restoring his horse to life. In some versions of the tale, Dhyanu actually cuts off his head, which the goddess subsequently restores. This is the version usually shown in pictures, Dhyanu kneeling in front of the goddess, offering her his head on a platter. Just outside the entrance of the Bajreśvarī-devī temple in Kangra is a sculpted head said to be that of Dhyanu. A large tableau in a recessed niche of the temple also depicts this incident. Dhyanu kneels before the goddess holding his severed head in his two hands. The practice of cutting out one's tongue, I was told, is done to this day at Jvālāmukhī temple. Just as the goddess restored Dhyanu's head, so she is supposed to restore the devotee's tongue in recognition of his or her devotion.

A story similar to Dhyanu's is associated with the Maihar-devī temple near Allahabad in Uttar Pradesh. Once upon a time, there was a wrestler who wished to achieve supremacy in his chosen vocation. He propitiated the goddess for a long time, but she did not appear to him. In desperation and determination, he cut off his own head as a final act of devotion to her. The goddess then appeared and, pleased with his devotional sincerity, reattached his head.

In the Chinnamastā icon, the theme of devotional head offering to a goddess is, of course, reversed. It is the goddess who offers her head to her devotees, who in turn sometimes seem to be offering heads to her. The self-decapitating impulse is attributed to the goddess herself rather than to her devotees.

Heads as Power Objects

The Chinnamastā icon raises questions about detached heads,[20] which also play an important role in the iconography and *sādhanā* of other Mahāvidyās. Kālī, Tārā, and others often wear garlands of severed heads or skulls. Tārā's crest is decorated with skulls. Kālī and Tārā nearly always hold a freshly severed head in one hand. The heads are often said to have belonged to enemies who were killed by the goddess in question. But sometimes they are said to represent the letters of the alphabet, particularly when the heads number fifty or fifty-two and are threaded as a garland around a goddess's neck. As sounds or letters they are sometimes referred to as *matṛkās*, "mothers." They give birth to the creation in the form of sound, that is. They are also said to represent, especially in the case of Kālī and Tārā, who hold heads in their lower left hands, the chopped off bonds that prevented a *sādhaka* from achieving spiritual success.

Heads, or more usually skulls, are also commonly used in tantric *sādhanā*. The cremation ground at Tārāpīṭh in Bengal is highly favored by *tāntrikas*, partly because of the ready availability of both skulls and corpses (as many as 60 percent of the dead here are buried rather than cremated). One scholar comments:

> The disruption of graves [the same ground is used repeatedly for burials] also leads to the digging up of many human skulls. *Muṇḍāsanas*, or seats on skulls, are the most favoured *asanas* for Tantric *sādhanā*, and their availability in a place heightens the attraction to *sādhakas*. In Tārāpīṭh about ten *sadhus* of various kinds reside in and around the cremation ground, some of whom collect the skulls for use in their daily routines. Most have five neatly arranged skulls in their huts, each decorated with flowers and a *tilaka* (coloured marking between the eyebrows, or sockets in this case). One *sadhu* had built an entire wall of his hut out of skulls using mud as mortar, and another wandered about the village with a skull as a begging bowl.[21]

It seems clear that in some sense skulls and severed heads are power objects containing special qualities, particularly for ritual purposes. Their use in iconography to represent letters or sounds, the "seeds" from which all creation proceeds, is no doubt connected to the head and mouth as the source of language or sound. The head as the chief of the body's parts also houses the person's essential being. Without the head, a person is without identity. This is made clear in stories concerning transposed heads in which the identity of the person follows the head, not the rest of the body.[22] In some cases devotees may use skulls as seats, bowls, or ritual implements, in imitation of Śiva himself as Kāpālika, "the one who bears a skull." In this case, the skull represents something powerfully polluted, because in Śaivite mythology the skull is that of Brahmā, whom Śiva has decapitated. It represents the heinous crime of Brahmacide and sticks to Śiva's hand until, after eons, he atones for the act.[23] Skulls and severed heads also may represent "the forbidden." They are "out of place," liminal objects. They belong somewhere else, with a body. They are "out of bounds," which is where tantric *sādhakas* want to get. There, "out of bounds," *sādhakas* can transform themselves, unhampered by social limits and constraints.

The chopped-off head also may represent liberation, a particular state of expanded, awakened consciousness. This interpretation is particularly likely in the Buddhist context, which we will discuss below.

Overcoming Desire

Another particularly striking feature of the Chinnamastā icon is often mentioned in her *dhyāna* mantras and *stotras:* she stands on the copulating couple Kāma and Rati. Kāma (whose name means "sexual desire") and Rati (whose name means "sexual intercourse") are almost always shown having sex with Rati on top, the same position Kālī assumes with Śiva. They are usually shown lying on a lotus, but sometimes on a cremation pyre. There are two quite different interpretations of this aspect of Chinnamastā iconography. One interpretation understands it as a symbol of control of sexual desire, the other as a symbol of the goddess's embodiment of sexual energy.

Certainly the most common interpretation of Chinnamastā's standing (or sometimes sitting) on Kāma and Rati is that she is defeating what they represent, namely, sexual desire, sexual energy, sexual force. She symbolizes self-control, which must be achieved before undertaking successful yogic practice. Swami Annapurnananda of the Ramakrishna Math in Varanasi told me that Chinnamastā sacrifices herself to her devotees in a great act of love for them and is able to do this because she has overcome or controlled sexual and selfish desires, as is symbolized by her standing on Kāma and Rati.[24] She represents yogic control and repression of sexual energy. In her hundred-name hymn in the *Śākta-pramoda*, she is called Yoginī (female yogi) and Yoganiratā (she who practices yoga).[25] The same hymn also calls her Madanāturā (she who cannot be overcome by Kāma),[26] suggesting her control of sexual desire. In her hymn of one-thousand names, she is called Yogamārgapradāyinī (she who bestows the yogic path, name 745), Yogagamāyā (follower of yoga, name 747), Yogamayī (she who embodies yoga, name 751), and Yogānandapradāyinī (she who gives bliss through yoga, name 759).[27]

One commentator on this aspect of the Chinnamastā icon has argued that her worship is particularly appropriate for those in the military. An effective warrior must overcome lust and the desire to indulge in sexual play before committing himself to battle. In battle, he must cultivate an attitude of self-surrender so that he can give his life freely for the benefit of others. Both of these themes are embodied in Chinnamastā, he says. Her control of lust is represented by her standing on Kāma and Rati, and her perfection of self-surrender, fearlessness of death, and self-sacrifice for others is seen by her cutting off her own head to feed her hungry companions.[28] The same commentator says that devotion to Chinnamastā is both dangerous and rare. It is dangerous because it demands much of the devotee, namely, renouncing sexual desire and cultivating self-surrender for the benefit of others. He also says that only those of heroic nature worship Chinnamastā, and those of heroic nature are particularly apt to be found in the military.[29] Her nudity, according to this commentator, represents truthfulness and heedlessness, yielding oneself to danger for others. The worshiper of Chinnamastā perfects self-control, if not self-annihilation, and in this way becomes a very effective warrior. Her thousand-name hymn, in fact, calls her Raṇotkaṇṭhā (battle cry, name 768), Raṇasthā (battlefield, name 769), and Raṇajaitrī (victorious in war, name 772).[30] It also calls her the slayer of various demons.

Sexual Vitality

A quite different interpretation of the presence of Kāma and Rati in the Chinnamastā icon emphasizes that the goddess is being charged with the sexual power of the copulating couple. On the analogy of a lotus seat conferring its qualities and power on a deity, Chinnamastā may be thought of as acquiring the sexual energy of the copulating couple upon whom she stands or sits. Surging up through her body, which is usually described as a naked, sixteen-year-old girl's, that energy gushes out of her head in the form of blood to feed her devotees and replenish herself. In this interpretation the copulating couple is not opposed to the goddess but an integral part of a rhythmic flow of energy symbolized by sex and blood.

Reinforcing this interpretation are images or descriptions of Chinnamastā sitting, rather than standing, on Rati and Kāma (figure 23).[31] In this type of image, it is less likely that Chinnamastā is to be understood

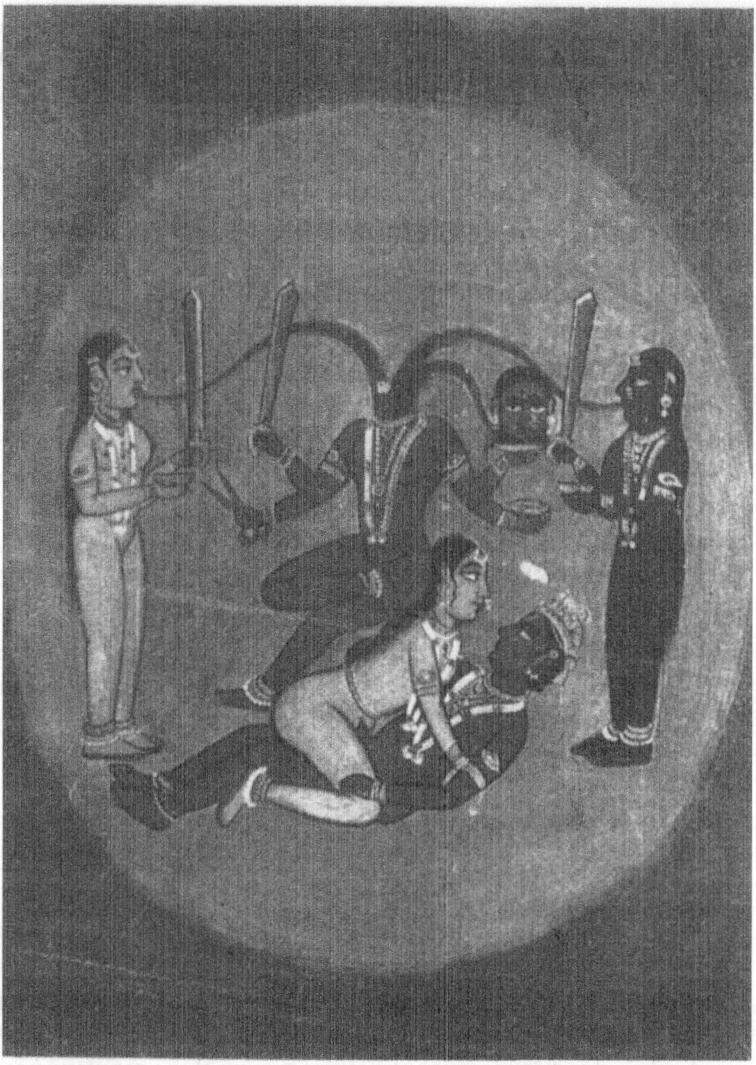

Fig. 23. Chinnamastā, by Bhatuk Ramprasad, early twentieth century. Printed with the permission of Dr. Bhanu Shanker Mehta, Varanasi.

as overcoming or suppressing the copulating couple. In still other renderings of Chinnamastā, she is shown squatting above Śiva, having sexual intercourse with him (figure 24). In these images Kāma and Rati have been replaced with Śiva. It is clear that Śiva is not being suppressed, defeated, or overcome. The goddess is on top of him, to be sure, but this is typical in tantric imagery, indicating the priority of the goddess; there is no suggestion of yogic suppression of sexual desire. Śiva is not being suppressed by the goddess; he is being energized by her.

The sexual themes in Chinnamastā's iconography are reinforced by the fact that *klīm*, the seed syllable of the deity Kāma, the god of sexual lust (and also, appropriately, the seed syllable of Kṛṣṇa), features in Chinnamastā's mantra: "Śrīm hrīm klīm aim Vajravairocanīye hum hum phat svāhā."[32] It is equally relevant to note that the invocation of this mantra is said to attract and subjugate women.[33] Chinnamastā's erotic nature is also suggested in some of the names contained in her hundred- and thousand-name hymns. In her hundred-name hymn she is called Kāmeśvarī (goddess of desire, name 76), Kāmarūpa (she whose form is desire, name 79), and Kāmakautukakāriṇī (she who creates the eagerness of desire, name 81).[34] In her thousand-name hymn she is called Madonmatta-svarūpiṇī (she whose form is intoxicated with delight, name 725), Ratirāga-vivṛddhinī (she who is engaged in the realm of *rati* [sexual intercourse or desire], name 762), and Puṣpāyudhadharā (she who holds a flower weapon [that is, who is like Kāma-deva, the god of lust], name 896).[35]

Symbol of the Living Creation

The Chinnamastā icon conveys the idea of reality as the coincidence of sex and death, creation and destruction, giving and taking. Chinnamastā is probably the most stunning representation in the Hindu pantheon of the truth that life, sex, and death are part of an interdependent, unified system. One writer says: "She simply represents the continued state of self-sustenance of the created world in which are seen continuous self-destruction and self-renewal, in a cyclic order."[36] The stark contrasts in this iconographic scenario—the gruesome decapitation, the copulating couple, the cremation ground, the drinking of fresh blood, all arranged in a delicate, harmonious pattern—jolt the viewer into an awareness of the truths that life feeds on death, is nourished by death, and necessitates death and that the ultimate destiny of sex is to perpetuate more life, which in turn will decay and die in order to feed more life. As arranged in most renditions of the icon, the lotus and the copulating couple appear to channel a powerful life force into the goddess, who is standing or sitting on the back of the copulating woman. The couple enjoying sex convey an insistent, vital urge to the goddess; they seem to

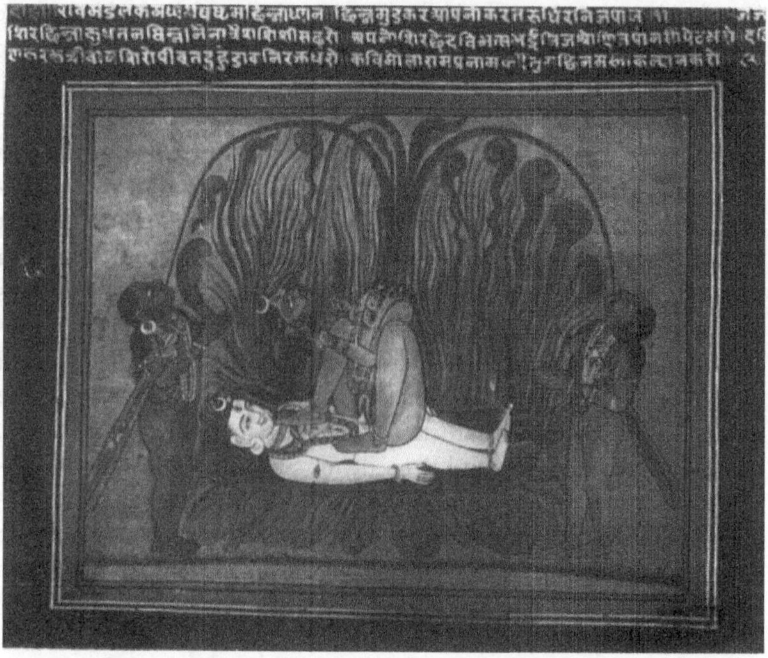

Fig. 24. Chinnamastā, by Molaram, late eighteenth century, Garwahl, Himachal Pradesh. Bharat Kala Bhavan, Benares Hindu University, Varanasi.

pump her with energy. And at the top, like an overflowing fountain, her blood spurts from her severed neck, the life force leaving her, but streaming into the mouths of her devotees (and into her own mouth as well) to nourish and sustain them. The cycle is starkly portrayed: life (the couple making love), death (the decapitated goddess), and nourishment (the flanking *yoginīs* drinking her blood).

Certain other fierce Hindu goddesses, such as Kālī, sever the heads of others to nourish themselves, or devotees offer heads and blood to the goddesses. The offerings may be voluntary (in the case of devotees) or involuntary (in the case of sacrificial victims), but the message is clear that such goddesses like, and probably need, blood. These goddesses, representing the vital forces of the cosmos, need regular nourishment; sacrificing oneself to them is a way of acknowledging that one is obliged to give life back to them because one has received life from them. This imagery conveys the truth that such goddesses are ever hungry, as Kālī's lolling tongue indicates, and demand blood in order to be satisfied.

The Chinnamastā image reverses some of these motifs but ultimately teaches similar truths. She simply represents the alternate phase of an ever-recurring sequence. The cosmic process—the rhythms of creation and destruction, the universal economy—is a harmonious alternation of giving and taking, of life and death. Kālī's need for blood, or conversely the ever-fecund, ever-bountiful nature of goddesses such as Annapūrṇā or Śatākṣī, represents only one aspect of the process of giving and taking. Chinnamastā shockingly presents both aspects together and in such a way that the viewer can grasp the interconnectedness of the different stages in the process. Chinnamastā takes life and vigor from the copulating couple, then gives it away lavishly by cutting off her own head to feed her devotees. Such is the way of a world where life must be sustained by organic matter, where metabolism is maintained only by ingesting the corpses of other beings.

The Upward Flow of the *Kuṇḍalinī*

The Chinnamastā icon also suggests certain aspects of *kuṇḍalinī* yoga, in which spiritual energy is awakened, traverses the subtle body, pierces the different centers of energy called *cakras* in its ascent to the top of the skull, unites with Śiva in the thousand-petaled lotus *cakra*, and then creates a flood of nectar that flows downward, drenching the practitioner in bliss. Chinnamastā, in her hymns and *stotras*, is identified or associated with the *kuṇḍalinī* and this process of spiritual ascent. She is called, for example, Suṣumnāsvarabhāsinī (she who understands the sound of the *suṣumnā nāḍī* [the central channel up which the *kuṇḍalinī* travels], name 803), Sahasradalamadhyasthā (she who is established in the thousand-petaled lotus, name 804), and Sahasradalavarttinī (she who abides in the thousand-petaled lotus, name 805).[37]

A contemporary author is explicit in his identification of Chinnamastā with this process, specifically with the awakened *kuṇḍalinī śakti*. He says that there are knots in the body called *granthis* that keep a person weak, ignorant, and sorrowful. They are located in the *cakras*. When the *kuṇḍalinī* is awakened, she rises through the *cakras* and cuts these knots, freeing the person from their binding effects.[38]

The Chinnamastā icon can be understood as a dramatic representation of this yogic process. In this interpretation, the copulating couple, Kāma and Rati, represent the awakened *kuṇḍalinī* in the *mūlādhāra cakra*.

Like Kāma and Rati, the *kuṇḍalinī* has been aroused. Normally, she sleeps curled up there in the form of a serpent. She is roused by tantric yogic exercises, such as *japa* mantra, *nyāsa*, and *pūjā*. This also might be thought of as the first awakening of one's spiritual consciousness in preparation for a spiritual ascent that will result in infinitely expanded awareness. The blood spurting from Chinnamastā's severed throat represents the upward-flowing *kuṇḍalinī* that has broken through all the knots (*granthis*) of the *cakras* and has cleared the central passage, the *suṣumnā nāḍī*. Her severed head, which she holds in her left hand, in this interpretation represents transcendent consciousness (see also the Buddhist interpretation below). The power of the upward-flowing *kuṇḍalinī*, the power of the rising spiritual consciousness, hits the topmost *cakra*, the thousand-petaled lotus, with such force that it blows her head right off, that is, it transforms all conventional, habitual, limited mental structures. The three jets of downward-flowing blood going into the three mouths, her own and those of her two flanking companions, represent the flow of nectar that drenches the *sādhaka* after the union of *kuṇḍalinī* and Śiva in the topmost *cakra*.

Another related interpretation of Chinnamastā and her two flanking figures, Ḍākinī and Varṇinī, is that they represent the three principal channels, the *nāḍīs*, in the subtle spiritual body. Chinnamastā, the central figure, represents the opened and flowing *suṣumnā nāḍī* achieved by means of spiritual techniques, while Ḍākinī represents the *iḍā nāḍī* and Varṇinī the *piṅgalā nāḍī*.[39]

It is tempting to see in the Chinnamastā icon a further possibility, related to the interpretation of it as a symbol of the rising *kuṇḍalinī*. A common theme in Hindu spirituality is the retention of semen as necessary for spiritual awakening and maturity or as a symbol of spiritual progress. The idea is often expressed in terms of redirecting sexual energy upward instead of downward. The retained semen becomes spiritually potent energy, by means of which a male gains expanded consciousness, spiritual powers, and enlightened awareness.[40]

But what might be the female equivalent of this? In some cases, menstrual blood is seen as the corresponding sexual fluid of women and its release as an expression of sexual power, similar to the release of semen.[41] In some Indian traditions, the flow of menstrual blood is believed to signify that a woman is fertile and desirous of sex. If menstrual blood is the equivalent of male semen for a woman, then the retention of menstrual blood might also result in spiritual awakening and power. When a woman becomes pregnant, menstrual blood ceases to flow, and the result of the retained blood is dramatically evident: a new being is formed inside her. Another dramatic result of retained menstrual blood and pregnancy is the creation of milk in the breasts. It is as if the blood has been transformed into milk. Might not the Chinnamastā image represent the generation of spiritual power in a female, the rising of the *kuṇḍalinī*, by means of the retention of her sexual fluids and the transformation of them into nourishing fluid?

Chinnamuṇḍā and the Buddhist Meditative Tradition

Chinnamastā is prominent in tantric Buddhism and probably was known in Buddhism before her appearance in Hinduism.[42] Buddhist materials usually refer to her as Chinnamuṇḍā or as a form of Vajrayoginī or Vajra-varāhī, but she is clearly identifiable as Chinnamastā. She has decapitated herself, holds her severed head in her left hand, and is feeding her head and two flanking female attendants with three jets of blood from her severed neck. As in Hindu iconography, she and her companions are naked, have disheveled hair, and wear garlands of skulls. Unlike the Hindu depiction of Chinnamastā, however, she is not shown standing or sitting on a copulating couple.

Certain stories concerning Buddhist spiritual masters suggest that Chinnamuṇḍā in the tantric Buddhist context symbolizes spiritual accomplishment, especially the ability to control the "internal winds" or the *kuṇḍalinī* power. This is clear in the story of two female devotees of Kṛṣṇācarya, Mekhalā and Kanakhalā. The two were sisters and resisted the attempts of their parents to marry them off. Instead they retreated from the world to become Buddhist spiritual practitioners. Under the guidance of Kṛṣṇācarya, they soon mastered the most difficult spiritual accomplishments. Subsequently, while trying to convert Lalitacandra, the king of Bengal, to Buddhism, Krsnācarya asked the two girls to chop off their own heads to demonstrate their spiritual mastery and impress the king. They did so and then danced off on a heavenly path through the sky. Following this incident, many spiritual practitioners tried to repeat this feat. Indeed, according to the story, Vajra-varāhī herself appeared in a self-decapitated form, thus lending the practice a certain prestige.[43]

Another Buddhist story describes a female adept's self-decapitation as a magical spiritual power. In the story, a woman devotee of Padmasambhava tells of an incident from one of her past lives. Once upon a time, she displeased her father, who was a king, and he sentenced her to severe punishment. She told him, however, that he need not inflict punishment on her, as she would do so herself. She thereupon decapitated herself with a golden razor and walked around the city holding her head. The citizens of the town called her Chinnamuṇḍā.[44]

In the *Trikāyavajra-yoginī*, a Buddhist text dealing with the worship of Chinnamuṇḍā, the goddess is interpreted, in typically Mahāyāna Buddhist fashion, as a symbol of compassion who destroys worldly suffering: "The red blood which gushes from her severed neck symbolizes compassion and she drinks for peace. She extinguishes the sufferings of the worlds, destroys the four Maras, and severs with her scimitar the mental difficulties."[45] Although the text does not specifically relate the theme of compassion to Chinnamuṇḍā feeding her two female companions with her own blood, its emphasis on her compassion calls to mind the Hindu stories about Chinnamastā's origin, in which she decapitates herself as the direct result of her starving devotees' plea for food.

Getting Rid of False Consciousness

It is tempting to interpret the Chinnamastā icon, particularly the central feature of self-decapitation, in terms of removing false notions, ignorance, and limited consciousness. The iconography and the myths that refer to it are unanimous in asserting that the violent act does not result in the death or destruction of the goddess. Indeed, the Buddhist sources emphasize the magical or spiritual ability involved in being able to cut off one's head without destroying oneself. Particularly in the Buddhist materials, the themes of offering one's head to a goddess and of the goddess's self-sacrifice are weak. The principal interpretation seems to focus on self-decapitation as a spiritual or meditative ability. It is rarely stated in either Hinduism or Buddhism that this ability is related to getting rid of false notions, although this is implied when the self-decapitation is associated with the awakening of the *kuṇḍalinī*. One Buddhist text, however, explicitly links cutting off one's head and gaining spiritual wisdom. The tale concerns a disciple of Milarepa, Gam-po-pa, and his attempts to gain enlightenment.

Thereupon Gam-po-pa set up his hermitage three miles removed from Milarepa's cave and began meditating. After six weeks, he had visions; the first day the Buddha appeared, the second day a *maṇḍala*, and so on. Each time, he reported his visions to Milarepa, who kept on saying, "It is nothing! Go back to your practise." After a few more weeks, Gam-po-pa had a vivid vision of all six worlds, and naturally he thought that he had hit the mark. He ran to Milarepa to report, but Milarepa was at the time sleeping. The excited meditator woke up the master, and narrated the wonderful vision. Milarepa merely said, "Let me sleep! I am not a scholar like you. But I know that the Prajñāpāramitā says all this is mere illusion. I suggest that you go back and practise!" Gam-po-pa, crestfallen and frustrated, returned to his meditation. At length, he dreamt one day that he had cut off his own head and that he saw it rolling down the hill. Thereafter there were no more visions, for the root of "ātmagraha" [egoism] was cut off.[46]

In both Hinduism and Buddhism, false consciousness represents the obstacle to liberation or enlightenment. To awaken, to become enlightened, to realize the underlying nature of reality, is to overcome an ego-centered view of the world, according to which the individual is at the center of the universe and reality is understood as specially arranged to be at the ego's disposal. To be ego ridden is to be under the veil of *māyā* (self-infatuation). The image of cutting off one's own head might be taken as a dramatic rendering of the enlightenment process: the adept or devotee completely destroys false consciousness by "decapitating" himself or herself, getting rid of his or her own ego-ridden mind, which was the hindrance to a true apprehension of reality.

Worship of Chinnamastā

Tantric manuals such as the *Śākta-pramoda*, *Tantrasāra*, and *Mantra-mahodadhiḥ* give the details for worship of Chinnamastā, just as for all Mahāvidyās and other deities. The invocation of her mantra, the meditation on her form, the construction and worship of her yantra, and so on, are more or less the same as for the other goddesses in the group. It is easy to get the impression that her worship is not much different from what is prescribed for other deities and that it might be as widespread. The usual rewards for her worship are cited: poetic speech, well-being and security, control over one's enemies, the ability to attract others (specifically women), the ability to influence kings, and liberation (*mokṣa* or *mukti*).

In fact, however, worship of Chinnamastā, at least at the public level, is extremely rare. It is probably also uncommon at the private level. This is not so surprising, given Chinnamastā's particularly fierce nature. In her hundred-name hymn, for example, she is called: Mahābhīmā (great terrible one, name 3), Caṇḍeśvarī (fierce goddess, name 5), Caṇḍamātā (mother of fierce beings, name 6), Mahācaṇḍā (great fierce one, name 8), Krodhinī (wrathful one, name 12), Krodharūpā (wrathful in form, name 14), Kopāturā (afflicted with rage, name 17), Pretāsanā (who sits on a ghost, name 31), Ghorarūpā (of terrific form, name 37), Ghoraṭṭiṣṭā (terrific to behold, name 38), Ghorarāvā (having a terrific roar, name 39), Raktapānaparāyaṇā (gulping blood continuously, name 61), Bhairavī (formidable one, name 66), Bhūtabhairavasevitā (served by fierce ghosts, name 68), and Dṛṣṭisamhārakāriṇī (she who causes destruction by her glance, name 99).[47] Her thousand-name *stotra* invokes many more names in a similar vein: Mahābhayaṅkarī-devī (very frightening goddess, name 19), Bhayarūpā (who has a fearful form, name 22), Ghoraghurghurnādinī (whose fierce roar is frightening, name 182), Ghorasattva (who embodies fierceness, name 189), Ghorattattvamayī-devī (the goddess who embodies a fierce form, name 199), Ghoramantrayutā (who is worshiped with a fierce mantra, name 209), Naramānsapriyānityā (who is always pleased with human flesh, name 622), Nararaktapriyāsadā (who is always pleased with human blood, name 623), Pretāsananivāsinī (who lives among ghosts, name 642), Lomamāṇsaprapūjitā (who is worshiped with body hair and flesh, name 810), and Palalādipriyānityā (who is always pleased with meat, name 930).[48]

Some other Mahāvidyās are also fierce, particularly Kālī and Tārā, and Dhūmāvatī is clearly a goddess with many inauspicious connotations and associations. Chinnamastā, though, seems to have the strongest reputation for being a dangerous goddess to worship or approach, and her many fierce epithets indicate this. She has exceedingly few temples or shrines, and it is often said that those who do worship her must be either yogis or world renouncers or of a particularly heroic nature. The only shrine I have been able to find to Chinnamastā in the Varanasi area, which is a veritable ocean of Hindu temples, is very small and located in the northeast corner of the compound of the Durgā temple in Ramnagar (across the Ganges River from Varanasi). The *pūjarī* (priest) there told me that the goddess is only worshiped by *tāntrikas* and that when she is worshiped the *sādhaka* uses a corpse. The shrine is said to have been built by a *tāntrika* from Madras. The goddess's image is of white marble, and she is flanked by the usual two figures (see figure 25). There are also temples of Chin-

Fig. 25. White marble image of Chinnamastā in a shrine in the compound of the Durgā temple, Ramnagar. Photograph by Hillary Rodrigues.

namastā in Bihar. One is located on top of a hill, Nandan Parvat, northeast of Vaidyanath.[49] Another is located in Ranchi, where there are shrines to all ten Mahāvidyās. There are shrines to each of the other Mahāvidyās, including Chinnamastā, at the Kāmākhyā-devī temple at Kāmarūpa in Assam.[50] I have also been told of a Chinnamastā temple in Vishnupur in West Bengal at which daily worship takes place.

Chinnamastā generally is not casually approached, and some texts indicate that this might be because of the inherent dangers of her worship. The *Bhairava-tantra*, as cited in the *Śākta-pramoda*, says in reference to Chinnamastā's worship: "Whoever performs this worship without meditating on Chinnamastā, the Goddess will sever one's head and drink one's blood."[51] The *Śākta-pramoda* also distinguishes between the worship of Chinnamastā by renouncers and householders,[52] implying that there are different styles of worship and that renouncers pursue a more heroic path. Indeed, many people have told me that only those of particularly heroic nature dare worship Chinnamastā.

The *Śaktisaṁgama-tantra* stipulates which path is appropriate for worshiping each of the Mahāvidyās. Chinnamastā is to be worshiped by the left-handed path alone.[53] The only other goddess to be so worshiped is Bhairavī. The others are to be worshiped by the right-handed path or by both paths. A consistent theme in tantric texts is that only those with the nature of the *vīra* (hero) are qualified to undertake *sādhanā* of the left-handed type and that those who are not qualified should not attempt it. Left-handed worship of Chinnamastā involves sexual intercourse with a woman who is not one's wife, according to both the *Mantra-mahodadhiḥ*[54] and the *Śākta-pramoda*.[55] The *Śākta-pramoda* also says that, in making fire offerings to Chinnamastā, one should offer her meat and wine at night.[56]

In conclusion, Chinnamastā has few shrines or temples and is probably worshiped in tantric fashion by a few particularly brave individuals who are bold enough to engage this fearsome deity.

Bhairavī

The Fierce One

She has a luminous complexion like a thousand rising suns. She wears silken red clothes and a garland of severed heads. Her breasts are smeared with blood. She has four arms: in two of her hands she holds a rosary and a book, and with her other two hands she makes the gestures of assurance and conferring boons. She has three eyes that resemble large lotuses. On her forehead is the half-moon and on her head a jeweled crown. She smiles.[1]

She is brilliant like the rising sun and wears the moon crest on her head. She has three eyes and is lovely in her various ornaments. She is the destroyer of enemies. She wears a garland of freshly severed heads that are still vomiting blood. She wears red clothes. She has ten hands and carries a trident, small drum, sword, club, bow, arrows, noose, goad, book, and rosary. She is seated on a corpse throne.[2]

A Hymn in Praise of Bhairavī

I have been unable to find any myths concerning the origin or emergence of Bhairavī, which is surprising in view of her widespread popularity in Nepal. As a way of introducing her multifaceted nature, therefore, it may be helpful to quote a relatively early hymn in her praise from the *Śāradā-tilaka* (this ninth-century C.E. text is attributed to Lakṣmaṇa Deśikendra, the guru of the tenth-century Kashmiri philosopher Abhinavagupta).

Fig. 26. Bhairavī. Ajit Mookerjee Collection of Tantric Art, National Museum, Delhi.

> You are so subtle that the gods cannot describe you. You are the source of the world and have no beginning. You have three eyes, a beautiful face, and four hands in which you hold a book and a rosary and with which you make the signs of assurance and giving favors. You are the source of speech, of everything graceful, the source of the universe itself. You wear the moon as a crest in your hair and have a white complexion like the autumn moon. You hold a jar of *amṛta* [immortality nectar] and make the gesture of exposition/teaching. When Śiva and Viṣṇu are worshiped, you are there to be worshiped as well. You are also Brahmā, where speech abides. You are the nature of consciousness; you control the vital air, and by granting yogic powers you defeat the six kinds of passions: sexual lust, greed, delusion, intoxication, jealousy, and anger. Śiva, having obtained half of your body [in his half-man/half-woman form], was then empowered to create the world. The world cannot be created without you. After worshiping you, the wives of the *siddhas* [heavenly beings] become red eyed because of drinking too much wine. They sing your names along with the *kinnaras* [heavenly beings]. We worship you who as the coiled serpent *(kuṇḍalinī)* goes to the city of Śiva after passing along the *suṣumnā nāḍī* making all the lotuses bloom [an allusion to the awakening and rising of the *kuṇḍalinī*, representing consciousness]. We worship you who are bathed with a flow of nectar. You are the source of all Vedas; your form is consciousness itself. You are the creator of the world in the form of sound and meaning. You maintain the world by your power as the sun, and you dissolve the world in your form as fire. Narāyaṇī, Gaurī, and Sarasvatī are also your names.[3]

This hymn emphasizes the cosmic aspect of Bhairavī, not her fearsome nature (which is mentioned in later texts and suggested in her name itself, "the fierce one"), nor her role as the consort of Bhairava (a fierce form of Śiva, which is also implied in her name). The hymn primarily describes Bhairavī in a position of cosmic preeminence: as overseeing or empowering the three male deities usually associated with creation, maintenance, and destruction or as assuming these roles herself. She is not a consort but is independent of the gods and transcends them. This is a common emphasis in many goddess texts and hymns, especially those pertaining to the Mahāvidyās.

The hymn also emphasizes her beauty and power to cause erotic excitement. Heavenly beings are intoxicated by worshiping her, and her face and form are described as beautiful. On the other hand, she is said to control passion as well as arouse it. Through yoga, she gives the power to overcome worldly passions. She is also cast in the role of revealer and teacher. She creates the Vedas, the source of all knowledge and wisdom; she is shown making the gesture of teaching and is said to carry a book.

The hymn also identifies Bhairavī with *kuṇḍalinī śakti* and thereby with the inherent power of awakened consciousness that is cultivated in tantric *sādhanā* (spiritual practice). In this respect she is affirmed to exist inwardly, as the inherent spiritual power that can be aroused in an individual by means of meditation or other spiritual techniques or rituals. This aspect of Bhairavī complements her transcendent, cosmic aspect, lending her an intensely immanent presence.

The Goddess of Destruction

At the close of the hymn from the *Śāradā-tilaka* we hear of Bhairavī's destructive aspect: at the end of the cosmic cycle, in her form as fire, she dissolves the world. As the universe-ending fire, she resembles Śiva in his form as the destroyer. Her destructive nature, though, is a very minor theme in the *Śāradā-tilaka* hymn. Some recent interpretations, however, focus on Bhairavī's name, "the fierce one," on her association with fierce forms of Śiva, and on her often fierce appearance.

One scholar interprets Bhairavī as a female version of Śiva in his destructive form as Kāla-bhairava, in which he punishes people both living and dead. He notes that Kāla-bhairava is closely associated with Yama, lord of death, who lives in the south, and says this is why Śiva is also known as Dakṣiṇamūrti, "whose form faces southward." Kāla-bhairava's consort, he says, is Tripura-bhairavī, who is constantly occupied with destroying the three worlds; hence her name, "she who is fierce in the three worlds." Creation and destruction are the two essential aspects of the universe, which is continually subject to their alternating rhythms. The two are equally dominant in the world and indeed depend upon each other in symbiotic fashion. Bhairavī embodies the principle of destruction. Tripura-bhairavī arises or becomes present when the body declines and decays, which is a natural, inevitable, and irresistible force. She is also evident in self-destructive habits, such as eating *tāmasic* food (food having a quality associated with ignorance and lust) and drinking liquor, which wear down the body and mind. She is present, he says, in the loss of semen, which weakens males. Anger, jealousy, and other selfish emotions and actions strengthen Bhairavī's presence in the world. Righteous behavior, conversely, makes her weaker. In short, she is an ever-present goddess who manifests herself in, and embodies, the destructive aspects of the world. Destruction, however, is not always negative, this interpreter says: creation cannot continue without it. This is most clear in the process of nourishment and metabolism, in which life feeds on death; creation proceeds by means of transformed energy given up in destruction.[4]

A second contemporary author interprets Bhairavī in a similar vein. According to this writer, Bhairavī is identical with Kālarātri, a name often associated with Kālī that means "black night [of destruction]" and refers to a particularly destructive aspect of Kālī. She is also identified with Mahāpralaya, the great dissolution at the end of a cosmic cycle, during which all things, having been consumed by fire, are dissolved in the formless waters of precreation. She is the force that tends toward dissolution. This force, furthermore, which is actually Bhairavī herself, is present in each person as one gradually ages, weakens, and finally dies. Destruction is apparent everywhere, and therefore Bhairavī is present everywhere.[5]

Bhairavī's fierce, terrible, or destructive nature is emphasized in some of her descriptions; for example, she is said to wear a garland of freshly severed heads that gush blood over her breasts and to be seated on a corpse (see the *dhyāna* mantra of Rudra-bhairavī, preceding note 2 above). This aspect of Bhairavī is also mentioned fairly often in her thousand-name hymn from the *Viśvasāra-tantra*, where she is called Extremely Terrible (Ghora-tārā), Black Night (Kālarātri), Fierce One (Caṇḍī), She Who Creates Fear and Awe, Who Has a Terrible Face, Who Has the Face of a Ghost, Who Arises from the Body of a Corpse, Who Likes Blood, Who Drinks Blood, Who Destroys the Body, and Who Is the Cause of Mahāpralaya.[6] This hymn also often identifies her with the sun and fire, which may have destructive functions but are not specifically mentioned as destructive forces when she is associated with them.[7] She is said to dwell in cremation grounds (Śmaśāna-vāsinī, Śmaśānālaya-vāsinī) and to have a corpse as a seat (Śavāsana).[8] Her thousand-name hymn in the *Śākta-pramoda* says that she sits on a corpse, eats the flesh of a corpse, is fond of flesh, drinks blood, and destroys those who criticize the offering of blood (perhaps the Vaiṣṇavas). She is also called Koṭarākṣi, "whose eyes are sunken" (probably from being emaciated),[9] which associates her with the terrible forms of Kālī and Cāmuṇḍā, who are often described as having sunken eyes. In short, Bhairavī is strongly associated with destruction, is often said to have a fierce, terrible, frightening nature, and is fond of meat and blood. In Nepal, the "Bhairavī of Nawakot . . . is believed annually to disseminate *awal* (malaria) in the Triśūlī Valley lowlands, sparing only those who adequately appease her."[10] In these respects, she fulfills the promise of her name, Bhairavī, "the fierce one."

The Goddess of Many Forms

Bhairavī has several distinct forms, some of which have separate mantras and yantras in tantric manuals. Other goddesses among the Mahāvidyās have more than one form, but none has as many as Bhairavī. The *Tantrasāra* describes twelve separate forms of Bhairavī, and taken together they suggest a multifaceted goddess, a goddess who is certainly not limited to being the embodiment of destruction.[11] The names of several of her forms stress that she gives a range of blessings. As Sampatpradā-bhairavī she gives riches, as Sakalasiddhi-bhairavī she is the one who grants every perfection, as Bhayavidhvaṁsinī-bhairavī she destroys all fears, as Caitanya-bhairavī she gives awakened consciousness, as Bhuvaneśvarī-bhairavī she is present in creation and engenders growth, as Kāmeśvarī-bhairavī she kindles sexual desire and grants sexual gratification, and as Annapūrṇeśvarī-bhairavī she gives food. These last two forms deserve some comment, as they present such a strong contrast to the destructive aspect that tends to dominate her character.

Kāmeśvarī denotes a form of Bhairavī who is mistress of Kāma-deva, the god of sexual desire, namely, Rati (whose name means "sexual intercourse"). As Kāmeśvarī, she embodies sexual desire and lends to creation its distinctive quality of being pervaded by the mutual attraction of the sexes. One of her *dhyāna* mantras, that of Sampatpradā-bhairavī, says that she is intoxicated with her youth, and most descriptions of her, despite her associations with destruction, say that she is attractive, young, and shapely. Bhairavī's association with sexual desire and fulfillment is mentioned often in her thousand-name hymns. In the *Śākta-pramoda*, for example, she is called She Who Is Fond of Semen and Menstrual Blood and She Who Is Worshiped by Those Who Worship with Semen.[12] In her thousand-name hymn in the *Viśvasāra-tantra*, she is called Lovely One, She Whose Form Is Semen, Who Produces Semen, Who Gives Love, Who Enjoys Sexual Intercourse, Who Is Dear to Kāma, and Who Dwells in the Yoni.[13]

At one point, the *Tantrasāra* says that Bhairavī is the consort of Kāmadeva and stipulates that the adept imagine and interiorize the five different forms of the love god with the corresponding five forms of Rati, his consort.[14] Bhairavī is also worshiped through *bāṇa nyāsa* (*nyāsa* is a ritual by means of which one divinizes the body with mantras and *mudrās*). In *bāṇa nyāsa*, the adept places the five flower arrows of Kāma in the fingers of both hands and empowers himself or herself in the arts of love.

Fig. 27. Bhairavī on Śiva. Ajit Mookerjee Collection of Tantric Art, National Museum, Delhi.

Each of the flower arrows produces an intoxicating emotion of love and desire, such as excessive agitation, a melting sensation, an irresistible attraction to another, and stupefaction.[15]

Annapūrṇeśvarī-bhairavī reveals a quite different dimension of Bhairavī by identifying her with the well-known goddess Annapūrṇā. Annapūrṇā-devī, the goddess "who is filled with food," is strongly associated with Śiva and a domestic setting. She is a goddess of the kitchen, as it were, whose basic function is to satisfy the hunger of her husband, and by extension, as he is Paśupati, "lord of creatures," to satisfy the hunger of all creatures. Bhairavī's fearsome aspects are here completely submerged. The *dhyāna* mantra from the *Tantrasāra* describes her thus:

> She is golden in color and wears the moon crest on her forehead. She is covered with nine kinds of jewels and is dressed in multicolored clothes. She has three eyes, which are wide and long, and golden jarlike breasts. She is with Pañcamukha-śiva [Śiva having five faces], who is white in color and has a smiling face and a blue throat. He wears an animal hide and serpents for clothing, and he shines like the *kunda* flower [a bright white blossom]. Looking on the goddess, he dances in delight. She is pleasing in appearance and wears a golden girdle that adorns her full buttocks. She is giving food to Śiva. Flanking her are the goddesses Śrī and Bhūmi [goddess of the earth].[16]

The presence of Śrī and Bhūmi in the company of Annapūrṇeśvarī is significant; they are both strongly identified with Viṣṇu. Although Annapūrṇā-devī is well known as the consort of Śiva, or a form of his consort, Annapūrṇeśvarī is associated with a range of Vaiṣṇavite deities. In constructing her yantra physically or mentally, in addition to invoking Śrī and Bhūmi, the adept invokes other deities associated with Viṣṇu: Varāha, Narayāṇa, and Kamalā. The worshiper prays to them for plentiful food so that he or she can provide for others.[17] The presence of the Vaiṣṇava deities, who are generally benign and concerned with worldly blessings, as opposed to Śaivite deities, who have more pronounced ascetic tendencies, is probably meant to underline Annapūrṇeśvarī's nature as a beneficent provider.[18]

Cosmic Dimensions

Bhairavī has facets and epithets that assert her cosmic importance, if not supremacy. A commentary on the *Paraśurāma-kalpasutra* says that the name Bhairavī is derived from the words *bharaṇa* (to create), *ramaṇa* (to protect), and *vamana* (to emit or disgorge).[19] The commentator, that is, seeks to discern the inner meaning of Bhairavī's name by identifying her with the cosmic functions of creation, maintenance, and destruction. The image of the basic cosmic rhythm as one of inhaling and exhaling is perhaps suggested by the commentator's use of the term *vamana* and may reflect the Kashmir Śaivite emphasis on the rhythm of breathing as a metaphor for the nature of ultimate reality, which alternately reveals or emanates itself and then withdraws and obscures itself.

In her thousand-name hymn from the *Viśvasāra-tantra*, Bhairavī has several names that identify her with philosophical or cosmic absolutes. She is called Parameśvarī (mistress of all), Jaganmātā (mother of the world), Jagaddhātrī (world nurse or she who nourishes the world), Paramā (she who is the highest), Parabrahmasvarūpiṇi (she whose form is the highest *brahman*), and Sṛṣṭisaṁhārakāriṇī (she who is the cause of creation and destruction).[20] These names, like her many forms, emphasize that she is a complete goddess, as it were, not just a goddess associated with destructive energy.

Dhūmāvatī

The Widow Goddess

Dhūmāvatī is ugly, unsteady, and angry. She is tall and wears dirty clothes. Her ears are ugly and rough, she has long teeth, and her breasts hang down. She has a long nose. She has the form of a widow. She rides in a chariot that has a banner on top decorated with a crow emblem. Her eyes are fearsome, and her hands tremble. In one hand she holds a winnowing basket, and with the other hand she makes the gesture of conferring boons. Her nature is rude. She is always hungry and thirsty and looks unsatisfied. She likes to create strife, and she is always frightful in appearance.[1]

Dhūmāvatī has two hands, which hold a skull bowl and a spear. Her complexion is black, she wears ornaments made of snakes, and her dress is made of rags taken from the cremation ground.[2]

The goddess should be imagined in the following way. Her complexion is like the black clouds that form at the time of cosmic dissolution. Her face is very wrinkled, and her nose, eyes, and throat resemble a crow's. She carries a broom, a winnowing fan, a torch, and a club. Her face has a venomous expression. She is very old, and she wears the plain clothes of a mendicant. She has disheveled hair, and her breasts are dry and withered. She is without mercy. She frowns.[3]

Nirṛti, Jyeṣṭhā, and Alakṣmī

Dhūmāvatī is barely known outside the Mahāvidyās. If she had an independent cult prior to her inclusion in the group, we know nothing about it. However, Dhūmāvatī bears striking similarities to

Fig. 28. Dhūmāvatī, contemporary black and white drawing.

certain goddesses who appeared very early in the Hindu tradition and who had cults or myths prior to and separate from the Mahāvidyās; some contemporary authors identify Dhūmāvatī with them. In particular, Dhūmāvatī is said to be the same as Nirṛti, Jyeṣṭhā, and Alakṣmī.[4] All three of these goddesses, as we shall see, are inauspicious, dangerous, and avoided by people.

Nirṛti is known in the earliest Vedic text, the Ṛg-veda, as a dangerous and inauspicious goddess. Just one hymn mentions her (10.59), and its concern is to seek protection from her or to ask that she be driven away. She is equated with death, bad luck, and destruction. The hymn sums up Nirṛti's nature very well. After four verses asking the gods for renewed life, wealth, food, glorious deeds, youth, and continued long life, the following refrain is invoked: "Let Nirṛti depart to distant places." That is, Nirṛti is identified with the opposites of the blessings sought: she is decay, need, anger, cowardice, decrepitude, and death.

Later Vedic literature describes Nirṛti in more detail and mentions her more frequently than does the Ṛg-veda. She is said to be dark, to dress in dark clothes, and to receive dark husks as her share of the sacrifice,[5] although one passage says that she has golden locks.[6] She lives in the south, the direction of the kingdom of the dead,[7] is associated with pain,[8] and is repeatedly given offerings with the specific intention of keeping her away from the sacrificial rituals and from the affairs of people in general. Nirṛti continues to be known in the later Hindu tradition. Her nature has not changed; she is still associated with negative qualities and bad luck.

The goddess Jyeṣṭhā also appears very early in the Hindu tradition.[9] She seems to have enjoyed a quite widespread cult during some periods. Many images of her have been found, and during the seventh and eighth centuries she seems to have been widely known in South India.[10] In physical appearance she bears some similarities to Dhūmāvatī. She is described as having "large pendulous breasts descending as far as her navel, with a flabby belly, thick thighs, raised nose, hanging lower lip, and is in colour as ink."[11] She is black, or sometimes red, holds a lotus and a waterpot, and sometimes makes the sign of protection. She wears many kinds of ornaments, as well as a *tilaka* (an ornamental mark on her forehead), which identifies her as a married woman. Her hair is usually braided and piled on top of her head or wound around her head. She has a banner depicting a crow. Sometimes a crow stands next to her. She rides a donkey or is drawn in a chariot by lions or tigers. She carries a broom.[12]

According to the *Liṅga-purāṇa*, she was born when the gods and demons churned the ocean to obtain the nectar of immortality. She was given in marriage to the sage Dussaha, who soon discovered that his unattractive wife could not bear the sound or sight of any kind of pious activity. When he complained to Viṣṇu, Viṣṇu told Dussaha to go with his wife only to places where inauspicious things occur—hence Jyeṣṭhā's popular epithet Alakṣmī, "she who is inauspicious." Among the places specifically mentioned as appropriate residences for her are homes where family members quarrel and elders eat food while disregarding the hunger of their children. Eventually Dussaha abandoned Jyeṣṭhā. She complained to Viṣṇu that she could not sustain herself without a husband, and he dictated that she would be sustained by offerings from women.[13] Although the text does not say so, it is probably understood that Jyeṣṭhā will not enter the homes of those who propitiate her. It is also significant, as a link between Jyeṣṭhā and Dhūmāvatī, that her name means "elder" or "eldest." Dhūmāvatī, as we shall see, is usually shown as an old woman.

Alakṣmī, the third goddess with whom Dhūmāvatī is identified by contemporary authors, is mentioned as early as the *Śrī-sūkta*, a very early hymn in praise of the goddess Śrī. In that hymn, Śrī is asked to banish her sister, Alakṣmī (vv. 5, 6, and 8).[14] Alakṣmī is said to appear in such inauspicious forms as need, poverty, hunger, and thirst. Lakṣmī, or Śrī, is her exact opposite, and the two do not dwell in the same place at the same time; by their natures they are incompatible and are unable to exist where the other is present. Alakṣmī is described as "an old hag riding an ass. She has a broom in her hand. A crow adorns her banner."[15] The crow and the broom, as we shall see, are associated with Dhūmāvatī.

The contrast between Alakṣmī and Lakṣmī is dramatically evident in the festival of Dīvalī (also known as Dīpāvalī) and the rituals and practices leading up to it. The ghosts of the dead are said to return during the three days before Dīvalī, which takes place in the autumn on the night of a new moon.[16] The demon Bali emerges from the underworld to rule for three days, and goblins and malicious spirits are abroad, including Alakṣmī.[17] People invoke Lakṣmī to drive these spirits away and light lamps to frighten the demons. In general, evil spirits are exorcised, especially Alakṣmī, who is believed to have reigned on earth during the past four months, when the gods were sleeping. In addition to the lighted lamps, which Alakṣmī dislikes, people bang pots and pans or play on instruments to frighten her off.[18] On another occasion in Bengal, an image of Alakṣmī is made and ceremoniously disfigured by cutting off her nose and ears, after which an image of Lakṣmī is installed to signify the triumph of good luck over bad in the future.[19]

In reading descriptions of Dhūmāvatī, it is clear that she shares many characteristics with Nirṛti, Jyeṣṭhā, and Alakṣmī. Like Nirṛti and Alakṣmī, she is associated with poverty and need, or is said to be poor herself; with hunger and thirst, or is said to be constantly hungry and thirsty; and with inauspicious things and bad luck. Like Nirṛti and Jyeṣṭhā, she is sometimes said to have a dark complexion. Like Jyeṣṭhā and Alakṣmī, she is said to have a banner with a crow on it and, sometimes, to carry a broom. Like Jyeṣṭhā, she causes quarrels and has a bad temper. And finally, like Alakṣmī, she is described as an old hag and is said to rule during the four months prior to *śukla ekādaśi* (the eleventh day of the waxing moon) of the month of Kārtik, the date when Viṣṇu wakes up after a four-month sleep. During the four months when Viṣṇu is asleep, the soul lacks its usual luster, and auspicious events, such as weddings, are not performed.[20]

While the similarities between Dhūmāvatī and these three goddesses are unmistakable, and sometimes striking, and while it is likely that some modern writers are consciously patterning Dhūmāvatī on them, especially Alakṣmī, there are some important differences between Dhūmāvatī and her prototypes. One of the most distinguishing and consistent features of Dhūmāvatī is that she is a widow. Jyeṣṭhā is married and has a *tilaka* and braided hair, signs of a married woman. I have found no mention of Nirṛti or Alakṣmī as widows.

Dhūmāvatī is also described as ugly more often and more consistently than the other three goddesses. Her breasts are dried and withered, her face is nasty and wrinkled, her teeth are crooked or missing, her hair is gray and disheveled, and her clothes are dirty and worn.[21] Although the other goddesses are certainly not said to be attractive, there is a stronger insistence on Dhūmāvatī's unattractive appearance in most written descriptions of her.

Dhūmāvatī is also described as fierce, frightening, and fond of blood, characteristics that are not emphasized in descriptions of the other three goddesses. Dhūmāvatī, for example, crushes bones in her mouth, and the sound is awful. She is also said to make the noises of drums and bells, which are frightening and warlike. She wears a garland of skulls, chews the corpses of the demons Caṇḍa and Muṇḍa, and drinks a mixture of blood and wine.[22] Her eyes are glaring red, stern, and without tenderness. She carries Yama's buffalo horn in her hand, symbolizing death. She dwells with widows, in ruined houses, and in wild, uncivilized, dangerous places such as deserts.[23] Also, unlike the other three goddesses, Dhūmāvatī is related to Śiva, albeit indirectly in some cases, and to his spouse Satī.

Finally, Dhūmāvatī is not identified with these three goddesses in contexts where one might expect it. For example, in her *nāma stotras* (hymns invoking her many names), where she is identified with numerous other goddesses, the names of Nirṛti, Jyeṣṭhā, and Alakṣmī are not included, a remarkable omission. Dhūmāvatī, as we shall see, also has certain important positive characteristics and is interpreted by some as an effective symbol or power for achieving spiritual knowledge and liberation. None of the other three goddesses has such positive aspects.

Dhūmāvatī, then, probably stands in a tradition of inauspicious goddesses, like Nirṛti, Jyeṣṭhā, and Alakṣmī, who symbolize the more difficult and painful aspects of life and reality generally. It is also possible, even likely, that Dhūmāvatī has been consciously modeled on these three goddesses. That she is "the same," however, seems to me to be an exaggeration, particularly in light of some of her characteristics that they do not share and in light of her positive aspects in the context of the Mahāvidyās.

Origin Myths

There are two myths that tell of Dhūmāvatī's origin, and they suggest significant aspects of her character. The first says that she was born when Satī burned herself to death on her father's sacrificial fire or was burned on that fire after she committed suicide by willing her own death. Dhūmāvatī was created from the smoke of Satī's burning body. "She emerged from that fire with blackened face; she appeared from that smoke."[24] Born in such circumstances, embodying both the mood of the insulted, outraged goddess Satī at the time of her death and her funeral smoke, Dhūmāvatī has, in the words of the priest at the Dhūmāvatī temple in Varanasi, "a sad frame of mind." In this version, then, Dhūmāvatī is a form of Satī, indeed the physical continuation of her in the form of smoke. She is "all that is left of Satī": sad smoke.

The second myth that tells of Dhūmāvatī's origin says that once, when Śiva's spouse Satī was dwelling with him in the Himalayas, she became extremely hungry and asked him for something to eat. When he refused to give her food, she said, "Well, then I will just have to eat you." Thereupon she swallowed Śiva. He persuaded her to disgorge him, and when she did he cursed her, condemning her to assume the form of the widow Dhūmāvatī.[25] In this myth, Dhūmāvatī is associated with Śiva. She represents an aggressive, assertive aspect of Satī. When Śiva does not acquiesce to her wish, she turns on him and consumes him. This echoes the theme in the origin myth of the Mahāvidyās as a group, in which the goddesses are formed when Satī is thwarted by Śiva and she grows angry. The myth underlines Dhūmāvatī's destructive bent. Her hunger is only satisfied when she consumes Śiva, who himself contains or creates the world. One author, commenting on her perpetual hunger and thirst, which is mentioned in many places, says that she is the embodiment of "unsatisfied desires."[26] The myth also emphasizes that Dhūmāvatī as a widow is inauspicious. This is compounded by the fact that she has also been cursed and rejected by her husband. Her status as a widow in the myth is curious. She makes herself one by swallowing Śiva, an act of self-assertion, and perhaps independence. On the other hand, she does not assume the form of a widow until Śiva curses her.

Symbol of Inauspiciousness as Transformative

There can be no question that Dhūmāvatī is a figure who vividly symbolizes all that is conventionally affirmed to be inauspicious. She is often shown sitting in a chariot that has nothing to pull it, and she is a widow. In the context of Hindu society, she is a woman going nowhere, the ultimate symbol of all that is unlucky, unattractive, and inauspicious. She is a nobody socially; she has no place; she does not fit. The crow, which appears as the emblem on her banner or atop her chariot or as her mount (*vāhana*), is a carrion eater and symbol of death. Indeed, she herself is sometimes said to resemble a crow. The *Prapañcasārasāra-saṁgraha*, for example, says that her nose and throat resemble a crow's.[27] She lives in cremation grounds and is so depicted in a painting of her by a contemporary Varanasi artist (figure 31).[28] In this picture she is surrounded by four cremation fires; on top of each one sits a crow. Her thousand-name hymn says that her house is in the cremation ground, that she sits on a corpse, wears ashes from the cremation ground, and blesses those who haunt cremation grounds.[29] She also wears a dress taken from a corpse in the cremation ground.[30] She is said to be the embodiment of the *tamas guṇa*, the aspect of creation associated with lust and ignorance.[31] Her thousand-name hymn says that she likes liquor and meat,[32] both of which are *tāmasic*. According to a scholar of Tantrism in Varanasi, Dhūmāvatī is "the aspect of reality that is old, ugly, and unappealing. The Mahāvidyās are supposed to represent the diversity of reality, so we have in female form the young and beautiful forms and the ugly and fearsome forms."[33] Dhūmāvatī is generally associated with all that is inauspicious: she dwells in areas of the earth that are perceived to be desolate, such as deserts, in abandoned houses, in quarrels, in mourning children, in hunger and thirst, and particularly in widows.[34]

The inauspicious, if not dangerous, overtones of Dhūmāvatī as a widow also might be suggested by the Nepalese belief in *boksis*, a class of dangerous, inimical spirit beings who possess widows. To become a *boksi* it is necessary for a woman to sacrifice her husband or son.[35] Widows are here associated with the murder of their husbands and sons, with willful evil. They are understood as bringing about their own inauspicious condition by despicable acts or as being vulnerable to possession by evil spirits who will prompt them to undertake such acts. Widows, by definition, are suspect as dangerous beings who are likely to cause trouble and who therefore should be avoided. As the divine widow, the symbolic widow par excellence, Dhūmāvatī is to be feared.

Like the three inauspicious goddesses to whom she is sometimes compared or with whom she is sometimes identified, it seems that Dhūmāvatī is primarily a being to keep at bay. Indeed, the majority of people are advised not to worship her, and married people, in particular, should keep her at a distance.[36] That anyone would approach her, worship her, or cultivate a relationship with her seems, at first glance, highly unlikely.

In several places, however, it is said that she grants *siddhis* to those who worship her, that she rescues her devotees from all kinds of trouble, and that she grants all rewards and desires, including ultimate knowledge and liberation. The details for her worship are stipulated, and it must be assumed that at least some adepts worship her and cultivate a rapport with her, indeed, seek to become united with her and to realize her presence in themselves according to the logic of tantric *sādhanā*.

An inkling of Dhūmāvatī's positive aspect is suggested in a comment made to me by a priest serving the Dasamāhavidyā *pandal* (a temporary shelter for worship) on S. N. Banerjea Street during Kālī Pūjā in Calcutta. After telling me that she is a vision of old age and decay—that she is nearly blind and has loose, wrinkled skin, sagging breasts, and no teeth—and that furthermore she looks fierce, he said that inside she is tenderhearted. The priest at the Dhūmāvatī temple in Varanasi, Panalal Gosvami, after telling me about all the inauspicious aspects of the goddess, and emphasizing that she should not be approached by happily married men like me, said that she gives "anything the devotee wants," which he said was unusual among deities. He also said that her worship instills a feeling of wanting to be alone and a distaste for worldly things. In this vein, he said, her worship is appropriate for world renouncers. He also said that Dhūmāvatī is partial to unmarried people and to those who have been widowed. He insisted that only unmarried people could withstand her great power and successfully spend a night alone in her temple. For a married person to do this, he said, would result in death.

These comments are suggestive. According to this priest, Dhūmāvatī attracts and probably encourages and reinforces a certain kind of independence, or solitariness, that is experienced outside marriage. Whether this solitariness implies and affirms independence is not clear. It is important to remember, though, that the highest stages of the spiritual quest in many traditional Hindu texts can only be undertaken alone, after the aspirant has left home and family. It is also important to realize that many of the most pious Hindus one sees today in India are widows who have vowed to spend the rest of their lives undertaking pilgrimages to sacred centers or performing religious rituals at such sites. In most respects these women are living the life of the traditional Hindu world renouncer. Indeed, one text says that Dhūmāvatī wears a "dress like a mendicant's."[37]

The priest's comment that Dhūmāvatī instills a distaste for worldly things also relates to the highest stages of the spiritual quest in traditional Hinduism. The world renouncer seeks to achieve a frame of mind that does not covet the comforts and joys of the worldly life, a frame of mind in which he or she is content with what comes to hand, with minimal food, clothing, and shelter. Like Dhūmāvatī herself, who in the form of smoke is ever moving, never still, the traditional *sannyasī* wanders the world, never remaining in one place for more than a few days.

Why Dhūmāvatī in particular might be effective in instilling these kinds of feelings or bringing about a frame of mind that is indifferent to the world is perhaps explained in the same way as the symbolism of the goddess Kālī and the logic that underlies the *pañca tattva* ritual (the ritual of the five forbidden things): Dhūmāvatī is able to inculcate indifference to the world because she so unambiguously reveals the negative aspects of life. Like Kālī, with whom she is sometimes identified,[38] she forces her worshipers to acknowledge the inherent miseries of existence and thus encourages an indifference to or distaste for the world. In the logic of the *pañca tattva* ritual, according to which it is spiritually transformative to confront what is forbidden, Dhūmāvatī may be understood as a dramatic symbol of all that is socially rejected. To seek to identify with her by undertaking her worship is to partake of the "forbidden" and to realize that it is primarily a manifestation of false human categories, that underlying what is thought to be pure and impure, auspicious and inauspicious, is a unity that transcends such artificial dichotomies. Beyond desire for worldly blessings, beyond avoidance of what is thought to be polluting and dangerous, is indifference to these distinctions, is the knowledge of the ultimate, which is without name and form.

In a more positive vein, as a socially marginal being for whom worldly concerns are past, Dhūmāvatī encourages spiritual awakening. Although others may consider the widow unfortunate, she is free to undertake spiritual pursuits, such as pilgrimage, that were difficult or impossible in her younger, socially responsible days. For women whose marriages prove oppressive, the widow may be a liberating figure. Like the traditional world renouncer, she is outside society and free of its constraints and obligations.

Dhūmāvatī is often said to be manifest in Mahāpralaya, the great dissolution of the universe at the end of the great cosmic age. In the *Prapañcasārasāra-saṁgraha* she is said to have a complexion that is "black like the accumulated clouds during dissolution."[39] In her thousand-name hymn she is called She Whose Form is *Pralaya*, Who Is Occupied with *Pralaya*, Who Creates and Causes *Pralaya*, and Who Walks About in *Pralaya*.[40] One author says that she appears at the end of time, when even Mahākāla, Śiva himself, has disappeared. Since she is alone, she appears as a widow and in this form represents "the Power of Time, outside Time and Space."[41] Another scholar says that Dhūmāvatī "personifies the destruction of the world by fire, when only smoke from its ashes remains."[42] Beyond name and form, beyond human categories, alone and indivisible, as the great dissolution, she reveals the nature of ultimate knowledge, which is formless and knows no divisions into good or bad, pure and impure, auspicious and inauspicious.

The Dhūmāvatī Temple in Varanasi

Dhūmāvatī temples are few and far between. In Varanasi I visited one of these rare temples on several occasions.[43] Although the central image there is covered with clothing, the priest assured me that it represents Dhūmāvatī. He described her as a widow, riding a chariot; in three of her hands she holds a winnowing fan, a broom, and a pot, and with the fourth she makes the fear-not *mudrā*. The image is of black stone with large eyes and red lips. She receives as offerings the usual things, such as flowers and fruit, but also likes liquor, *bhāng* (a form of hashish), cigarettes, and meat. Blood sacrifices are performed occasionally at this temple. She does not like offerings burnt in a fire that is not smokey, so the priest said he is always careful to create a lot of smoke. She also likes smoke from incense, offerings, and cremation fires. Smoke attracts her because it suggests destruction. She herself, the priest said, exists in the form of smoke, and like smoke she drifts everywhere at will.

Paintings of the other Mahāvidyās adorn the inner walls, although some have been effaced. Mātaṅgī, Chinnamastā, Ṣoḍaśī, Bhuvaneśvarī, and Bagalāmukhī still remain. The priest said the temple exists on the spot (*pīṭha*) where a piece of Satī's body fell to earth and was founded a long time ago by the sage Dhurvāsā, who had an irascible disposition, appropriate for a devotee of Dhūmāvatī, who causes such irascibility in those who worship her. The priest said that the goddess tends to be in a sad frame of mind and is quarrelsome, that her lips are red because they are covered with blood, and that she is the same as Śmaśāna-kālī (Kālī who lives in the cremation ground). The priest said that world renouncers and *tāntrikas* worship at this temple and implied that Dhūmāvatī is partial to them. He also insisted that married people, like me, should not cultivate a relationship with Dhūmāvatī, as she produces in her devotees a desire to be alone, inappropriate for a married person; she has an affinity for unmarried people. The priest himself, however, is married and has five children.

Despite the priest's comments about the typical worshipers being single and the goddess preferring this, the regular flow of visitors to the temple on the occasions when I was there consisted primarily of married men and women; I saw very few widows, though one might assume that widows would feel a special affinity to this goddess. It is difficult to imagine that people who attend the temple do not, on occasion, ask for the usual worldly favors: children (male children, usually), good fortune, a good marriage partner for their children, success on exams and in business, and so on. Indeed, the priest admitted that most of the regular worshipers are locals and that stories of the goddess's grace are common among these people.

As the priest described Dhūmāvatī's local significance, it became clear that she plays the role of a guardian deity, or village deity, who looks after the people of her locale first and foremost and whose lives she supports with worldly blessings. It is also interesting to note that a Śiva *liṅgam* is enshrined directly behind the image of Dhūmāvatī, implying the presence in the temple of Śiva and all that he represents. When I asked about the *liṅgam*, I was told that, although it represents Śiva, it does not indicate that he is married to Dhūmāvatī. It is an independent shrine that arose at the same time that the Dhūmāvatī temple appeared. It is also interesting to see that both inside and outside the temple are images of a lion, the vehicle (*vāhana*) of Durgā in her various manifestations. The *liṅgam* and the lion associate Dhūmāvatī with the creative male power of Śiva and the demon-slaying, dharma-supporting role of the goddess. These two aspects of Dhūmāvatī, as Śiva's consort and as a manifestation of Durgā, are both clearly present in her *nāma stotras*, where many epithets identify her with Pārvatī or Satī or as a slayer of demons.

The priest at her temple said that Dhūmāvatī appears in many forms and read me sections of her hymns to illustrate this. In the morning she appears as a young maiden, at noon as a married woman (her image was usually draped in a red *sārī*, the color for a married woman), and in the evening as a widow. In this public temple cult, it is clear that Dhūmāvatī has taken on an approachable character. She is no longer simply the inauspicious, dangerous goddess who can be approached only by heroic tantric adepts. Here she is a neighborhood deity who favors and protects those who live near her and seek her shelter and blessing. Indeed, a benign, approachable, even auspicious facet of Dhūmāvatī is clear in her thousand-name hymn. She is frequently said to bestow favors, and in many pictures of her she makes a boon-conferring gesture. Her thousand-name hymn says that she lives in the midst of women and is worshiped by women (vv. 80–81), and her hundred-name hymn says that she bestows children (v. 16).[44]

Unusual Portraits of Dhūmāvatī

Among the many pictures I have seen of Dhūmāvatī and the many descriptions I have read of her, three relatively recent paintings are striking, suggesting facets of the goddess that are not usually apparent. One painting is by the eighteenth-century painter Molaram of Himachal Pradesh (figure 29), another is from an eighteenth-century illuminated Nepali manuscript (figure 30), and the third, done around 1915, is by a Varanasi artist, Batuk Ramprasad (figure 31).

Molaram's painting of Dhūmāvatī shows her on a chariot being pulled by two enormous birds. Although they are not crows, their hooked beaks suggest carrion-eating birds, perhaps buzzards or vultures, which would

Fig. 29. Dhūmāvatī, by Molaram, late eighteenth century, Garwahl, Himachal Pradesh. Bharat Kala Bhavan, Benares Hindu University, Varanasi.

be appropriate to Dhūmāvatī's generally inauspicious associations. She holds a large winnowing basket in her left hand, and her right hand is raised, perhaps in the gesture of conferring boons. She has fangs, and her tongue lolls out in the fashion of Kālī and Tārā. None of this is unusual for Dhūmāvatī (except for the lolling tongue). What is striking about the picture is the elaborate ornamentation of the goddess. She wears bracelets, earrings, armbands, a necklace, and a pendant. She also wears elegant clothes. Her breasts are not pendulous but high and round. She is portrayed as young and full of life. Her appearance contrasts sharply with descriptions of her as ugly, withered, and wearing the soiled clothes of a widow.

The Nepali painting of Dhūmāvatī is equally uncharacteristic, if we take the descriptions in her *dhyāna* mantras to be normative. In this striking picture, Dhūmāvatī stands, legs apart as if striding, on a peacock, which in turn rests on a lotus. She is naked except for a necklace of pearls and a circle of pearls crowning her hair. Her yoni is clearly exposed. Her breasts are high and not pendulous. Her hair is light in color and elaborately

Fig. 30. Dhūmāvatī and her yantra, Nepali Manuscript. Bharat Kala Bhavan, Benares Hindu University, Varanasi.

braided. She is looking at herself in a mirror, which she holds in her left hand. She is encircled by a ring of fire, which is a typical feature of Nepali iconography and many represent cremation fires. This image bears no similarities to any of Dhūmāvatī's *dhyāna* mantras with which I am familiar. In this image she conveys a rather erotically alluring presence.

In the painting by Batuk Ramprasad, Dhūmāvatī is again pictured in a style that deviates markedly from her *dhyāna* mantras and from most depictions of her with which I am familiar. She is dressed in white and sits astride a huge crow. Surrounding her are what appear to be cremation fires, with a crow sitting on top of each one. Her complexion is black, and she holds a trident, sword, winnowing fan, and bowl in her four hands. Her breasts are somewhat pendulous. Again, what is striking is that she is heavily adorned with ornaments—bracelets, armlets, anklets, toe rings, earrings, a nose ring, necklace, and pendant—and is wearing an elegant, diaphanous upper garment and a gold-hemmed lower garment, hardly the dress of a widow.

What might be the significance of these paintings? It is possible that there is another tradition, which I have not been able to find, in which Dhūmāvatī is not a widow and is not described as ugly and clothed in soiled, worn garments. Barring this, a plausible interpretation of the paintings might well relate to the reputation of widows as dangerous to men. Attractive young widows, who in most upper castes are prevented from remarrying, are considered particularly threatening. Because her husband has died, the widow is a woman who has lost her social identity, at least from the point of view of the Hindu law books. From the male perspective, she is a social misfit, and if she is attractive and still in her childbearing years, she represents a temptation. She might also be understood to have strong, unsatisfied sexual longings, particularly in light of the claim made in many (male authored) texts that females are sexually insatiable. In short, the widow is understood to be sexually tempting to males. A saying popular in Varanasi captures this: "Widows, bulls, stairs, and Sannyāsis / If you can save yourself from these, / for you awaits the liberation of Kashi."[45] Widows here are put on a par with such notorious dangers in Varanasi as wandering bulls, dilapidated stairs at the bathing ghats, and unscrupulous "holy men."

Hints that Dhūmāvatī possesses sexual attractiveness and allure can be found in her thousand-name hymn. She is said to give enjoyment (v. 10), to be completely beautiful (v. 15), to be lovely (v. 20), and to be doe-eyed (v. 71). She is also said to create dance and to be a leader of dancers (vv. 76–77) and to be adorned with new garlands, clothes, and ornaments

Fig. 31. Dhūmāvatī, by Bhatuk Ramprasad, early twentieth century. Printed with the permission of Dr. Bhanu Shanker Mehta, Varanasi.

(vv. 77–78). She is also called She Whose Form Is Rati (either Kāmadeva's wife or, literally, "sexual intercourse," v. 82) and is said to enjoy sexual intercourse, to be present where sexual activity is, and to be occupied with sex (vv. 81–83). She is also said to have disheveled hair, which suggests a certain wildness, perhaps sexual wildness (v. 8), to like liquor and to be intoxicated (vv. 87–88), to be worshiped by intoxicated people

(v. 112), and to partake constantly in the five forbidden things (*pañca tattva*) (v. 92).[46]

Her generally ugly, decrepit, inauspicious, cranky, cronelike nature, then, is tempered or even offset by other qualities suggested in this hymn. In particular, she is said to be beautiful and to have erotic power, aspects of Dhūmāvatī that are featured in the three paintings. While these contrasting qualities may reflect the common tendency to portray a goddess, particularly in her thousand-name hymn, as "complete," as having many facets, both terrible and benign, the mention of erotic qualities may also suggest the sexual appeal, and perhaps sexual danger, of widows.

Bagalāmukhī

The Paralyzer

In the middle of the ocean is a pavilion of jewels with an altar inside it. On the altar is a lion throne on which the goddess Bagalāmukhī is seated. Her complexion is completely yellow, perfectly yellow, and she wears a yellow dress, yellow ornaments, and a yellow garland. I call to mind she who holds the tongue of the enemy in her left hand and a raised club in her right hand.[1]

She has assumed a serious mood and is maddened with intoxication. Her brilliance reflects the golden hue of her body. She has four arms and three eyes and is seated on a lotus. On her forehead is the crescent moon, which is yellow in color. She wears yellow clothes, has high, firm breasts, and wears golden earrings.[2]

Origin Myths

I have found three myths concerning the origin of Bagalāmukhī. According to the first myth, once upon a time in the Kṛta Yuga a cosmic storm threatened to destroy the universe. Many creatures were killed, and Viṣṇu, who was reclining on the cosmic serpent, Śeṣa, was himself disturbed. He went to a sacred pond named Haridrā (turmeric) and undertook austerities to find a solution to the problem. (Viṣṇu himself is often called Pītāmbarā, "he who wears yellow clothes.") He prayed to Tripura-sundarī, who appeared and lit up the entire world with her presence. She brought forth Bagalāmukhī, who sported in that pond of turmeric and then calmed the storm with her great powers.

Fig. 32. Pītāmbarā (Bagalāmukhī), by Bhatuk Ramprasad, early twentieth century. Printed with the permission of Dr. Bhanu Shanker Mehta, Varanasi.

She is also known as Pītāmbarā-devī because she appeared in a lake of turmeric.[3]

In the second myth, a demon named Madan undertook austerities and won the boon of *vāk siddhi*, according to which anything he said came about. He abused this *siddhi* by killing people. Enraged by his mischief, the gods worshiped Bagalāmukhī. She stopped the demon's rampage by taking hold of his tongue and stilling his speech. Before she could kill him, however, he asked to be worshiped with her, and she relented. That is why he is depicted with her.[4]

The third myth touches on the origins of both Bagalāmukhī and Dhūmāvatī. Once upon a time, Śiva was living on Mount Kailasa with Pārvatī. She became so hungry that her body was racked with pain. She complained to Śiva, asking him for something to eat: "O Śiva," she said, "give me some food. I am famished." Śiva told her to be patient and wait a bit, after which he would give her anything she wanted. But having said this, Śiva ignored her and went back to doing yoga. She appealed to him again, saying that she was desperate for food. He again asked her to wait awhile. She protested that she could not wait, that she was starving to death. When he still was uncooperative, she put Śiva himself into her mouth to devour him. After a little while smoke began to issue from Pārvatī's body. This smoke was her *māyā* (magic power of illusion). Then Śiva emerged from Pārvatī and said: "Listen, O Goddess, a woman without a husband, as you just were, is called a widow and must strip herself of the adornments and marks of a married woman. That woman, you, who left her husband by swallowing him, will be known as Bagalāmukhī. And the smoke that came from her will be known as the goddess Dhūmāvatī."[5]

These three myths are so dissimilar that it is difficult to think of them as variants of each other. They seem to represent three different meditations on Bagalāmukhī's origin. In the first myth, Bagalā is associated with Viṣṇu and plays a role similar to one of his *avatāras*. That is, a cosmic crisis arises, and Viṣṇu initiates action to meet it. Bagalā emerges to restore cosmic stability. This myth does not overtly emphasize her ability to stun or paralyze (*stambhana*), for which she is famous, but the stilling of the storm does imply this power. The myth also promotes the superiority of a goddess over an eminent male deity, in this case Viṣṇu, by implying that he could not deal with a situation and had to summon the goddess for help.

In the second myth, Bagalā is again propitiated by the gods (the implication is that the male deities collectively petition her) to rescue the world from a power-crazed demon whose very words can kill and destroy. She stops the demon's rampage by grasping his tongue, preventing him from further speech. She is almost always portrayed in this act. In this myth her power to paralyze is explicit and stressed. She is often said to give the power of paralyzing the movements and activities of enemies.

She is also said to be the giver of *vāk siddhi*, the power of superior speech by which all opponents can be defeated. In this myth, by stopping the demon's tongue, she exercises her peculiar power over speech and her power to freeze, stun, or paralyze.

In the third myth, Bagalā is cast in the familiar role of Śiva's wife. As in the version of the origin of the Mahāvidyās as a group in which Satī challenges Śiva to allow her to attend her father's sacrifice even though Śiva has not been invited, so here Pārvatī and Śiva are at odds. Pārvatī is hungry and wants to eat at once, while Śiva, apparently indifferent to her hunger and impatience, puts her off and ignores her, or at least ignores the intensity of her need. As in the Satī myth, Pārvatī directly challenges Śiva: she satisfies her hunger by eating him. Although the denouement of the story asserts Śiva's primacy by having him, in effect, curse Pārvatī, condemning her to assume the forms of Bagalāmukhī and Dhūmāvatī, Pārvatī's power over Śiva is dramatic and memorable. The myth also hints at the meaning of Bagalāmukhī's name, which may be translated as "she who has the head or face of a crane." Like a crane, she swallowed whole what she ate—her husband—and perhaps this is why she is called Bagalāmukhī.

The Names Bagalāmukhī and Pītāmbarā

One of Bagalāmukhī's most-used epithets is Pītāmbarā-devī. Both names are strikingly distinctive, suggesting peculiar and particular characteristics. The significance of the names is far from clear, however. The name Bagalāmukhī probably means "she who has the face of a crane" or "the crane-faced one" (from Sanskrit *baka*, "crane"). Indeed, some scholars describe Bagalāmukhī as having the head of a crane.[6] She is in fact shown with the head of a crane in at least one painting I have seen, which has been identified as from Kangra, about the year 1800.[7] Other sources, however, say that she has the head of a duck[8] and the nose of a parrot.[9]

Some assume that the name is a corruption and that the original meaning had nothing to do with her having a bird face. Rama Shankar Tripathi of the Kāśi Viśvanāth temple in Varanasi told me that her name is actually Valgāmukhī (*valga* means "bit" in Sanskrit) and that the name refers to her ability to control one's enemies. Just as a bit in a horse's mouth controls it, so through the power of Bagalāmukhī one can control others. Another informant agreed that her name originally was Valgāmukhī but said that *valga* means "to paralyze" and refers to Bagalāmukhī's giving the *siddhi* of *stambhana*, "paralysis."[10]

What is troubling about interpreting Bagalāmukhī's name as meaning "crane faced" is that iconographically she is rarely shown with a bird head. In the Bagalāmukhī temple in Bankhandi in Himachal Pradesh, a framed picture of Bagalā hangs just outside the *garbha gṛha*. In this image, she sits on a crane that is attacking the demon with its beak and claw. A second crane is flying to the attack. In another image the pavilion in which she sits is decorated with swans.[11] There are examples of other Hindu goddesses having bird heads. Some of the sixty-four *yoginīs*, for example, are said to have bird heads: parrot, hawk, peacock, eagle, pigeon, or owl. Other goddesses are associated with birds as their *vāhanas* (vehicles). Sarasvatī is associated with a swan, Mātaṅgī with a parrot, Dhūmāvatī with a crow, and Lakṣmī with an owl. But in the scene of her afflicting the demon, Bagalā is almost always depicted anthropomorphically and without any bird symbolism. It is also difficult to interpret her name as a corruption of *valgā*, meaning either "bit" or "to paralyze," as she is never shown employing a bit, and the derivation of "paralyze" from *valgā* is etymologically dubious.

Perhaps the best we can do is speculate on the significance of her name, taking all of the above opinions into account. Bagalāmukhī is strongly associated with supernatural or magical powers, the ability to immobilize and attract others. Such uncanny abilities may be associated with birds, who perceive more acutely than humans. This is the interpretation of at least one author, who says that crows, for example, give advance information of people's arrival.[12] The crane, in its ability to stand absolutely still while hunting, is a symbol of intense concentration. In this sense, the crane is an appropriate symbol of the yogi.[13] The crane also seems to be able to attract prey to itself by remaining motionless. It is perhaps these kinds of perfections or "magical powers" that Bagalāmukhī possesses and gives to her devotees. The parrot, on the other hand, which in at least one case is said to be the type of bird's head Bagalāmukhī possesses, might suggest her ability to grant *vāk siddhi*, the power to make everything come true that one says (the very power with which the demon Madan caused such trouble in the world that Bagalāmukhī destroyed him).

The attempt to interpret Bagalāmukhī's name as implying her ability to rein in an enemy by means of a bit also stresses her association with magical powers of control. Even if the etymology is mistaken, it underlines this aspect of her cult. The imagery of the bit also suggests the theme of mounting and riding another being, a common image in shamanistic possession. The idea here is that one being (usually a spirit) controls or possesses another as a rider controls and possesses a horse. The image of mastery or control is vivid here. It may be that Bagalāmukhī is invoked to aid a worshiper in gaining possession of or control over another being or spirit.

Bagalāmukhī is also often known as Pītāmbarā-devī, "she who is dressed in yellow." She is often said to like yellow, to be dressed in yellow, and to prefer yellow offerings. In her *pūjā paddhati* (instructions for her worship), the worshiper is directed to offer her yellow items whenever possible, to wear yellow clothes while worshiping her, to sit on a yellow garment, and to use turmeric beads (which are yellow) when doing *japa* (repeated recitations) of her mantra.[14] In her *upāsanā paddhati*, or special *pūjā*, use of yellow is compulsory.[15] Her temples are often painted yellow. That is, the name Pītāmbarā-devī reflects a striking feature of her cult and worship. Unlike the name Bagalāmukhī, which does not seem to have any obvious connection with her worship and cult, Pītāmbarā-devī is born out in practice. The problem with this epithet, however, is understanding the significance of yellow for this particular goddess. That she likes yellow, wears yellow, and prefers yellow offerings is something most texts and informants mention. The reason, however, is rarely commented upon.

Mahant Rama Shankar Tripathi told me that women in South India wear yellow and that it is an auspicious color. He also suggested that yellow symbolizes the sun and gold. He said that the lust for money paralyzes people (hence Bagalāmukhī's ability to paralyze) and that the sight of yellow, which represents gold, has the same effect. I have also been told that yellow is the color of ripe grain and fire, the former suggesting abundance and the latter purity. The four yugas, or world ages, have the following colors: Kṛta, white; Tretā, yellow; Dvāpara, red; and Kali, black.[16] In this system, yellow is next to white in excellence, as the yugas decline in purity from the Kṛta, which is the best, to the Kali, which is the worst. The five *bhūtas*, or elements of creation (earth, fire, water, wind, and space), are denoted by colors and shapes. Earth is designated as yellow. This may imply that Pītāmbarā-devī is associated with the earth and worldly blessings. Bagalāmukhī's yantra, interestingly, shows two squares superimposed on each other at an angle, which may also imply her association with the earth, the square being the shape for the earth element.[17] Turmeric is also associated with marriage, particularly in South India.

"Turmeric, which gives the yellow colour, is par excellence the colour and symbol of marriage in the south (and in other parts of India as well) generally."[18] Although yellow seems auspicious or pure in most of these cases, its exact relation to Bagalāmukhī remains obscure.

Magical Powers

More than any of the other Mahāvidyās, Bagalāmukhī is associated with magical powers, which are sometimes referred to as *siddhis*, "accomplishments" or "perfections."[19] Among her epithets in her hymn of a thousand names are She Who Gives the Eight *Siddhis*, She Who Gives Magical and Mystical Powers (*ṛddhis* and *siddhis*), and She Who Gives All *Siddhis*.[20] The invocation written around the edge of an amulet containing her yantra in the *Tantrasāra* reads: "O Bagalāmukhī, please arrest the speech of wicked people, paralyze their faces, fix their tongues and destroy their intellect."[21] At the end of her *stotra* (hymn) in the *Rudrayāmala*, it is said that those who worship her will be able to make their enemies deaf and dumb, destroy their intelligence, and turn their wealth to poverty. Worshiping her will also make hostile people friendly toward the adept.[22] One author says that Bagalāmukhī is worshiped to gain control over one's enemies, to paralyze others, to attract others, to bring about the death of another, to counter the influence of the planets, to get wealth, and to win court cases.[23] Her paralyzing power applies to motion, thought, and initiative. In the hymn of her hundred names in the *Rudrayāmala*, she is called She Whose Form Is the Power to Paralyze and She Who Paralyzes.[24] She gives the ability to stupefy. She also gives the power of forceful and intelligent speech by which one can defeat any opponent, no matter how brilliant.[25]

In the *Sāṅkhyāyana-tantra* she is compared to the Brahmāstra, the missile of Brahmā, a supernatural weapon used by the god in war.[26] In fact, one of her most common epithets is She Who Is the Form of the Brahmāstra (Brahmāstra-rūpiṇī).[27] The *Sāṅkhyāyana-tantra* also has a special section about worshiping her for the acquisition of magical powers.[28] In some texts, specific recipes for worship are given for the different *siddhis* sought from Bagalāmukhī. If, for example, one wishes the *siddhi* of *māraṇa* (the power to kill an enemy by simply willing it), one should make a burnt offering. In this case, though, the sacrificial fire should be the fire of the cremation ground. In this fire one should offer mustard oil and the blood

Fig. 33. Bagalāmukhī, by Molaram, late eighteenth century, Garwahl, Himachal Pradesh. Bharat Kala Bhavan, Benares Hindu University, Varanasi.

of a she-buffalo. For *uccāṭana* (upsetting or ruining a person) one should burn the feathers of a crow and a vulture, and so on for the other *siddhis*.[29]

A contemporary author tries to explain the nature of the *siddhis* Bagalāmukhī bestows on her devotees by comparing them to the ability of certain animals to detect the presence of other creatures in situations where human beings would not be able to. They seem to have either more-acute senses or extrasensory perception. He explains that every living creature gives off subtle waves that pervade its whole body and permeate the environment it occupies. These waves linger for awhile after the departure of the creature who made them, he claims, and can be detected by dogs and crows, for example. Bagalāmukhī bestows such heightened sensory abilities on her devotees, and with them her devotees can overcome, outwit, and control other people.[30]

In the case of each of the Mahāvidyās, and indeed in the case of almost every Hindu deity, rewards can be expected from correct and sincere worship. Similarly, in the ancient meditative tradition of Hinduism, going all the way back to the earliest texts on yoga, one finds the assumption that worldly benefits, rewards, and special powers may be achieved through meditation. These are the eight *siddhis*, in fact. That Bagalāmukhī should be associated with such pragmatic and practical rewards and accomplishments, then, is neither surprising nor unusual; it is merely explicit. Positive or negative interpretations can be placed on this aspect of Bagalāmukhī. One author says that she "represents the ugly side of living creatures, like jealousy, hatred and cruelty."[31] Another informant, also by coincidence a monk of the Ramakrishna order, says that Bagalāmukhī's powers of *stambhana*, "paralyzing," represent her control over the five *prāṇas* (breaths) inside us. "She controls the vital breath; she conquers the tongue, which means self-control over greed, speech, and taste."[32] Indeed, we find in Bagalāmukhī's epithets references to both her power to give worldly enjoyment and her power to grant wisdom, knowledge, and liberation. In her thousand-name hymn, for example, she is called She Who Gives *Mokṣa* to All, She Who Is the Bestower of Ultimate Liberation, and She Who Gives Wisdom.[33] On the other hand, she is also called She Who Bestows Ultimate Enjoyment, Giver of Wealth, and Giver of the Pleasures of Dharma and *Artha* (power).[34]

Bagalāmukhī's associations with sexual desire and pleasure probably can be understood as part of her bestowing the power of attracting others, including sexually attracting them. Several of her epithets in her thousand-name hymn associate her directly with *kāma*, "sexual desire," or the god of sexual desire, Kāma-deva. She is called, for example: She Who Dwells Where There Is Sexual Desire, Who Likes Sexual Desire, Whose Form Is Sexual Desire, Whose Eyes Are Full of Desire, Who Gives Sexual Desire, and Who Takes Pleasure in Sexual Play.[35] Another string of epithets associates and identifies her with the female sexual organ: She Whose Form Is the Yoni, Who Dwells in the Yoni, Whose Form is the *Liṅgam* and Yoni, Who Has a Garland of Yonis, Who Is Adorned with Yonis, Who Enjoys the Union of the *Liṅgam* and Yoni, Who Is Worshiped with the *Liṅgam* and Yoni, and Who Is Absorbed with the *Liṅgam* and Yoni.[36]

Śava Sādhanā

In many depictions of Bagalāmukhī and in some of her *dhyāna* mantras, she is sitting on a corpse.[37] A hymn to her in the *Rudrayāmala*, for example, describes her as having her seat on a platform set in the middle of the ocean of nectar. The throne is decorated with red lotuses, and she sits on the corpse of an enemy she has killed and tossed onto the throne.[38] At the same time, she is pulling the tongue of a man or a beastlike creature. This combination of the goddess seated on a corpse while pulling the tongue of a demon suggests certain features of *śava sādhanā* (spiritual practice using a corpse), which is described in some tantric texts.

The presence of corpses in the iconography and worship of several of the Mahāvidyās is striking. Kālī, Tārā, Bagalāmukhī, Chinnamastā, Mātaṅgī, and Bhairavī are often pictured or described as standing or seated on a corpse or a *preta* (ghost). Others, such as Dhūmāvatī, although not seated or standing on a corpse, are sometimes said to be surrounded by funeral pyres or to be worshiped in cremation grounds. This association with corpses can be interpreted in several ways.

First, many informants say that the corpse is that of a demon whom that particular goddess has defeated in combat. This interpretation is usually cast in the framework of Vaiṣṇavite *avatāra* mythology: the goddess emerges to protect the cosmic order by killing a demon who has usurped the gods. The myth of Bagalāmukhī's origin that features the demon Madan supports this explanation.

Second, the corpse may be said to represent ignorance or the passions that the goddess has defeated or controlled. Swami Annapurnananda, for example, explained the demon and corpse in the Bagalāmukhī image as the bodily rhythms being mastered by yogic control.

A third interpretation is that the corpse represents the male pole in the Śiva-Śakti vision of reality, in which the male tends toward the static and the female toward the dynamic. This is exactly how the image of Dakṣiṇā-kālī is usually interpreted. She represents the underlying rhythm and power of the creation, which invigorates and empowers all beings and represents life itself, while the "corpse," Śiva, represents the unchanging, immobile, eternally blissful aspect of reality.

The corpse also might be interpreted as a reference to *śava sādhanā* (spiritual endeavor employing a corpse), which is described in detail in several tantric texts. The *Tantrasāra* of Kṛṣṇānanda Āgamavāgīśa[39] describes this practice as follows: The *sādhaka* is to take care, first of all, to select the right location, the right time, and the proper type of corpse with which to undertake this worship. A deserted house, the bank of a river, a mountain, a sacred place, the root of a *bilva* tree, a forest, and a cremation ground are all recommended as suitable. The best time is said to be the eighth lunar *tithi* (a lunar day), bright or dark, on a Tuesday night. The corpse itself should be intact and should belong to a young member of the Caṇḍāla caste (a low caste) who drowned, committed sui-

Fig. 34. Bagalāmukhī, contemporary lithograph.

cide, or was killed by a spear, lightning, a snake, or on the battlefield facing the enemy. The *sādhaka* should avoid using the corpse of a person who was very attached to a spouse, lived an immoral life, was prominent, or died of famine.[40]

The *sādhaka* takes the corpse to the place of worship, reciting a mantra to purify it as he does so (let us assume the adept in the following ritual is a male). He offers the corpse three handfuls of flowers and makes obeisance to it saying: "You are the lord of all heroic persons, lord of *kulas*, blissful, you are the form of Ānanda-bhairava (a form of Śiva), and you are the seat of the goddess. I am heroic myself, and I bow to you. Please arise for the purposes of making my worship of Caṇḍikā fruitful."[41] The *sādhaka* bathes the corpse with perfumed water while uttering mantras, then makes a bed of *kuśa* grass and places the corpse on it with its head toward the east. Having put some betel nut in the corpse's mouth, he turns the corpse over and smears sandal paste on its back, making a square in the middle of which he draws a yantra with an eight-petaled lotus and four gates. He puts a woolen cloth over the yantra, and if the corpse moves he spits on the corpse. He then worships the guardians of the directions and the sixty-four *yoginīs* with vegetable offerings. Next he worships the *śava āsana* (corpse seat) and sits on it, mounting it as he would a horse.[42] He expresses his intention (*saṇkalpa*), saying what he desires as a result of the worship. He then ties the corpse's hair into a knot. Next he makes offerings to the deity, placing them in the mouth of the corpse. Getting off the corpse, he binds its feet with a silken cord and draws a triangle around them. Remounting the corpse, he presses its hands firmly down on the *kuśa* grass, practices *prāṇayāma* (breath control), and meditates on his guru and the deity in his heart, repeating the deity's mantra fearlessly. While doing so, he scatters mustard and sesame seeds in all directions. Again getting down from the corpse, he takes seven steps and, returning, repeats the deity's mantra. If he hears a voice asking him to make some offerings, he should reply: "Next time I shall offer an elephant and other things." Then he should say: "Who are you and what is your name? Please give me a blessing." After this, he unbinds the feet of the corpse, bathes it, and buries it or places it in a body of water.

It is not clear in this description of *śava sādhanā* exactly whom the *sādhaka* might be worshiping and whom he might be trying to control. At some points it seems clear that he is propitiating the corpse itself or the corpse as the seat or location of a deity. At other points it seems as if he is trying to control the corpse or the spirit that may inhabit it. The image of mounting the corpse in the fashion of riding a horse is particularly vivid and reminds one of possession cults, such as voodoo, in which spirits are said to mount those whom they possess. The tying of the corpse's feet and the pressing down of its hands seem to indicate that the *sādhaka* is trying to control or tame the corpse or the corpse's spirit.

It is also not clear whose voice addresses the *sādhaka* in this corpse ritual. It might be the deity whose mantra he is reciting, or the spirit of the corpse, or a *preta* or *bhūta* (ghost) associated with the corpse.

The *Tantrasāra* mentions another possibility: a goddess named Karṇa-piśācī, who lives in the heart of a corpse. She favors the successful *sādhaka* by coming invisibly to him and whispering in his ear the correct answer to any question. The text says: "Ascending her, getting her power, he [the *sādhaka*] can go anywhere and see the past, present, and future."[43] Perhaps this deity is summoned or commanded by *śava sādhanā* and it is she whom the aspirant seeks to contact through this rite. Karṇa-piśācī is also described and discussed by a contemporary tantric practitioner as a deity whom one encounters in the cremation ground and from whom one may obtain knowledge of the present and past.[44] This deity has clear shamanistic overtones. A central theme in shamanism is the acquisition of a spirit who gives the shaman special or mystical knowledge from the spirit world. Both in *śava sādhanā* and in the propitiation of Karṇa-piśācī, it seems that the *sādhaka* is interested in gaining access to such a spirit.[45] It is in cooperation with, or through the power of, this spirit that the adept comes to possess magical powers for overcoming, controlling, or defeating his enemies.[46] This is the possible connection between Bagalāmukhī, who is so consistently associated with granting magical powers, and *śava sādhanā*.

The image of Bagalāmukhī seated on a corpse while pulling the tongue of an "enemy" might also relate to the themes evident in *śava sādhanā*. A description of *śava sādhanā* by a contemporary adept often mentions the possibility of the corpse reviving or becoming aggressive. This particular *sādhaka* stresses the importance of remaining fearless in such circumstances and facing and overcoming the corpse, the corpse's spirit, or the spirit possessing the corpse. Describing his own experience with this ritual, he tells how he was instructed to deal with the eventuality of the corpse becoming enlivened. "The old man had warned me that if she [the corpse was a young female] tried to get up I should knock her down and pin her firmly."[47] He was also warned that the corpse often begins to growl and scream at the *sādhaka* who is seeking to control it.[48] In Tibetan Buddhist tantric corpse *sādhanā* (*chod* rites) the adept is warned that if the corpse comes to life it must be subdued, which may involve biting off its protruding tongue before the ghost can devour the adept.[49]

The "enemy" that Bagalāmukhī beats sometimes has animal characteristics, which may suggest its ghost or spirit nature. A painting in a private collection in Bharat Kala Bhavan in Varanasi shows Bagalāmukhī pulling the hair of a demon who has a tail and a dark complexion (see figure 32). In another painting of Bagalāmukhī in Bharat Kala Bhavan, the demon she abuses is monkeylike in appearance (see figure 33). It may be that the depiction of Bagalāmukhī seated on a corpse while afflicting a "demon" is meant to suggest that she overcomes or controls the corpse's spirit, which has been revived or summoned by means of tantric rituals such as *śava sādhanā*. By bringing the spirit under her control, she becomes the mistress of magical powers, as does the *sādhaka* who worships her.

This analysis of corpse imagery also might be relevant to other Mahāvidyās. Kālī and Tārā are often said to stand or sit on corpses, Chinnamastā sometimes stands on a corpse being consumed in a funeral pyre, and Dhūmāvatī is sometimes pictured in cremation grounds. This is a striking aspect of the Mahāvidyās and begs for interpretation. In *śava sādhanā* it is specified that the corpse should be fresh, for then the spirit of the dead person is still nearby. The ghost of the corpse has not been settled and lingers in the liminal area between life and death. It still dwells in the land of the living, not being able to depart for the land of the dead until the appropriate *śrāddha* rituals have been performed. In this sense, the spirit of the dead person is a potential *preta* or *bhūta*, an unhappy spirit that can cause trouble for the living. The spirit of a person recently killed, especially if the death has been violent, is a preeminent example of a liminal being, a being betwixt and between identities, realms, structured contexts.[50] Such a spirit, like *pretas* and *bhūtas*, who are stuck permanently between worlds, does not belong anywhere. They are outside all structures.

Victor Turner has argued that many religious rituals, beliefs, and practices seek to create liminal situations or to transform human beings into liminal figures. The reason for this, he argues, is that transformation of consciousness or identity, which is the goal of many rituals and beliefs, cannot take place easily, if at all, within the structures of the normal world. In many cultures, for example, initiation rituals often take place outside the normal confines of society—in the bush, the woods, or specially prescribed places—in liminal space. The rituals often use the imagery of rebirth to speak of the aim of the rites, which is to transform the initiates.

Similarly, perhaps, tantric rituals aim at transforming the aspirant, awakening in him or her an expanded consciousness and the acquisition of a new identity. An appropriate place to undertake such rituals is the cremation ground, the liminal place par excellence. To associate or identify with a fresh corpse, to employ one as a "seat" for ritual purposes, or to court the company of ghosts and troublesome spirits, enhances the liminal context of tantric rituals, instilling them with transformative potential.

Bagalāmukhī Temples

Shrines dedicated to Bagalāmukhī are not very common; her worship is undertaken primarily through individual *sādhanā*, which does not require a public shrine or temple. I have, however, heard of and visited a few Bagalāmukhī-Pītāmbarā temples.

One is in the old part of Varanasi, not far from Manikarnika Ghat. The temple is attached to a private house, and I was told by the priest there that it was a "private temple" but open to the public. The image of the goddess is normally kept hidden, which is typical in goddess temples. This one is covered with clothing and a silver mask. The priest told me, however, that the image underneath depicts Bagalāmukhī in her familiar form, namely, pulling the tongue of a demon and about to strike him with a club. The priest said that the goddess gives the *siddhis* of detachment and *māraṇa* (the ability to kill by simply willing it). He did not mention *stambhana*, which is the *siddhi* usually associated with Bagalāmukhī. To the right of the goddess is an image of Śiva and on her left an image of Ganeśa. The statue of a crouching lion faces the goddess, which is typical in goddess temples. Pictures of the ten *avatāras* of Viṣṇu hang in the adjoining hall, and outside the temple, on the porch, are large paintings of Garuḍa and Kṛṣṇa. The goddess, then, has strong associations at this temple with both Śiva and Viṣṇu. The large painting of Garuḍa; Pakṣarāja (the king of birds), may be significant in light of Bagalāmukhī's association with the crane, although the priest did not comment on this association. According to the priest, *tāntrikas* do not worship at this temple, and *bali* (blood offerings) are not offered there. It is used primarily by ordinary householders and residents of the area. The sandals of the founding *mahant* (chief temple priest) are prominently enshrined in the hall adjoining the main sanctuary that houses the image of the goddess. None of the other Mahāvidyās is enshrined or depicted at this temple, and the goddess's association with this group is nowhere in evidence.

Another temple to Bagalāmukhī is located in Bankhandi, Himachal Pradesh. Bankhandi, "where the arrow split the ground," so named because long ago a sadhu established a spring by repeatedly jabbing an arrow into the ground, is a small town, and the temple is located outside it in the woods. According to the temple priest, the goddess came from Tibet, where she had killed demons who were assaulting her devotees. The tradition that Bagalāmukhī came from the north is interesting and is supported by her popularity in Nepal. The king of Kangra became the goddess's devotee and established her worship there. Since that time, the priest said, she has been the protective deity of the area. The priest said that the temple was "four or five hundred years old." The goddess grants all desires and gives protection from all harm and blesses people with children (all standard functions of a goddess). She is unmarried, according to the priest, and there was no sign of a *liṅgam* nor any image of a male consort. The priest said that her *vāhana* is sometimes a crane, and indeed a framed painting in the temple showed Bagalāmukhī seated on one. The crane is attacking the demon with its beak, and another crane is flying to join in. The priest said that the goddess likes yellow, which is the color of a crane's beak. The entire temple, inside and out, is painted yellow. The actual image of the deity, which the priest assured me resembled in detail the descriptions of the goddess in her *dhyāna* mantras, was not visible except for the head, which was of rough, black stone.

The most famous temple to Bagalāmukhī is at Datiya in Madhya Pradesh, which I have not visited. It was established sometime in the 1930s by a sadhu who eventually became known as Pūjā Swami. Bagalāmukhī was his *iṣṭa devata* (chosen deity), and he established her image to benefit India, which at that time was in the throes of the Independence movement. Patriotism remained a strong theme in the *sādhanā* of this founder priest, and I have been told that he undertook special worship to invoke Bagalāmukhī's power of *stambhana* against the enemies of India (both internal and external) on several occasions. An image of Dhūmāvatī is also installed at this temple, and it seems clear that Bagalāmukhī's association with the Mahāvidyās is emphasized there. According to one report, left-handed tantric worship of Dhūmāvatī takes place at this shrine, although the founding priest did not practice it himself. This same description says that Bagalāmukhī's image is beautiful and she is associated with material blessings and welfare, while Dhūmāvatī's image is terrible and she is associated with destruction.[51]

Mātaṅgī

The Outcaste Goddess

She is seated on a corpse. Her clothes and all her ornaments are red. She wears a garland of *guñja* seeds [a small forest seed]. She is sixteen years old and has full breasts. She holds a skull and a sword in her two hands. She should be offered leftovers [*ucciṣṭa*].[1]

She is blue in color and has the disc of the moon on her forehead. She has three eyes, is seated on a jeweled throne, and is adorned with jeweled ornaments. She has a very thin waist, and her breasts are round and firm. She has a smiling face and holds a noose, a sword, a goad, and a club in her four hands.[2]

She is seated on an altar and has a smiling face and a greenish complexion. She is worshiped by gods and demons. Around her neck is a garland of *kadamba* flowers. Her hair is long, and the disk of the moon adorns her forehead. She perspires slightly around her face, which makes her more beautiful and bright. Below her navel are three horizontal lines [from the folds of her skin] and a thin vertical line of fine hair. She wears a girdle of jeweled ornaments, as well as bracelets, armlets, and ear ornaments. Her eyes are intoxicated. She represents the sixty-four arts, and she is flanked by two parrots.[3]

Intimations of Mātaṅgī in a Buddhist Tale

In the *Divyāvadāna*, a Buddhist collection of stories concerning previous lives of the Buddha that was probably written around 250–300 C.E., there is a tale of a hunter king named Mātaṅga and his daughter. Certain details of the story bear such a striking similarity to

Fig. 35. Mātaṅgī, by Bhatuk Ramprasad, early twentieth century. Printed with the permission of Dr. Bhanu Shanker Mehta, Varanasi.

later characteristics of the goddess Mātaṅgī's nature and mythology that it is relevant to mention it as a possible intimation, or very early version, of the Mahāvidyā goddess.

Once upon a time, the Buddha's disciple Ānanda went out begging for food. After getting some, he became thirsty. He saw a girl drawing water from a well, approached her, and asked for water. The girl answered:

"My name is Prakṛti [nature], and I am a Caṇḍāla [a very low caste], the daughter of Mātaṅga. Should I give you water?" Ānanda replied: "I am not asking what your caste is, I am only asking for water." He took water from her, and as he drank Prakṛti admired his youthful body and became fascinated by him. Her desire for him grew, and she yearned to have him as her husband.

After Ānanda had returned to the monastery, Prakṛti asked her mother, Mahāvidyādharī (she who is skilled in the great mantras), if she would attract Ānanda to her by the appropriate rituals and mantras. Her mother hesitated: she feared trouble from the local king, who was a devotee of the Buddha, and she also doubted whether her magic could overcome the power of the Buddha to protect his disciples. At first she refused her daughter, but when Prakṛti threatened suicide if she could not have Ānanda, her mother agreed to try to capture him by magic. The mother cleaned an area near her house, built an altar, offered up flowers in the fire on the altar, and began to recite mantras to attract Ānanda to her daughter. So adept was she, and so powerful the mantras, that she was able to harness the forces of the lightning and rain to help her.

By her magic, Ānanda's heart became agitated as he remembered Prakṛti's charm, and he left the monastery to seek her out. As he approached Prakṛti's home, her mother saw him coming and instructed Prakṛti to beautify herself and prepare a bed for lovemaking, which she did. Arriving there, Ānanda stood near the mother's altar and began to weep. He prayed to the Buddha to rescue him, and the Buddha, aware of his predicament, nullified the power of the Caṇḍāla woman's mantras. Ānanda became calm and returned to the monastery.

When Prakṛti discovered that the Buddha had overcome her mother's magic, she went herself to the Buddha, who asked what she wanted. She was frank and said that she desired Ānanda for her husband. The Buddha told her that the only way she could share Ānanda's company was to become a nun herself. Prakṛti, seeing the shortsightedness of her craving for Ānanda, and impressed with the teachings of the Buddha, agreed to be initiated as a nun. Her hair was cut off, and she was given the simple garb of a Buddhist nun.

After Prakṛti's entrance into the Buddhist order, the Buddha told her a story that put the attraction between her and Ānanda in perspective. Once in the past, Triśaṅku was king of elephant hunters (Mātaṅga-rāja). He had a son, Śārdūlakarṇa, for whom he wished to find a suitable bride. Triśaṅku heard of a Brahman's daughter, named Prakṛti, who he thought would be suitable for his son, so he set out to arrange a wedding. He traveled with an entourage of his ministers and his many dogs. When the Brahman saw that Triśaṅku was an elephant hunter of low caste, he was disdainful of him and rejected his proposal for a marriage. In a subsequent conversation, however, Triśaṅku impressed him with his vast knowledge of spiritual matters and the arts and sciences. The Brahman relented and allowed the marriage to take place.

That Brahman's daughter was the same Prakṛti who in this life desired Ānanda, the Buddha said. And Triśaṅku's son, Śārdūlakarṇa, was Ānanda in that life. This explained the mutual attraction of the pair in this life. And the elephant-hunter king, the Buddha said, was he himself.[4]

This story, which was made popular in recent times by Rabindranath Tagore's story *Caṇḍālikā*, has several intriguing points that are relevant to our consideration of the Mahāvidyā goddess Mātaṅgī. First, the heroine's father is named Mātaṅga, and in the story of her previous birth, her father-in-law is said to be king of the elephant hunters (Mātaṅga-rāja). In the context of the Mahāvidyās, as we shall see, Mātaṅgī is often said to be the daughter of Mātaṅga, who is either a sage or a hunter. Second, the heroine is of low caste, a Caṇḍāla. This is an important, if not central, feature of the goddess Mātaṅgī. Third, the heroine's name, Prakṛti, which may be translated as "nature," identifies her with the jungle, the forests, and hunting culture, again an important aspect of the later goddess. Fourth, rites aimed at attracting another person and forcing him to do one's will are an important part of the story and remind us of Mātaṅgī's power to attract and control others. And, fifth, the name of Mātaṅgī's mother, Mahāvidyādharī (she who is skilled in the great mantras), and her use of magical powers to infatuate Ānanda, relate the story to the Mahāvidyās.

We do not have the goddess Mātaṅgī in this early Buddhist tale. What we probably have is a source that contributed to the eventual emergence of the goddess. The story contains early intimations of the later goddess.

Origin Myths

There are several myths concerning the origin or appearance of Mātaṅgī, and taken together they tell us a good deal about the type of goddess she is. As will be apparent, some of the themes and details of the Buddhist tale of Prakṛti, the daughter of Mātaṅga, also show up in these myths.

The first myth dealing with Mātaṅgī's origin is found in the *Śakti-saṁgama-tantra* and concerns the appearance of Uccịṣṭa-mātaṅginī, one of Mātaṅgī's most common forms. Once upon a time, Viṣṇu and Lakṣmī went to visit Śiva and Pārvatī. Viṣṇu and Lakṣmī gave Śiva and Pārvatī fine foods, and some pieces dropped to the ground. From these remnants arose a maiden endowed with fair qualities. She asked for leftover food (*ucciṣṭa*). The four deities offered her their leftovers as *prasāda* (food made sacred by having been tasted by deities). Śiva then said to the attractive maiden: "Those who repeat your mantra and worship you, their activities will be fruitful. They will be able to control their enemies and obtain the objects of their desires." From then on this maiden became known as Ucciṣṭa-mātaṅginī. She is the bestower of all boons.[5]

The second version of Mātaṅgī's origin is found in the *Prāṇatoṣinī-tantra.* Once upon a time, Pārvatī was seated on Śiva's lap. She said to him that he always gave her anything she wanted and that now she had a desire to return to her father's home for a visit. Would he consent to her visiting her father, Himālaya, she asked? Śiva was not happy about granting her this wish but eventually complied, saying that if she did not come back in a few days, he would go there himself to ask for her return. Pārvatī's mother sent a crane to carry Pārvatī back to her family home. When she did not return for some days, Śiva disguised himself as an ornament maker and went to Himālaya's house. He sold shell ornaments to Pārvatī and then, seeking to test her faithfulness, asked that she have sex with him as his payment. Pārvatī was outraged at the merchant's request and was ready to curse him, but then she discerned with her yogic intuition that the ornament vendor was really her husband, Śiva. Concealing her knowledge of his true identity, she replied: "Yes, fine, I agree. But not just now."

Sometime later, Pārvatī disguised herself as a huntress and went to Śiva's home, where he was preparing to do evening prayer. She danced there, near Mānas Lake. She wore red clothes, and her body was lean, her eyes wide, and her breasts large. Admiring her, Śiva asked: "Who are you?" She replied: "I am the daughter of a Caṇḍāla. I've come here to do penance." Then Śiva said: "I am the one who gives fruits to those who do penance." Saying this, he took her hand, kissed her, and prepared to make love to her. While they made love, Śiva himself was changed into a Caṇḍāla. At this point he recognized the Caṇḍāla woman as his wife Pārvatī. After they had made love, Pārvatī asked Śiva for a boon, which he granted. Her request was this: "As you [Śiva] made love to me in the form of a Caṇḍālinī [Caṇḍāla woman], this form will last forever and will be known as Ucciṣṭa-caṇḍālinī.

Only after performing suitable worship to this form will you [Śiva] be worshiped and your worship be made fruitful."[6]

The third myth that deals with Mātaṅgī's origin is from the *Svatantra-tantra*. Once upon a time Mātaṅga undertook austerities in order to gain the power to subdue all creatures. He persisted in his ascetic exercises for thousands of years until finally, in a burst of bright light, the goddess Tripura-sundarī appeared before him. She emitted brilliant rays from her eyes, and the goddess Kālī emerged. Kālī then took on a greenish complexion and assumed the form of Rāja-mātaṅginī. With the help of this goddess, Mātaṅga was able to realize his desire to control all creatures.[7]

A fourth story concerning the creation of Mātaṅgī, told to me by an informant in Varanasi, is associated with a small temple dedicated to Kauri-bai, a form of Mātaṅgī, located in a low-caste area of Varanasi. According to this myth, Kauri-bai (whose name associates her with the cowrie shell) was Śiva's sister. She was particularly fastidious and was preoccupied, in a high-caste Brahman sort of way, with purity and pollution. She was annoyed with Śiva, who had many habits that she considered disgusting, such as spending time in the cremation ground, imbibing intoxicants, and associating with ghosts and goblins. He was completely inconsiderate of her attempts to keep their house pure and would often track ashes from the cremation ground into her freshly cleaned house. After Śiva married Pārvatī, Pārvatī made polite overtures to Kauri-bai, inviting her to visit them. Kauri-bai, however, refused all these friendly gestures, complaining bitterly to Pārvatī about Śiva's disgusting habits. Finally, like a good wife, Pārvatī took umbrage at the abuses being leveled at her husband and cursed Śiva's sister to be reborn in an untouchable community and to spend her entire life there. And so she was reborn in the untouchable area of Varanasi and in such polluted circumstances found herself very unhappy. She went to Śiva, the lord of Varanasi (Kāśi Viśvanātha), who gave her the boon that people on pilgrimage to Varanasi would have to worship at her shrine before their journey could be considered complete.[8]

The Goddess Who Prefers Pollution

In these otherwise dissimilar myths, several important themes are emphasized that seem central to Mātaṅgī's character. The first myth stresses Mātaṅgī's association with leftover food, which is normally

Fig. 36. Mātaṅgī, Nepali Manuscript. American Institute of Indian Studies, Ramnagar.

considered highly polluting. Indeed, she herself actually arises or emerges from Śiva and Pārvatī's table scraps. And the first thing she asks for is sustenance in the form of leftover food (*ucciṣṭa*).[9]

Not only does Mātaṅgī request *ucciṣṭa* in this story, but texts describing her worship specify that devotees should offer her *ucciṣṭa* with their hands and mouths stained with *ucciṣṭa;* that is, worshipers should be in a state of pollution, having eaten and not washed.[10] This is a dramatic reversal of the usual protocols for the worship of Hindu deities. Normally, devotees are careful to offer particularly pure food or food that the deity especially likes. After the deity has eaten it (consumed its spiritual essence), the food is returned to the worshiper. This leftover food (*ucciṣṭa*, although it is not called this) is referred to as *prasāda* (grace). The ritual give-and-take in this case emphasizes the inferior position of the devotee, who serves the deity and accepts the deity's leftover food as something to be cherished. In the case of Mātaṅgī, worshipers present her with their own highly polluted leftover food and are themselves in a state of pollution while doing so. In one case, a devotee offers Ucciṣṭa-mātaṅginī a piece of clothing stained with menstrual blood in order to win the boon of being able to attract someone.[11] Menstrual blood is regarded in almost all Hindu texts and contexts as extremely polluting, and menstruating women are forbidden to enter temples or otherwise serve the deities. In the case of Mātaṅgī, these strict taboos are disregarded, indeed, are flaunted.

Worship manuals also specify that no fasting is required before worshiping Mātaṅgī, although it is often desirable in the case of other deities; that vows of any type are not necessary in seeking her blessing (devotees typically agree to perform some pious deed, such as fasting or making a pilgrimage, in return for a deity's favor); and that worshipers need not observe any rituals of purification prior to her worship. Similarly, anyone may recite her mantra, even those who are not initiated or who would not be considered qualified to undertake any other goddess's worship.[12]

In a society such as that of high-caste Hindus, who are probably the authors of most of the texts concerning Mātaṅgī, preoccupation, indeed obsession, with purity and pollution dominates almost every facet of daily life. Keeping track of what is clean and what is unclean, who is clean and who is not and under what circumstances, and how clean one is oneself at any given time and in any given circumstance, becomes oppressive at times. For such purity-minded individuals, furthermore, polluted persons and objects may be regarded with fear bordering on awe, as having the power to completely devastate one and make one unfit for normal social life. For some Hindus, it is exhilarating, if not spiritually liberating, to intensely embrace the forbidden, to come to terms with it once and for all and in so doing to overcome its hold over them. Ucciṣṭa-mātaṅginī, as the embodiment of the polluted, is the goddess by means of whom one can come directly to terms with pollution. As such, she is both powerful and liberating.[13]

The Outcaste/Low-Caste Goddess

The second myth concerning the origin of Mātaṅgī also touches on the theme of the polluted or forbidden by associating the goddess with Caṇḍālas and with hunting culture, as in the Buddhist tale of Prakṛti. By disguising herself as a Caṇḍālinī, Pārvatī assumes the identity of a very low-caste person, and by being attracted to her, Śiva allows himself to be intensely polluted. Both deities self-consciously and willingly associate themselves with the periphery of Hindu society and culture. The Caṇḍāla identity is sacralized, as it were, in the establishment of the goddess Ucciṣṭa-caṇḍālinī. This goddess, a form of Mātaṅgī, sums up in her name the polluted and the forbidden: *ucciṣṭa* and Caṇḍāla, polluted, dangerous food and polluted, dangerous people.

In this story, Mātaṅgī is born when Pārvatī adopts a Caṇḍāla identity. The story makes the point that Pārvatī has a facet that is outside normal society; in her character is an "other" identity that transgresses propriety and caste-bound society. This affirmation of Pārvatī's "forest" or "hunter" or "Caṇḍālinī" identity can actually be traced to the *Mahābhārata* (3.40.1–5), where Arjuna encounters Śiva and Pārvatī in the guise of hunters in the Himalayas. Given Śiva's strong identity as an outsider in many texts, this is not surprising. Traditionally, Śiva and Pārvatī's home lies somewhere outside normal society—in the forest, in the mountains, among tribal, low-caste, or outcaste people. This myth reasserts this aspect of their marital history.

The fourth version of Mātaṅgī's origin, in which she is said to have been Śiva's purity-minded sister, cursed by Pārvatī to be reborn in an untouchable community, also emphasizes Mātaṅgī's association with pollution and low castes. Indeed, a central message of the myth is that an undue obsession with purity can be dangerous and destructive. The myth also emphasizes that it can be transformative, indeed, even necessary, to associate with that which is polluted or to worship a deity who is closely identified with those who are of low caste. Śiva and Pārvatī, by implication, are not as preoccupied with pollution as Kauri-bai; Śiva is even said to make contact purposely with polluting things and people. As Kauri-bai, then, Mātaṅgī is clearly identified with a goddess who lives among low castes in a polluted environment and who earned this dubious distinction by being overly preoccupied with avoiding pollution.

Mātaṅgī's association with low castes and pollution is also clear in the ways in which polluted substances are handled among certain communities in Nepal. The lowest group of castes in Nepal, the Pore, includes sweepers, cleaners of latrines, and fishermen. These castes have the important job of collecting and accumulating the polluted and polluting detritus of other castes and getting rid of it. They not only collect physically impure things, such as human waste, but are also thought to accumulate pollution associated with death and bad luck. They are required to live outside the village and in this sense define the boundaries of "pure" society. That society cannot, in fact, function without them: they provide the valve through which it rids itself of its own pollution. This role of low castes is a common theme in Hindu ideas of caste and pollution. What is particularly interesting for our purposes is that members of this group of castes are also known by the caste name Mātaṅgī.[14]

In the Nepalese context, polluted substances and items are also associated with special rocks called *chwāsas* that are set up at crossroads (a very common location for getting rid of dangerous things). Remains of sacrificial animal heads offered to deities, clothes worn by people just before they died, and other such things are disposed of at the *chwāsas*. According to some people, the deity associated with these *chwāsas* "is the dangerous goddess, Mātaṅgī," who is believed to consume these dangerous materials.[15] Like the untouchables among whom she is found, that is, she gets rid of pollution by accepting it as an offering and in so doing lives up to her name Ucciṣṭa-mātaṅginī.

The second version of Mātaṅgī's origin also emphasizes sexual tension between husband and wife. It contains the familiar theme (in stories of the Mahāvidyās) of Pārvatī (or Satī) asking Śiva for permission to return to her paternal home and Śiva's reluctance to grant it. Śiva, in disguise, seeks to test and seduce his own wife, while she in turn does the same thing to him. They present themselves to each other as "the forbidden" and, perhaps inadvertently (it is not clear), make themselves more sexually appealing to each other. Pārvatī agrees to have sex with the ornament merchant, and Śiva lusts after the Caṇḍāla huntress. One of the central tensions in the story is the lure and attractiveness of illicit sex. In the *pañca tattva* ritual, the woman with whom *maithuna* (sexual intercourse) is performed is not one's wife and can be from a low caste. In both the story and the *pañca tattva* ritual, the power of illicit sex is transformative in one way or another. Śiva is actually transformed into a Caṇḍāla in the act of sex, while the *sādhaka* who performs *maithuna* with a low-caste woman seeks spiritual transformation. The name Mātaṅgī reinforces this aspect of the goddess as erotically powerful. Her name literally means "she whose limbs are intoxicated (with passion)" and most commonly refers to an impassioned female elephant.

Fig. 37. Mātaṅgī, contemporary lithograph.

Mātaṅgī is closely identified with a goddess named Śavareśvarī (mistress of the Śavaras). The Śavaras are a tribal people often mentioned in Sanskrit literature, and they typify forest culture, life beyond the boundaries of civilized society.[16] Śavareśvarī is described as sixteen and short in stature. She is entirely clothed in leaves and wears a garland of *guñja* seeds and earrings of creepers. She holds a basket made of vines, is collecting fruit with her right hand, and is smiling and singing.[17] This goddess, or this form of Mātaṅgī, puts into sharp focus one aspect of Mātaṅgī, her association with the forest. In her thousand-name hymn from the *Nandyāvarta-tantra*, Mātaṅgī bears several epithets that associate her with Śavareśvarī. She is called She Who Lives in the Forest, Who Walks in the Forest, Who Knows the Forest, Who Enjoys the Forest (v. 4), and Śavarī (v. 103).[18] In her hundred-name hymn from the *Rudrayāmala*, she is said, like Śavareśvarī, to love music (v. 13).[19] In her *dhyāna* mantra in the *Śāradā-tilaka-tantra*, Rāja-mātaṅgī is said to listen to the chattering of green parrots, to play a *vīṇā*, to have paintings of leaves on her forehead, and to wear flower garlands in her hair and conch shells as earrings.[20] She is also said to control all wild animals.[21] This association with Śavareśvarī affirms and reinforces Mātaṅgī's identity with the forest and with tribal culture, both of which are strongly "other" from the point of view of high-caste Brahman society.[22]

The Goddess of Magical Powers

The third story points to another aspect of Mātaṅgī, namely, her association with magical powers, particularly the power to exert control over others. The sage Mātaṅga subjects himself to austerities to gain this power, and Mātaṅgī appears as a manifestation of Kālī in order to enable Mātaṅga to realize his wish. Like other goddesses among the Mahāvidyās, particularly Bagalāmukhī, Mātaṅgī is worshiped in order to gain certain magical or psychic powers. In a prayer in the *Mahābhāgavata-purāṇa*, the Mahāvidyās are typified according to their peculiar natures and powers. The *sādhaka* asks to be like Chinnamastā in showing generosity to others, like Bagalāmukhī in battle, like Dhūmāvatī when angry, in kingly functions like Tripura-sundarī, in times of peace like Bhuvaneśvarī, and in controlling enemies like Mātaṅgī.[23] The *Tantrasāra* at several points says that by meditating upon, reciting the mantra of, or worshiping Mātaṅgī one gains power over others, the power of having everything one says come true, and the power of attracting people.[24]

Texts devoted to the Mahāvidyās often contain a section called *prayog vidhi*, "concerning the acquisition of desires." It is here that the different "recipes" are given for achieving specific benefits in return for worshiping the goddess in question. While Mātaṅgī is not at all unique in terms of being approached for certain desires, she is definitely associated with acquiring magical powers and granting favors. It is useful in getting a more complete picture of Mahāvidyā worship to discuss in some detail this aspect of her cult.

Certain preliminary rites are necessary before making the specific offerings to obtain what one wants. First, and of essential importance, is the empowerment of the goddess's mantra (*puraścarna*), in this case Mātaṅgī's mantra, which will be an indispensable part of subsequent rituals. The *sādhaka* empowers the mantra by performing the following rituals: (1) reciting the mantra itself ten thousand times, (2) offering flowers mixed with honey and ghee in a fire while saying the mantra one thousand times, (3) pouring purified water (*tarpaṇa*, often done for spirits of the ancestors) one hundred times while reciting the mantra, (4) sprinkling water ten times while saying the mantra, and finally (5) offering food to ten Brahmans. The mantra is now empowered and is referred to as a *siddha* mantra.[25]

The initial empowering of the mantra need not be done every time it is used. On subsequent occasions, the *sādhaka* need only recite the mantra ten thousand or one thousand times in order to "recharge" it, as it were, restoring it to its full power. Next is performed the worship of the *pīṭha*, or place, within which the offerings will be made for the desired boons. After the *pīṭha* has been made pure by banishing inimical spirits and summoning protective deities (the guardians of the ten directions), the goddess's yantra is duly constructed (either physically or mentally). On this yantra altar the *sādhaka* kindles a fire. Depending upon what it is the *sādhaka* wishes, different elements or combinations of elements are offered up in the fire, accompanied by the recitation of Mātaṅgī's mantra. Sometimes certain times of day or night, and sometimes also special places, such as cremation grounds, river banks, forests, or crossroads, are specified as the most effective for the performance of the ritual. The following twelve "recipes" are prescribed:

1. If *homa* (fire sacrifice) is done with *mallikā* flowers (a small, white, fragrant flower—not jasmine), the *sādhaka* will acquire success in yoga.
2. If offerings of *bel* flowers are made, the *sādhaka* will acquire the power to rule over others, kingship.
3. If offerings of *palās* flowers or leaves are made, the *sādhaka* will acquire control over others.
4. If another type of plant is used, diseases will be destroyed.
5. If *nīm* twigs with rice are offered up in the fire, the worshiper will obtain great wealth.
6. If *nīm* oil and salt are offered, the *sādhaka* will be able to destroy enemies, and his or her store of grain will increase.
7. If salt alone is offered, the *sādhaka* will gain the power to control others.
8. If turmeric powder (which is bright yellow and hence favored by Bagalāmukhī) is offered, the worshiper will acquire the power to paralyze others (Bagalāmukhī's special power, *stambhana*).
9. If eight different fragrant items, including red and white sandal paste, saffron, and camphor, are offered, the *sādhaka* will be at-

tractive to people. If the mantra is recited an additional one hundred times and sandal paste put on the worshiper's forehead, he or she will become attractive to the whole world.

10. If salt mixed with honey is offered up in the fire and the mantra is recited 108 times at night, the *sādhaka* will acquire the power to attract others.
11. If the *sādhaka* makes rice powder and with this makes bread and then eats it while reciting the Mātaṅgī mantra, he will control women. In this case there is no *homa* offering.
12. Finally, any person can be made the *sādhaka*'s servant if the following rites are performed: In the dark of night put a conch in a (presumably dead) crow's stomach, wrap the crow in blue thread, and then burn it on a cremation fire. Meditate on the ashes of the burned crow while invoking Mātaṅgī's mantra one thousand times. Anyone to whom the ashes are given will become the worshiper's servant. No *homa* accompanies this recipe, although the burning of the crow on the cremation fire might be thought of as a fire offering to Mātaṅgī.[26]

In the *Tantrasāra* we are told that at night, in a cremation ground or at a crossroads, the *sādhaka* should offer fish, meat, cooked rice, milk, and incense to Mātaṅgī to acquire poetic talent and victory over enemies and to become a second Bṛhaspati (the gods' priest-guru). We are also told in the same text that to achieve the highest knowledge of the scriptures, Mātaṅgī should be offered *ucciṣṭa*, cat meat, and goat meat.[27] In the *Puraścaryārṇava*, Karṇa-mātaṅgī is invoked in the hope that she will whisper in the *sādhaka*'s ear the truth about some question posed by the *sādhaka*.[28] We are told elsewhere that those who recite Mātaṅgī's mantra one hundred thousand times, offer ten thousand flowers in the sacrificial fire, and worship her yantra will get great wealth, will be able to control an angry king and his children, will be immune to the troubles caused by evil spirits, and will themselves become like deities. In this case, to insure the success of their *sādhanā*, worshipers are cautioned to refrain at all times from criticizing women and to treat them like goddesses.[29]

Fig. 38. Lakṣmī, contemporary lithograph.

Kamalā

The Lotus Goddess

She has a beautiful golden complexion. She is being bathed by four large elephants who pour jars of nectar over her. In her four hands she holds two lotuses and makes the signs of granting boons and giving assurance. She wears a resplendant crown and a silken dress. I pay obeisance to her who is seated on a lotus in a lotus posture.[1]

Let Kamalā protect us by her wonderful side-glances that delight the heart of Viṣṇu. She is seated on a lotus, has a smiling face, and with her four hands holds two lotuses and makes the signs of giving favors and granting assurance. Her complexion is like the brightness of lightning. Her breasts are firm and heavy and are decorated with garlands of pearls.[2]

She is resplendent like the rising sun and wears a bright moon disc on her brow. She is adorned with a crown and necklace of jewels. She is bent down due to the weight of her large breasts, and in her hands she holds two lotuses and two bunches of rice shoots. She has three lotuslike eyes. She wears the *kauṣṭubha* gem and has a smiling face.[3]

The name Kamalā means "she of the lotus" and is a common epithet of the goddess Lakṣmī or Śrī, who is said to adore lotuses and to be lotus eyed and surrounded by lotuses. Indeed, Kamalā is none other than the goddess Lakṣmī. She is usually listed as the tenth and last of the Mahāvidyās. Of all goddesses in the Mahāvidyā group, Kamalā is the best known and most popular and has the oldest tradition of worship outside the Mahāvidyā context. Her usual position as last in line of the Mahāvidyās (which is often interpreted as meaning the least significant, or the lowest, in a spiritual hierarchy) is in direct contrast with her importance outside the group. Compared to Kālī, who is usually named as the first of the Mahāvidyās, Kamalā is a goddess with almost completely auspicious, benign, and desirable qualities. As we shall see below, she is associated or identified with a number of worldly blessings that preoccupy human beings and their ordinary religious practice: wealth, power, good luck, and safety.

The Early History of Śrī

Early references to Kamalā call her Śrī and consistently associate her with positive qualities. Indeed, the name Śrī means "auspicious." For example, in the *Śatapatha-brāhmaṇa* (11.4.3.1 ff.), she is identified with food, royal power, luster, fortune, and beauty. Her positive qualities and auspicious nature are elaborated in the *Śrī-sūkta*, an early hymn in her praise probably dating back to pre-Buddhist times.[4] She gives wealth and other desired objects to her devotees (vv. 1, 5, 10, 14), is beautiful and adorned with costly ornaments (vv. 1, 4, 6, 13), and is associated with fertility and growth (vv. 9, 11, 13).

This hymn also associates Śrī with the lotus and the elephant, both of which became central in her subsequent history and suggest important aspects of her character. The lotus seems to have two general meanings. First, it is related to life and fertility.[5] On a cosmic scale, the lotus represents the entire created order. The cosmos as lotuslike suggests a world that is organic, vigorous, and beautiful. It is the fecund vigor suggested by the lotus that is revealed in Śrī. She is the life force that pervades creation.

Second, especially in relation to Śrī, the lotus suggests spiritual purity, power, and authority. The lotus seat is a common theme in Hindu and Buddhist iconography. Gods and goddesses, Buddhas and bodhisattvas, are typically shown seated or standing on a lotus. Like the lotus, which is rooted in the mud but whose blossoms are uncontaminated by it, these spiritual beings are understood to transcend the earthly limitations of the world (the mud of existence, as it were). Śrī's association with the lotus suggests that she symbolizes a certain perfection or state of refinement that transcends the material world, yet is rooted in it.

Śrī's association with the elephant suggests other aspects of her character that are ancient and persistent. One of the most common representations of Śrī shows her flanked by two elephants that are showering her with water from their trunks.[6] The elephants have two meanings. According to Hindu tradition, elephants are related to clouds and rain, and hence fertility.[7] Second, elephants suggest royal authority. Kings kept stables of elephants, which they rode in processions and used in military campaigns. Kings were also held responsible for bringing timely rains and for the fertility of the land generally; their possession of elephants is probably related to that role too.[8]

Śrī-Lakṣmī's Association with Male Deities

Śrī (also known consistently as Lakṣmī at a fairly early date in her history) is associated with several male deities, each of whom suggests aspects of her character. One of her earliest associations is with the god Soma, who is identified with plants and vegetative vigor. It is appropriate that Śrī-Lakṣmī, who is also identified with the vitality of plants, should be linked with him.[9] Some texts say that Śrī-Lakṣmī is the wife of Dharma. The connection here seems to relate proper social conduct (dharma) to obtaining prosperity (*śrī*).[10]

Many texts emphasize that in her relationship with the god Indra, royal authority and fertility are central.[11] Indra's political fortunes are directly related to Śrī-Lakṣmī in several myths. When she dwells with him, he prospers politically and economically. When she abandons him, or lives with one of his adversaries, he is bereft of royal authority and wealth. The myths make it clear that kingly power, authority, and prosperity are directly related to Śrī and that without her a king cannot succeed.[12]

Śrī-Lakṣmī's association with Indra also underlines her identity with fertility and growth. The pair complement and reinforce each other in this respect, as he is strongly identified with bringing rain, a symbol of fertility, and his favorite weapon is the thunderbolt. There also seems to be phallic symbolism in his identification with the plow.

Śrī-Lakṣmī's association with the god Kubera is yet another example of her identification with wealth and vegetative growth and fertility. Kubera is related to wealth; he is said to be the possessor and distributor of wealth and to possess and guard the earth's treasure. He is also said to be leader of the *yakṣas*, creatures who dwell in the woods and forests and promote the growth of plants.[13]

Śrī-Lakṣmī and Viṣṇu

Śrī-Lakṣmī's connection with the god Viṣṇu is one of the most important features of her mythology and cult. In Hindu myth, their association begins as a result of the churning of the ocean of milk by the gods and demons, who seek the elixir of immortality (*amṛta*). In the process of churning, they stir up desirable objects and beings, among whom is Lakṣmī. The lovely goddess is granted to Viṣṇu, who is the leader of the gods in this myth.

In Hindu tradition, Viṣṇu is strongly associated with kingship. He is depicted as a divine king. His *avatāras* ("descents" or incarnations) all serve to uphold the social and political order and promote dharma. He supports righteous kings on earth, through whom he is said to uphold society.[14] Lakṣmī, as the embodiment of royal authority, is appropriately linked to Viṣṇu. Where she is present, royal authority prospers; where she is absent, it weakens and disappears.

Lakṣmī is often portrayed as Viṣṇu's loyal, modest, and loving wife. She is described as occupied with domestic chores, such as cooking,[15] and is typically depicted as subservient to her husband. Iconographically, she is often shown massaging Viṣṇu's feet and is much smaller than he. Her submissive position is clearly conveyed in an image from Bādāmī, in which he sits on a high stool while she sits on the ground and leans on him, her right hand on his knee.[16]

In the Pañcarātra school of thought, Lakṣmī, along with Viṣṇu, assumes a central cosmological role. Although Viṣṇu is said to be the ultimate reality, he is almost entirely inactive, standing aloof from the cosmogonic process in which Lakṣmī plays an active role.[17] Her cosmic role is particularly striking in the *Lakṣmī-tantra*, a popular Pañcarātra text, which says that she singlehandedly undertakes the creation of the universe with only one-billionth part of herself (14.3). The text describes Lakṣmī as pervading the entire created order and as regulating the social and moral orders as well. In effect, in this text she takes over the roles of Viṣṇu as creator of the universe and regulator of dharma.[18]

Lakṣmī plays a quite different, but important, role in the Śrī Vaiṣṇava school of South India. In this case, Śrī (Lakṣmī) has a minor cosmological place, but a crucial role in the devotional economy of the school. She is the mediator between devotees and Viṣṇu. Through her grace devotees are allowed to approach the Lord. She is described as an indulgent, forgiving mother who pleads the case of devotees to her husband. In the mythology of this school, Viṣṇu is usually described as a just, mighty king who does not tolerate impurity or sin, who is inclined to punish devotees for the slightest offense. His stern, righteous character is balanced and moderated by Lakṣmī.[19]

The Worship of Lakṣmī

It is quite likely that Lakṣmī is the most popular of all Hindu deities. Associated as she is with wealth, prosperity, good luck, and fertility, she is very appealing and is known in every corner of the Indian subcontinent. She is as popular in the North as in the South and is as widely adored in cities as in small villages. Her images are everywhere.

Several annual festivals are given in her honor. Of these, the Dīvalī festival is the best known and most widely celebrated. The festival links Lakṣmī to three important and interrelated themes: prosperity and wealth, fertility and crops, and good luck during the coming year. During this festival, many people, especially merchants, worship their account books, invoking Lakṣmī to reside in them.[20] Farmers are enjoined to worship their crops as imbued with Lakṣmī's presence. Cow dung is also worshiped as an embodiment of Lakṣmī's fecund power.[21] Lakṣmī's association with good luck in the coming year is stressed in injunctions to gamble during Dīvalī. She is also called upon to drive away her sister Alakṣmī, who is associated with bad luck and misfortune.

Kamalā among the Mahāvidyās

Kamalā's role among the Mahāvidyās is a recent and minor part of her cult and worship in the Hindu tradition. Unlike other Mahāvidyās, such as Dhūmāvatī, Bagalāmukhī, and Mātaṅgī, who are barely known outside the Mahāvidyā group, Lakṣmī is an ancient and extremely popular goddess, worshiped throughout India in a variety of contexts and sectarian movements. Indeed, her inclusion among the Mahāvidyās is not easily explained, and her place in Tantrism, the primary context of the Mahāvidyās, seems somewhat out of character. It is also clear that Kamalā has been selectively appropriated as a Mahāvidyā. That is, her iconography and her descriptions in *dhyāna* mantras leave out certain aspects of her character and minimize certain roles that are important in her history and cult.

It is striking, for example, that as a Mahāvidyā Kamalā is never shown iconographically or described in her *dhyāna* mantras as accompanying Viṣṇu. He may be mentioned, as in her *dhyāna* mantras from the *Śāradātilaka*, which say that she has glances that please Viṣṇu or is called the beloved of Viṣṇu,[22] but for the most part he is absent. In this respect, Kamalā is almost entirely removed from marital and domestic contexts. Her central role as mediator between devotees and Viṣṇu in Śrī Vaiṣṇavism is completely missing in her Mahāvidyā incarnation. She does not play the role of model wife in any important way, and her association with proper dharmic or social behavior, either as an example of it or as the rewarder of it, is not important in the Mahāvidyā context.

Her association with elephants persists. In Mahāvidyā iconography and written descriptions, she is typically flanked by two or four elephants pouring water or nectar onto her from golden or jeweled containers. Thus the Gaja-lakṣmī motif, one of her most ancient aspects, remains central in her Mahāvidyā form. As symbols of sovereignty and fertility, the elephants convey Lakṣmī's association with these highly desirable qualities, which are often sought after or mentioned as rewards in the *phala stotras*, the hymns concerning rewards (or "fruits") that conclude many Mahāvidyā liturgical texts.

Kamalā is often pictured or described as sitting alone on a lotus in the midst of a pond, with neither Viṣṇu nor elephants. This is to be expected in the context of the Mahāvidyās, where a premium seems to be put on the independence of the goddesses. For the most part, the Mahāvidyās are seen as powerful goddesses in their own right. Their power and authority do not derive from association with male deities. Rather, it is their power that pervades the gods and enables them to perform their cosmic functions. When male deities are shown, they are almost always in supporting roles (literally, as when they are shown supporting Tripura–sundarī's throne) and are depicted as subsidiary figures.

It is also interesting to note that Vaiṣṇava connections do not dominate Kamalā's incarnation as a Mahāvidyā. Although she is linked to Viṣṇu from time to time, she is rarely associated with Vaiṣṇava *avatāras* or their consorts, as one might expect. She is rarely identified with Sītā, Rādhā, or Rukmiṇī, although she is sometimes associated with Varāhī and Vaiṣṇavī, two of the Saptamātṛkās (seven mothers), with which group the Mahāvidyās as a group are sometimes linked. In fact, Kamalā in her Mahāvidyā form seems to be associated or identified as frequently with Śiva or Śiva's consort as she is with Viṣṇu. Her thousand-name hymn in the *Śākta-pramoda*, for example, calls her Śivā, Raudrī, Gaurī, She Whose Bliss Is Śiva, She Who Is Dear to the One Who Does the *Tāṇḍava* Dance, Satī, and Kapālī.[23] Again, this is in keeping with the tendency in Mahāvidyā texts to associate the goddesses with Śiva, and consistent, too, with the accounts of the origins of the Mahāvidyās, which usually feature Śiva.

As a Mahāvidyā, Kamalā also has become associated with fearsome qualities, which are almost entirely lacking in her cult and worship outside this context. Her hundred- and thousand-name hymns in the *Śākta-pramoda*, for example, call her Kālarātri (a fearsome name for Kālī), She Who Wears a Garland of Skulls, She Whose Form Is Very Terrible, Ghorā (awful), Bhimā (terrible), and Tāmasī (darkness; literally, "she who is the *tamas guṇa*").[24] Although benign and auspicious qualities dominate her character as a Mahāvidyā, a fearsome, dangerous dimension is suggested in these epithets.

Another feature that characterizes the Mahāvidyā Kamalā but is weak or absent from her worship and cult outside the Mahāvidyās is her role as a demon slayer. Outside the Mahāvidyās, Lakṣmī is strongly associated with both Viṣṇu and Durgā, who are the demon slayers par excellence in Hindu mythology. Lakṣmī herself, however, does not take an active part. She is primarily a witness to Viṣṇu or his *avatāras* while they slay demons or is displayed with Durgā during Durgā Pūjā, when she is said to be Durgā's daughter. There are female Vaiṣṇavite goddesses who slay demons in the *Devī-māhātmya*, namely, Vaiṣṇavī, Varāhī, and Narasiṁhī, but none of these is directly identified with Lakṣmī in that text. Her hundred- and thousand-name hymns in the *Śākta-pramoda*, however, at times give her epithets that directly identify her with the demon-slaying goddess Durgā or one of Durgā's demon-slaying helpers. She is called, for example, Slayer of Madhu and Kaiṭabha, Slayer of Śumbha and Niśumbha, and Durgā. Her thousand-name hymn also identifies her with the fierce Vaiṣṇava goddesses Narasiṁhī and Varāhī.[25]

As in the Pañcarātra tradition, where Lakṣmī assumes a preeminent cosmic role, several epithets in her name hymns in the *Śākta-pramoda* emphasize her elevated position as a cosmic queen or a transcendent philosophical absolute. She is called, for example, Mother of the World, Creator of All the Gods, Mistress of All, Mahāśakti, Prāṇaśakti (the life principle), Mahāmāyā, She Who Is Situated in the Middle of Countless Universes, Whose Form Is the Creation, Who Is the Cause of Creation, Who Is without Support (that is, who supports everything else and alone transcends the need for support), Who Is the Form of Highest Spiritual

Fig. 39. Kamalā, by Bhatuk Ramprasad, early twentieth century. Printed with the permission of Dr. Bhanu Shanker Mehta, Varanasi.

Bliss, Who Is the Three *Guṇas* (the constituents of matter), Who Creates All, Whose Form Is Everything, and several other such designations.[26]

Kamalā is also identified in these name hymns with several of the other Mahāvidyās, most of whom share few characteristics with her and are notable for their fearsomeness. She is called, for example, Mātaṅgī, Dhūmāvatī, Tāriṇī, Bhadra-kālī, Mahākālī, and Bhairavī.[27]

In appropriating the great and widely worshiped goddess Śrī-Lakṣmī as a Mahāvidyā, the formulators of the Mahāvidyā tantric texts modified and tailored her character, it seems, to make her more suitable to the group. They stressed her independence from Viṣṇu (as well as any other male consort with whom she is linked outside the Mahāvidyās), although she is not entirely disassociated from him; they gave her fierce attributes; and they connected her with Śiva. She retains her character, no doubt. She is definitely recognizable as Śrī-Lakṣmī, but her portrait has been drawn selectively.

Finally, Kamalā's usual place as the tenth Mahāvidyā deserves some comment. In almost all lists of the Mahāvidyās, Kamalā is the last of the group. If this position is meant to convey her subsidiary or inferior position (or conversely, her superior position) in the group, the texts themselves do not comment upon it. Indeed, in those tantric texts that discuss and describe Kamalā, she, like each of the others, is hailed as a great goddess and identified with absolute philosophical principles and transcendent cosmic functions. However, every one of my informants in Varanasi interpreted her tenth position as an indication that she is inferior to the other Mahāvidyās and represents realities that are distant or opposite from Kālī, who is taken to be the ultimate or highest expression of truth among the Mahāvidyās.

A contemporary *śākta* informant contrasts tantric religion in the South, which he calls Śrī *kula*, with tantric religion in the North, which he calls Kālī *kula*. He describes Śrī *kula* as the worship of Lakṣmī and as seeking wealth and worldly comfort. Kālī *kula*, on the other hand, is heroic and boldly confronts the darkness, demanding ultimate knowledge. Kālī is described as a goddess with whom one must struggle, Lakṣmī as one who pampers her devotees but ultimately is incapable of giving such supreme blessings as liberating knowledge.[28]

Swami Annapurnananda of the Ramakrishna Mission in Varanasi also said that Kamalā represents a state of consciousness preoccupied with material well-being and security. That is, she represents the normal state of consciousness in almost all people and, as such, the starting point in the process of spiritual maturation. Kamalā consciousness is what one seeks to restrain, overcome, and finally transcend. Kālī consciousness, represented by the first of the Mahāvidyās, is the ultimate goal.

PART III

Concluding Reflections

Having focused on the Mahāvidyās as a group and on each of them individually, I would like to comment on a few particularly striking features or motifs and seek to answer certain questions related to these features.

Corpses and Cremation Grounds

Corpses are remarkably often associated with the Mahāvidyās, and cremation grounds seem to be highly favored as places in which to worship them. Kālī, Tārā, Bagalāmukhī, Tripura-sundarī, Mātaṅgī, and Bhairavī are all said to stand or sit upon corpses. Kālī, Tārā, Chinnamastā, and Dhūmāvatī are often described or pictured as dwelling in cremation grounds. On several occasions the *Mantra-mahodadhiḥ* stipulates that *sādhanā* (spiritual endeavor) should be done while sitting on a corpse or on a place where a corpse has recently been buried. For example, in an almost matter-of-fact way, the text says: "Bringing a corpse on a Tuesday or Saturday, . . . bury it one foot deep in the ground beneath the door of the house. Then, sitting on that spot, . . . perform 108 Japas [repetitions] every day. . . . Through such a Japa for eight days the [*sādhaka*, "adept"] becomes the lord of various Siddhis ["perfections," magical powers]."[1] The same text, again, instructs the *sādhaka* as follows: "Sitting on a Śavāsana [a corpse seat] . . . the Sādhaka should begin the Japa at sunrise and continue it without break till the next sunrise.

Through such a [process] the Sādhaka becomes fearless and master of various Siddhis."[2] In discussing the empowerment or perfection of mantras, which is accomplished primarily by repetition, the *Mantra-mahodadhiḥ* says: "A Sādhaka who, sitting on a corpse, performs one lakh (100,000) [repetitions] of this mantra, his mantra becomes potent and all his cherished desires are soon fulfilled."[3] In discussing the relative power of different "seats," the *Mantra-mahodadhiḥ* describes the *komalāsana*, which uses an aborted fetus or the corpse of a five-year-old child, and the *viṣṭarāsana*, which is made of woven grass and "consecrated with a corpse."[4] The *Tantrasāra*, a text devoted primarily to the Mahāvidyās, has detailed descriptions of both *śavā sādhanā* (spiritual endeavor with a corpse)[5] and *citā sādhanā* (spiritual endeavor on a cremation pyre).[6] These rituals are not described as applicable to a particular goddess among the Mahāvidyās, so probably both techniques are appropriate in the worship of any, or at least several, of the Mahāvidyās.

It is important to reflect on these associations if we wish to come to an understanding of certain individual Mahāvidyās and of the group as a whole. As a group, they seem to be associated with a type of spirituality that relies heavily on death imagery. This is perhaps most explicit in the case of Kālī, the first and most important of the group. But corpses and cremation grounds are central in descriptions of several of the other goddesses as well, and worship of nearly all of them is said to be most effective if undertaken in a cremation ground.

It is tempting to suppose that this death imagery belongs to the ascetic, world-denying vein of Hinduism, in which renunciation of worldly desire is central. In such a context, death imagery and death rituals make sense: they reinforce the renunciant's decision to pursue spiritual liberation by giving up the lures of the world. Meditation upon death puts worldly pleasures in a perspective where their attraction can be minimized or subverted altogether.[7] And surely corpses and cremation grounds do play this role in Mahāvidyā *sādhanā*.

The cremation ground also plays the role of a "forbidden thing," a kind of sixth *tattva*, which the heroic *sādhaka* must confront in order to glimpse the underlying nature of reality, which is that all things, no matter how polluted or terrible, are pervaded by *śakti* (energy or power) (see the chapter on Kālī). To meditate upon, to meditate in, or to live in a cremation ground functions as a spiritual test. In what has been termed the "*samādhi* [heightened or intensified consciousness] of horror,"[8] the adept discovers a distaste for the world, which encourages him or her to see beyond or through its lures to underlying spiritual truths. The goddess herself is sometimes described as putting the male gods through similar tests. In the *Mahābhāgavata-purāṇa*, she assumes a terrible form to test Brahmā, Viṣṇu, and Śiva. To avoid looking at her, Brahmā turns his head away, and Viṣṇu closes his eyes and plunges into the water. Only Śiva is able to continue to gaze on her, and for this heroic ability she gives him the blessing of becoming a great yogi.[9] In a similar scenario, the goddess appears to the three male gods as a rotting corpse. Śiva thinks her stench is fragrant incense, and he takes her corpse on his breast. The goddess blesses him by placing his *liṅgam* in her yoni.[10] The tantric *sādhaka* is tested, as it were, in the cremation ground. The challenge is for the spiritual aspirant to be able to perceive the presence of the goddess even in the most terrible and polluting objects and places.

There is some evidence that cremation grounds are sometimes used for initiation into certain tantric cults.[11] Insofar as initiation rites often involve the symbolic death and rebirth of the initiate,[12] a cremation ground seems an appropriate venue. It is a place of transformation, where people die to one mode of being and are born to another. It is the locale of the greatest human transformation, that from life to death. If the candidate's initiation into a tantric cult is meant to signify dramatic transformation, the cremation ground is a most suitable place for it.

However, something beyond this seems to be involved in the use of corpses and cremation grounds, for it is often clear that people undertaking these rituals are householders who have not renounced the world, are not engaged in ascetic practices, do not seem primarily concerned with affirming the underlying divinity of the forbidden or the polluted, and are not undergoing initiation into a tantric cult. It is also clear that the desires that motivate this type of spirituality are often worldly: power over one's enemies, kingly authority, eloquence in speech, and so on. The aim of this *sādhanā*, that is, seems to be, not so much to triumph over the lures of the world or even to see through its illusory facade to its underlying reality as *śakti*, but rather to gain success and well-being in the world. Corpses and cremation grounds seem to function as more than dramatic reminders of the transience of worldly existence and the futility of physical and mental desires, and thus as appropriate accoutrements or contexts for the spiritual quest. They also seem to function as objects and places of power by means of which or in which extraordinary achievements may be accomplished. Power seems to accrue to the individual who associates with corpses and frequents cremation grounds. Why might this be so?

It is clear that texts describing the Mahāvidyās and their worship as-

Fig. 40. Tārā on Śiva in cremation ground, contemporary lithograph.

sume the existence of a world of spirits that is parallel to the physical world and impinges upon it. This assumption persists in and to a great extent dominates contemporary Hinduism in both its popular and its refined, literary forms. The inhabitants of this world include gods, goddesses, *rākṣasas, asuras, vetālas, yoginīs, ḍākinīs, gandharvas, kinnaras, siddhas, bhūtas, pretas, piśācas, nāgas,* and other classes of beings that are not visible under usual conditions but that appear from time to time in the physical world. All of these beings are more powerful than humans or have some ability or cunning that surpasses normal human abilities. Their eruptions into the visible world of human beings can be beneficial or harmful, unexpected or willed. Examples of harmful and unexpected eruptions are illnesses, bad luck, and accidents. These are often attributed to the actions of *bhūtas* and *pretas* (spirits of the dead, ghosts), but also to other inimical spirits or deities. Such eruptions may result from either bad karma on the part of the victim (who caused the disease by wicked deeds or thoughts) or unsatisfied passions or desires on the part of the spirit being, who tries to fulfill them by possessing the human victim. Much of Hindu belief and practice concerns warding off or dealing with such inimical intrusions into human affairs.

On the other hand, another large part of Hindu ritual and practice deliberately seeks contact with this invisible world for a variety of purposes, and it is in this context that much tantric ritual probably should be understood. Tantric rituals in many cases are clearly aimed at crossing the barrier between the visible and invisible worlds, either by allowing the *sādhaka* to enter the spirit world or by enticing or forcing spirit beings to appear in the visible world. The goal of the *sādhaka* is often made explicit: to gain a blessing, usually in the form of some kind of power or ability, from a being in the spirit world, usually a deity, often one of the Mahāvidyās. Contacting the spirit world deliberately (as opposed to being contacted by it unexpectedly) is also assumed to be both difficult and dangerous, and often terrifying. This is where the importance of corpses and cremation grounds becomes understandable in tantric worship.

Where might one hope to contact the unseen, spiritual world? Where might the barrier between the visible and invisible worlds be most permeable? One place is certainly the cremation ground. It is where all human beings eventually and inevitably make contact with the spirit world as they pass from life to death. Indeed, to a great extent this is precisely what death is, the transition from one mode of being to another, from that of a physical to a nonphysical being. The cremation ground is the "terminal" where such transitions routinely take place. In this sense, it represents a more-or-less-permanent "opening" to the spirit world and the beings that inhabit it. It is a place of spirit traffic, of coming and going from one world to another.[13] It is a liminal place,[14] betwixt and between worlds, where radical transformations take place and contact between worlds is relatively common.

Corpses, particularly of the recent dead, are vehicles with which one can move from one world to the other. A recently dead person, particularly if the proper death rituals have not yet been done, still hovers in the physical world while already having been transformed into a spirit being. He or she is a liminal being, with a foot in both worlds, as it were. He or she is on the way to the "other world"; to ride that person's corpse, or otherwise associate with or dominate it, is to make that transition also. References to reviving or gaining control over a corpse, or the spirit that inhabits it, are not infrequent. The *Uḍḍīśa-tantra* gives mantras for reviving a corpse.[15] The *Kathāsaritsāgara* also mentions revitalizing corpses, gaining control over them in order to use them at will, and acquiring the ability to fly by eating human flesh.[16] Elsewhere we read: "Dead and putrefying corpses submerged near cremation grounds are still brought to life by the force of the sādhaka's mantras, and made to render aid to sādhanā and siddhi."[17] These references make clear that a corpse is a numinous object particularly useful for making contact with the spirit world and acquiring powers and abilities associated with spirit beings.

Skulls and Severed Heads

Another remarkable feature of Mahāvidyā iconography is the prevalence of skulls and chopped-off heads. Kālī, Tārā, Chinnamastā, Mātaṅgī, and Bhairavī all wear garlands of skulls or severed heads and are often said to hold a freshly cut head or a skull in their hands. Skulls also adorn Tārā's forehead and sometimes Kālī's hair. Some texts devoted to worship of the Mahāvidyās also prescribe skulls as seats upon which effective *sādhanā* may be performed. The *Mantra-mahodadhiḥ* stipulates that the *sādhaka* should bring a human skull to a remote place in the woods, purify it, bury it, and perform worship while seated on that spot.[18] The most dramatic example of a chopped-off head in the context of the Mahāvidyās, of course, is that of Chinnamastā, who has severed her own head. Although I commented upon the significance of skulls and chopped-off heads in the discussion of Chinnamastā,[19] their prevalence among the Mahāvidyās generally deserves further comment.

Perhaps the most obvious interpretation of these skulls and heads concerns head offerings. Animal (and sometimes human) sacrifice was fairly common in the Hindu tradition, and the typical way of killing the victim was by decapitation. During the Vedic period, animal sacrifices were commonly offered to many deities; later, most blood sacrifices were directed to goddesses. In contemporary Hinduism, which continues a tradition that is hundreds of years old, blood sacrifice is still almost invari-

Fig. 41. Kālī in cremation ground, Pahari painting. Ajit Mookerjee Collection of Tantric Art, National Museum, Delhi.

ably associated with certain goddesses. At some goddess temples, daily sacrifices are made, usually of goats and chickens. In almost all cases the animal's head is cut off and offered to the image of the goddess, often on a platter. The *Tantrasāra* devotes a section to *bali*, "blood sacrifice," and makes it clear that the proper method of killing the victim (which according to the text may be a human being) is by decapitation.[20] The chopped-off heads that several of the Mahāvidyās wear or sit upon can be thought of as sacrificial offerings. That these human heads are always male in Mahāvidyā iconography is still reflected in contemporary practice, which uses male animals almost exclusively.

Another interpretation of skulls and severed heads also seems possible, however, and is more in line with the importance of corpses and cremation grounds in Mahāvidyā worship and iconography. The severed head (or skull), especially when worn as an ornament by one of the Mahāvidyā goddesses, might be thought of as symbolic of transformed consciousness. By means of spiritual exercises in the cremation ground and with corpses, the *sādhaka* seeks a direct encounter with the spirit world in order to acquire powers associated with spirit beings: superior power, or even omnipotence; expanded knowledge, or omniscience; transcendence of time and space, including precognition and clairvoyance; and the ability to change form at will, to become small or light, or to fly.[21] In short, the adept seeks to transcend in some manner the limitations of the physical, earth-bound human condition by direct association with the spirit world.

That these spirit powers often denote transcendence of corporeal limitations and the expansion of consciousness, the ability of the consciousness to drift free of the body and roam at will, suggests a divorce of body and mind, the liberation of the mind from the body. Those chopped-off heads and skulls might be symbolic of *sādhakas* who, by a particular goddess's blessing or their own efforts, have accomplished these feats. They might be thought of as symbolic of transformed consciousness in two ways: First, they have achieved the status of spirit beings by having died; the theme of symbolic death in many religions functions in just this way, namely, to dramatically denote a drastic change in status.[22] Second, the severed heads may denote consciousness that has transcended the limitations of physical, worldly existence: the mind (symbolized by the head) has left the body and is no longer attached to or limited by it.

A common motif in the world's religions is the quest by a spiritual master to acquire techniques for transcending the human condition. The shaman and the mystic are examples of this. Both undertake spiritual journeys to achieve an unmediated and transformative experience of the spirit world, and to achieve it they must often undergo a symbolic death and dismemberment. The shaman is often said to be torn asunder by spiritual beings, who then reconstitute his or her body with indestructible pieces, signifying a new, transcendent condition. Just such a dismemberment was described by Pāgal Haranāth (b. 1865), a Bengali Vaiṣṇava. While traveling in Kashmir, he fell into a deep trance. Caitanya, the famous Bengali Vaiṣṇava reformer, appeared to him, divided his body into sixty-four parts, and then proceeded to clean and purify them. When his body was reassembled, Haranāth had acquired magical, shamanic powers, that is, expanded consciousness.[23]

Mystics often pass through a "dark night of the soul," in which they feel as if they have died, before experiencing the bliss of union with the divine. In the cremation ground, in association with corpses, tantric *sādhakas* undergo a symbolic death before entering the spirit world, where they are reconstituted as spiritual beings equipped with spiritual powers that go beyond the limitations of earthly existence. The severed heads that the goddesses wear might signify both the symbolic death and the transcendent consciousness of successful *sādhakas*. That all of these chopped-off heads seem to wear a look of peace and satisfaction seems to confirm this interpretation.

Sexuality and Awakened Consciousness

Mahāvidyā iconography, mythology, worship, and ritual are dominated by implicit and explicit sexual symbolism. Sexual intercourse is explicitly portrayed in the *dhyāna* mantras and portraits of Kālī, Chinnamastā, and Tārā,[24] and most of the individual Mahāvidyās are described as sexually attractive and powerful. The mythology concerning the origin of certain individual Mahāvidyā goddesses (for example, Chinnamastā and Mātaṅgī) stresses sexual tension. The yantras that represent the Mahāvidyās contain implicitly sexual symbols, and the central metaphor of awakening *kuṇḍalini śakti* may be interpreted as the arousal of sexual energy. It is also the case that most of the Mahāvidyās may be worshiped through the *pañca tattva* ritual, in which sexual intercourse is the culminating act. The centrality of sexual imagery in Mahāvidyā worship and iconography deserves further comment and analysis at this point.

Sexual imagery in Mahāvidyā materials must be related to the tantric philosophy and ritual that are its primary religious context. This imagery can be understood on several different, but related, levels. On the most abstract level, sexual imagery reflects the tantric vision of reality as the dynamic interaction and tension between the two great principles, Śiva and Śatki. As the basic underlying principles of reality, the basic components of the essential texture of the cosmos, Śiva and Śakti obviously may be understood in a wide variety of ways. Several sophisticated philosophical systems have been constructed on the meaning and interpretation of these two principles, Kashmir Śaivism perhaps being the most impressive. Śiva and Śakti are present in the mutual attraction and complementarity of the sexes. At the level of human existence and human relationships, they are inherent and embodied in individual males and females. In the context of Tantra, sexual attraction, sexual behavior, and sexual intercourse suggest the underlying texture of reality, which is the manifestation of the dynamic, energetic, creative, and harmonious interaction of Śiva and Śakti.

At a more concrete, but still fairly coded, level, sexual imagery suffuses the yantras and *maṇḍalas* associated with all of the Mahāvidyā goddesses (as it does tantric *maṇḍala* structure and symbolism generally). The dominant forms of the yantra—the triangle and the lotus—both have sexual connotations. The triangle, particularly when it is pointing downward, is symbolic of the vulva. An upward-pointing triangle is sometimes held to represent the phallus. When the two are superimposed on each other, as in most of the yantras representing the individual Mahāvidyās, they denote sexual union. Another feature of yantra design is the presence of a small dot, called a *bindu*, in the very center of the diagram. This dot is often said to represent either the two principles of Śiva and Śakti in union or the male seed, particularly when it is enclosed in a downward-pointing triangle at the center of the yantra. The lotus also has sexual connotations. It is often a symbol of generation, that from which all creation proceeds or that in which all creation is contained. As it opens and blossoms, the cosmos emerges. In this sense it represents the womb from which the world is born and may be associated with the womb or sexual organ of Śakti, from whom creation emerges and in whom it is contained.

The yantras representing the Mahāvidyās are also charged with a group of powers—male and female deities—who are located at various points in the design. The *sādhaka* places these powers in the yantra while either drawing or imagining it during *sādhanā*. In many of the Mahāvidyā yantras, the petals of the inner lotus are charged with the presence of different forms of Rati and Kāma, deities associated in particular with sexual vitality and desire. In general structure, then, the Mahāvidyā yantras may be understood as schematic renderings of sexual imagery and containers of sexual power. As schematic representations of both the goddess in question and the cosmos generally, which she is held to embody, the yantra again expresses the idea that reality in its basic nature is sexually charged.

The yoni, in turn, is interpreted as a yantra. It is said to contain, in essential form, all aspects of the cosmos in microcosm. The *Yoni-tantra*, in describing yoni *pūjā*, says that the yoni is a manifestation of the Devī (the Great Goddess). The Devī, furthermore, is said to manifest herself in the form of the Mahāvidyās. Each of the Mahavidyās is identified with a different part of the yoni.[25]

In Mahāvidyā iconography, sexual imagery is often explicit. Kālī and Tārā are sometimes shown copulating with Śiva; a copulating couple, usually identifiable as Kāma and Rati, figures in Chinnamastā and Tārā iconography. Sexual motifs and activity also figure prominently in certain tantric rituals associated with the Mahāvidyās. In the *pañca makāra* or *pañca tattva* ritual, the culminating act, the fifth *makāra*, is *maithuna*, in which the *sādhaka* and his *śakti* perform sexual intercourse. This act as described in the *Tantrasāra* is highly ritualized.[26] It involves the careful purification of many elements and a lengthy worship by the *sādhaka* of his female companion (the text is written from the male point of view). Some interpreters have suggested that the primary aim of the ritual is for the *sādhaka* to demonstrate that he has mastered his sexual desires. They claim that the male does not ejaculate during intercourse but redirects his semen "upward" or inward, thereby controlling and channeling his sexual energy to achieve spiritual ends.[27] In the *Tantrasāra*, however, it is clear that the man ejaculates into the woman; as he does so, he says a particular prayer comparing his ejaculation to an offering: "The fire of *ātman* has been made blazing by the offering of clarified butter; by means of my mind ladle I am ever engaged in offering the modality of my senses through the *suṣumnā* channels."[28] This utterance implies, not that the *sādhaka* withholds his semen, but that he interprets his ejaculation as part of a process that awakens *kuṇḍalinī śakti*. It is not sublimated or curbed sexual activity that awakens the *kuṇḍalinī* but sexual activity properly understood or perhaps properly appreciated.[29]

Sexual imagery in Mahāvidyā iconography and worship plays a symbolic role. It may be understood metaphorically as suggesting the dynamic polar rhythm of reality, the interaction of Śiva and Śakti that creates and suffuses the cosmos. The *Kulārṇava-tantra* says that the world does not bear the likeness of the *cakra*, the lotus, or the thunderbolt but rather the likeness of the *liṅgam* and yoni, thus reflecting the form of Śiva and Śakti; wherever there is the union of the two, "the devotee experiences deep trance [*samādhi*]."[30] Sexual imagery may also symbolize awakening consciousness. The rising of *kuṇḍalinī śakti* and the bliss of her union with Śiva in the *sahasrāra cakra* may be symbolized by sexual union. Sexual activity seems an appropriate metaphor for the rousing of the *kuṇḍalinī*, as both are highly energetic processes accompanied by heightened awareness.

It seems likely that in some cases sexual imagery reflects actual practice, as in the *pañca tattva* ritual, where sexual intercourse may be used as a means of awakening *kuṇḍalinī śakti*. Substitutes may be used in the ritual, however, which implies that sexual intercourse is not necessary to the awakening of the *kuṇḍalinī*. Tantric texts sometimes warn that only those of a certain accomplished character and heroic nature should engage in this ritual. To suggest that explicit sexual activity is a necessary part of Mahāvidyā worship would be an exaggeration. On the other hand, sexual practices clearly have a role, and for some *sādhakas* in some situations, sexual intercourse may lead to an intense spiritual experience.

The Conjunction of Death and Sexual Imagery

It is striking that imagery of both sex and death should be so central in Mahāvidyā materials and that both are so often juxtaposed in the characterization of a goddess and in certain rituals of worship. Kālī, Tārā, and Chinnamastā, in particular, often combine both types of imagery in their icons. In an eighteenth-century Kangra painting, Tārā stands on Kāma and Rati, who are copulating on a cremation fire.[31] Kālī is sometimes shown copulating with Śiva in a cremation ground,[32] and Chinnamastā decapitates herself while standing or sitting on Rati, who is having sexual intercourse with Kāma. It is not unusual for the copulating couple on whom Chinnamastā stands or leans to be lying on a cremation fire. There are also examples of Chinnamastā having intercourse with Śiva while he lies on a cremation pyre and she decapitates herself (see figure 24).

These are only the most dramatic examples of the juxtaposition of death and sexual imagery. Certain Mahāvidyā texts prescribe equally shocking juxtapositions in their descriptions of rituals appropriate to

Mahāvidyā worship. In its section on Tārā, for example, the *Mantra-mahodadhiḥ* says that the *sādhaka* who seeks lordship should sit naked on the heart of a corpse in a cremation ground and offer the goddess one thousand flowers, each covered with his semen, while reciting her mantra.[33] The same section of the text describes a ritual in which the *sādhaka* should imagine the goddess seated on the chest of a corpse engaged in sex with her consort on a fifteen-petaled lotus while the *sādhaka* is also having sexual intercourse.[34] Also in the section on Tārā, the *Mantra-mahodadhiḥ* mentions a ritual in which the *sādhaka* places a human skull at the place where he is to recite the goddess's mantra. Then, while repeating the mantra, he is to gaze upon, touch, and sexually enjoy a woman.[35] The *Uḍḍīśa-tantra* gives directions for improving the erotic appeal of a woman, which are followed immediately by rules governing *śava sādhanā* (spiritual endeavor using a corpse).[36]

What might this juxtaposition of sex and death imagery mean? I would suggest two interpretations. First, tantric *sādhanā*, which is so intimately associated with Mahāvidyā worship, places a premium upon direct, unmediated experience. As mentioned above, tantric *sādhanā* is secret and private. It is undertaken by an individual in a lonely place. Priests are not necessary, and while the *sādhaka*'s guru may be present, or the *sādhaka* may take part in a collective ritual on rare occasions, it is primarily a lone adept who undertakes the rituals described in Mahāvidyā and related tantric texts. The texts are also explicit concerning at least one of the aims of *sādhanā:* to become one with the deity being worshiped, or to be blessed with a vision of the deity—a transformative and probably intense experience. We may typify the tantric *sādhaka* as someone who seeks concrete religious experience, for whom rituals are a means to experiencing an intensity of feeling and emotion. Both dying and sex are overwhelming human experiences that can leave a person uprooted from and unprotected by social conventions and ritual insulation. Both, of course, are highly ritualized in almost every culture, precisely because the intense emotions they engender are so apt to cause social disruption. But no amount of ritual can guarantee the taming or orderly channeling of either of these basic human experiences. It is the "explosive" nature of death and sex imagery that makes them so central in tantric *sādhanā*, which puts such a premium on achieving transformative religious experiences. As symbols they are particularly powerful in evoking feelings that can deeply affect and alter a person; they can trigger the kind of experience the *sādhaka* seeks.

Second, the juxtaposition of death and sex imagery appropriately expresses the nature of reality as constant and simultaneous inception-

creation and destruction. The waxing and waning of all beings and all things, from individual organisms to the infinite cosmos itself, is appropriately suggested in the simultaneous presentation of sex and death imagery. If such juxtaposed imagery shocks us, it is because we are in the habit of masking the destructive dimension of reality so insistently that its inevitable appearance is upsetting. That sex and death imagery "do not belong together," that we find the juxtaposition in "bad taste," is simply an admission that our view of reality is warped and unrealistic. Those Mahāvidyā goddesses who juxtapose sex and death imagery are icons of revelation to the *sādhaka*, who seeks an expanded consciousness, an awareness of the truth of things that does not pander to wishful thinking concerning one's own mortality and frailty. They are images that help the *sādhaka* tear the veil of *māyā* (illusion grounded in self-infatuation).

The Roles of Women and Reverence for Women

It is striking how central female imagery and women are in Mahāvidyā and related tantric materials. Theologically, the goddess, or Śakti, in one form or another is equal or superior to a male deity or principal, usually Śiva. She is usually identified with the origin of the cosmos and is said to infuse it and contain it. Frequently in Mahādevī texts she empowers the male gods to create, maintain, and consume the creation, or she undertakes these functions herself. Iconographically, the individual Mahāvidyā goddesses are shown dominating male deities. Kālī and Tārā stand on, sit on, or have sex astride Śiva. Other Mahāvidyās sit on male corpses. Tripura-sundarī sits on the body of Śiva, which in turn rests on a couch whose legs are four male deities. None of the Mahāvidyās is shown in the role of a traditional Hindu wife or consort. Even Lakṣmī, who is widely known for her loyal and subservient position as Viṣṇu's wife, is shown alone. It is also noteworthy that the severed heads that decorate the goddesses' bodies are male, as are the corpses that lie beneath them. When animal sacrifice is included in worship, male animals are offered.

Moreover, Mahāvidyā and related tantric texts often mention the importance of revering women.[37] The *Kaulāvalī-tantra* says that all women should be looked upon as manifestations of the Mahādevī (great goddess).[38] The *Nīla-tantra* says that one should desert one's parents, guru, and even the deities before insulting a woman.[39]

Several rituals involve the worship of individual women. At several points in the *pañca tattva* ritual, particularly during *maithuna*, the *sādhaka* does elaborate worship of his *śakti*. According to the description of the ritual in the *Tantrasāra*, he begins by mentally worshiping the goddess and several different groups of women: dancing girls, Kāpālikas ("those who bear skulls," a particular type of religious adept), prostitutes, and women of the barber, washerman, and cowherd castes.[40] These groups are all either low caste or socially or religiously liminal. It is from one of these groups that the *sādhaka* recruits the woman who is to be his *śakti* in the ritual. The significance of the low-caste or liminal status of these women may relate to a general theme of the ritual, which affirms as sacred what is ordinarily viewed as forbidden or polluting and uses it to worship the goddess, who pervades all things. By worshiping women of lower castes, or women who are socially or religiously marginal, the adept reverses the normal hierarchy of respect. By revering such women, he affirms their underlying and essential divinity as concrete manifestations of the goddess. He affirms as divine that which is normally disdained or shunned.[41]

During the rituals directly related to *maithuna*, the theme of worshiping the woman as the goddess is persistent. Having performed *bhūta śuddhi* and *nyāsa* on her body to purify and divinize the woman, the *sādhaka* directs her to sit on a bed, which he then worships as a *pīṭha* of the goddess. This sacred spot is imagined to be the center of the world and is pictured as a lotus supported by the cosmic serpent in the depths of the cosmic ocean. On the lotus sits the goddess, represented by the *sādhaka*'s *śakti*. The *sādhaka* then worships the woman's body: By means of mantras, he "deposits" in her limbs the five forms of Kāma-deva, the god of sexual desire. Again using mantras, he divinizes her breasts or empowers them with sacred energy by "depositing" there the deities Vasanta (who personifies the amorous season of spring) and Kāma. Her forehead is imagined to have the moon adorning it (as is the case with many of the Mahāvidyā goddesses), and both her right and left sides are imagined as suffused with divine beings. The *sādhaka* then worships her vagina, which should be seen to have three channels, representing the moon, sun, and fire. From the moon channel flows water, from the sun channel flows menstrual fluid, and from the fire channel, which is in the middle, flows seed. He should then worship the two goddesses Bhagamālā and Bhagamālinī (both names mean "having a garland of yonis"), in addition to his own chosen deity, as residing in the *śakti*'s vagina.[42] He should also at this point worship his own penis as representing Śiva. In short, the *sādhaka* ritually transforms sexual intercourse into a cosmic event that unites Śiva and Śakti.

Some tantric texts also mention ritual worship of a woman preceding sexual intercourse outside the context of the *pañca tattva* ritual, which suggests that the tantric *sādhaka* should routinely view intercourse as a sacred ritual in which or by which one realizes one's cosmic identity. The *Guptasādhanā-tantra*, for example, directs the adept to worship his wife, or the wife of another, by washing her feet with water, then worshiping her forehead, face, throat, heart, navel, breasts, and vagina by repeating one hundred mantras of his chosen deity. At the time of ejaculation, the *sādhaka* is to offer his semen to Śiva and imagine the *śakti* as his chosen deity.[43] The *Kubjikā-tantra*, similarly, instructs the *sādhaka*, outside the context of the *pañca tattva* ritual, to worship his wife while she is drunk and lying on a bed. He is to view her as a goddess and, while repeating mantras, should touch her heart with his heart, her vagina with his penis, and her face with his face, thus symbolizing the uniting of Śiva and Śakti.[44]

The *Yoginī-tantra* says that yoni *pūjā*, worship of the vulva, is the best of all methods of worship.[45] The *Kāmākhyā-tantra* instructs the *sādhaka* to worship the goddess in the genitals of his *śakti*.[46] The *Māyā-tantra* enjoins the adept to imagine his chosen deity residing in the yoni of a woman "who is not his own" in order to obtain perfection.[47] The *Sarvollāsa-tantra* of Sarvānanda, citing the *Vṛhad-yoni-tantra*, discusses the downward-pointing triangle, the symbol of the yoni, as containing Brahmā, Viṣṇu, and Śiva on its three sides, and also most of the Mahāvidyās. In short, the text says, the triangle is the Great Goddess herself, the abode of all deities. Kālī is said to dwell on all three sides of the triangle, which is identical with the yoni. Tārā is above it, Bhuvaneśvarī and Tripura-sundarī are inside it, Bhairavī is at its root. Chinnamastā abides inside the hole in the triangle, and at the end (perhaps deep within) dwells Dhūmāvatī, who emerges from there (perhaps with menstrual flow).[48] At the root of the hair of the yoni dwells Mahākālī, while Mātaṅgī resides in the folds of skin below the navel. Covering the whole area are Kamalā and Kāmākhyā.[49] The same text, citing the *Vrhad-yoni-tantra*, also equates the yoni with sacred *tīrthas* ("crossings," or holy places), specifically certain holy rivers and ponds.[50] The text also says that worship of the yoni earns one the merit ordinarily obtained by making arduous pilgrimages to holy places, because the yoni itself contains all their sacred power.[51]

Another common ritual in which females are revered is *kumārī pūjā*.[52] In this ritual, prepubescent or virgin girls are offered *pūjā* and fed. In this case, females from high castes, usually Brahmans, are sometimes specified, while other texts say girls from any caste are suitable. This ritual is not specifically tantric or associated with the Mahāvidyās, although it occurs in tantric and Mahāvidyā materials. It is often done today during Durgā Pūjā, the great autumn festival in honor of Durgā. The underlying theme of individual females representing the pervasive divine female principle is again clearly expressed through this ritual.

That some of these rituals may not suggest reverence for women at all, but are simply examples of males setting up women as objects of sexual lust, is of course possible. Mainstream Hindu society has roundly criticized such tantric practices as excuses for sexual indulgence. It is clear, however, that these rituals fit a highly sophisticated general philosophy or theology of reality, and it is therefore unfair to suggest that they are undertaken solely for sexual gratification or involve the implicit or explicit abuse of women.

In some tantric traditions, women are said to be transmitters of doctrine, to play the role of teacher or guru. An example is the Paścimāmnāya Kaula tradition, which flourished in Kashmir and Nepal. According to the *Manthāna-bhairava-tantra* of this school, no distinction whatsoever should be made between the guru and the *yoginī* (female practitioner).

> The secret of all the scripture, the supreme essence of the oral tradition, is on the lips of the yoginī. Thus she is venerated as the Supreme Power which bestows bliss [knowledge] of the innate nature of things. . . . The yoginī is the womb from which the enlightened yogi is born and her mouth, from which issues the tradition, is the sacred matrix (*yoni*). . . . As the womb (*yoni*) of creation, it is the Lower Mouth (*ardhovaktra*) which is the essence of Kaula doctrine.[53]

In the Paścimāmnāya school, Śiva originally revealed the teachings to the *yoginīs*, who subsequently handed them down from generation to generation.[54] The implication here is that women, at least in this particular tantric tradition, have played an important, even central, role as sources of tantric instruction. According to the *Guptasādhanā-tantra*, initiation by a female guru leads to the achievement of all desires and is the initiate's great good fortune.[55] The *Prāṇatoṣinī*, citing the *Rudrayāmala*, discusses the conditions under which a female guru might perform initiation, and also the qualities that such a woman should possess. It is clear, in short, that females were gurus in at least some tantric cults.[56]

Even though goddesses play a central role in much tantric literature, particularly in Mahāvidyā texts; even though women are said to be revered generally in some tantric texts and are often worshiped as individuals; and even though in at least one tantric tradition women are said to be the source and transmitters of doctrine, it is not clear to what extent the Mahāvidyā materials, or even the related tantric materials, express female spirituality. The texts in most cases take a male point of view and seem to be written by males for males. Women are often described as objects of the male subjects, and the *sādhaka* is assumed to be male and his partner female. The rituals are described from his point of view.

Because the texts are preoccupied with goddesses, female imagery, and women, and usually view the female in a positive or affirmative fashion, and because we know that women were sometimes teachers and full participants in tantric *sādhanā*, it is possible that the spirituality described in tantric texts reflects women's religious experience as well as men's. Miranda Shaw has argued in the case of Buddhist Tantrism that the "male gaze," and male spirituality generally, might be understood to reflect female experience as well, insofar as women teach, fully participate in rituals with males, and sometimes write tantric texts.[57] The same may be the case in Hindu Tantrism,[58] and in Mahāvidyā worship specifically. While men wrote the great majority of tantric texts, it is possible that women wrote some of them, since they were sometimes teachers. It is also possible, as Shaw has argued for Buddhist Tantra, that male spirituality, as reflected in texts written by males, might be informed by female religious experience, especially in cases where both sexes were full participants in tantric rites. Thus far, however, I have been unable to find Hindu tantric texts that explicitly discuss or describe tantric rites from a female point of view. During my research I asked scholars and informants if they knew of any materials on the Mahāvidyās, or any Hindu tantric materials, that were written by, for, or about females. No one did.

This does not mean that such texts do not exist. Miranda Shaw's recent work on tantric Buddhism is sobering in this respect, illustrating how female sources have been almost entirely ignored by scholars of Buddhism. It seems unlikely that scholars of Hinduism have been any more assiduous than scholars of Buddhism in seeking female-authored texts or accounts of female spirituality. We can only hope that female-authored Hindu tantric texts will come to light in the near future.

The Potentially Liberating Nature of Social Antimodels

Finally, the question remains: Why would one wish to identify with, to actually become (in the logic of Tantra), a goddess such as Kālī, Chinnamastā, Dhūmāvatī, Bhairavī, or Mātaṅgī, each of whom dramatically embodies marginal, polluting, or socially subversive qualities? These goddesses are frightening, dangerous, and loathsome. They often threaten social order. In their strong associations with death, violence, pollution, and despised marginal social roles, they call into question such normative social "goods" as worldly comfort, security, respect, and honor. Seeking to identify with or become one with these goddesses suggests that the *sādhaka* in some fashion finds marginality, social taboos—the forbidden generally—spiritually refreshing or liberating. Wherein lies the potentially liberating power of what we might term social antimodels?

The answer, as I have suggested at several points throughout this book, probably lies in certain Hindu tantric emphases. These goddesses "fit" the logic of certain aspects of Tantra, especially left-handed Tantra, in which a central aim is to stretch one's consciousness beyond the conventional, to break away from approved social norms, roles, and expectations. By subverting, mocking, or rejecting conventional social norms, which seems to be the aim of the ritual of the five forbidden things (the *pañca tattva* ritual), the adept seeks to liberate his or her consciousness from the inherited, imposed, and probably inhibiting categories of proper and improper, good and bad, polluted and pure.

A principle aim in left-handed Tantra is to overcome what might be termed hardening of the categories. Living one's life according to rules of purity and pollution and caste and class that dictate how, where, and exactly in what manner every bodily function may be exercised, and which people one may, or may not, interact with socially, can create a sense of imprisonment from which one might long to escape. Perhaps the more marginal, bizarre, "outsider" goddesses among the Mahāvidyās facilitate this escape, as social antimodels who can effectively dislocate an individual. By identifying with one of them, the adept may experience expanded or liberated consciousness; by identifying with the forbidden or the marginalized, an adept may acquire a new and refreshing perspective on the cage of respectability and predictability.

The perspective from the cremation ground (Kālī, Tārā, and others), or the perspective of a polluted, culturally peripheral person of low caste

(Mātaṅgī) or of an inauspicious, marginalized widow who is shunned as an ill omen (Dhūmāvatī), offers tantric adepts a subversive vision of revered social values, cultural norms, and accepted frameworks of meaning. To take on such a perspective, to become one of these goddesses, might very well involve or imply a transformation of identity in which hardened categories are jettisoned and the emotions, mind, and spirit are stretched in exhilarating fashion.

Notes

Introduction

1. In a list of fifty-one goddesses in the *Mahākāla-saṁhitā*, nine of the ten Mahāvidyās are mentioned, Dhūmāvatī alone being absent. This text has been dated as early as the tenth century C.E. and may be the earliest mention of the Mahāvidyās as a group. *Mahākāla-saṁhitā* (Allahabad: Gāngānath Jha Research Institute, 1974), Kamakalā-khaṇḍa, pp. 65–66. Six of the ten Mahāvidyās—Kālī, Tārā, Mātaṅgī, Bhairavī, Chinnamastā, and Dhūmāvatī—are described in *upa tantras*, small sections dealing with each goddess, in the *Sammoha-tantra*, which was probably written in the fifteenth century. Prabodh Chandra Bagchi, *Studies in the Tantras* (Calcutta: University of Calcutta, 1975), p. 101.

2. See David Kinsley, *Hindu Goddesses: Visions of the Divine Feminine in the Hindu Religious Tradition* (Berkeley: University of California Press, 1986), chap. 9: "The Mahādevī."

The Mahāvidyās as a Group

1. *Kālikā-purāṇa* 74.90–94.

2. S. C. Banerjee, *A Brief History of Tantric Literature* (Calcutta: Naya Prokash, 1986), p. 30.

3. Ibid.

4. The list of the goddesses in one manuscript of the *Muṇḍamālā-tantra*, for example, varies in both number and sequence from the corresponding list in another. In the first list the Mahāvidyās are given as follows: Kālī, Tārā, Ṣoḍaśī, (Tripura-sundarī), Bhuvaneśvarī, Bhairavī, Chinnamastā, Dhūmāvatī, Bagalā, Mātaṅgī, and Kamalā. The second manuscript names thirteen: Kālī, Tārā, Tripura-sundarī, Bhairavī, Bhuvaneśvarī, Chinnamastā, Bagalā, Dhūmāvatī, Annapūrṇā, Durgā, Kamalā, Mātaṅgī, and Padmāvati. *Muṇḍamālā-tantra* (Calcutta: Nava Bharat, 1980), 1.7ff., 1.14ff.

5. Upendra Kumar Das, *Bhāratiya Śaktisādhanā*, 2 vols. (Santiniketan: Ranjit Rai Praksan, Visvabharati, 1967), p. 471, n. 5.

6. Narendra Nath Bhattacharyya, *History of the Tantric Religion: A Historical, Ritualistic and Philosophical Study* (New Delhi: Manohar Publishers, 1982), p. 348.

7. *Bṛhaddharma-purāṇa*, Madhya-khaṇḍa 25.58–68; *Bṛhaddharma Purāṇam*, ed. M. M. Haraprasad Sastri (Varanasi: Chaukhamba Amarabharati Prakashan, 1974), p. 379.

8. The group is the standard one, with the goddesses depicted in the following order, clockwise from left to right: Kālī, Tārā, Ṣoḍaśī, Bhuvaneśvarī, Bhairavī, Chinnamastā, Dhūmāvatī, Bagalā, Mātaṅgī, and Kamalā.

9. The group consists of the usual ten: Kālī, Tārā, Tripura-sundarī, Bhuvaneśvarī, Tripura-bhairavī, Chinnamastā, Dhūmāvatī, Bagalāmukhī, and Kamalā.

10. See D. C. Sircar, *The Śākta Pīṭhas* (Delhi: Motilal Banarsidass, 1973). The *śākta pīṭhas* are places sacred to the goddess because pieces of Satī's body fell on them. Viṣṇu dismembered Satī after she killed herself to avenge her father's insult to her. Traditionally there are said to be fifty-two such *pīṭhas.*

11. The pictures are actually numbered and show the Mahāvidyās in the following order: Kālī, Tārā, Ṣoḍaśī, Bhuvaneśvarī, Chinnamastā, Tripura-sundarī, Dhūmāvatī, Bagalāmukhī, Mātaṅgī, and Kamalā, which is the usual group of ten in a relatively common order.

12. They include the usual group and from left to right are: Kālī, Tārā, Ṣoḍaśī, Bhuvaneśvarī, Chinnamastā, Tripura-bhairavī, Dhūmāvatī, Bagalā, Mātaṅgī, and Kamalā.

13. My description of the place of the Mahāvidyās at Kāmākhyā is based on a paper by Patricia Dold, "The Mahāvidyās at Kāmarūpa" (presented at the annual meeting of the Canadian Association for Asian Studies, Ottawa, June 1993).

14. The *Mahābhāgavata-purāṇa*, ed. Pushpendra Kumar (Delhi: Eastern Book Linkers, 1983), 77.9–11, which tells the origin of the Mahāvidyās, locates them at Kāmarūpa, saying that Kālī is in the center there, surrounded by the other goddesses.

15. At the larger of the two temporary *pandals* housing the Mahāvidyās, located on S. N. Banerjea Road, ten goddesses were arranged as follows, from left to right: Dhūmāvatī, Chinnamastā, Tārā, Bhuvaneśvarī, Kālī, Mātaṅginī (Mātaṅgī), Ṣoḍaśī, Bagalā, and Kamalā. At the other shrine, nine goddesses were arranged, from left to right, as follows: Kāminī (Ṣoḍaśī), Dhūmāvatī, Bhairavī, Kamalā, Kālī (in the center and much larger than the others), Bhuvaneśvarī, Tārā, Bagalā, and Kāmākhyā-devī. The goddesses Mātaṅgī and Chinnamastā were absent, and the goddess Kāmākhyā was added to the usual group.

16. See David Kinsley, *Hindu Goddesses: Visions of the Divine Feminine in the Hindu Religious Tradition* (Berkeley: University of California Press, 1986), chap. 9: "The Mahādevī."

17. For example, *Devī-māhātmya* 11.38–50.

18. For example, Vedamūrti Taponiṣṭa, *Tantra-mahāvijñana*, 2 vols. (Bareli, U.P.: Saṁskṛti Saṁsthān, 1971), vol. 2, p. 389, says of the Great Goddess: "All women are your different forms."

19. Sircar, *The Śākta Pīṭhas*, p. 48.

20. Teun Goudriaan and Sanjukta Gupta, *Hindu Tantric and Śākta Literature* (Wiesbaden: Otto Harrassowitz, 1981), p. 81.

21. Govinda Sastri, "Karuṇāmayi Tārā," *Caṇḍi* 6, no. 7 (1946): 231.

22. Kālī is Kṛṣṇa, Tārā is Rāma, Bhuvaneśvarī is Varāha, Tripura-sundarī is Nṛsiṁha, Dhūmāvatī is Vāmana, Chinnamastā is Paraśurāma, Kamalā is Matsya, Bagalāmukhī is Kūrma, Mātaṅgī is the Buddha, and Ṣoḍaśī is Kalki.

23. As follows: Kālī is Kṛṣṇa, Tārā is Rāma, Chinnamastā is Narasiṁha, Bhuvaneśvarī is Vāmana, Bagalā is Kūrma, Dhūmāvatī is Matsya, Sundarī is Paraśurāma, Bhairavī is Halī (a personified and deified constellation), and Lakṣmī is the Buddha. Taponiṣṭa, vol. 2, p. 390.

24. Lakṣmī Narayana Śarmā, *Tantra Vidyā* (Delhi: World Book Co., 1986), p. 37.

25. Dhūmāvatī's spreading of disease might be understood on the analogy of the Buddha as an *avatāra* of Viṣṇu. When the Buddha is included as an *avatāra*, as he is in some late Vaiṣṇava texts, the purpose of his incarnation is to delude wicked people so that they will get their just deserts.

26. See Sircar, *The Śākta Pīṭhas.*

27. The accounts are found in *Bṛhaddharma-purāṇa*, Madhya-khaṇḍa 6.73–133, and *Mahābhāgavata-purāṇa* 8.45–9.82.

28. 6.78.

29. *Bṛhaddharma-purāṇa*, Madhya-khaṇḍa 6.128–31. The locations and names of the Mahāvidyās in the *Mahābhāgavata-purāṇa* account (77.31–34) are somewhat different: Tārā is to the east, Ṣoḍaśī to the southeast, Dhūmāvatī to the south, Bhairavī to the southwest, Bhuvaneśvarī to the west, Chinnamastā to the northwest, Bagalāmukhī to the north, Tripura-sundarī to the northeast, and Mātaṅgī above. Kālī is said to be present in all the directions.

30. As follows: Tārā is to her left (east), Bhuvaneśvarī to her right (west); in the southeast is Ṣoḍaśī; in the southwest, Bhairavī; in the northwest, Chinnamastā; in the north, Bagalā; in the northeast, Sundarī; and in the south, Dhūmāvatī.

31. Madhya-khaṇḍa 8.66–67.

32. *Mahābhāgavata-purāṇa* 8.71.

33. Madhya-khaṇḍa 6.132.

34. *Bṛhaddharma-purāṇa*, Madhya-khaṇḍa 6.133.

35. Ibid. 6.139–40.

36. 9.79.

37. Madhya-khaṇḍa 6.124–26.

38. William Sax, *Mountain Goddess: Gender and Politics in a Himalayan Pilgrimage* (New York: Oxford University Press, 1991), pp. 91ff.

39. Another example of a group of goddesses personifying magical powers is found in the tale of Birobā, a regional deity of western India. In his wanderings, Birobā encounters seven female deities, from whom he acquires magical powers. "But in a broader sense, the seven goddesses are also the personified, supernatural, feminine powers, the seven—or rather, eight—*siddhis*, who serve the one who wins them by his asceticism or in some other way." Gunther-Dietz Sontheimer, *Pastoral Deities in Western India*, trans. Anne Feldhaus (New York: Oxford University Press, 1989), pp. 92–95.

40. Madhya-khaṇḍa 6.132.

41. *Śaktisaṁgama-tantra*, vol. 4: *Chinnamastā Khaṇḍa*, ed. B. Bhattacharyya and Vrajavallabha Dvivedi (Baroda: Oriental Institute of Baroda, 1978), 2.89–91.

42. Vibhuti Narayana Dvivedi and Harisankara Upadhyay, *Śrī Tārā-sādhanā* (Vindhyacal: Śrī Tārā Mandir, 1988), p. 14.

43. *Vāmana-purāṇa* 29.1–30.73; *Śiva-purāṇa* 5.47.1–48.50; *Skanda-purāṇa* 7.3.24.1–22; and several *upa purāṇas*.

44. For the nine Durgās, see Diana Eck, *Banaras, City of Light* (Princeton, N.J.: Princeton University Press, 1982), pp. 268–69.

45. Śarmā, *Tantra Vidyā*, p. 37.

46. See Thomas B. Coburn, *Encountering the Goddess: A Translation of the Devī-Māhātmya and a Study of Its Interpretation* (Albany: State University of New York Press, 1991).

47. The classic statement of Vaiṣṇava *avatāra* theology is in *Bhagavad-gītā* 4.7–8.

48. This characteristic of the Mātṛkās is found in other *purāṇic* accounts of them, for example, *Matsya-purāṇa* 179.8–90 and *Varāha-purāṇa* 17.33–37.

49. *Śākta-pramoda* (Bombay: Khemrāja Śrīkṛṣṇadāsa Prakāśān, 1992), p. 268.

50. *Sahasranāma stotra* from the *Rudrayāmala;* Rājeś Dīkṣit, *Bhuvaneśvarī evam Chinnamastā Tantra Śāstra* (Agra: Braj Printers, 1988), pp. 46–52.

51. The Mahāvidyās are closely associated with Durgā in Nepal. A recent scholarly work refers to them as "an unstable set of Durgā manifestations," by which the author means that the number and identity of the group vary, including at times Annapūrṇā and Mahiṣamardinī, a form of Durgā herself. Mary Shepherd Slusser, *Nepal Maṇḍala: A Cultural Study of the Kathmandu Valley*, 2 vols. (Princeton, N.J.: Princeton University Press, 1982), vol. 1, p. 322.

52. See "The Mahāvidyās as Forms of the Mahādevī" in Part I.

53. The magical power that enables one to become small is called *anima siddhi* and is sometimes represented as a goddess, along with other *siddhis;* see Douglas Brooks, *Auspicious Wisdom: The Texts and Traditions of Śrīvidyā Śākta Tantrism in South India* (Albany: State University of New York Press, 1992), p. 142.

54. Dīkṣit, *Bhuvaneśvarī evam Chinnamastā*, v. 36, p. 49.

55. Ibid., v. 7, p. 47.

56. *Devī-bhāgavata-purāṇa* 7.28; *The Sri Mad Devi Bhagavatam*, trans. Swami Vijnanananda (Allahabad: Sudhindra Nath Vasu, 1921–23), pp. 688–92.

57. For a discussion of the *Devī-bhāgavata-purāṇa*, see C. Mackenzie Brown, *The Triumph of the Goddess: The Canonical Models and Theological Visions of the Devī-Bhāgavata Purāṇa* (Albany: State University of New York Press, 1990).

58. Goudriaan and Gupta, p. 195.

59. Dīkṣit, *Bhuvaneśvarī evam Chinnamastā*, pp. 45–51.

60. Eck, *Banaras, City of Light*, p. 360.

61. Private communication from Hillary Rodrigues.

62. Taponiṣṭa, p. 73.

63. Pranab Bandyopadhyay, *The Goddess of Tantra* (Calcutta: Punthi Pustak, 1990), pp. 19–24.

64. Dīkṣit, *Bhuvaneśvarī evam Chinnamastā*.

65. Sir John Woodroffe, *Śakti and Śākta, Essays and Addresses* (Madras: Ganesh & Co., 1987), p. 361. The same grouping of the Mahāvidyās is given in Sarbeswar Satpathy, *Dasa Mahavidya and Tantra Sastra* (Calcutta: Punthi Pustak, 1992), pp. 56–57.

66. *Mahānirvāṇa-tantra* 13.4; N. Bhattacharyya, *History of the Tantric Religion*, p. 348.

67. *Kālikā-purāṇa* 60.55ff.; Bani Kanta Kakati, *The Mother Goddess Kāmākhyā* (Gauhati, Assam: Lawyer's Book Stall, 1948), pp. 36–37.

68. *Kālikā-purāṇa* 78.86; Kakati, pp. 51–52.

69. For examples, see the works by Pushpendra Kumar listed in the Bibliography.

70. See Banerjee, *A Brief History of Tantric Literature*, p. 28.

71. *Śaktisaṁgama-tantra*, Tārā-khaṇḍa 1.84–90; N. Bhattacharyya, *History of the Tantric Religion*, p. 343.

72. There are often said to be three types of aspirants, each of whom reflects a different *bhava* (mentality): *divya* (said to be superior and associated with the *sattva guṇa*), *vīra* (said to be the appropriate type of spirituality for engaging in left-handed tantric rites and sometimes associated with the *rajas guṇa*), and *paśu* (the lowest, "beastly," type of person or spirituality). There are appropriate paths for each type of aspirant, and perhaps appropriate types of goddesses, although I have not yet found clear examples of the Mahāvidyās being related to the three *bhavas*. See Sures Chandra Banerji, *Tantra in Bengal: A Study of Its Origin, Development and Influence* (Calcutta: Naya Prokash, 1977), pp. 155–56.

73. See Kamalakar Mishra, *Significance of the Tantric Tradition* (Varanasi: Arddhanarisvara Publications, 1981), pp. 38, 76–77, and Satpathy, *Dasa Mahavidya and Tantra Sastra*, p. vii.

74. For a detailed interpretation of Kālī and the other Mahāvidyās according to this approach, see the treatment of the individual Mahāvidyās in Part II.

75. See June McDaniel, *The Madness of the Saints: Ecstatic Religion in Bengal* (Chicago: University of Chicago Press, 1989), pp. 132–33, where she discusses the famous Bengali *śākta* saint, Bāmākhepa.

76. This is exactly the interpretation proposed by K. Mishra, *Significance of the Tantric Tradition*, pp. 140ff. See also Sarbeswar Satpathy, *Sakti Iconography in Tantric Mahāvidyās* (Calcutta: Punthi Pustak, 1991), pp. 151–53, where the Mahāvidyās and the seven *cakras* are said to reflect the evolution-devolution of consciousness in much the same way as in Sāṁkhya philosophy.

77. Taponiṣṭa, vol. 2, p. 470.

78. Ibid., p. 471.

79. *Śākta-pramoda*, p. 270.

80. Kālī-khaṇḍa 3.32; Banerjee, *A Brief History of Tantric Literature*, p. 31.

81. *Mahānirvāṇa-tantra* 10.112; Banerjee, *A Brief History of Tantric Literature*, p. 31

82. Brooks, *Auspicious Wisdom*, pp. 136, 141–42.

83. N. Bhattacharyya, *History of the Tantric Religion*, pp. 322–25.

84. In the *Muṇḍamālā-tantra*, in the *Dasamahāvidyā-stotra*, chap. 11, there is an implied hierarchy. Kālī and Tārā are called Mahāvidyās; Ṣoḍaśī, Bhuvaneśvarī, Bhairavī, Chinnamastā, and Dhūmāvatī are called Vidyās; and Bagalāmukhī, Mātaṅgī, and Kamalā are called Siddhi-vidyās; *Kalyāṇa, Tīrtha Aṅk* (Gorakhpur: Gita Press, 1957), pp. 696–97. Pushpendra Kumar, *Sakti Cult in Hinduism*, p. 155, also identifies the Mahāvidyās with these categories but does not cite any textual reference. In neither the *Muṇḍamālā-tantra* nor Kumar, however, is there any comment on the meaning of these three designations or the distinctions they

denote. It is likely that Kālī and Tārā as Mahāvidyās are understood to be superior in some sense to the other Mahāvidyās, but this is not made explicit.

85. *Sāmanya pūjā* to the goddess is described in K. R. Van Kooij, *Worship of the Goddess according to the Kālikāpurāṇa* (Leiden: E. J. Brill, 1972), pp. 72–90; tantric worship is also described in *Kaulāvalī*, ed. Arthur Avalon (Delhi: Bharatiya Vidya Prakashan, 1985), chaps. 2–8.

86. The importance of purification in tantric worship is discussed by K. Mishra, *Significance of the Tantric Tradition*, pp. 148–50.

87. Uccișṭa-mātaṅgī, a form of the Mahāvidya Mātaṅgī, may be related to such goddesses insofar as she is often described as fierce and is said to prefer leftovers, *uccișṭa*, for offerings.

88. See K. Mishra, *Significance of the Tantric Tradition*, pp. 60ff.

89. For the achievement of *siddhis* and other powers as distractions from the spiritual quest in yoga, see Alain Daniélou, *Yoga: The Method of Re-integration* (New York: University Book Publishers, 1955), pp. 118–22, and Mircea Eliade, *Yoga: Immortality and Freedom* (New York: Pantheon Books, 1958), pp. 85–90.

90. *Dāmara-tantra*, ed. and trans. Ram Kumar Rai (Varanasi: Pracya Prakashan, 1988), pp. 15, 18, 51, and passim.

91. Chap. 3; Goudriaan and Gupta, p. 116.

92. Goudriaan and Gupta, p. 117.

93. Ibid., p. 119.

94. Ibid., p. 121.

95. Ibid., p. 122.

96. V. B. Mishra, *Religious Beliefs and Practices of North India* (Leiden: E. J. Brill, 1973), p. 56.

97. *Bṛhaddharma-purāṇa*, Madhya-khaṇḍa 6.133.

98. Brooks, *Auspicious Wisdom*, p. 142.

99. See *pūjā vidhi* (rules on worship) for Mātaṅgī in *Śākta-pramoda*, p. 332.

100. See Goudriaan and Gupta, pp. 193–94.

101. *Śākta-pramoda*, p. 285.

102. Ibid., p. 226.

103. Acarya Pandita Sri Sivadattamisra Sastri, *Bagalāmukhī-rahasyam* (Varanasi: Thakur Prasad Pustak Bharadar, 1951), pp. 11–13.

104. *Śākta-pramoda*, pp. 173–74.

105. Hemendra Nath Chakravarty and Mark Dyczkowski.

106. T. V. Kapali Sastry, *Sidelights on Tantra* (Pondicherry, 1971), p. 16; cited in Brooks, *Auspicious Wisdom*, p. 82.

107. Jan Gonda, "The Indian Mantra," *Oriens*, vol. 16 (1963); reprinted in J. Gonda, *Selected Studies IV* (Leiden: E. J. Brill, 1975), p. 252; cited in Brooks, *Auspicious Wisdom*, p. 81.

108. See Harold G. Coward, *Bhartṛhari* (Boston: Twayne, 1976), for a discussion of the Sphoṭa school and the creative role of sound generally in Hinduism.

109. Swami Harshananda, *Hindu Gods and Goddesses* (Mylapore: Sri Ramakrishna Math, 1988), p. 107.

110. Ajit Mookerjee and Madhu Khanna, *The Tantric Way: Art, Science, Ritual* (Delhi: Vikas Publishing House, 1977), p. 190.

111. Pushpendra Kumar, *Sakti Cult in Ancient India* (Banaras: Bharatiya Publishing House, 1974), p. 155.

112. Banerjee, *A Brief History of Tantric Literature*, p. 28.

113. Taponiṣṭa, vol. 2, pp. 384–89.

114. *Devī-māhātmya* 1.60, 4.4, 5.14, 11.7.

115. For example, Gaṇeśa-khaṇḍa 45.4; Kṛṣṇajanma-khaṇḍa 41.78, 86.97, 109.20.

116. Cheever MacKenzie Brown, *God as Mother: A Feminine Theology in India* (Hartford, Vt.: Claude Stark & Co., 1974), p. 165.

117. *Lalitā-sahasranāma with Bhāskararāya's Commentary*, trans. R. Ananthakrishna Sastry (Madras: Theosophical Publishing House, 1951).

118. *Sri Mad Devi Bhagavatam*, pp. 1, 3, 11, 15, 16, 57, 121, 126, 130, 136, 167, 194, 201, 216, 303, 323, 419–20.

119. Diana Eck, "India's *Tīrthas*: 'Crossings' in Sacred Geography," *History of Religions* 20, no. 4 (May 1981): 323–44.

120. This is a term used by Eck, ibid.

121. See Kinsley, *Hindu Goddesses*, chaps. 2 and 8.

Kālī

1. *Dhyāna* mantra of Dakṣiṇā-kālī from the *Kālī-tantra:* Kṛṣṇānanda Āgamavāgiśa, *Bṛhat Tantrasāra* (Calcutta: Navabharat Publishers, 1984), pp. 387–88.

2. *Dhyāna* mantra of Guhya-kālī; *Tantrasāra*, p. 406.

3. *Dhyāna* mantra of Śmaśāna-kālī; *Tantrasāra*, p. 461.

4. Sir John Woodroffe, *Śakti and Śākta, Essays and Addresses* (Madras: Ganesh & Co., 1987), p. 361; Rājeś Dīkṣit, *Kālī Tantra Śāstra* (Agra: Sumit Prakashan, 1987), p. 1.

5. Vibhuti Narayana Dvivedi and Harisankara Upadhyay, *Śrī Tārā-sādhanā* (Vindhyacal: Śrī Tārā Mandir, 1988), p. 14.

6. *Mahābhāgavata-purāṇa* 8.48–53.

7. *Skanda-purāṇa* 5.82.1–21.

8. *Śaktisaṁgama-tantra*, vol. 4: *Chinnamastā Khaṇḍa*, ed. B. Bhattacharyya and Vrajavallabha Dvivedi (Baroda: Oriental Institute of Baroda, 1978), 9.7–8.

9. *Agni-purāṇa* 133, 134, 136; *Garuḍa-purāṇa* 38.

10. *Bhāgavata-purāṇa* 5.9.12–20.

11. For the Thugs, see Francis Tuker, *The Yellow Scarf* (London: J. M. Dent & Sons, 1961).

12. Teun Goudriaan and Sanjukta Gupta, *Hindu Tantric and Śākta Literature* (Wiesbaden: Otto Harrassowitz, 1981), p. 219.

13. *Mānasāra-śilpa-śāstra* 9.289.

14. R. Nagaswamy, *Tantric Cult of South India* (Delhi: Agam Kala Prakashan, 1982), p. 26.

15. Ibid., p. 26.

16. Ibid., p. 27.

17. Ibid., p. 28.

18. *Liṅga-purāṇa* 1.106.

19. Ibid. 1.72.66–68.

20. *Vāmana-purāṇa* 25–29.

21. *Skanda-purāṇa* 5.82.1–21.

22. This story is told in the *Adbhūta Rāmāyaṇa*, Sāralā-dāsa's Oriyan *Rāmāyaṇa*, and the Bengal *Jaiminibhārata Rāmāyaṇa*. Narendra Nath Bhattacharyya, *History of the Śākta Religion* (New Delhi: Munshiram Manoharlal Publishers, 1974), p. 149.

23. See C. Sivaramamurti, *Nataraja in Art, Thought and Literature* (New Delhi: National Museum, 1974), p. 138.

24. *Bhavabhūti's Mālatīmādhava with the Commentary of Jagaddhara*, ed. and trans. M. R. Kale (Delhi: Motilal Banarsidass, 1967), pp. 44–48.

25. N. Bhattacharyya, *History of the Śākta Religion*, p. 136.

26. Mark S. G. Dyczkowski, *The Doctrine of Vibration: An Analysis of the Doctrines and Practices of Kashmir Shaivism* (Delhi: Motilal Banarsidass, 1989), p. 16.

27. Ibid., pp. 117–24.

28. See Sures Chandra Banerji, *Tantra in Bengal: A Study of Its Origin, Development and Influence* (Calcutta: Naya Prokash, 1977), pp. 85–86; Sarbeswar Satpathy, *Sakti Iconography in Tantric Mahāvidyās* (Calcutta: Punthi Pustak, 1991), pp. 120–22; N. Bhattacharyya, *History of the Śākta Religion*, p. 136.

29. *Principles of Tantra: The Tantratattva of Śrīyukta Śiva Candra Vidyārnava Bhattācārya Mahodaya*, ed. Arthur Avalon (Madras: Ganesh & Co., 1960), pp. 327–28.

30. *Hymn to Kālī (Karpurādi-stotra)*, ed. and trans. Arthur Avalon (Madras: Ganesh & Co., 1965), p. 34.

31. Ibid.

32. Ibid.

33. For example, *Mahānirvāṇa-tantra* 5.140–41, 6.68–76, 10.102.

34. Ibid. 4.30–34.

35. For the *pañca tattva* ritual, see *ibid.* 5–6; Agehananda Bharati, *The Tantric Tradition* (London: Rider, 1965), pp. 228–78; Mircea Eliade, *Yoga: Immortality and Freedom* (New York: Pantheon Books, 1958), pp. 254–62; and Heinrich Zimmer, *Philosophies of India* (Cleveland: World Publishing Co., 1956), pp. 572–80.

36. *Hymn to Kālī*, pp. 84, 86.

37. Dīkṣit, *Kālī Tantra Śāstra*, pp. 119–31.

38. Jeffrey J. Kripal, "Kālī's Tongue and Ramakrishna: 'Biting the Tongue' of the Tantric Tradition," *History of Religions* 34, no. 2 (November 1994): 152–89.

39. Frédérique A. Marglin, *Wives of the God-King: The Rituals of the Devadasis of Puri* (New York: Oxford University Press, 1985), pp. 214–15.

40. Kripal, p. 167.

41. Ram Chandra Datta, *Śrīśrīrāmakṛṣṇa Paramahaṁsadever Jīvanavṛttāta*, 5th ed. (Calcutta: Yogadyana, 1935), p. 19; cited in Kripal, p. 168.

42. "Till recently, in Kerala, older women would disapprove of young females leaving their hair loose when they were in a public place. A woman with loose hair was often equated in literature and common parlance with a loose woman, an actress, a professional dancer, a woman out to seduce." Savithri Shanker de Tourreil, "Nayars in a South Indian Matrix: A Study Based on Female-Centered Ritual" (Ph.D. diss., Concordia University, Montreal, 1995), p. 129, n. 2.

43. "Hindu women are normally expected to keep their hair tied up, that is,

'under control.' Keeping the hair loose is a sign of impurity, as after the death of a close relative or during menstruation." Kathleen M. Erndl, *Victory to the Mother: The Hindu Goddess of Northwest India in Myth, Ritual, and Symbol* (New York: Oxford University Press, 1993), p. 165, n. 2.

44. Alf Hiltebeitel, "Draupadī's Hair," *Puruṣārtha* 5 (1981): 186–87.

45. See P. Hershman, "Hair, Sex and Dirt," *Man* 9 (1974): 282–83. For rules concerning menstruation in Hinduism, see Pandurang Vaman Kane, *History of Dharmaśastra*, vol. 2 (Poona: Bhandarkar Oriental Research Institute, 1974), pt. 2, pp. 802–5.

46. Dīkṣit, *Kālī Tantra Śāstra*, p. 130.

47. Ibid., p. 125.

48. The details of the following interpretation are particularly dependent on interviews I had with Swami Annapurnananda of the Ramakrishna Mission in Varanasi and on the observations by Dīkṣit, *Kālī Tantra Śāstra*, pp. 3–7; Caman Lal Gautam, *Kālī Siddhi* (Bareli, U.P.: Saṁskṛti Saṁsthān, 1984), pp. 91–117; Satpathy, *Sakti Iconography in Tantric Mahāvidyās*, pp. 118–21; and other sources, who spoke on the condition of anonymity.

49. June McDaniel, *The Madness of the Saints: Ecstatic Religion in Bengal* (Chicago: University of Chicago Press, 1989), p. 87, citing an interview with a contemporary devotee.

50. Dīkṣit, *Kālī Tantra Śāstra*, p. 3.

51. Swami Annapurnananda.

52. Dīkṣit, *Kālī Tantra Śāstra*.

53. Gautam.

54. Swami Annapurnananda.

55. Dīkṣit, *Kālī Tantra Śāstra;* Gautam.

56. Swami Annapurnananda.

57. Dīkṣit, *Kālī Tantra Śāstra;* Swami Annapurnananda. This is a strikingly different interpretation of Kālī's lolling tongue from that of Kripal cited above.

58. Gautam.

59. Dīkṣit, *Kālī Tantra Śāstra*.

60. Gautam.

61. Ibid.

62. Dīkṣit, *Kālī Tantra Śāstra*.

63. Ibid.

64. Swami Annapurnananda.

65. N. N. Bhattacharyya, in a conversation with me in Calcutta in October 1992—appropriately, during Kālī Pūjā—said that Kālī's standing on Śiva, as in the Dakṣiṇa-kālī image, symbolizes her being above him during intercourse. Such sexual union between the two is often actually shown and is sometimes part of the *dhyāna* mantras of other forms of Kālī.

66. See Satpathy, *Sakti Iconography in Tantric Mahāvidyās*, p. 121.

67. In a commentary to the *Karpūrādi-stotra*, the *Niruttara-tantra*, and the *Kāmadhenu-tantra;* Guy L. Beck, *Sonic Theology: Hinduism and Sacred Sound* (Columbia: University of South Carolina Press, 1993), p. 145.

68. Dīkṣit, *Kalī Tantra Śāstra;* Swami Annapurnananda.

69. Swami Annapurnananda.

70. See the *Tantrasāra* on Guhya-kālī; see also Chintaharan Chakravarti, *Tantras: Studies on Their Religion and Literature* (Calcutta: Punthi Pustak, 1963), pp. 90–91.

71. Drinking blood results in intoxication in many myths featuring Kālī and other goddesses. She gets drunk on fresh blood and behaves in wild, unpredictable, dangerous ways.

72. Dyczkowski, *The Doctrine of Vibration*, pp. 124–25; K. C. Pandey, *Abhinavagupta: An Historical and Philosophical Study*, 2d ed. (Varanasi: Chowkhamba Sanskrit Series Office, 1963), pp. 513–21.

Tārā

1. Stephan Beyer, *The Cult of Tārā: Magic and Ritual in Tibet* (Berkeley: University of California Press, 1973), p. 7.

2. John Blofeld, *Boddhisattva of Compassion: The Mystical Tradition of Kuan Yin* (Boulder, Colo.: Shambala Publications, 1978), p. 53; Heinrich Zimmer, *Philosophies of India* (Cleveland: World Publishing Co., 1956), p. 534.

3. Beyer, pp. 8–10.

4. Ibid., p. 4.

5. For references on the history of Tārā in Tibet, see ibid., p. 469.

6. Ibid., p. 12.

7. Ibid., p. 13.

8. For a description of the "eight terrors" from which Tārā is said to save, see Giuseppe Tucci, *Tibetan Painted Scrolls*, 2 vols. (Rome: Libraria dello Stato, 1949), *tanka* 44, pl. 78, discussed in vol. 2, pp. 403ff.

9. For example, see Beyer, pp. 233–40, and Blofeld, pp. 55–71.

10. Beyer, pp. 386–88.

11. Ibid., p. 386.

12. See Blofeld, p. 59, where Tārā blesses a young couple with a child after rescuing them from calamity.

13. Beyer, pp. 212–13.

14. Beyer, p. 302, shows quite clearly that Kurukullā was originally an Indian tribal deity.

15. Ibid., p. 303; see also Benoytosh Bhattacharyya, *The Indian Buddhist Iconography: Mainly Based on the Sādhanamālā and the Cognate Tāntric Texts of Rituals* (Calcutta: Firma K. L. Mukhopadhyaya, 1968), pp. 147–52.

16. Beyer, p. 302.

17. Ibid., p. 306.

18. B. Bhattacharyya, *Indian Buddhist Iconography*, pp. 134–46.

19. Beyer, p. 292.

20. B. Bhattacharyya, *Indian Buddhist Iconography*, p. 190; see also Nalini Kanta Bhattasali, *Iconography of Buddhist and Brahmanical Sculptures in the Dacca Museum* (Dacca: Rai S. N. Bhadra Bahadur, 1929), pl. 71(a), facing p. 206.

21. Pushpendra Kumar, *Tārā: The Supreme Goddess* (Delhi: Bharatiya Vidya Prakashan, 1992), pp. 103–4.

22. This myth is found in the first and second chapters of the *Brahmayāmala*

and the tenth chapter of the *Rudrayāmala*. This elaborated version of the story is from Rasmohan Cakravarti, "Mahāvidyā Tārā ki Sādhanā," *Caṇḍi* 6, no. 7 (1946): 216–20.

23. Note that the Buddha is included in some late lists of the *avatāras* of Viṣṇu. In such cases, the role of the Buddha is to delude sinners with his false teachings so that they will receive their appropriate karmic rewards.

24. Mahidhara, *Mantra Mahodadhiḥ*, vol. 1, ed. and trans. Ram Kumar Rai (Varanasi: Prachya Prakashan, 1992), pp. 179–80. I have edited the translation.

25. "Tārā Aṣṭakam," from the *Bṛhannīla-tantra*; Rājeś Dīkṣit, *Tārā Tantra Śāstra* (Agra: Sumit Prakashan, 1987), pp. 115–16.

26. Kṛṣṇānanda Āgamavāgiśa, *Bṛhat Tantrasāra* (Calcutta: Navabharat Publishers, 1984), p. 415.

27. Dīkṣit, *Tārā Tantra Śāstra*, pp. 128, 130.

28. For the poetry of Ramprasad and his use of the epithets Kālī and Tārā, see *Rama Prasada's Devotional Songs: The Cult of Shakti*, trans. Jadunath Sinha (Calcutta: Sinha Publishing House, 1966), passim. For his use of "Tārā" to suggest the benign aspect of the goddess, see song 221, pp. 118–19, where he refers to Tārā as the "doer of good, the good of all, grantor of safety," and as having a "smiling face."

29. Dīkṣit, *Tārā Tantra Śāstra*, p. 117.

30. Ibid., pp. 128–33.

31. See the discussion of this myth below.

32. *Liṅga-purāṇa* 1.106.

33. Dīkṣit, *Tārā Tantra Śāstra*, pp. 108, 132.

34. *Kalyāṇa*, *Śakti Aṅk* (Gorakhpur: Gita Press, 1934), p. 404.

35. Dīkṣit, *Tārā Tantra Śāstra*, p. 6.

36. Ibid.

37. Ibid.

38. Robert E. Svoboda, *Aghora: At the Left Hand of God* (Albuquerque, N.M.: Brotherhood of Life, 1986), p. 79.

39. Ibid., p. 80.

40. Swami Annapurnananda.

41. Swami Annapurnananda.

42. Dīkṣit, *Tārā Tantra Śāstra*, pp. 128–34.

43. *Kalyāṇa*, *Śakti Aṅk*, "Tārā-rahasya," p. 224.

44. Ibid.

45. Dīkṣit, *Tārā Tantra Śāstra*, p. 131.

46. *Kalyāṇa*, *Śakti Aṅk*, p. 225.

47. Dīkṣit, *Tārā Tantra Śāstra*, p. 10.

48. *Nīla-tantra* 31.12–18, 21–23; Kumar, *Tārā*, p. 101.

49. E. Alan Morinis, *Pilgrimage in the Hindu Tradition: A Case Study of West Bengal* (Delhi: Oxford University Press, 1984), pp. 166–67.

50. Ibid., p. 167. See also June McDaniel, *The Madness of the Saints: Ecstatic Religion in Bengal* (Chicago: University of Chicago Press, 1989), p. 89. In McDaniel's account, which is based on an interview with a devotee, it is Kālī who comes to Śiva's rescue. She changes her form to Tārā, she says, because "I cannot nurse my own husband."

51. Svoboda, pp. 77–80.
52. *Kalyāna, Sakti Aṅk*, p. 404.
53. Morinis, p. 182, says that the stone image is actually ill defined and that the devotee must use considerable imagination to detect Tārā nursing Śiva.
54. Ibid., p. 171.
55. Ibid., pp. 184–85.
56. See David Kinsley, *The Divine Player: A Study of Kṛṣṇa Līlā* (Delhi: Motilal Banarsidass, 1979), pp. 205–52.
57. Morinis, p. 177.
58. Ibid., pp. 178–79.

Tripura-Sundarī

1. Rājeś Dīkṣit, *Ṣoḍaśī Tantra Śāstra* (Agra: Sumit Prakashan, 1991), p. 1.
2. Interview with Swami Annapurnananda.
3. *Śākta-pramoda* (Bombay: Khemrāja Śrīkṛṣṇadāsa Prakāśān, 1992), p. 153.
4. *Lalitā-sahasranāma*, name 52; Douglas Renfrew Brooks, *Auspicious Wisdom: The Texts and Traditions of Śrīvidyā Śākta Tantrism in South India* (Albany: State University of New York Press, 1992), p. 64.
5. Dīkṣit, *Ṣoḍaśī Tantra Śāstra*, p. 137. In this description, Tripura-sundarī is described as a female version of Śiva.
6. Kṛṣṇānanda Āgamavāgiśa, *Bṛhat Tantrasāra* (Calcutta: Navabharat Publishers, 1984), pp. 356–58.
7. Ibid., p. 358.
8. This was described in Part I. The following discussion of Tripura-sundarī, particularly her place in South India, follows the excellent work done on her cult by Brooks in *Auspicious Wisdom*.
9. Ibid., p. 56.
10. Ibid., p. 72.
11. Ibid., p. 71.
12. *Kalyāṇa, Śakti Aṅk* (Gorakhpur: Gita Press, 1934), p. 670.
13. Conversation with T. K. Biswas, Joint Director, Bharat Kala Bhavan, Varanasi, December 1992.
14. Robert I. Levy, *Mesocosm: Hinduism and the Organization of a Traditional Newar City in Nepal* (Delhi: Motilal Banarsidass, 1992), pp. 229–31.
15. Ibid., p. 230.
16. From *Lalitopākhyāna* 30.56; summarized in Brooks, *Auspicious Wisdom*, pp. 68–69.
17. Dīkṣit, *Ṣodaśī Tantra Śāstra*, pp. 7–10, following the *Tripurā-rahasya* of the Māhātmya-khanda of the *Brahmānda-purāna*.
18. Dīkṣit, *Ṣodaśī Tantra Śāstra*, p. 139.
19. See "The One Hundred and Eight Names of Ṣoḍaśī" from the *Brahmayāmala* and the *Sahasranāma* from the *Vāmakeśvara-tantra;* ibid., pp. 136, 137–49.
20. *Prapañcasāra-tantra*, ed. John Woodroffe (Delhi: Motilal Banarsidass, n.d.), 9.23–24, translated by Woodroffe in his introduction to the text, p. 28.

21. Dīkṣit, *Ṣoḍaśī Tantra Śāstra*, pp. 147–48.

22. *Kālikā-purāṇa* 78.100; Bani Kanta Kakati, *The Mother Goddess Kāmākhyā* (Gauhati, Assam: Lawyer's Book Stall, 1948), pp. 45–46.

23. *Yoginī-tantra* 1.6.17; Kakati, p. 50.

24. *Tripurā-rahasya* 10.14; Kakati, pp. 50–51.

25. Dīkṣit, *Ṣoḍaśī Tantra Śāstra*, p. 140.

26. Ibid., p. 137.

27. Ibid., pp. 137, 143.

28. Ibid., p. 139, where she is called Kālī, Kālikā, and Kālaratri.

29. Upendra Kumar Das, *Bhāratiya Śaktisādhanā*, 2 vols. (Santiniketan: Ranjit Rai Prakasan, Visvabharati, 1967), vol. 1, pp. 525–26.

30. Ibid., p. 525.

31. Conversation with a tantric scholar in Varanasi, January 1993.

32. Das, p. 525.

33. T. V. Sastry, *Sidelights on Tantra* (Pondicherry, 1971), p. 254; cited in Brooks, *Auspicious Wisdom*, p. 77.

34. Sastry; cited in Brooks, *Auspicious Wisdom*, p. 79.

35. Sastry, p. 254; cited in Brooks, *Auspicious Wisdom*, p. 77.

36. *Nityaṣoḍaśikārṇava* 1.12; Brooks, *Auspicious Wisdom*, p. 77.

37. *Prānatoṣinī* 5.6; Das, p. 526.

38. Swami Annapurnananda.

39. Mark Dyczkowski and Hemendra Nath Chakravarty, two scholars of Tantra, private conversations in Varanasi, 1993.

40. Brooks, *Auspicious Wisdom*, p. 107.

41. Commentary on the *Lalitā-sahasranāma*; Brooks, *Auspicious Wisdom*, p. 76, citing Sastry.

42. "In Śrī-Vidyā ideology, there is no disparate existence of signifying sound and the signified object; and the expressing consciousness and the expressed energy are fundamentally one. The universe of experience . . . is nothing other than the expressive sounds that constitute the alphabet. . . . The 36 letters (15 vowels taken as one, and the consonants 35) of the alphabet correspond to the 36 principles (*tattvas*) that underlie the constitution and function of the universe." S. K. Ramachandra Rao, *Śrī-Cakra: Its Yantra, Mantra and Tantra* (Bangalore: Kalpatharu Research Academy, 1982), p. 38.

43. Brooks, *Auspicious Wisdom*, p. 60.

44. *Varivasyā-rahasya* 2.163; Brooks, *Auspicious Wisdom*, p. 108.

45. Brooks, *Auspicious Wisdom*, p. 109.

46. Douglas Renfrew Brooks, *The Secret of the Three Cities: An Introduction to Hindu Śākta Tantrism* (Chicago: University of Chicago Press, 1990), p. 118.

47. A. L. Basham, *The Wonder That Was India* (New York: Grove Press, 1959), p. 162; cited in Brooks, *Auspicious Wisdom*, p. 93.

48. Brooks, *Auspicious Wisdom*, pp. 93–94.

49. Ibid., pp. 90–91.

50. Ibid., pp. 99–101.

51. For a description and interpretation of the Śrī *cakra*, see the *Kāmakalā-vilāsa*, summarized in S. C. Banerjee, *A Brief History of Tantric Literature* (Calcutta: Naya Prokash, 1986), pp. 208–12, and Ajit Mookerjee and Madhu Khanna,

The Tantric Way: Art, Science, Ritual (Boston: New York Graphic Society, n.d.), pp. 59–62.

52. Brooks, *Auspicious Wisdom*, pp. 140–41.

Bhuvaneśvarī

1. *Dhyāna* mantra from *Mantramahārṇava* (Bombay: Khemraj Śrīkṛṣṇadas Publishers, 1990), p. 471.

2. *Muṇḍamālā-tantra* (Calcutta: Nava Bharat, 1980), 6.5–8.

3. Rājeś Dīkṣit, *Bhuvaneśvarī evam Chinnamastā Tantra Śāstra* (Agra: Braj Printers, 1988), p. 17.

4. From her thousand-name hymn; ibid., pp. 47–52.

5. From the *Rudrayāmala-tantra; Mantramahārṇava*, p. 472; see also Kṛṣṇānanda Āgamavāgiśa, *Bṛhat Tantrasāra* (Calcutta: Navabharat Publishers, 1984), p. 467.

6. *Śākta-pramoda* (Bombay: Khemrāja Śrīkṛṣṇadāsa Prakāśān, 1992), pp. 204–5.

7. *The Sri Mad Devi Bhagavatam*, trans. Swami Vijnanananda (Allahabad: Sudhindra Nath Vasu, 1921–23), 3.4, pp. 128–29.

8. Ibid., 4.19, p. 319.

9. *Prapañcasāra-tantra*, ed. John Woodroffe (Delhi: Motilal Banarsidass, n.d.); the hymn is found in 11.49–68 and is translated by Woodroffe in his introduction, pp. 29–37.

10. Ibid. In the English translation, Woodroffe numbers the verses of the hymn beginning with 1, which corresponds to verse 49 in the text.

11. Ibid.

12. Ibid.

13. Ibid.

14. See *Tantrasāra*, p. 176 (blue form), and *Mantramahārṇava*, pp. 468–69 (golden form) and 471 (vermillion form).

15. *Mantramahārṇava*, p. 472.

16. Dīkṣit, *Bhuvaneśvarī evam Chinnamastā*, p. 21.

17. 1.26–28, p. 12.

18. *Mantramahārṇava*, p. 468.

19. 6.5, p. 499.

20. 2.5; Teun Goudriaan and Sanjukta Gupta, *Hindu Tantric and Śākta Literature* (Wiesbaden: Otto Harrassowitz, 1981), p. 89.

21. Dīkṣit, *Bhuvaneśvarī evam Chinnamastā*, pp. 47–52.

22. Ibid., pp. 45–51.

23. Hundred-name hymn from the *Rudrayāmala;* ibid., p. 45.

24. *Bhuvaneśvarī-stotra* from the *Rudrayāmala; Mantramahārṇava*, p. 472.

25. *Prapañcasāra-tantra*, chap. 3, and Introduction, p. 19.

26. Vedamūrti Taponiṣṭa, *Tantra-mahāvijñāna*, 2 vols. (Bareli, U.P.: Saṁskṛti Saṁsthān, 1971), p. 470.

27. The following description is found in the *Tantrasāra*, pp. 173–75; the interpretation follows that of Hemendra Nath Chakravarty, a scholar of Tantrism

in Varanasi. The yantra itself is also pictured in the *Śākta-pramoda*, p. 194. See also Ajit Mookerjee, *Tantra Āsana: A Way to Self-Realization* (Basel: Ravi Kumar, 1971), pl. 38, p. 67, an eighteenth-century Bhuvaneśvarī yantra from Rajasthan. Here the names of the deities, *śaktis*, and guardians are actually written out.

28. Hemendra Nath Chakravarty, private conversation.

29. Mahidhara, *Mantra Mahodadhiḥ*, vol. 1, ed. and trans. Ram Kumar Rai (Varanasi: Prachya Prakashan, 1992), pp. 234–47.

30. Ibid., p. 261.

31. *Tantrasāra*, p. 468.

32. *Śākta-pramoda*, pp. 204–5.

33. Dīkṣit, *Bhuvaneśvarī evam Chinnamastā*, p. 18.

34. Ibid.

35. Taponiṣṭa, p. 471.

36. Hundred-name hymn from the *Rudrayāmala; Śākta-pramoda*, p. 205.

Chinnamastā

1. From a hymn addressed to Chinnamastā; Teun Goudriaan and Sanjukta Gupta, *Hindu Tantric and Śākta Literature* (Wiesbaden: Otto Harrassowitz, 1981), p. 207.

2. Mahidhara, *Mantra Mahodadhiḥ*, vol. 1, ed. and trans. Ram Kumar Rai (Varanasi: Prachya Prakashan, 1992), p. 256.

3. *Dhyāna* mantra of Chinnamastā; *Śākta-pramoda* (Bombay: Khemrāja Śrīkṛṣṇadāsa Prakāśān, 1992), p. 221.

4. Jagdish Narain Tiwari, "Studies in Goddess Cults in Northern India, with Reference to the First Seven Centuries A.D." (Ph.D. diss., Australian National University, n.d.), pp. 312–37.

5. Ibid., pp. 313–15.

6. Ibid., p. 317.

7. The following names and their numbers are from Elisabeth Anne Benard, "Chinnamastā: The Awful Buddhist and Hindu Tantric Goddess" (Ph.D. diss., Columbia University, New York, 1990). In Chinnamastā's 108-name hymn from the *Śākta-pramoda*, for example, she is called Killer of the Demons Caṇḍa and Muṇḍa (name 7), and in her thousand-name hymn from the *Śākta-pramoda* she is called Killer of the Demon Keśī (name 90), She Who Is the Battle Cry (name 767), She Who Is the Battlefield (name 768), and several other epithets that associate her with demon slaying.

8. Tiwari, p. 334.

9. *Prāṇatoṣinī-tantra* (Calcutta: Basumati Sahitya Mandir, 1928), p. 378; translated by Benard, pp. 35–36. This version is also told, with slight modifications, in Śrī Swami Ji Mahārāja Datiya, *Śrī Chinnamastā Nityārcana* (Prayag: Kalyan Mandir Prakasan, 1978), p. 5.

10. *Prāṇatoṣinī-tantra*, p. 378; translated by Benard, p. 36.

11. *Śaktisaṁgama-tantra*, vol. 4: *Chinnamastā Khaṇḍa*, ed. B. Bhattacharyya and Vrajavallabha Dvivedi (Baroda: Oriental Institute of Baroda, 1978), 5.152–73.

12. See also *Devī-bhāgavata-purāṇa* 5.28–29 and *Vāmana-purāṇa* 30.

13. P. Pal, *Hindu Religion and Iconology* (Los Angeles: Vichitra Press, 1981), p. 82.

14. Several examples of human sacrifice to goddesses are mentioned in Bani Kanta Kakati, *The Mother Goddess Kāmākhyā* (Gauhati, Assam: Lawyer's Book Stall, 1948), pp. 61–64.

15. R. Nagaswamy, *Tantric Cult of South India* (Delhi: Agam Kala Prakashan, 1982), p. 26.

16. Ibid.

17. See J. P. Vogel, "The Head-Offering to the Goddess in Pallava Sculpture," *Bulletin of the School of Oriental Studies* (London) 6: 539–43, and U. N. Ghosal, *Studies in Indian History and Culture* (Bombay: Orient Longman, 1965), pp. 333–40.

18. Ghosal, pp. 335–36; Ramendra Nath Nandi, *Religious Institutions and Cults of the Deccan* (Delhi: Motilal Banarsidass, 1973), pp. 145–46.

19. Prince Ilango Adigal, *Shilappadikaram*, trans. Alain Daniélou (New York: New Directions Book, 1965), pp. 539–43.

20. Head symbolism is discussed by Benard, pp. 243–61.

21. E. Alan Morinis, *Pilgrimage in the Hindu Tradition: A Case Study of West Bengal* (Delhi: Oxford University Press, 1984), p. 187.

22. For examples, see "Jambhaladatta's Version of the Vetalapañcavimsati," trans. M. B. Emeaneau, *American Oriental Society* 4 (1934): 59–63 (this story of transposed heads is originally from *Kathāsaritsāgara* 6.80), and Wendy O'Flaherty, *Origins of Evil in Hindu Mythology* (Berkeley: University of California Press, 1976), p. 351, for the story of Renukā's beheading.

23. See David N. Lorenzen, *The Kāpālikas and Kālāmukhas: Two Lost Śaivite Sects* (Berkeley: University of California Press, 1972), for details of why Śiva carries a skull after killing Brahmā by chopping off his head.

24. Datiya, p. 7.

25. *Śākta-pramoda*, p. 234.

26. Ibid., p. 235.

27. Translated by Benard, p. 171.

28. Acarya Ananda Jha, "Chinnamastā Tattva," *Sanmarg—Tantraviseś Aṅk* (Varanasi), July 26, 1979, pp. 69–71.

29. Ibid.

30. *Śākta-pramoda*; translated by Benard, p. 172.

31. Kṛṣṇānanda Āgamavāgiśa, *Bṛhat Tantrasāra* (Calcutta: Navabharat Publishers, 1984), p. 374.

32. *Tantrasāra*, p. 371; *Śākta-pramoda*, p. 222.

33. *Tantrasāra*, p. 371.

34. *Śākta-pramoda*; translated by Benard, p. 143.

35. *Ibid.*, pp. 170, 172, 176.

36. Swami Harshananda, *Hindu Gods and Goddesses* (Mylapore: Sri Ramakrishna Math, 1988), p. 108.

37. From her thousand-name hymn from the *Śākta-pramoda*; translated by Benard, p. 173.

38. Vedamūrti Taponiṣṭa, *Tantra-mahāvijñana*, 2 vols. (Bareli, U.P.: Saṁskṛti Saṁsthān, 1971), pp. 479–80.

39. Benard, pp. 276–77.

40. See Wendy Doniger O'Flaherty, *Sexual Metaphors and Animal Symbols in Indian Mythology* (Delhi: Motilal Banarsidass, 1981), pp. 44–49, 269–72.

41. Ibid., pp. 35–44.

42. On the basis of Chinnamastā's appearance in the teachings of a ninth-century C.E. Buddhist devotee, Lakṣmīṅkarā, Benard, p. 58, concludes that Chinnamastā appeared in Buddhist sources at least a century before she did in Hindu materials.

43. The story is told in Benard, pp. 40–41.

44. Ibid., p. 43.

45. Translated by Benard, p. 211.

46. S. K. Rao, *Tibetan Tantric Tradition* (New Delhi: Arnold-Heinemann, 1977), p. 87; quoted by Benard, p. 249.

47. *Śākta-pramoda;* translated by Benard, pp. 133–35.

48. Ibid., pp. 140, 147, 148, 167, 174, 178.

49. Jagannath Prasad Sharma, *Bhārat Tīrth Darśan* (Varanasi: Bhola Yantralaya, 1984), p. 355.

50. There is some evidence that the Cintpūrṇī temple in Himachal Pradhesh was once a Chinnamastā temple. The name Chinnamastā is written on the gateway to the temple, and according to one of the priests at the temple, Chinnamastā "is the original name of Cintpūrṇī." The worship of Cintpūrṇī today is nontantric, exoteric, and completely ordinary (*sādhāran*) or vegetarian (Vaiṣṇava). Cintpūrṇī is described as benign and similar to Durgā in appearance. Kathleen M. Erndl, *Victory to the Mother: The Hindu Goddess of Northwest India in Myth, Ritual, and Symbol* (New York: Oxford University Press, 1993), p. 51.

51. Benard, p. 92.

52. Ibid., pp. 93–94.

53. *Śaktisaṁgama-tantra* 6.79–82.

54. Mahidhara, pp. 266–67.

55. Chinnamastā *stotra*, v. 8; Benard, p. 105.

56. *Śākta-pramoda*, p. 228.

Bhairavī

1. *Dhyāna* mantra of Bhairavī, *Śāradā-tilaka* 12.31; *Śāradā Tilaka Tantram*, ed. Arthur Avalon (Delhi: Motilal Banarsidass, 1982), p. 525.

2. *Dhyāna* mantra of Rudra-bhairavī; Kṛṣṇānanda Āgamavāgīśa, *Bṛhat Tantrasāra* (Calcutta: Navabharat Publishers, 1984), p. 308.

3. *Śāradā-tilaka* 12.81–95, pp. 534–37.

4. Vedamūrti Taponiṣṭa, *Tantra-mahāvijñāna* (Bareli, U.P.: Saṁskṛti Saṁsthān, 1971), pp. 486–89.

5. Rājeś Dīkṣit, *Bhairavī evam Dhūmāvatī Tantra Śāstra* (Agra: Dīp Publication, 1988), p. 1.

6. Ibid., pp. 57–58, 61, 64.

7. Ibid., p. 61; see also her thousand-name hymn in the *Śākta-pramoda* (Bombay: Khemrāja Śrīkṛṣṇadāsa Prakāśān, 1992), p. 288, where she is said to exist in a circle of fire, to be a circle of fire, and to be destructive fire.

8. Dīkṣit, *Bhairavī evam Dhūmāvatī*, p. 57.

9. *Śākta-pramoda*, pp. 265, 266, 268.

10. Mary Shepherd Slusser, *Nepal Maṇḍala: A Cultural Study of the Kathmandu Valley*, 2 vols. (Princeton, N.J.: Princeton University Press, 1982), vol. 1, p. 328.

11. *Tantrasāra*, pp. 295–315.

12. *Śākta-pramoda*, p. 266.

13. Dīkṣit, *Bhairavī evam Dhūmāvatī*, pp. 58, 60, 62, 64.

14. *Tantrasāra*, p. 297.

15. Ibid.

16. Ibid., p. 315; see also *Śāradā-tilaka* 10.110.

17. *Tantrasāra*, p. 315.

18. Conversation with Hemendra Nath Chakravarty.

19. Upendra Kumar Das, *Bhāratiya Śaktisādhanā*, 2 vols. (Santiniketan: Ranjit Rai Prakasan, Visvabharati, 1967), p. 535.

20. Dīkṣit, *Bhairavī evam Dhūmāvatī*, pp. 56, 60, 61, 64.

Dhūmāvatī

1. *Dhyāna* mantra of Dhūmāvatī; Rājeś Dīkṣit, *Bhairavī evam Dhūmāvatī Tantra Śāstra* (Agra: Dīp Publication, 1988), p. 152.

2. *Prapañcasārasāra-saṁgraha*, ed. Gīrvānendra Sarasvatī, 2 parts (Thanjavur: T.M.S.S. Library, pt. 2, 1980), p. 236.

3. Ibid., pp. 234–35.

4. Dīkṣit, *Bhairavī evam Dhūmāvatī*, pp. 141–42

5. *Taittirīya-brāhmaṇa* 1.6.1.4.

6. *Atharva-veda* 5.7.9.

7. *Śatapatha-brāhmaṇa* 5.2.3.3.

8. Ibid. 9.1.2.9.

9. She is mentioned in the *Baudhayana-gṛhyasūtra*, which can be dated between 600 and 300 B.C.E.; Kane, *History of Dharmaśāstra*, 2.1:xi; cited in Julia Leslie, "Śrī and Jyeṣṭhā: Ambivalent Role Models for Women," in Julia Leslie, ed., *Roles and Rituals for Hindu Women* (Delhi: Motilal Banarsidass Publishers, 1992), p. 113.

10. Leslie, p. 114.

11. T. A. Gopinatha Rao, *Elements of Hindu Iconography*, 2d ed., 2 vols. (New York: Paragon Books, 1914–16), vol. 1, pt. 2, p. 393.

12. Leslie, pp. 115–19.

13. *Liṅga-purāṇa* 2.6.83–87.

14. For the text and translation of the *Śrī-sūkta*, see Bandana Sarasvati, "The History of the Worship of Śrī in North India to cir. A.D. 550" (Ph.D. diss., University of London, 1971), pp. 22–31.

15. Swami Harshananda, *Hindu Gods and Goddesses* (Mylapore: Sri Ramakrishna Math, 1988), p. 94.

16. Upendra Nath Dhal, *Goddess Lakṣmī: Origin and Development* (New Delhi: Oriental Publishers, 1978), p. 179.

17. Ibid., p. 178.

18. Ibid., pp. 150–56, 177–78.

19. M. C. P. Srivastava, *Mother Goddess in Indian Art, Archaeology and Literature* (Delhi: Agam Kala Prakashan, 1979), p. 190.

20. *Kalyāṇa, Śakti Aṅk* (Gorakhpur: Gita Press, 1934), p. 264; Dīkṣit, *Bhairavī evam Dhūmāvatī*, p. 152.

21. *Prapañcasārasāra-saṁgraha*, p. 234.

22. Dhūmāvatī *stotra; Śākta-pramoda* (Bombay: Khemrāja Śrīkṛṣṇadāsa Prakāśān, 1992), pp. 283–84.

23. Sarbeswar Satpathy, *Sakti Iconography in Tantric Mahāvidyās* (Calcutta: Punthi Pustak, 1991), pp. 147–48.

24. *Śaktisaṁgama-tantra*, vol. 4: *Chinnamastā Khaṇḍa*, ed. B. Bhattacharyya and Vrajavallabha Dvivedi (Baroda: Oriental Institute of Baroda, 1978), 6.24–25. This myth was also told to me by the priest at the Dhūmāvatī temple in Varanasi.

25. *Prāṇatoṣinī-tantra* 5.6; Upendra Kumar Das, *Bhāratiya Śaktisādhanā*, 2 vols. (Santiniketan: Ranjit Rai Prakasan, Visvabharati, 1967), p. 542.

26. Ajit Mookerjee and Madhu Khanna, *The Tantric Way: Art, Science, Ritual* (Delhi: Vikas Publishing House, 1977), p. 191.

27. *Prapañcasārasāra-saṁgraha*, p. 234.

28. The painting of Dhūmāvatī by Batuk Ramprasad is discussed later (see figure 31).

29. Vv. 95–97; Dīkṣit, *Bhairavī evam Dhūmāvatī*, p. 167.

30. *Prapañcasārasāra-saṁgraha*, p. 236.

31. According to the priest at the Dhūmāvatī temple in Varanasi.

32. Vv. 87 and 92; Dīkṣit, *Bhairavī evam Dhūmāvatī*, pp. 166–67.

33. Conversation with Kamalakar Mishra, October 1992.

34. Sarbeswar Satpathy, *Dasa Mahavidya and Tantra Sastra* (Calcutta: Punthi Pustak, 1992), p. 70.

35. Mary Shepherd Slusser, *Nepal Maṇḍala: A Cultural Study of the Kathmandu Valley*, 2 vols. (Princeton, N.J.: Princeton University Press, 1982), vol. 1, pp. 333–34.

36. According to the priest at the Dhūmāvatī temple in Varanasi.

37. *Prapañcasārasāra-saṁgraha*, p. 234.

38. Thousand-name hymn, v. 32; Dīkṣit, *Bhairavī evam Dhūmāvatī*, p. 162. The priest at the Dhūmāvatī temple said that she is the same as Śmaśāna-kālī, "Kālī who lives in the cremation ground."

39. *Prapañcasārasāra-saṁgraha*, p. 234.

40. Vv. 125–26; Dīkṣit, *Bhairavī evam Dhūmāvatī*, p. 169.

41. Pushpendra Kumar, *The Principle of Śakti* (Delhi: Eastern Book Linkers, 1986), p. 122.

42. Harshananda, p. 108.

43. There are also small Dhūmāvatī temples at Ranchi in Bihar and near the Kāmākhyā-devī temple near Gauhati in Assam.

44. Dīkṣit, *Bhairavī evam Dhūmāvatī*, pp. 166, 159.

45. Shiv Prasad Mishra Kahikey, "Bahati Ganga (The Flowing Ganges)," trans. Paul R. Golding and Virendra Singh (MS, Varanasi, n.d.), p. 69.

46. Dīkṣit, *Bhairavī evam Dhūmāvatī*, pp. 160–67.

Bagalāmukhī

1. *Dhyāna* mantra of Bagalāmukhī; Kṛṣṇānanda Āgamāvagīśa, *Bṛhat Tantrasāra* (Calcutta: Navabharat Publications, 1984), pp. 463–64.

2. Ibid., p. 465.

3. *Śaktisaṁgama-tantra*, vol. 4: *Chinnamastā Khaṇḍa*, ed. B. Bhattacharyya and Vrajavallabha Dvivedi (Baroda: Oriental Institute of Baroda, 1978), 6.1–10; see also Acarya Pandita Sri Sivadattamisra Sastri, *Bagalāmukhī-rahasyam* (Varanasi: Thakur Prasad Pustak Bharadar, 1951), p. 81, and Upendra Kumar Das, *Bhāratiya Śaktisādhanā*, 2 vols. (Santiniketan: Ranjit Rai Prakasan, Visvabharati, 1967), p. 544.

4. A. Sastri, *Bagalāmukhī-rahasyam*, p. 82.

5. Sri Bankhandesvara, *Mahāvidyā Catustayam: Tārā, Dhūmāvatī, Bhuvaneśvarī, Mātaṅgī* (Dattiya, M.P.: Pitambara Pith, n.d.), p. 23.

6. For example, Swami Harshananda, *Hindu Gods and Goddesses* (Mylapore: Sri Ramakrishna Math, 1988), p. 108, and Alain Daniélou, *Hindu Polytheism* (New York: Bollingen Foundation, 1964), p. 283.

7. Ushā P. Shāstrī and Nicole Menant, trans., *Hymnes à la déesse* (Paris: Le Soleil Noir, 1980), pl. 12, p. 103.

8. A. Sastri, *Bagalāmukhī-rahasyam*, p. 11.

9. Swamiji, a tantric informant in Varanasi.

10. Vedamūrti Taponiṣṭa, *Tantra-mahāvijñana* (Bareli, U.P.: Saṁskṛti Saṁsthān, 1971), vol. 2, p. 492, also says the name of the goddess was originally Valgāmukhī.

11. *Kalyāṇa, Śakti Aṅk* (Gorakhpur: Gita Press, 1934), facing p. 320.

12. Taponiṣṭa, pp. 494–95.

13. Conventionally, in fact, cranes are taken as symbols of *false* yogis or holy men in Hindu culture. The crane appears to be rapt in meditation, like a yogi, while in fact its entire attention is directed toward capturing and devouring fish. The false yogi is not actually meditating; he is pretending to meditate while conniving to cheat or seduce unwitting people.

14. A. Sastri, *Bagalāmukhī-rahasyam*, pp. 11–30; see also *Tantrasāra*, p. 465.

15. A. Sastri, *Bagalāmukhī-rahasyam*, p. 15.

16. *Mahābhārata* 3.187.31–39; John E. Mitchener, *Traditions of the Seven Ṛṣis* (Delhi: Motilal Banarsidass, 1982), p. 68.

17. See *Tantrasāra*, p. 466, for her yantra.

18. Savithri Shanker de Tourreil, "Nayars in a South Indian Matrix: A Study Based on Female-Centered Ritual" (Ph.D. diss., Concordia University, Montreal, 1995), p. 198; see also pp. 176, 179, and 204.

19. The tradition of acquiring magical powers is ancient in India and pervades tantric literature in particular. For a discussion of magical powers in Hinduism, see N. N. Bhattacharyya, *History of the Tantric Religion: A Historical, Ritualistic and Philosophical Study* (New Delhi: Manohar Publishers, 1982), pp. 149–51.

20. Rājeś Dīkṣit, *Bagalāmukhī evam Mātaṅgī Tantra Śāstra* (Agra: Sumit Prakashan, 1989), pp. 83, 84, 88.

21. *Tantrasāra*, p. 466.

22. Vv. 5–6; Dīkṣit, *Bagalāmukhī evam Mātaṅgī*, p. 64.

23. A. Sastri, *Bagalāmukhī-rahasyam*, p. 11.

24. Dīkṣit, *Bagalāmukhī evam Mātaṅgī*, p. 73.

25. *Pītāmbarī-upaniṣad;* ibid., p. 57.

26. Teun Goudriaan and Sanjukta Gupta, *Hindu Tantric and Śākta Literature* (Wiesbaden: Otto Harrassowitz, 1981), p. 89.

27. See her hundred names from the *Rudrayāmala;* Dīkṣit, *Bagalāmukhī evam Mātaṅgī,* p. 73.

28. Goudriaan and Gupta, p. 81.

29. A. Sastri, *Bagalāmukhī-rahasyam,* p. 13.

30. Dīkṣit, *Bagalāmukhī evam Mātaṅgī,* pp. 1–2.

31. Harshananda, p. 108.

32. Swami Annapurnananda.

33. Dīkṣit, *Bagalāmukhī evam Mātaṅgī,* pp. 84, 88, 89.

34. Ibid., pp. 88–89.

35. Ibid., p. 76.

36. Ibid., pp. 80–81.

37. *Kalyaṇa, Śakti Aṅk,* "Śrī Bagalāmukhī Upāsanā," p. 506.

38. V. 4; Dīkṣit, *Bagalāmukhī evam Mātaṅgī,* p. 63.

39. *Tantrasāra,* pp. 438–44; see also *Kaulāvalī,* ed. Arthur Avalon (Delhi: Bharatiya Vidya Prakashan, 1985), chap. 15, and *Nīla-tantra,* chap. 16, summarized in S. C. Banerjee, *A Brief History of Tantric Literature* (Calcutta: Naya Prokash, 1986), pp. 251–52.

40. *Tantrasāra,* pp. 438–39.

41. At many points in this ritual it appears that the *sādhaka* is seeking to revive or control the spirit of the corpse, which will then be used as a "power instrument," as it were, to bring about desired goals. See N. Bhattacharyya, *History of the Tantric Religion,* pp. 137–41.

42. This is also specifically mentioned in the *Kaulāvalī* description of the ritual, p. 15.

43. *Tantrasāra,* p. 468.

44. Robert E. Svoboda, *Aghora: At the Left Hand of God* (Albuquerque, N.M.: Brotherhood of Life, 1986), p. 195.

45. *Kaulāvalī,* chap. 19, describes gaining power from a corpse by reviving it. The particular power (*siddhi*) mentioned in this case is the ability to see through solid objects and substances. See also June McDaniel, *The Madness of the Saints: Ecstatic Religion in Bengal* (Chicago: University of Chicago Press, 1989), pp. 120–21, concerning gaining power from a corpse by means of cremation-ground rites.

46. Attempts to converse with and control spirits in the cremation ground, the different kinds of spirits that are present there, and the dangers inherent in such practices are described in Svoboda, pp. 187–209.

47. Ibid., p. 49.

48. Ibid.

49. P. H. Pott, *Yoga and Yantra: Their Interrelation and Their Significance for Indian Archaeology* (The Hague: Martinus Nijhoff, 1966), p. 78.

50. The idea of liminality is developed in Victor W. Turner, *Dramas, Fields, and Metaphors: Symbolic Action in Human Society* (Ithaca, N.Y.: Cornell University Press, 1974).

51. *Kalyāṇa, Śakti Aṅk,* p. 407; Kulsekar Śrī Maheś Candra Garg, "Pūjā Swamiji aur Śrī Pītāmbarā Pīth Datiya," *Caṇḍī* 7, no. 40 (October 1981): 17–21.

Mātaṅgī

1. *Dhyāna* mantra of Ucciṣṭa-mātaṅginī; Kṛṣṇānanda Āgamavāgīśa, *Bṛhat Tantrasāra* (Calcutta: Navabharat Publishers, 1984), p. 449.

2. *Dhyāna* mantra of Mātaṅgī from the *Puraścaryārṇava; Tantrasāra*, p. 447.

3. *Dhyāna* mantra of Rāja-mātaṅgī from *Puraścaryārṇava*, chap. 9; Upendra Kumar Das, *Bhāratiya Śaktisādhanā* (Santiniketan: Ranjit Rai Prakasan, Visva-bharati, 1967), pp. 546–47. In *Śāradā-tilaka* 12.128, Rāja-mātaṅgī's *dhyāna* mantra adds that she plays the *vīṇā*, wears flower garlands and conch-shell earrings, and has her forehead decorated with paintings of flowers.

4. *Divyāvadāna*, ed. P. L. Vaidya (Darbhanga: Mithila Research Institute, 1959), story 33: "Śārdūlakarna," pp. 314–25.

5. *Śaktisaṁgama-tantra*, vol. 4: *Chinnamastā Khaṇḍa*, ed. B. Bhattacharyya and Vrajavallabha Dvivedi (Baroda: Oriental Institute of Baroda, 1978), 6.30–38.

6. *Prāṇatoṣinī-tantra* (Calcutta: Basumati Sahitya Mandir, 1928), pp. 379–81. The story of Pārvatī returning to her father's house because of her pique over Śiva's philandering, Śiva's appearance at her father's house disguised as a seller of shell bangles, and Pārvatī's subsequent disguise as a low-caste woman (in this case a *bāgdinī*) whom Śiva tries to seduce is found in the Bengali *maṅgal kāvyas*. See Asutosh Bhattacharya, *Bangla mangal-kavyer itihasa* (Calcutta: E. Mukharji and Co., 1939), pp. 205ff., and D. Zbavitel, *Bengali Literature* (Wiesbaden: Otto Harrassowitz, 1976), pp. 156–58. In these accounts, however, Pārvatī is not identified with Mātaṅgī.

7. *Svatantra-tantra;* Das, p. 545.

8. Told to me by Ram, an informant in Varanasi. During a visit to this temple I was not able to confirm Kauri-bai's identification with Mātaṅgī. The story of the origin of the temple also differed in several ways from the story told by Ram. The story I was told at the temple did not mention the tension between Śiva and Kauri-bai, and Pārvatī, in her form as Annapūrṇā, cursed Kauri-bai to live in the jungle, not a low-caste area, because of Kauri-bai's preoccupation with purity, which left her no time even to eat a meal (which insulted Annapūrṇā, the goddess who gives food). The temple is, in fact, in a neighborhood housing low-caste people, but it now also includes some modern development with upper-caste residents. That the area was formerly "jungle" is credible, as the location of the temple is in the southern part of Varanasi, which was uninhabited not very long ago.

9. The leftovers or residue of sacrificial offerings (*ucciṣṭa*) are regarded as possessing great spiritual potency in some Vedic texts. The *Atharva-veda* (11.7.1–3, 16), for example, celebrates the sacrificial residue as containing cosmic creative force. Stella Kramrisch, *The Presence of Śiva* (Princeton, N.J.: Princeton University Press, 1981), p. 66.

10. For example, *Tantrasāra*, p. 449, and Rājeś Dīkṣit, *Bagalāmukhī evam Mātaṅgī Tantra Śāstra* (Agra: Sumit Prakashan, 1989), pp. 138–39.

11. Dīkṣit, *Bagalāmukhī evam Mātaṅgī*, p. 140.

12. *Tantrasāra*, p. 449; Dīkṣit, *Bagalāmukhī evam Mātaṅgī*, p. 140.

13. In many festivals celebrating village goddesses in South India, a low-caste woman called a *mātaṅgī* plays a central role. During the festival, the *mātaṅgī*

represents the goddess. Possessed by the goddess, she dances wildly, uses obscene language, drinks intoxicants, spits on spectators, and pushes people about with her backside. She seems to take special delight in abusing members of the high castes. During this festival an inversion of the usual social codes and rules takes place. The *mātaṅgī* personifies social topsy-turvy. Exactly what the connection might be between these low-caste women and the goddess Mātaṅgī is not clear. See Wilber Theodore Elmore, *Dravidian Gods in Modern Hinduism: A Study of the Local and Village Deities of Southern India* (Hamilton, N.Y.: Published by the author, 1915), p. 31; see also Edgar Thurston, *Castes and Tribes of Southern India*, 7 vols. (Madras: Madras Government Press, 1909), vol. 4, pp. 295–307, 316–17.

14. Robert I. Levy, *Mesocosm: Hinduism and the Organization of a Traditional Newar City in Nepal* (Delhi: Motilal Banarsidass, 1992), pp. 84–85.

15. Ibid., p. 263.

16. The leader of the Śabaras (Śavaras) in Bana's *Kādambarī* is named Mātaṅga. *The Kādambarī of Bana*, trans. C. M. Ridding (London: Royal Asiatic Society, 1896), p. 28.

17. *Mahākāla-saṁhitā* (Allahabad: Gāṅgānath Jha Research Institute, 1974), p. 106.

18. Dīkṣit, *Bagalāmukhī evam Mātaṅgī*, pp. 149, 157.

19. Ibid., p. 147.

20. *Śāradā-tilaka* 12.128.

21. Ibid. 12.98.

22. The spiritually transformative role of female hunters, who would be regarded as marginal and polluted by high-caste Hindu society, is emphasized in the story of the Buddhist tantric yogi Maitrīpa, who travels into the mountains of South India in search of Śavari, a well-known tantric teacher (whose name associates him with the Śavaras, a tribal people). Maitrīpa finds Śavari in the company of two female hunters, who have long, matted hair, wear bark and leaves as clothing, carry hunting gear, and have freshly killed game at their feet. At first Maitrīpa is repulsed by the women, but later he learns that they are advanced spiritual teachers. It is from them that Maitrīpa eventually gains illumination. Miranda Shaw, *Passionate Enlightenment: Women in Tantric Buddhism* (Princeton, N.J.: Princeton University Press, 1994), p. 50.

23. *Mahābhāgavata-purāṇa*, Madhya-khaṇḍa 2.69–72.

24. *Tantrasāra*, pp. 446, 448.

25. Dīkṣit, *Bagalāmukhī evam Mātaṅgī*, p. 104.

26. Ibid., p. 105.

27. *Tantrasāra*, p. 449.

28. Das, p. 548.

29. Dīkṣit, *Bagalāmukhī evam Mātaṅgī*, p. 128.

Kamalā

1. *Dhyāna* mantra of Kamalā; *Śākta-pramoda* (Bombay: Khemrāja Śrīkṛṣṇadāsa Prakāśān, 1992), p. 353.

2. *Dhyāna* mantra of Kamalā; *Śāradā Tilaka Tantram*, ed. Arthur Avalon (Delhi: Motilal Banarsidass, 1982), p. 420.

3. *Dhyāna* mantra of Mahālakṣmī; *Śāradā Tilaka Tantram*, p. 424.

4. For the text and translation of this hymn, see Bandana Saraswati, "The History of the Worship of Śrī in North India to cir. A.D. 550" (Ph.D. diss., University of London, 1971), pp. 22–31.

5. For the symbolism of the lotus, see F. D. K. Bosch, *The Golden Germ* (The Hague: Mouton, 1960), pp. 81–82.

6. For a discussion of these images, referred to as Gaja-lakṣmīs, see Niranjan Ghosh, *Concept and Iconography of the Goddess of Abundance and Fortune in Three Religions of India* (Burdwan, West Bengal: University of Burdwan, 1979), pp. 75–87; Saraswati, pp. 159–61; and Kiran Thaplyal, "Gajalakṣmī on Seals," in D. C. Sircar, ed., *Foreigners in Ancient India and Lakṣmī and Sarasvatī in Art and Literature* (Calcutta: University of Calcutta, 1970), pp. 112–25.

7. Heinrich Zimmer, *The Art of Indian Asia*, 2 vols. (New York: Pantheon Books, 1955), vol. 1, pp. 160–61.

8. Jan Gonda, *Ancient Indian Kingship from the Religious Point of View* (Leiden: E. J. Brill, 1969), pp. 7–8.

9. Upendra Nath Dhal, *Goddess Lakṣmī: Origin and Development* (New Delhi: Oriental Publishers, 1978), pp. 65–66; Saraswati, pp. 150–53.

10. Dhal, pp. 68–69.

11. See Saraswati, pp. 138–47.

12. See particularly the myths of the demons Bali and Prahlāda in Saraswati, pp. 138–47, and Dhal, pp. 68–69.

13. Dhal, pp. 91–93; Saraswati, pp. 173–77; Ananda Coomaraswamy, *Yakṣas*, 2 parts (Delhi: Munshiram Manoharlal, 1971), pt. 1, pp. 32ff.

14. Jan Gonda, *Aspects of Early Viṣṇuism*, 2d ed. (Delhi: Motilal Banarsidass, 1969), pp. 164–67.

15. K. S. Behera, "Lakṣmī in Orissan Literature and Art," in Sircar, ed., *Foreigners in Ancient India*, p. 101.

16. Saraswati, p. 242.

17. F. Otto Schrader, *Introduction to the Pañcarātra and the Ahirbudhnya Saṁhitā* (Madras: Adyar Library, 1916), pp. 34–35.

18. See *Lakṣmī Tantra, a Pañcarātra Text*, trans. Sanjukta Gupta (Leiden: E. J. Brill, 1972).

19. For Śrī-Lakṣmī in Śrī Vaiṣṇavism, see John Carman, *The Theology of Rāmānuja* (New Haven, Conn.: Yale University Press, 1974), pp. 238–44; Vasudha Narayanan, "The Goddess Śrī: The Blossoming Lotus and Breast Jewel of Viṣṇu," in John Stratton Hawley and Donna Marie Wulff, eds., *The Divine Consort: Rādhā and the Goddesses of India* (Berkeley, Calif.: Berkeley Religious Studies Series, 1982), pp. 224–37; and Vasudha Narayanan, "*Karma* and *Kṛpa*. Human Bondage and Divine Grace: The Teṅkalai Śrī Vaiṣṇava Position" (DePaul University, Chicago, n.d.).

20. M. C. P. Srivastava, *Mother Goddess in Indian Art, Archaeology and Literature* (Delhi: Agam Kala Prakashan, 1979), p. 189.

21. Dhal, p. 176.

22. *Śāradā Tilaka Tantram*, pp. 420, 432.

23. *Śākta-pramoda*, pp. 373–76, 378.
24. Ibid., pp. 369, 375, 377.
25. Ibid., pp. 369, 374, 375.
26. Ibid., pp. 370–74, 379.
27. Ibid., pp. 373–75, 379.
28. Cited in June McDaniel, *The Madness of the Saints: Ecstatic Religion in Bengal* (Chicago: University of Chicago Press, 1989), p. 150.

Concluding Reflections

1. Mahidhara, *Mantra Mahodadhiḥ*, vol. 1, ed. and trans. Ram Kumar Rai (Varanasi: Prachya Prakashan, 1992), p. 214.
2. Ibid., p. 146; see also p. 145.
3. Ibid.
4. Ibid., p. 198.
5. Kṛṣṇānanda Āgamavāgīśa, *Bṛhat Tantrasāra* (Calcutta: Navabharat Publishers, 1984), pp. 438–44.
6. Ibid., pp. 434–38.
7. See David Kinsley, " 'The Death That Conquers Death': Dying to the World in Medieval Hinduism," in Frank E. Reynolds and Earle H. Waugh, eds., *Religious Encounters with Death: Insights from the History and Anthropology of Religions* (University Park: Pennsylvania State University Press, 1977), pp. 97–108.
8. P. H. Pott has used the term in reference to rituals in cremation grounds by tantric Buddhists in Nepal; *Yoga and Yantra: Their Interrelation and Their Significance for Indian Archaeology* (The Hague: Martinus Nijhoff, 1966), p. 77.
9. *Mahābhāgavata-purāṇa* 3.15–70; Wendy Doniger O'Flaherty, *Sexual Metaphors and Animal Symbols in Indian Mythology* (Delhi: Motilal Banarsidass, 1981), p. 98.
10. *Bṛhaddharma-purāṇa* 2.31.16–36; O'Flaherty, *Sexual Metaphors*, p. 99.
11. Mark S. G. Dyczkowski, *The Canon of the Śaivāgama and the Kubjikā Tantras of the Western Kaula Tradition* (Albany: State University of New York Press, 1988), pp. 6–7.
12. See Mircea Eliade, *Rites and Symbols of Initiation: The Mysteries of Birth and Rebirth* (New York: Harper & Row, 1958).
13. For a vivid description of the cremation ground as the locale of a host of spirits, see Mary Shepherd Slusser, *Nepal Maṇḍala: A Cultural Study of the Kathmandu Valley*, 2 vols. (Princeton, N.J.: Princeton University Press, 1982), vol. 1, p. 333; see also Robert E. Svoboda, *Aghora: At the Left Hand of God* (Albuquerque, N.M.: Brotherhood of Life, 1986), pp. 187–210, for a discussion of making contact with spirits in the cremation ground.
14. See Victor Turner, *The Ritual Process: Structure and Anti-structure* (Harmondsworth, U.K.: Penguin, 1969), for a definition and discussion of the "liminal" as central to many sets of rituals.
15. *Uḍḍīśa-tantra*, chap. 9; S. C. Banerjee, *A Brief History of Tantric Literature* (Calcutta: Naya Prokash, 1986), p. 325.
16. Banerjee, *A Brief History of Tantric Literature*, pp. 496–97.

17. June McDaniel, *The Madness of the Saints: Ecstatic Religion in Bengal* (Chicago: University of Chicago Press, 1989), p. 112.

18. Mahidhara, p. 214.

19. See the discussion of chopped-off heads in the chapter on Chinnamastā.

20. *Tantrasāra*, pp. 682–83; see also *Paraśurāma-kalpasūtra*, ed. A. N. Jani (Baroda: University of Baroda, 1979), pp. 222, 245, 253.

21. The *aṣṭa siddhis*, which are superior powers or "perfections" achieved by means of yoga, include some of these abilities and are ancient in the Hindu tradition. A well-known example of the ability to change form at will, including changing into animal form, is Mahiṣāsura, the buffalo demon whom Durgā slays in the *Devī-māhātmya*.

22. Kinsley, " 'The Death that Conquers Death.' "

23. McDaniel, p. 58.

24. Ajit Mookerjee and Madhu Khanna, *The Tantric Way: Art, Science, Ritual* (Delhi: Vikas Publishing House, 1977), pl. 3, which is identified as Kālī but is actually Tārā.

25. *The Yonitantra*, ed. J. A. Schoterman (New Delhi: Manohar, 1980), 3.14, p. 23.

26. *Tantrasāra*, pp. 692–702.

27. For example, Mookerjee and Khanna, pp. 166–67, 185.

28. *Tantrasāra*, p. 702.

29. Miranda Shaw, *Passionate Enlightenment: Women in Tantric Buddhism* (Princeton, N.J.: Princeton University Press, 1994), argues that sexual complementarity and sexual union are central to Buddhist tantric spirituality and that sexual union is used to clear the central channel (*avadhūtī*) of all obstructions and "knots." Sexual union, she argues, is a meditative technique whereby illumination is achieved (pp. 147, 160, 171, 186–88).

30. *Kulārṇava-tantra* 108–9; McDaniel, p. 111.

31. See Mookerjee and Khanna, pl. 3, p. 83.

32. In one rendition of Kālī and Śiva, he is lying beneath her feet on a cremation pyre that is surrounded by bones, crows, and jackals. He is naked and has an erection. Philip Rawson, *Oriental Erotic Art* (New York: A and W Publishers, 1981), fig. 16, p. 22.

33. Mahidhara, p. 145.

34. Ibid.

35. Ibid., p. 181.

36. *Uddīśa-tantra*, chaps. 7–9; Banerjee, *A Brief History of Tantric Literature*, p. 325.

37. For example, *Kaulāvalī*, ed. Arthur Avalon (Delhi: Bharatiya Vidya Prakashan, 1985), chap. 10, p. 12; Mahidhara, p. 181; and *Kaṅkālamālinī-tantra*, chap. 4; for a brief discussion of women in tantric literature, see Banerjee, *A Brief History of Tantric Literature*, pp. 499–503.

38. *Kaulāvalī-tantra*, chap. 10; Banerjee, *A Brief History of Tantric Literature*, p. 217.

39. Chap. 16; Banerjee, *A Brief History of Tantric Literature*, p. 253.

40. *Tantrasāra*, p. 694.

41. It is not fair to conclude from this text, however, that only low-caste or

socially marginal women took part in tantric *sādhanā*. Nor would it be fair to say that low-caste or socially marginal women were never full participants in tantric *sādhanā* (as opposed to being simply "used" by male *sādhakas*). See Shaw, passim, esp. pp. 35–68.

42. *Tantrasāra*, p. 701.

43. *Guptasādhanā-tantra*, chap. 4; Banerjee, *A Brief History of Tantric Literature*, pp. 184–85.

44. *Kubjikā-tantra*, chap. 16; Banerjee, *A Brief History of Tantric Literature*, p. 223.

45. *Yoginī-tantra*, chap. 7; Banerjee, *A Brief History of Tantric Literature*, p. 347.

46. *Kāmākhyā-tantra* 36; McDaniel, p. 122.

47. *Māyā-tantra* 6; McDaniel, p. 123.

48. *Yoni-tantra* 6.5 (*The Yonitantra*, p. 20) specifies that yoni *pūjā* should be undertaken during menstruation.

49. *Sarvollāsa-tantra* (Calcutta: Harambacandra Bhattacharya, 1953), 50.30–32, p. 202; see also *The Yonitantra*, pp. 23–24.

50. *Sarvollāsa-tantra* 50.40–42.

51. Ibid. 50.37.

52. See *Kaulāvalī-tantra*, chap. 15; *Gandharva-tantra*, chap. 18; *Kāmākhyā-tantra*, chap. 11; *Kubjikā-tantra*, chap. 7; and *Nīla-tantra*, chap. 15, where this rite is described as being undertaken on a corpse; Banerjee, *A Brief History of Tantric Literature*, p. 251.

53. Dyczkowski, *The Canon of the Śaivāgama*, p. 64.

54. Ibid., p. 65.

55. Banerjee, *A Brief History of Tantric Literature*, p. 184. Mark Dyczkowski, the author of several books on Hindu Tantrism, has told me that both Hindu and Buddhist tantric lineages mention female teachers, although they are clearly in the minority.

56. *Prāṇatoṣinī-tantra* (Calcutta: Basumati Sahitya Mandir, 1928), 2.2, p. 96. It is also clear in this passage that the discussion is very much from a male point of view. The conditions under which a female may function as a guru depend on whether her husband is a guru, whether she is a widow (and, if so, whether she has a son), and so on. Similarly, among her commendable qualities, loyalty to her husband is mentioned first. See also N. N. Bhattacharyya, *History of the Tantric Religion: A Historical, Ritualistic and Philosophical Study* (New Delhi: Manohar Publishers, 1982), p. 121: "In the Tantric religious system a woman has the right of initiating persons into the secrets of the cult and acting as guru."

57. Shaw, p. 174 and passim.

58. For a discussion of tantric female spirituality in the Hindu tradition, see Sanjukta Gupta, "Women in the Śaiva/Śākta Ethos," pp. 193–210, and Lynn Teskey Denton, "Varieties of Hindu Female Asceticism," pp. 225–27, both in Julia Leslie, ed., *Roles and Rituals for Hindu Women* (Delhi: Motilal Banarsidass, 1992).

Glossary

Simplified pronunciation guide: the letter *c* should be pronounced *ch*. The letters *ś* and *ṣ* should be pronounced *sh*.

adharma	Evil, immorality
Alakṣmī	"She who is inauspicious," a goddess; Lakṣmī's sister
amṛta	Nectar (of immortality)
Annapūrṇā	"She who is full of food," a goddess
āsana	Seat, used in reference to spiritual practice
ātman	"Self" or soul; the spiritual essence of a person
avatāra	"Descent" or incarnation of a deity
avidyā	Ignorance
Bagalāmukhī	"She who is crane faced," one of the Mahāvidyās
bali	Blood offerings
Bāmākhepa 1843–1911	A famous Bengali devotee of Kālī
Bhairava	A fierce form of Śiva
Bhairavī	"The fierce one," one of the Mahāvidyās
bhava	Spiritual mood; mentality
bhūta	one of the five elements; also, a ghost
bhūta śuddhi	A ritual in which the adept imagines the dissolution and re-creation of the cosmos
Bhuvaneśvarī	"Mistress of the world," one of the Mahāvidyās
bīja	Seed syllable, sound seed
bīja mantra	Seed mantra

bindu	Seed, dot, or essence; a component of yantras
Brahmā	One of the gods of the male *trimūrti;* the creator
brahman	The absolute; ultimate reality. See also *nirguṇa brahman*, *śabda brahman*
Brahman	A member of the priestly caste
cakra	A spiritual center within the body
Caṇḍālas	A very low caste
Chinnamastā	"She who has severed her head," one of the Mahāvidyās
dakṣiṇa	South; right; clockwise; also the gift given to a priest after a ritual
darśan	Viewing of a deity's image
devī	Goddess
Devī-māhātmya	The most revered of Hindu *śākta* texts; probably written around the sixth century C.E.
dharma	Cosmic and moral order
Dhūmāvatī	"She who abides in smoke," one of the Mahāvidyās
dhyāna	Meditation
dhyāna mantra	A meditation mantra, which often describes the physical appearance of a deity
Durgā	A demon-slaying goddess
Durgā Pūjā	A festival in honor of Durgā; also known as Navarātra, the festival of nine nights
Gaja-lakṣmī	An image of Lakṣmī flanked by elephants
gandharvas	Celestial beings
Gaṇeśa	An elephant-headed deity
garbha gṛha	"Womb room," the inner shrine of a temple
Gaurī	"The golden one," an epithet of Pārvatī
guṇas	Qualities or constituents that constitute all matter: *sattva* (spiritual, pure), *rajas* (energetic, powerful), and *tamas* (lustful, ignorant)
Himālaya	The Himalayan mountains personified as a god
Indra	Ruler of the city of the gods
indriya	A physical sense; sensory perception
Jagaddhātrī	"World nurse," "she who nurses the world," a goddess
japa	Repetition

Jayā	One of two females flanking the goddess Chinnamastā
jīva	Life force
jñāna	Liberating wisdom; knowledge
Kālī	"She who is black," one of the Mahāvidyās
Kālighāṭ	Kalī's most famous temple, for which Calcutta is named
Kālī Pūjā	A festival in honor of Kālī
Kālī Yuga	The present cosmic era, in which morality has declined; the last of the four yugas
kāma	Sexual desire
Kāma or Kāma-deva	The god of love
Kāmākhyā	"She whose eyes are filled with desire," a goddess; also the place where she is worshiped in Assam
Kamalā	"She of the lotus," one of the Mahāvidyās; also known as Śrī or Lakṣmī
Kāmarūpa	A goddess center in Assam
Kāpālika	"One who bears a skull," the name of a type of religious ascetic; also an epithet of Śiva
Kṛṣṇa	"The black one," a deity
Kubera	A deity associated with wealth
kula	"Family," a lineage or group of worshipers
kuṇḍalinī	An inner power in the form of a serpent that is aroused in tantric yoga
kuṇḍalinī śakti	*Kuṇḍalinī* as a female power or deity
kvaca	"Armor," a type of protective invocation
Lakṣmī	Also known as Śrī or Kamalā; one of the Mahāvidyās
Lalitā	"Soft and delicate," "she who is lovely," an epithet of Tripura-sundarī, one of the Mahāvidyās
Lalitā-sahasranāma	"The thousand names of Lalitā," a famous goddess hymn
Mahādevī	"Great goddess"; an overarching, transcendent female reality
mahant	The chief priest at a temple
Mahāvidyā	"Great knowledge," "great mantra," an epithet of a goddess
Mahāvidyās	A group of ten tantric goddesses
Mahiṣamardinī	"Slayer of Mahiṣa," an epithet of Durgā
maithuna	Sexual intercourse

maṇḍala	A graphic and symbolic representation of the cosmos
maṅgal kāvyas	"Auspicious poems," a genre of Bengali literature
mantra	A sacred verbal formula; a deity in verbal form
Mantra-mahodadhiḥ	A tantric manual
māraṇa	The power to cause a person's death simply by willing it
Mātaṅgī	One of the Mahāvidyās
matṛkās	"Mothers," sounds or letters that give birth to the creation
Mātṛkās	A fierce band of goddesses
māyā	False consciousness, self-infatuation, magic power of illusion
mokṣa	Spiritual liberation from rebirth
mudrās	Hand gestures
mukti	Liberation, freedom from rebirth
mūlādhāra cakra	The lowest *cakra*, where the *kuṇḍalinī* sleeps
mūrti	An image
nāḍī	A vein or artery
nāma stotras	Hymns consisting of names or epithets
nirguṇa	Without or beyond qualities, beyond all quality and form
nirguṇa brahman	Ultimate reality without qualities
Nirṛti	An inauspicious goddess
nirvāṇa	Final liberation and freedom from rebirth
nyāsa	A ritual in which one suffuses one's body with the seed syllables of deities or divinizes one's body with mantras and *mudrās*
pañca makāra ritual	See *pañca tattva* ritual
pañca tattva ritual	A ritual in which the aspirant partakes of five forbidden things
Pārvatī	"She of the mountains," a goddess, Śiva's spouse
pati vratā	A wife devoted to her husband
piśācas	Flesh-eating demons
Pītāmbarā	"She who is dressed in yellow," an epithet of Bagalāmukhī
pīṭha	A seat, shrine, or sacred center, usually associated with a goddess

prakṛti	Nature or the physical world
pralaya	Cosmic dissolution
Prāṇatoṣinī or *Prāṇatoṣinī-tantra*	A tantric digest probably written in Bengal in the seventeenth century
Prapañcasārasāra-saṁgraha	A tantric digest
Prapañcasāra-tantra	An early South Indian tantric text attributed to Śankara
preta	A ghost
Pṛthivī	The goddess Earth
pūjā	Worship
purāṇa	A genre of medieval texts that include mythology, ethics, legend, and ritual instructions
Rājarājeśvarī	"Queen of kings," a common epithet of Tripura-sundarī
rajas	Energy, one of the three *guṇas*
Rāma	The hero of the *Rāmāyaṇa*
Ramakrishna 1836–86	A famous Bengali devotee of Kālī
Rāmāyaṇa	A Hindu epic
Rati	"Sexual intercourse," wife of Kāma, the god of love
śabda brahman	The underlying essence of reality as manifest in sound
saccidānanda	"Being, consciousness, and bliss," a common definition of *brahman*
sādhaka	A religious adept
sādhanā	Religious endeavor; spiritual exercise
sahasranāma stotra	Thousand-name hymn
sahasrāra cakra	The topmost *cakra*, depicted as a thousand-petaled lotus located just above the crown of the head
Śākambharī	"She who bears vegetables," a goddess
śākta	Pertaining to *śakti;* partial to *śakti*
śākta pīṭhas	"Seats of Śakti," places sacred to goddesses
Śākta-pramoda	A tantric digest or manual
śakti	Energy, power
Śakti	The embodied form of *śakti* as a goddess
Śaktisaṁgama-tantra	A tantric digest
saṁsāra	The realm of rebirth; this world

Śankara 788–820	A famous Hindu philosopher
Śāradā-tilaka-tantra	A tantric digest
Sarasvatī	Goddess of wisdom and learning
Satī	Wife of Śiva; source of the Mahāvidyās in some accounts
sattva	Purity, one of the three *guṇas*
sattvic	Spiritual
Satya Yuga	The first and most perfect of the four periods of a world cycle
Saundaryalaharī	A famous goddess hymn attributed to Śankara
śava sādhanā	Spiritual practice using a corpse
siddhas	Celestial beings
siddhis	"Perfections," magical powers
Sītā	A goddess, heroine of the *Rāmāyaṇa*, wife of Rāma
Śiva	A deity associated with the Mahāvidyās, asceticism, yoga, and cosmic destruction
śmaśāna sādhanā	Spiritual practices appropriate to cremation grounds
Ṣoḍaśī	"She who is sixteen," "the sixteenth," "she who has sixteen (good) qualities"; an epithet of Tripura-sundarī, one of the Mahāvidyās
Śrī	"Auspicious"; another name for Kamalā, one of the Mahāvidyās
Śrī-sūkta	An ancient hymn to the goddess Śrī
Śrīvidyā	The form of the goddess Tripura-sundarī as mantra; also, a school of Tantrism
stambhana	The power to immobilize or paralyze a person
sthūla	The physical, anthropomorphic, "gross" aspect of a deity
stotra	A hymn
suṣumnā nāḍī	The central vein or channel of the subtle body in tantric yoga
svarūpa	The essential form
Svatantra-tantra	A tantric digest
tamas	Ignorance, one of the three *guṇas*
Tantra	A form of Hindu and Buddhist religious practice
tantras	A genre of scriptures concerned with tantric practice and theory

Tantrasāra	A tantric digest or manual
tāntrika	One who practices Tantra
Tantrism	A form of Hindu and Buddhist religious practice
Tārā	One of the Mahāvidyās
tattva	Thing or truth
tattvas	Categories of creation
tīrthas	"Crossings," sacred centers
tithis	The thirty days of the waxing and waning moon
trimūrti	"Having three forms"; the Hindu triad of Brahmā, the creator; Viṣṇu, the maintainer; and Śiva, the destroyer
Tripura-sundarī	"She who is lovely in the three worlds," one of the Mahāvidyās
uccāṭana	The power to make one's enemy sick by willing it; the power to eradicate
ucciṣṭa	Leftover food
upa purāṇas	Lesser or "younger" *purāṇas*, usually briefer and more recent than principal *purāṇas*
vāhana	Vehicle of a deity, usually an animal
Vaiṣṇava	Pertaining to Viṣṇu, partial to Viṣṇu
vāk siddhi	The power by which whatever one says comes true; the power of superior speech
Vāmācāra	The left-handed path in Tantrism
vidyā	Knowledge; in tantric contexts, mantra
vīra	"Hero"; a type of religious practitioner qualified to undertake certain left-handed tantric practices
Viṣṇu	One of the three great male deities of Hinduism, the maintainer
yakṣas	Supernatural beings often associated with the forest or with heavenly places
Yama	King of the dead and ruler of the south
yantra	A schematic rendering of a deity or the cosmos
yoginī	A female practitioner
yoginīs	Female beings associated with magical powers
yugas	The periods or stages of the world or universe

Tantrasara	A tantric digest or manual
tantrika	One who practices Tantra
Tantrism	A form of Hindu and Buddhist religious practice
Tara	One of the Mahavidyas
tattva	"Thing of truth"
tattvas	Categories of creation
tirthas	"Crossings," sacred centers
tithis	The thirty days of the waxing and waning moon
trimurti	"Having three forms"; the Hindu triad of Brahma, the creator, Visnu, the maintainer, and Siva, the destroyer
Tripura-sundari	"She who is lovely in the three worlds," one of the Mahavidyas
uccatana	The power to make one's enemy sick by yelling at the power to eradicate
ucchista	Leftover food
upa-puranas	Lesser or "younger" *puranas*, usually briefer and more recent than principal *puranas*
vahana	Vehicle of a deity, usually an animal
Vaisnava	Pertaining to Visnu, partial to Visnu
vak-siddhi	The power by which whatever one says comes true; the power of superior speech
Vamacara	The left-handed path in Tantrism
vidya	Knowledge; in tantric contexts, mantra
vira	"Hero"; a type of religious practitioner qualified to undertake certain left-handed tantric practices
Visnu	One of the three great male deities of Hinduism, the maintainer
yaksas	Supernatural beings often associated with the forest or with heavenly places
Yama	King of the dead and ruler of the south
yantra	A schematic rendering of a deity or the cosmos
yogini	A female practitioner
yoginis	Female beings associated with magical powers
yugas	The periods or stages of the world or universe

Bibliography

Adigal, Prince Ilango. *Shilappadikaram*. Translated by Alain Daniélou. New York: New Directions Book, 1965.

Agni-purāṇa. Poona: Anandasrama Sanskrit Series, 1957.

Agni Puranam. Translated by Manmatha Nath Dutt Shastri. 2 vols. Varanasi: Chowkhamba Sanskrit Series Office, 1967.

Bagchi, Prabodh Chandra. *Studies in the Tantras*. Calcutta: University of Calcutta, 1975.

Bana. *The Kādambarī of Bana*. Translated by C. M. Ridding. London: Royal Asiatic Society, 1896.

Banabhaṭṭa. *Kādambarī*. Bombay: Mathurānāth Śastrī, 1940.

Bandyopadhyay, Pranab. *The Goddess of Tantra*. Calcutta: Punthi Pustak, 1990.

Banerjee, S. C. *A Brief History of Tantric Literature*. Calcutta: Naya Prokash, 1986.

Banerji, Sures Chandra. *Tantra in Bengal: A Study of Its Origin, Development and Influence*. Calcutta: Naya Prokash, 1977.

Bankhandesvara, Sri. *Mahāvidyā Catustayam: Tārā, Dhūmāvatī, Bhuvaneśvarī, Mātaṅgī*. Dattiya, M.P.: Pitambara Pith, n.d.

Basham, A. L. *The Wonder That Was India*. New York: Grove Press, 1959.

Beck, Guy L. *Sonic Theology: Hinduism and Sacred Sound*. Columbia: University of South Carolina Press, 1993.

Behera, K. S. "Lakṣmī in Orissan Literature and Art." Pp. 91–105 in D. C. Sircar, ed. *Foreigners in Ancient India and Lakṣmī and Sarasvatī in Art and Literature*. Calcutta: University of Calcutta, 1970.

Benard, Elisabeth Anne. "Chinnamastā: The Awful Buddhist and Tantric Goddess." Ph.D. diss., Columbia University, New York, 1990. Published as *Chinnamastā: The Aweful Buddhist and Tantric Goddess*. Delhi: Motilal Banarsidass Publishers, 1994.

Beyer, Stephan. *The Cult of Tārā: Magic and Ritual in Tibet*. Berkeley: University of California Press, 1973.

Bhāgavata-purāṇa. Gorakhpur: Gita Press, Samvit 2021.

The Bhagavata Purana. Translated and annotated by Ganesh Vasudeo Tagare. 4 vols. Delhi: Motilal Banarsidass, 1976.

Bharati, Agehananda. *The Tantric Tradition*. London: Rider, 1965.

Bhattacharya, Asutosh. *Bangla mangal-kavyer itihasa*. Calcutta: E. Mukharji and Co., 1939.

Bhattacharyya, Benoytosh. *The Indian Buddhist Iconography: Mainly Based on the Sādhanamālā and the Cognate Tāntric Texts of Rituals*. Calcutta: Firma K. L. Mukhopadhyaya, 1968.

Bhattacharyya, Narendra Nath. *History of the Śākta Religion*. New Delhi: Munshiram Manoharlal Publishers, 1974.

———. *History of the Tantric Religion: A Historical, Ritualistic and Philosophical Study*. New Delhi: Manohar Publishers, 1982.

Bhattasali, Nalini Kanta. *Iconography of Buddhist and Brahmanical Sculptures in the Dacca Museum*. Dacca: Rai S. N. Bhadra Bahadur, 1929.

Bhavabhūti's Mālatīmādhava with the Commentary of Jagaddhara. Edited and translated by M. R. Kale. Delhi: Motilal Banarsidass, 1967.

Blofeld, John. *Bodhisattva of Compassion: The Mystical Tradition of Kuan Yin*. Boulder, Colo.: Shambala Publications, 1978.

Bosch, F. D. K. *The Golden Germ*. The Hague: Mouton, 1960.

Brahma-vaivarta-purāṇa. Poona: Ānandāśrama Sanskrit Series, 1935.

Brahma-Vaivarta Puranam. Translated by Rajendra Nath Sen. 2 parts. Allahabad: Sudhindra Nath Vasu, 1920, 1922.

Bṛhaddharma Purāṇam. Edited by M. M. Haraprasad Sastri. Varanasi: Chaukhamba Amarabharati Prakashan, 1974.

Brooks, Douglas Renfrew. *Auspicious Wisdom: The Texts and Traditions of Śrīvidyā Śākta Tantrism in South India*. Albany: State University of New York Press, 1992.

———. *The Secret of the Three Cities: An Introduction to Hindu Śākta Tantrism*. Chicago: University of Chicago Press, 1990.

Brown, Cheever Mackenzie. *God as Mother: A Feminine Theology in India*. Hartford, Vt.: Claude Stark & Co., 1974.

———. *The Triumph of the Goddess: The Canonical Models and Theological Visions of the Devī-Bhāgavata Purāṇa*. Albany: State University of New York Press, 1990.

Cakravarti, Rasmohan. "Mahāvidyā Tārā ki Sādhanā." *Caṇḍī* 6, no. 7 (1946).

Carman, John. *The Theology of Rāmānuja*. New Haven, Conn.: Yale University Press, 1974.

Chakravarti, Chintaharan. *Tantras: Studies on Their Religion and Literature*. Calcutta: Punthi Pustak, 1963.

Coburn, Thomas B. *Devī-Māhātmya: The Crystallization of the Goddess Tradition*. Delhi: Motilal Banarsidass, 1984.

———. *Encountering the Goddess: A Translation of the Devī-Māhātmya and a Study of Its Interpretation*. Albany: State University of New York Press, 1991.

Coomaraswamy, Ananda. *Yakṣas*. 2 parts. Delhi: Munshiram Manoharlal, 1971.

Coward, Harold. *Bhartṛhari*. Boston: Twayne Publishers, 1976.

Dāmara-tantra. Edited and translated by Ram Kumar Rai. Varanasi: Pracya Prakashan, 1988.

Daniélou, Alain. *Hindu Polytheism*, Bollingen Series LXXIII. New York: Bollingen Foundation, 1964.

———. *Yoga: The Method of Re-integration*. New York: University Book Publishers, 1955.

Das, Upendra Kumar. *Bhāratiya Śaktisādhanā*. 2 vols. Santiniketan: Ranjit Rai Prakasan, Visvabharati, 1967.

Datiya, Śrī Swami Ji Mahārāja. *Śrī Chinnamastā Nityārcana*. Prayag: Kalyan Mandir Prakasan, 1978.

Denton, Lynn Teskey. "Varieties of Hindu Female Asceticism." Pp. 211–31 in Julia Leslie, ed. *Roles and Rituals for Hindu Women*. Delhi: Motilal Banarsidass, 1992.

de Tourreil, Savithri Shanker. "Nayars in a South Indian Matrix: A Study Based on Female-Centered Ritual." Ph.D. diss., Concordia University, Montreal, 1995.

Devī-bhāgavata-purāṇa. Varanasi: Pandita Pustakalaya, 1969.

[*Devī-bhāgavata-purāṇa*]. *The Sri Mad Devi Bhagavatam*. Sacred Books of the Hindus, vol. 26. Translated by Swami Vijnanananda. Allahabad: Sudhindra Nath Vasu, 1921–23.

Devī-māhātmya. See Coburn and below.

[*Devī-māhātmya*]. *The Glorification of the Great Goddess*. Edited and translated by Vasudeva S. Agrawala. Varanasi: All-India Kashiraj Trust, 1963.

Dhal, Upendra Nath. *Goddess Lakṣmī: Origin and Development*. New Delhi: Oriental Publishers, 1978.

Dīkṣit, Rājeś. *Bagalāmukhī evam Mātaṅgī Tantra Śāstra*. Agra: Sumit Prakashan, 1989.

———. *Bhairavī evam Dhūmāvatī Tantra Śāstra*. Agra: Dīp Publication, 1988.

———. *Bhuvaneśvarī evam Chinnamastā Tantra Śāstra*. Agra: Braj Printers, 1988.

———. *Kālī Tantra Śāstra*. Agra: Sumit Prakashan, 1987.

———. *Ṣoḍaśī Tantra Śāstra*. Agra: Sumit Prakashan, 1991.

———. *Tārā Tantra Śāstra*. Agra: Sumit Prakashan, 1987.

Divyāvadāna. Edited by P. L. Vaidya. Buddhist Sanskrit Series, no. 20. Darbhanga: Mithila Research Institute, 1959.

Dold, Patricia. "The Mahāvidyās at Kāmarūpa." Paper presented at the annual meeting of the Canadian Association for Asian Studies, Ottawa, June 1993.

Dvivedi, Vibhuti Narayana, and Harisankara Upadhyay. *Śrī Tārā-sādhanā*. Vindhyacal: Śrī Tārā Mandir, 1988.

Dyczkowski, Mark S. G. *The Canon of the Śaivāgama and the Kubjikā Tantras of the Western Kaula Tradition*. Albany: State University of New York Press, 1988; Delhi: Motilal Banarsidass, 1989.

———. *The Doctrine of Vibration: An Analysis of the Doctrines and Practices of Kashmir Shaivism*. Albany: State University of New York Press, 1987; Delhi: Motilal Banarsidass, 1989.

Eck, Diana L. *Banaras, City of Light*. Princeton, N.J.: Princeton University Press, 1982.

———. "India's Tīrthas: 'Crossings' in Sacred Geography." *History of Religions* 20, no. 4 (May 1981): 323–44.

Eliade, Mircea. *Rites and Symbols of Initiation: The Mysteries of Birth and Rebirth.* New York: Harper & Row, Publishers, 1958.

———. *Yoga: Immortality and Freedom.* New York: Pantheon Books, 1958.

Elmore, Wilber Theodore. *Dravidian Gods in Modern Hinduism: A Study of the Local and Village Deities of Southern India.* Hamilton, N.Y.: Published by the author, 1915.

Erndl, Kathleen M. *Victory to the Mother: The Hindu Goddess of Northwest India in Myth, Ritual, and Symbol.* New York: Oxford University Press, 1993.

Garg, Kulsekar Śrī Maheś Candra. "Pūjā Swamiji aur Śrī Pītāmbarā Pīth Datiya." *Caṇḍī* 7, no. 40 (October 1981): 17–21.

Garuḍa-purāṇa. Edited by Ramshankar Bhattacarhya. Varanasi: Kashi Sanskrit Series, 1964.

The Garuda-Puranam. Translated by Manmatha Nath Dutt Sastri. Banaras: Chowkhamba Sanskrit Series Office, 1968.

Gautam, Caman Lal. *Kālī Siddhi.* Bareli, U.P.: Saṁskṛti Saṁsthān, 1984.

Ghosh, Niranjan. *Concept and Iconography of the Goddess of Abundance and Fortune in Three Religions of India.* Burdwan, West Bengal: University of Burdwan, 1979.

Ghoshal, U. N. *Studies in Indian History and Culture.* Bombay: Orient Longman, 1965.

Gonda, Jan. *Ancient Indian Kingship from the Religious Point of View.* Leiden: E. J. Brill, 1969.

———. *Aspects of Early Visnuism.* 2d ed. Delhi: Motilal Banarsidass, 1969.

———. "The Indian Mantra." *Oriens,* vol. 16 (1963). Reprinted in J. Gonda. *Selected Studies IV.* Leiden: E. J. Brill, 1975.

Goudriaan, Teun, and Sanjukta Gupta. *Hindu Tantric and Śākta Literature.* Wiesbaden: Otto Harrassowitz, 1981.

Gupta, Sanjukta. "Women in the Śaiva/Śākta Ethos." Pp. 193–210 in Julia Leslie, ed. *Roles and Rituals for Women.* Delhi: Motilal Banarsidass, 1992.

Harshananda, Swami. *Hindu Gods and Goddesses.* Mylapore: Sri Ramakrishna Math, 1988.

Hawley, John Stratton, and Donna Marie Wulff, eds. *The Divine Consort: Radhā and the Goddesses of India.* Berkeley, Calif.: Berkeley Religious Studies Series, 1982.

Hershman, P. "Hair, Sex and Dirt." *Man,* vol. 9 (1974).

Hiltebeitel, Alf. "Draupadī's Hair." *Puruṣārtha* 5 (1981): 179–214.

Hymn to Kālī (Karpurādi-stotra). Edited and translated by Arthur Avalon. Madras: Ganesh & Co., 1965.

The Hymns of the Rgveda. Translated by T. H. Griffith. 4th ed. 2 vols. Banaras: Chowkhamba Sanskrit Series Office, 1963.

"Jambhaladatta's Version of the Vetalapañcavimsati." Translated by M. B. Emeaneau. *American Oriental Society* 4 (1934): 59–63.

Jha, Acarya Ananda. "Chinnamastā Tattva." *Sanmarg—Tantraviseś Aṅk* (Varanasi), July 26, 1979, pp. 68–72.

Kahikey, Shiv Prasad Mishra. "Bahati Ganga (The Flowing Ganges)." Translated by Paul R. Golding and Virendra Singh. Manuscript, Varanasi, n.d.

Kakati, Bani Kanta. *The Mother Goddess Kāmākhyā*. Gauhati, Assam: Lawyer's Book Stall, 1948.

Kālikā-purāṇa. Bombay: Venkateśvara Press, 1891.

Kalyāṇa, Śakti Aṅk. Gorakhpur: Gita Press, 1934.

Kalyāṇa, Tīrtha Aṅk. Gorakhpur: Gita Press, 1957.

Kane, Pandurang Vaman. *History of Dharmaśāstra*. Vol. 2 Poona: Bhandarkar Oriental Institute, 1974.

Karpurādi-stotra. See *Hymn to Kālī*.

Kaulāvalī. Edited by Arthur Avalon. Delhi: Bharatiya Vidya Prakashan, 1985.

Kinsley, David. " 'The Death That Conquers Death': Dying to the World in Medieval Hinduism." Pp. 97–108 in Frank E. Reynolds and Earle H. Waugh, eds. *Religious Encounters with Death: Insights from the History and Anthropology of Religions*. University Park: Pennsylvania State University Press, 1977.

———. *The Divine Player: A Study of Kṛṣṇa Līlā*. Delhi: Motilal Banarsidass, 1979.

———. *Hindu Goddesses: Visions of the Divine Feminine in the Hindu Religious Tradition*. Berkeley: University of California Press, 1986.

Kramrisch, Stella. *The Presence of Śiva*. Princeton, N.J.: Princeton University Press, 1981.

Kripal, Jeffrey J. "Kālī's Tongue and Ramakrishna: 'Biting the Tongue' of the Tantric Tradition." *History of Religions* 34, no. 2 (November 1994): 152–89.

Kṛṣṇānanda Āgamavāgiśa. *Bṛhat Tantrasāra*. Calcutta: Navabharat Publishers, 1984.

Kumar, Pushpendra. *The Principle of Śakti*. Delhi: Eastern Book Linkers, 1986.

———. *Sakti Cult in Ancient India*. Banaras: Bharatiya Publishing House, 1974.

———. *Sakti Cult in Hinduism*.

———. *Tārā: The Supreme Goddess*. Delhi: Bharatiya Vidya Prakashan, 1992.

Lakṣmī Tantra, a Pañcarātra Text. Translated by Sanjukta Gupta. Leiden: E. J. Brill, 1972.

[*Lalitā-sahasranāma*]. *Sri Lalita Sahasranamam*. Translated by Chagany Suryanarayanamurthy. Madras: Ganesh, 1962.

Lalitā-sahasranāma with Bhāskararāya's Commentary. Translated by R. Ananthakrishna Sastry. Madras: Theosophical Publishing House, 1951.

Leslie, Julia. "Śrī and Jyeṣṭhā: Ambivalent Role Models for Women." Pp. 107–28 in Julia Leslie, ed. *Roles and Rituals for Hindu Women*. Delhi: Motilal Banarsidass Publishers, 1992.

———, ed. *Roles and Rituals for Hindu Women*. Delhi: Motilal Banarsidass Publishers, 1992.

Levy, Robert I., with the collaboration of Kedar Rāj Rājopādhyāya. *Mesocosm: Hinduism and the Organization of a Traditional Newar City in Nepal*. Berkeley: University of California Press, 1990; Delhi: Motilal Banarsidass, 1992.

Liṅga-purāṇa. Edited by J. V. Bhattacharya. Calcutta: J. V. Bhattacharya, 1885.

The Linga-Purana. Translated by a Board of Scholars. 2 parts. Delhi: Motilal Banarasidass, 1973.

Lorenzen, David N. *The Kāpālikas and Kālāmukhas: Two Lost Śaivite Sects.* Berkeley: University of California Press, 1972.

Mahābhāgavata-purāṇa. Edited by Pushpendra Kumar. Delhi: Eastern Book Linkers, 1983.

Mahābhārata. Edited by Vishnu S. Sukthankar et al. Poona: Bhandarkar Oriental Research Institute, 1933.

The Mahābhārata. Translated and edited by J. A. B. van Buitenen. Vol. 1: *The Book of the Beginning.* Vol. 2: *The Book of the Assembly Hall and the Book of the Forest.* Vol. 3: *The Book of Virāṭa and the Book of the Effort.* Chicago: University of Chicago Press, 1973, 1975, 1978. (Incomplete.)

The Mahabharata of Krishna-Dwaipayana. Translated by K. M. Ganguly. 12 vols. Calcutta: Oriental Publishing Co., n.d.

Mahākāla-saṁhitā. Allahabad: Gāngānath Jha Research Institute, 1974.

Mahānirvāna-tantra. See *Tantra of the Great Liberation.*

Mahidhara. *Mantra Mahodadhiḥ.* Vol. 1. Edited and translated by Ram Kumar Rai. Varanasi: Prachya Prakashan, 1992.

Mantramahārṇava. Bombay: Khemraj Śrīkṛṣṇadas Publishers, 1990.

Mantra-mahodadhiḥ. See Mahidhara.

Marglin, Frédérique Apffel. *Wives of the God-King: The Rituals of the Devadasis of Puri.* New York: Oxford University Press, 1985.

Matsya Puranam. Translated by a Taluqdar of Oudh. Allahabad: Sudhindra Nath Vasu, 1916.

McDaniel, June. *The Madness of the Saints: Ecstatic Religion in Bengal.* Chicago: University of Chicago Press, 1989.

McGee, Mary. "Feasting and Fasting: The Vrata Tradition and Its Significance for Hindu Women." Th.D. diss., Harvard University, 1987.

Menon, Usha, and Richard A. Shweder. "Kali's Tongue: Cultural Psychology and the Power of Shame in Orissa, India." Pp. 241–84 in Shinobu Kitayama and Hazel Rose Markus, eds. *Emotion and Culture: Empirical Studies of Mutual Influence.* Washington, D.C.: American Psychological Association, 1994.

Mishra, Kamalkar. *Significance of the Tantric Tradition.* Varanasi: Arddhanarisvara Publications, 1981.

Mishra, V. B. *Religious Belief and Practices of North India.* Leiden: E. J. Brill, 1973.

Mitchener, John E. *Traditions of the Seven Ṛṣis.* Delhi: Motilal Banarsidass, 1982.

Mookerjee, Ajit. *Tantric Āsana: A Way to Self-Realization.* Basel: Ravi Kumar, 1971.

Mookerjee, Ajit, and Madhu Khanna. *The Tantric Way: Art, Science, Ritual.* Delhi: Vikas Publishing House, 1977; London: Thames and Hudson, 1977; Boston: New York Graphic Society, n.d.

Morinis, E. Alan. *Pilgrimage in the Hindu Tradition: A Case Study of West Bengal.* Delhi: Oxford University Press, 1984.

Muṇḍamālā-tantra. Calcutta: Nava Bharat, 1980.

Nagaswamy, R. *Tantric Cult of South India.* Delhi: Agam Kala Prakashan, 1982.

Nandi, Ramendra Nath. *Religious Institutions and Cults of the Deccan.* Delhi: Motilal Banarsidass, 1973.

Narayanan, Vasudha. "The Goddess Śrī: The Blossoming Lotus and Breast Jewel of Viṣṇu." Pp. 224–37 in John Stratton Hawley and Donna Marie Wulff, eds. *The Divine Consort: Rādhā and the Goddesses of India.* Berkeley, Calif.: Berkeley Religious Studies Series, 1982.

———. "*Karma* and *Kṛpa.* Human Bondage and Divine Grace: The Teṅkalai Śrī Vaiṣṇava Position." DePaul University, Chicago, n.d.

O'Flaherty, Wendy. *Asceticism and Eroticism in the Mythology of Śiva.* London: Oxford University Press, 1973.

———. *Origins of Evil in Hindu Mythology.* Berkeley: University of California Press, 1976.

———. *Sexual Metaphors and Animal Symbols in Indian Mythology.* Delhi: Motilal Banarsidass, 1981. First published as *Women, Androgynes, and Other Mythical Beasts.* Chicago: University of Chicago Press, 1980.

Padma-purana. Edited by Khemaraj Srikrsnadas. Bombay: Venkatesvara Press, n.d.

Pal, P. *Hindu Religion and Iconology.* Los Angeles: Vichitra Press, 1981.

Pandey, K. C. *Abhinavagupta: An Historical and Philosophical Study.* 2d ed. Varanasi: Chowkhamba Sanskrit Series Office, 1963.

Paraśurāma-kalpasūtra. Edited by A. N. Jani. Baroda: University of Baroda, 1979. First published 1923.

Pott, P. H. *Yoga and Yantra: Their Interrelation and Their Significance for Indian Archaeology.* The Hague: Martinus Nijhoff, 1966.

Prāṇatoṣinī-tantra. Calcutta: Basumati Sahitya Mandir, 1928.

Prapañcasārasāra-saṁgraha. Edited by Gīrvānendra Sarasvatī. 2 parts. Tanjore Sarasvati Mahal Series, no. 98. Thanjavur: T.M.S.S. Library, 1976, 1980.

Prapañcasāra-tantra. Edited by John Woodroffe. Delhi: Motilal Banarsidass, n.d.

Principles of Tantra: The Tantratattva of Śrīyukta Śiva Candra Vidyārnava Bhattācārya Mahodaya. Edited by Arthur Avalon. Madras: Ganesh & Co., 1960.

Rama Prasada's Devotional Songs: The Cult of Shakti. Translated by Jadunath Sinha. Calcutta: Sinha Publishing House, 1966.

Ramayana. Edited by J. M. Mehta et al. Baroda: Oriental Institute, 1960.

The Ramayana of Valmiki. Translated by Hari Prasad Shastri. 3 vols. London: Shantisadan, 1957–62.

Rao, S. K. *Tibetan Tantric Tradition.* New Delhi: Arnold-Heinemann, 1977.

Rao, S. K. Ramachandra. *Śrī-Cakra: Its Yantra, Mantra and Tantra.* Bangalore: Kalpatharu Research Academy, 1982.

Rao, T. A. Gopinatha. *Elements of Hindu Iconography.* 2d ed. 2 vols. New York: Paragon Books, 1914–16.

Rawson, Philip. *The Art of Tantra.* London: Thames and Hudson, 1973.

———. *Oriental Erotic Art.* New York: A and W Publishers, 1981.

Ṛg-veda. See *The Hymns of the Rgveda.*

Śākta-pramoda. Bombay: Khemrāja Śrīkṛṣṇadāsa Prakāśān, 1992.

Śaktisaṁgama-tantra. Vol. 4: *Chinnamastā Khaṇḍa.* Edited by B. Bhattacharyya and Vrajavallabha Dvivedi. Baroda: Oriental Institute of Baroda, 1978.

Śāradā Tilaka Tantram. Edited by Arthur Avalon. Delhi: Motilal Banarsidass, 1982. First published in Calcutta, 1933.

Saraswati, Bandana. "The History of the Worship of Śrī in North India to cir. A.D. 550." Ph.D. diss., University of London, 1971.

Śarmā, Lakṣmī Narayana. *Tantra Vidyā*. Delhi: World Book Co., 1986.

Sarvollāsa-tantra. Calcutta: Harambacandra Bhattacharya, 1953.

Sastri, Acarya Pandita Sri Sivadattamisra. *Bagalāmukhī-rahasyam*. Varanasi: Thakur Prasad Pustak Bharadar, 1951.

Sastri, Govinda. "Karuṇāmayi Tārā." *Caṇḍi* 6, no. 7 (1946).

Sastry, T. V. Kapali. *Sidelights on Tantra*. Pondicherry, 1971.

Śatapatha-brāhmaṇa. Translated by Julius Eggeling. 5 vols. Delhi: Motilal Banarsidass, 1966.

Satpathy, Sarbeswar. *Dasa Mahavidya and Tantra Sastra*. Calcutta: Punthi Pustak, 1992.

———. *Sakti Iconography in Tantric Mahāvidyās*. Calcutta: Punthi Pustak, 1991.

The Saundaryalaharī or Flood of Beauty. Edited and translated by W. Norman Brown. Cambridge, Mass.: Harvard University Press, 1958.

Sax, William. *Mountain Goddess: Gender and Politics in a Himalayan Pilgrimage*. New York: Oxford University Press, 1991.

Schrader, F. Otto. *Introduction to the Pañcarātra and the Ahirbudhnya Saṁhitā*. Madras: Adyar Library, 1916.

Sharma, Jagannath Prasad. *Bhārat Tīrth Darśan*. Varanasi: Bhola Yantralaya, 1984.

Shāstrī, Ushā P., and Nicole Menant, trans. *Hymnes à la déesse*. Paris: Le Soleil Noir, 1980.

Shaw, Miranda. *Passionate Enlightenment: Women in Tantric Buddhism*. Princeton, N.J.: Princeton University Press, 1994.

Sircar, D. C. *The Śākta Pīṭhas*. Delhi: Motilal Banarsidass, 1973.

———, ed. *Foreigners in Ancient India and Lakṣmī and Sarasvatī in Art and Literature*. Calcutta: University of Calcutta, 1970.

Sivaramamurti, C. *Nataraja in Art, Thought and Literature*. New Delhi: National Museum, 1974.

Skanda-purāṇa. 5 vols. Calcutta: Mansukharaja Mora, 1959–62.

Slusser, Mary Shepherd. *Nepal Mandala: A Cultural Study of the Kathmandu Valley*. 2 vols. Princeton, N.J.: Princeton University Press, 1982.

Sontheimer, Gunther-Dietz. *Pastoral Deities in Western India*. Translated by Anne Feldhaus. New York: Oxford University Press, 1989.

Srivastava, M. C. P. *Mother Goddess in Indian Art, Archaeology and Literature*. Delhi: Agam Kala Prakashan, 1979.

Svoboda, Robert E. *Aghora: At the Left Hand of God*. Albuquerque, N.M.: Brotherhood of Life, 1986.

Taittīrya-brāhmana. 2 vols. Poona: Anandasrama Sanskrit Series, 1934, 1938.

Tantra of the Great Liberation (Mahanirvana-tantra). Translated by Arthur Avalon. New York: Dover Publications, 1972.

Tantrasāra. See Kṛṣṇānanda Āgamavāgīśa.

Taponiṣṭa, Vedamūrti [Śrīrām Śarmā Ācārya]. *Tantra-mahāvijñana*. 2 vols. Khavaja Kutub and Bareli, U.P.: Saṁskṛti Saṁsthān, 1971.

Thaplyal, Kiran. "Gajalakṣmī on Seals." Pp. 112–25 in D. C. Sircar, ed. *Foreigners in Ancient India and Lakṣmī and Sarasvatī in Art and Literature.* Calcutta: University of Calcutta, 1970.
Thurston, Edgar. *Castes and Tribes of Southern India.* 7 vols. Madras: Madras Government Press, 1909.
Tiwari, Jagdish Narain. "Studies in Goddess Cults in Northern India, with Reference to the First Seven Centuries A.D." Ph.D. diss., Australian National University, n.d.
Tucci, Giuseppe. *Tibetan Painted Scrolls.* 2 vols. Rome: Libraria dello Stato, 1949.
Tuker, Francis. *The Yellow Scarf.* London: J. M. Dent & Sons, 1961.
Turner, Victor W. *Dramas, Fields, and Metaphors: Symbolic Action in Human Society.* Ithaca, N.Y.: Cornell University Press, 1974.
———. *The Ritual Process: Structure and Anti-structure.* Harmondsworth, U.K.: Penguin, 1969.
Vāmana-purāṇa. Edited by Anand Swarup Gupta. Translated by S. M. Mukhopadhyaya and others. Varanasi: All-India Kashiraj Trust, 1968.
Van Kooij, K. R. *Worship of the Goddess according to the Kālikāpurāṇa.* Leiden: E. J. Brill, 1972.
Varāha-purāṇa. Mathura: Gita Press, n.d.
Viṣṇu-purāṇa. Gorakhpur: Gita Press, Samvit 2024.
The Vishnu Purana, a System of Hindu Mythology and Tradition. Translated by H. H. Wilson. 3d ed. Calcutta: Punthi Pustak, 1961.
Vogel, J. P. "The Head-Offering to the Goddess in Pallava Sculpture." *Bulletin of the School of Oriental Studies* (London) 6: 539–43.
Woodroffe, Sir John. *Śakti and Śākta, Essays and Addresses.* Madras: Ganesh & Co., 1987. First published in 1927.
Yogini Tantra. Edited by Biswanarayan Shastri. Delhi: Bharatiya Vidya Prakashan, 1982.
The Yonitantra. Edited by J. A. Schoterman. New Delhi: Manohar, 1980.
Zbavitel, D. *Bengali Literature.* Wiesbaden: Otto Harrassowitz, 1976.
Zimmer, Heinrich. *The Art of Indian Asia.* 2 vols. New York: Pantheon Books, 1955.
———. *Philosophies of India.* Cleveland: World Publishing Co., 1956.

Index

Note: Page numbers of illustrations are italicized.